POLITICS AND ETHICS OF THE INDIAN CONSTITUTION

Politics and Ethics of the Indian Constitution

edited by
RAJEEV BHARGAVA

OXFORD
UNIVERSITY PRESS

OXFORD
UNIVERSITY PRESS

Oxford University Press is a department of the University of Oxford.
It furthers the University's objective of excellence in research, scholarship,
and education by publishing worldwide. Oxford is a registered trademark of
Oxford University Press in the UK and in certain other countries

Published in India by
Oxford University Press
22 Workspace, 2nd Floor, 1/22 Asaf Ali Road, New Delhi 110002, India

© Oxford University Press 2008

The moral rights of the authors have been asserted

First Edition published in 2008
30ᵗʰ impression 2024

ISBN-13: 978-0-19-806355-1
ISBN-10: 0-19-806355-5

Typeset in Dante MT 10.5/12.5
by Sai Graphic Design, New Delhi 110 055
Printed in India by Manipal Technologies Limited, Manipal

Contents

Acknowledgements

This book consists of papers which were first presented at a conference on the Political Philosophy of the Indian Constitution held in Goa in September 2001. Both the conference and the book were an integral part of my commitment as a C.R. Parekh Fellow at the Centre for the Study of Developing Societies. My foremost gratitude is due therefore to the Nirman Foundation that instituted the C.R. Parekh Fellowship at the CSDS.

Though I am indebted to every participant in the seminar, I need to make special mention of Andrew Sharp and Rainer Bauböck who made presentations in Goa but for the sake of the book's overall coherence offered to leave out their own important contributions. Peter deSouza deserves to be singled out for more than one reason. Without his help and emphatic presence, the conference would not have had an idyllic setting. Another friend, Philip McDonagh chipped in with significant moral support.

Special thanks are owed to Bhikhu Parekh and Dhirubhai Sheth, partners in an ongoing conversation on political theory, Indian politics, and the identity-constituting features of the Indian Constitution. Without them, this book is inconceivable.

Finally, I would like to thank several of my students: Rinku Lamba, Rajesh Seth, Swaha Das, V. Sriranjini, Jaya Gupta, and Aparajita Narain who began to collectively work on the Constituent Assembly Debates a couple of years before the conference as well as Manash Bhattacharya, E. Arvind, Aryama, and Monika Dhami. All of them made learning as much of a joy in my last few years at the Jawaharlal Nehru University as it was when I first began teaching there. Another student, Jaby Mathew of the University of Delhi helped to give final shape to the book. Anthony Stephen always makes me computer-friendly. Without him, I cannot respond to any computer.

As always, Tani Sandhu provided indispensable ground support.

Introduction[*]
Outline of a Political Theory of
the Indian Constitution

Rajeev Bhargava

In 1950, for the first time in their history, a diverse collection of individuals
and groups became the people of a single book, one that reflects their
commitment to protect their mutual rights and which articulates a
collective identity. This volume deals with some aspects of that unique
document.

I

WHY AN INDIAN POLITICAL THEORY?

Our collective endeavour and quite certainly one of my own primary
motivations behind this seminar was ambitious: to try and resuscitate
political theory in India (an objective I shared with many of the
participants, particularly Bhikhu Parekh) and to eventually evolve a form
of political theory that is suitable to us and which simultaneously opens
up Western political theory as it exists today. This is neither insignificant
nor easy. A cursory glance at contemporary political theory is sufficient
to show that though some of its content may have universal reach, its
form remains parochial. Political philosophy as it exists today takes little
inspiration from non-Western societies, hardly refers to their problems

[*] I would like to thank my students Aryama, E. Arvind, and Jaby Mathew, as
well as Tani Sandhu and Anthony Stephen, for their help in preparing the
introduction.

and takes little notice of how cross-cultural issues imbibe distinct inflections or internal colourations at different places. The examples discussed in political philosophy hardly ever relate directly or immediately to the specific context of these societies. For all the talk of pluralism and multiculturalism in Western political theory, there is barely a mention of how these issues arise or are tackled in places such as India. Worse still, political philosophers show little curiosity about the experience of non-Western societies.

Take the philosophical debate on affirmative action. The Indian experience of this important issue is older than that of most countries, preceding by several decades the US experience, but the best articles written on this subject fail to take the Indian experiment into account. The story of other issues is no different. How can we not conclude that Western political theory remains Eurocentric or even Anglo-Saxon? This is not to say that the entire responsibility for this state of affairs rests with Western political theorists. Indian thinkers have contributed in no small measure to this state of affairs. We remain insulated from the experience of other Asian and African countries and have unthinkingly pursued an agenda shaped entirely by the concerns of a few Western countries—mainly Britain, the US, France, and maybe Germany.

My remarks above should not give rise to a misunderstanding. I am *not* suggesting that we must from now on ignore mainstream Western political theory; such a move would be suicidal for Indian political theorists. At any rate it is not a meaningful option before us. However, the almost exclusive attention bestowed on a small number of Western countries must surely be a matter of concern and self-reflection. Our blindness to other European countries is shocking. Consider the Belgium experience on the issue of language. India and Belgium can certainly learn a thing or two from one another about deep cultural differences that emanate from linguistic diversity. But can we think of a single book that discusses the comparative experience of linguistic diversity in India and Belgium? Has political theory been even faintly affected by a comparison of the experiences of these two countries? Or take the case of Switzerland. How many of us are aware of the interface and overlap of religion and language in Switzerland and their impact on Swiss politics. Quite clearly, the West towards which we remain almost permanently oriented comprises a handful of hegemonic countries.

Having assumed responsibility for the somewhat dismal state of Indian political theory and admitted a degree of collective guilt, I do not wish to let Western political theorists off the hook easily. I honestly believe that aspiring political philosophers anywhere in the world must take a crash-course in Indian politics, society, and culture. Furthermore, internationally known political theorists should consider a mandatory sabbatical in an Indian university to really come to grips with the deep diversity and the nearly incommensurable but co-existing worldviews and clusters of values that are an integral part of the daily life of India. Debates around group rights, self-determination, differentiated citizenship, gender equality, secularism, and constitutionalism will surely be considerably enriched by the Indian experience. A genuine search for trans-cultural ideals is impossible without such cross-references. The search for alternatives, a hallmark of the Centre for the Study of Developing Societies (CSDS), must also have an impact on political theory in India.

POLITICAL THEORY AND THE CONSTITUTION

It might now be asked why in order to revive interest in political theory, should we turn to the study of law and the Constitution. It is not my argument that only a study of the Constitution can refurbish political theory in India. However, a study of the Constitution would be particularly useful for two important reasons. First, debates in the Constituent Assembly are fascinating, rich in detail, and provide an extremely nuanced public discussion of issues that are the staple diet of political theory anywhere in the world. I cannot think of any other forum in which extensive political deliberation and argument over procedural and substantive issues relating to Indian society can be found. For one interested in reviving Indian political theory, the Constitution and the debates which preceded it are the most obvious sites to go.

This is obvious now, but only in hindsight, for the political theory of the Indian Constitution is among the most scandalously neglected topics. This need not have been the case. After all, in the period before Independence and in its immediate aftermath, the teaching of politics and law complimented one other. Not only was the study of law an integral part of the study of the political institutions, a detailed study of the Constitution was considered absolutely vital for the understanding of politics. But this was not the case after the 1960s. The focus had shifted from the study of political and legal institutions to large political processes and social movements. To be sure this was partly legitimate. But the pendulum had swung decisively in the more reductive direction. The internal logic and dynamics of constitutional law was suppressed and replaced by loose, speculative generalizations about social structures as if the nature of the legal system could simply be read off the social structure. By the late 1960s, law and political science were mutually estranged. The study of constitutions may not have been wholly neglected, but all the excitement centred on broadly conceived social structures and the study of constitutions gradually came to be considered boring and pedantic.

This was not the only problem. As current academic fashions began to see law as an ephiphenomenon of social relations and to view legal institutions as expressions of particular social interests, constitutions themselves came to be seen as embodiments of elite interests and strategies, as mere reflections of the interests of the propertied classes, indicative at best of a compromise between landlords and the bourgeoisie. If I am not mistaken, the otherwise admirable work of Shibani Chaubey and Shobhan Lal Dutta Gupta falls in this category.

The immediate consequence of this radically reductive treatment was that constitutions were rarely seen as moral texts, to be understood and interpreted in terms of values and ideals. To normatively inclined political theorists this was a disappointing outcome, particularly so because of their penchant for seeing moral values, ideals, conceptions of the good life on almost every inch of the social landscape. So the unchallenged reign of explanatory social science and legal positivism saw the systematic neglect of moral philosophy, normative political theory, liberalism, and the study of constitutional law. A distrust or unfamiliarity with normative concepts, the marginal place of political theory in social science, the inadequate manner in which political theory was itself imagined, all ultimately led to a blindness towards the moral resources of the Constitution. To students who naturally harbour high ideals at their age, a study of constitutions abstracted from ethical values could only appear pointless and tiresome, especially if it was further reduced to a tardy examination of its formulaic articles.

In short, it is important to see the Constitution as a moral document, as embodying an ethical vision. This is not to say that germinal work on the Indian Constitution is altogether absent. To begin with, there are historical studies that focus on the context that led to the framing of the Indian Constitution. Then there are politico-legal readings, somewhat technical and narrower in focus, that describe the character of the Indian polity, including the structures of governance. The work of Jennings[1] and C.H. Alexandrawicz[2] comes immediately to mind in this regard.

Other works see their defining characteristic in terms of an attempt to do both. Granville Austin[3] explicitly makes the claim that he is writing political history.

Though of very high calibre, these works are conspicuously non-theoretical and relatively indifferent to the moral concerns in the Constitution. True, there are exceptions. One scholar who immediately comes to mind in this regard is Upendra Baxi (a contributor to this volume), whose work was at once legal, political, and theoretical. In his contribution here, inspired by what he calls the Kabyle-Bourdieu perspective in contemporary social theory, he introduces an ethnographic approach to constitutions and attempts to make it relevant to comparative constitutional theory. However, even he would agree that most available work on the Indian Constitution is non-philosophical and under-emphasizes its normative potential. A political-theoretic approach to the Indian Constitution is therefore urgently required.

When I speak of the absence of a political-theoretic perspective on the Indian Constitution, I have three things in mind. First, existing work has insufficiently elaborated the conceptual structure of the Constitution and has shown little interest in the possible meanings or detailed analysis of frequently deployed terms such as 'rights', 'citizenship', 'minority', and 'democracy'. Furthermore, there is little attempt to construct a coherent vision of society and polity conditional upon an interpretation of the key concepts of the Indian Constitution.

The second weakness is that existing work on the Constitution *inadequately grasps the structure of ideals embedded in the Constitution.* I am not suggesting that the best work on the Constitution is silent on the values it upholds; nonetheless, it fails to properly articulate or provide a critical interpretation of these values. For example, Austin deploys the distinction between negative and positive liberty drawn by Isaiah Berlin and makes the useful point that the Indian Constitution is guided as much by the second as by the first. But this is where his discussion of normative values ends. My claim is that we need to move much further in this direction.

My third and final point is that the Indian Constitution must be read in conjunction with the Constituent Assembly Debates in order to refine and raise to a higher theoretical plane the *justification* of values that undergird it. A philosophical treatment of a value is woefully incomplete if a detailed justification for it is not provided. When the framers of the Constitution chose to guide Indian society and polity by a particular set of values rather than others, they could not have done so without a set of reasons, many of which are not made properly explicit. Howsoever sketchy and incomplete their arguments may have been, it is difficult to imagine that they did not exist. Political philosophers must articulate and refine these arguments so that an informed and meaningful debate on the character and value of the Indian Constitution may exist in future. I believe all the contributions in this volume go a long way towards not only making the competing arguments in the Constituent Assembly more explicit than they originally were but also in the direction of providing them a theoretical quality with as little distortion as possible.

WHAT DOES A POLITICAL-THEORETIC READING OF THE CONSTITUTION ENTAIL?

None of this is possible unless we begin a study of the Constitution with a great deal of hermeneutic charity. Thus, the first task before us is to ask just what it is that the Constitution is trying to say, to identify the broadest possible range within which all of us, coming as we do from diverse background and different presuppositions, try to fix the meaning of the text. We must not only identify the diverse overall meanings of the text but also its variable local meanings, the different ways in which each article specifies the meaning of a particular cluster of value terms. In the volume, a detailed discussion of equality is undertaken by Ashok Acharya. Upendra Baxi and Valerian Rodrigues elaborate the idea of citizenship. Sanjay Palshikar focuses on ideas of property in the Constitution. Suhas Palshikar outlines two distinct notions of the state, one which embodies the distinctly liberal idea of neutrality and the other which is more perfectionist and in his terms instrumentalist. He also speaks of different conceptions of democracy and welfare found in the Constitution. Rochana Bajpai discusses the notion of minority rights in great detail. Similar discussions of individual and group rights, procedural and substantive conceptions of democracy, and conceptions of negative and positive liberty are available in other contributions to this volume.[4]

We also need to ask questions that occur routinely to political philosophers. To take a random example, does the Constitution recognize all moral rights possessed by citizens? If not, which of them does it recognize? Are these rights only against the state or are they also against other fellow citizens? Must they be conceived as rights against anyone at all? What importance does the Constitution accord to the rights that it recognizes? Is the section on duties consistent with the section on

Fundamental Rights? In India, rights are often posed against duties, without adequate awareness that duties are a necessary correlate of rights. If this is indeed the case and if a tension between duties and rights nonetheless continues to exist, then what explains this tension? Perhaps it arises because the Constitution prescribes duties over and above rights? Or is the Indian Constitution predominantly rights-based? Is its liberalism compromised to the extent that it is not predicated on rights? What justifies this possible surplus? Does the Constitution support liberty, equality, and fraternity in equal measure? If so, how does it balance them? And what of power? Is the Constitution a framework for balancing liberty against power?

Also pertinent is the question concerning the overall character of the Constitution. Suppose that one says that broadly speaking, it is liberal-democratic. Is this sufficient? Probably not, because to many the real issue has to do with the interpretation and elaboration of the precise form of the liberal democracy enunciated by it, and more importantly the many ways in which it meaningfully challenges every single feature of liberal democracy as conventionally understood. If the challenge is successful, how much does it go in a communitarian direction? Or should it be read as anticipating, even espousing, a model of deliberative democracy along lines argued in the American context by political and legal theorists such as Cass Sunstein or Dennis Thompson and Amy Gutmann?

More to the point, some of the debates in the Constituent Assembly reflect a tussle between at least five competing visions. Two of these, the social-democratic vision of Nehru and the liberal-democratic Ambedkarite one, are closely related. The third is the non-modernist, quasi-communitarian vision of Gandhi, distinctly at odds with the other two but still inclusive. A fourth, represented by persons such as K.T. Shah, was radically egalitarian and came closest to the vision of the Left; and the fifth is what we have now come to call the Hindutva ideology. The articulation of these visions is the concern of several essays such as those by Peter deSouza and Thomas Pantham. But it constitutes the very core of Bhikhu Parekh's contribution to this volume.

However, Parekh focuses on only two of these visions. Parekh views the Constitution as a statement of national identity. The first important constituent of this identity is that it is self-determined. The India envisaged by the Constitution belongs to its people. Second, it is both a civilization and a nation-state. Third, it is committed to principles of justice, liberty, equality, fraternity, and the dignity of the individual. Although not specifically mentioned, secularism too was an important ingredient of this vision. Many of these principles were interlinked. For example, fraternity was not possible without some degree of equality. Likewise, for equality, liberty, and fraternity, it was crucial that the state did not belong exclusively to any one religious community; it had to be secular. Nehru put his weight behind this vision and further strengthened it. However, though inclusive and sensitive to the ethnic and cultural plurality of India, this vision which Nehru called the national philosophy of India had its limitations in that it was statist, elitist, 'insufficiently insensitive to rural India and to the religious aspirations of its people' (p. 48 of this volume), and tackled neither poverty nor illiteracy or ill health.

The other vision articulated throughout the first half of the twentieth century, within the Constituent Assembly Debates as well as in post-independent India, saw India as religiously and culturally exclusive, and was propelled by the upper castes. To some extent, it shared a status bias with the Nehruvian vision but it offered no strategy to tackle poverty, inequalities and the needs of minorities or the lower castes. It saw India as a strong, united and mighty economic and military power. As Parekh puts it, it 'militarizes the Indian psyche and ignores the moral core of Indian civilization'.

It is clear that Hindutva conflicts with 'the national philosophy of India'. But to what extent can we legitimately claim that the other four visions conflict with one another? For some contributors, such as Peter deSouza, there is a deep tension between Ambedkarite and Gandhian ideals. Indeed, for him the very idea of a Gandhian Constitution appears to be an oxymoron. deSouza claims that this tension was partially resolved only with the introduction of the Seventy-third Amendment in the 1980s. For other contributors, such as Thomas Pantham, the very idea of any such dichotomy between the Gandhian and the liberal–democratic Ambedkarite visions is deeply problematic. Pantham does not see these two constitutional visions in oppositional terms. Still others, such as Aditya Nigam, claim that all these visions were ultimately displaced by the nationalist and statist vision that was at least partially present in Nehru. Both Gandhi and Ambedkar, no matter how deep their differences, stood outside the logic of this perspective but their views were eventually co-opted within it. Other contributors may not explicitly discuss these visions or the possible tensions between them but they invariably figure as part of the backdrop of the issues on which they focus.

There is, then, a pressing need to excavate the moral values embedded in the Constitution, to bring out their connections, and to identify the coherent or not-so-coherent ethical worldviews contained within it. It is not implausible to believe that these values are simply out there, holding their breath and waiting to be discovered. The Constitution is a socially constructed object, and therefore it does not possess the hard objectivity of natural objects. This element of the Constitution is the ground for contesting interpretations. It is high time we identified these inter-pretations and debated their moral adequacy.

Several contributors draw our attention to such contesting inter-pretations of different features of the Constitution. Gopal Guru refers to the deep tension between a legal and a moral conception of rights. Sanjay Palshikar points out the opposition in the Constitution between a majoritarian conception of democracy and constitutionalism, as well as the tension between the negative freedom expressed largely in the section on Fundamental Rights and the positive freedom found in the Directive Principles of State Policy. Suhas Palshikar refers to the inherent tension between a conception of a state that purports to be strictly neutral and an alternative conception that, guided by a substantive conception of the good life, is not averse to intervening in society in order to reform it. Pratap Bhanu Mehta also draws our attention to an identical dilemma in the Constitution. According to him, the Constitution at once enjoins the state to leave religion alone as well as to make it an object of its interventionist reform.

We must study the Constitution not only to explore its multiple propositional content and to evaluate the many claims these propositions contain but also to use it to arbitrate between contesting interpretations of the many core values on which our polity is believed to be based. It is obvious that many of its ideals are currently disputed. They are not simply tucked away in the Constitution, fading away like dried flowers, but are taken in and out of the courts and have become an integral part of our political discourse, discussed, debated, and contested in different political arenas—in the legislatures, in party forums, in the press, in schools, and in universities. These ideals are variously interpreted and sometimes wilfully manipulated to suit partisan short-term interests or dictates of power. They are bandied about in conflictual political games that transform their meaning beyond recognition.[5] A need arises, therefore, to examine whether or not a serious disjunction exists between the constitutional ideal and its expression in other arenas. At any rate we need to evaluate the comparative worth of different interpretations of the same ideal embodied in different political institutions. Since an ideal acquires considerable, if not supreme, authority once it gets expressed in the Constitution, it must also be used, at least occasionally, to arbitrate in a conflict of interpretation over values. I believe that one significant reason for taking the Constitution seriously is that it can do this job of arbitration.

Let me give two examples. The first is the relationship between individual and group rights. On the one hand, there is the view that political discourse in India is dominated by community rights. When the language of rights arrived in India and was adopted in an Indian context charged with strong community values, it got detached from its individualist moorings and was applied to communities. On the other hand, another view exists that a characteristically un-Indian Constitution imposed an individualist morality on a community-oriented Indian society and did not care even to recognize group rights. Does the Constitution prioritize individual rights or group rights? Even a cursory glance of the Constitution dispels both these misinterpretations. In India, both sets of rights were recognized and no clear guideline was provided for just when one is to override the other, and no general criteria were provided to resolve conflicts between the divergent types of rights. An attempt was made instead to balance them, with the scales tilting marginally in favour of individual rights.

The second example is that of secularism. In India a fierce debate has raged over the value of secularism, but both those who support and those who oppose it assume that it is modelled exactly on the American variant, or rather on a particular interpretation of the American variant in which secularism is identified with a strict wall of separation between religion and state for the sake of individualistically construed values of freedom and equality. However, a close reading of the Constitution gives a different picture. Secularism in India has meant neither the mutual exclusion of religious and state institutions nor strict neutrality of the state with respect to all religious groups. Rather, it has meant what I have called principled distance, a value-based strategy that presupposes disestablishment and that enjoins the state to intervene in or abstain from such interventions depending upon whether specific values integral to the secular ideal are advanced.[6] Moreover, intervention does not always mean restrictions on religious activity but also includes support for them. Further, many of these values are also given a non-individualist interpretation. For example, religious liberty is also interpreted to mean the autonomy for groups to maintain their own religious practices. Another value—peace—is also conceived as a relation between communities, as communal harmony, and not in individualist Hobbesian terms. What is true of the ideas of rights and secularism may also hold for other concepts. In short, there is good reason to believe that attending closely to the Constitution would dispel misunderstandings of some of our key values and ideals.

In her essay for this volume, Gurpreet Mahajan appears to agree with my view, but others do not. For example Pratap Bhanu Mehta argues that the state's professed objective of respecting religion, by restraining itself from not interfering in it, is persistently at odds with its other objective of reforming it. Implicit in the idea of reform is disrespect for at least some of its features. The courts evade this dilemma by making a somewhat forced distinction between the essential and inessential features of religions and by taking recourse to the claim that its reformist measures are confined to a religion's inessential features—that by leaving the core of a religion untouched by intervention, no disrespect is shown to religion. This view is different from my own idea of principled distance, which embodies a critical respect towards religion. An appeal to the Constitution and the debates which preceded it might help decide whether separation in India was ever intended to mean the exclusion of religion or a principled distance towards it.

WHY STUDY THE CONSTITUENT ASSEMBLY DEBATES?

It might be agreed that we must conduct a philosophical and moral reading of the Constitution. But it might then be asked why must a study of this kind be accompanied by an examination of the debates in the *Constituent Assembly Debates*. Almost all the contributors to this volume, with the exception of Baxi and Mehta, refer to these debates. And only Nigam, at least partially, questions the validity of doing so. Is Nigam on the right track? Is it pointless looking backwards? Why risk committing the originalist fallacy? It may well be appropriate for the historian of legal and political ideas to look for original intentions. But why should the contemporary political theorist be interested in them? Why not take account of changed circumstances and redefine the normative function of the Constitution?

Broadly speaking, I agree with a view such as Dworkin's that judges must not transform themselves into conceptual historians who are hell-bent on rediscovering the world of the original framers and who evaluate current social practices in terms of laws as they were in the minds of those who first made them. We must abandon this project not because original intentions cannot be captured—to a large extent they can. However, current legal practice cannot be tied to original intentions for the simple reason that both the language and the world are likely to have radically transformed since the Constitution was written. In America, where the Constitution was written in late eighteenth century, it is surely absurd to apply values and standards of that era to the twenty-first century. However, in India, the world of the original framers and our own world may not be that different. Sixty years is a long time under conditions of modernity but not long enough to conceptually demarcate a society into two radically different worlds. I for one do not hold the view that our conceptions, values, and ideals have transformed so deeply to have separated us from the world of the Constituent Assembly. A history of our Constitution is still very much a history of the present.

Moreover, we may by now be suffering from amnesia about the real point underlying several of our legal and political practices, and have lapsed into a state of inarticulacy about why they are valued or justified, simply because somewhere down the road we began to take them for granted. These reasons have now slipped into the background and are screened off from our consciousness even though they continue to be the animating principle of current practices. This forgetting is harmless when the going is good. But when these practices are challenged or threatened, a sustained inarticulacy about their underlying purpose and justificatory reasoning can damage these practices even more. This can be prevented only when we undo this forgetting and retrieve the original articulations that may be much clearer and sharper precisely because they were achieved amidst debate and controversy and in much harder times. Consider the partition of India and the articulation of secularism in its immediate aftermath. The underlying point of secularism must have been articulated with a greater deal of perspicacity at that time than is possible even in this current phase of communalization. In short, to get a handle on current constitutional practices, to grasp their value and meaning, we may have no option but to go back in time to the Constituent Assembly Debates and perhaps even further back to the colonial era.

I have tried to unravel the complex motivations behind the seminar in which the papers in this volume were presented and to explain why a historical, normative, and political theory enquiry about the Constitution must begin collectively and earnestly in India. This idea of initiating such a process began to stir in the late 1980s but it was only in the early 1990s that some of us began to think seriously about it. The intellectual urgency for this and the discontent about the absence of a significant tradition of legal and political philosophy in India found expression at the end of a seminar organized on minority rights by Dhiru Bhai Sheth in Simla in November 1994. I still remember how for two wonderful hours on a car journey from Simla to Kalka we discussed the virtues and faults of the Indian Constitution and the urgency to explore its modern and liberal-democratic, as well as its culturally inflected, potential. It was then decided that a study week on the philosophy on the Indian Constitution should be proposed to the Institute of Advanced Study. I took upon myself the task of writing a brief proposal on this, but did nothing about it for the next few years.

Yet, it is a slight exaggeration to say that I did *nothing* about it. I may not have put down much about it on paper, but I talked freely and frequently about it. Potential participants were spoken to and the possibility of holding a workshop explored. Oxford University Press showed considerable interest in the topic. There was even talk of inaugurating a major project on the Constitution on the eve of 50 years of the birth of Constituent Assembly of India. That was in December 1996. But nothing happened thereafter. Then, as we neared 2000, a seminar was planned to commemorate 50 years of the Indian republic. This was discussed with friends but once again not put down on paper. Meanwhile others, better endowed in terms of efficiency and secretarial assistance, held seminar after seminar on the Indian Constitution. I even participated wistfully in some of them. In the spring of 2000, as a C.R. Parekh fellow at the CSDS, I was given the mandate and the finances to organize a seminar. The theme was already before me. And thus, first the seminar and then the book began to take definite shape.

II

WHY DO WE NEED CONSTITUTIONS?

Why did the leaders of the movement for national independence adopt a constitution? What was the point of binding ourselves with a constitution? Why do people have written constitutions anyway?

It is widely agreed that one reason for having constitutions is the need to restrict the exercise of power. Modern states are excessively powerful, and are believed to have a monopoly of force and coercion. What if the institutions of such states fall into the wrong hands, who then abuse this power? Many believe that this is not just a hypothetical possibility but inherent in the exercise of power and therefore in the nature of states. Even if these institutions were created for our safety and well-being, they can easily turn against us. Experience of state power the world over shows that most states are prone to harming the interests of at least some individuals and groups. If so, we need to draw the rules of the game in such a way that this tendency of states is continuously checked. Constitutions provide these basic rules and therefore prevent states from turning tyrannical.

This traditional reason is not the only one supporting constitutions. The framers of our Constitution were deeply aware of three other reasons, two of which were already known but had been systematically underemphasized and a third which they themselves helped shape. Traditionally, constitutions were meant to control the power of the state so as to enable people to live decently. But this idea presupposes an unbridgeable distance between people and the state. It assumes a powerless people who need the help of law to control state power. But what if people themselves have power? What if the power of the state comes from an original power that resides in the demos, the people? Why then would we need constitutions? Democracy, it might be argued, is an alternative to constitutionalism. State power might be limited not by some higher law but by the power of the people.

This is an attractive but flawed idea. It is flawed because in practice, power never really resides in all the people but largely in the majority. The tyranny of the non-democratic state of which individuals might be victims is replaced in democracies by the tyranny of the majority. If so, we need constitutions to check the tyranny of a majoritarian, democratic state. We need constitutions because they give us laws to protect not only individuals but also minority groups.

Moreover, constitutions are required not only to protect vulnerable individuals and groups but virtually everyone against human vulnerability in general. It is important not to forget that human beings are fallible, that they sometimes forget what is good for them in the long run, and that they yield to temptations which bring them pleasure now but pain later.[7] It is not unknown for people to acquire the mentality of the mob and act on the heat of the moment only to rue the consequences of the decision later. By providing a framework of law culled over from years of collective experience and wisdom, constitutions prevent people from succumbing to currently fashionable whims and fancies. Constitutions anticipate and try to redress the excessively mercurial character of everyday politics. They make some dimensions of the political process beyond the challenge of ordinary politics. The framers of the Indian Constitution were familiar with each of these three reasons for having a constitution. They understood that constitutions are needed both to check state power and majority tyranny and also to control the destabilizing swings generated by popular passion.

So far we have spoken of what constitutions dis-enable us from doing. However, constitutions also provide us with peaceful, democratic means with which to bring about profound social transformation. Moreover, for a hitherto colonized people, constitutions announce and embody the first real exercise of political self-determination. Nehru understood both these points well. The demand for a Constituent Assembly, he claimed, represented a collective demand for full self-determination, as only a Constituent Assembly of elected representatives of the Indian people had the right to frame India's Constitution, without external interference. Second, he argued, the Constituent Assembly is not just a body of people or a gathering of able lawyers. Rather, it is a 'nation on the move, throwing away the shell of its past political and possibly social structure, and fashioning for itself a new garment of its own making.' The Indian Constitution was designed to break the shackles of traditional social hierarchies and to usher in a new era of freedom, equality, and justice. Inscribed in the intentions of the framers of the Indian Constitution was the potential of a breakthrough in constitutional theory: constitutions exist not only to disenable people in power but also to empower those who traditionally have been deprived of it. Constitutions give vulnerable people the power to achieve collective good.

III

THE INDIAN CONSTITUTION

ACHIEVEMENTS

First, it is no mean achievement to have committed ourselves to universal franchise, especially amidst widespread belief that traditional hierarchies

in India are congealed and more or less ineliminable and when the right
to vote has only recently been extended to women and to the working
class in stable Western democracies. Franchise in India was restricted
before the adoption of the Constitution. Citizenship was based on what
Dahl calls 'the contingent principle of inclusion', that is, restricted to
only those qualified to rule and who could claim citizenship.[8] Citizenship
in the Constitution, is based instead on the categorical principle of
inclusion: to be an adult member in the society is sufficient qualification
for full citizenship of the state. Rights of citizenship, including the right
to vote, were justified by exclusive reference to this principle. In a society
ravaged by persistent social inequalities and marked by a subordinate
role for women within the patriarchal system, how could this come about?

I offer three possible reasons. The first is the influence of liberal
individualist ideas in which the self is constituted not by a place within
the group arena, but in abstraction from it. (Such ideas are unlikely to
have influenced those who played a key role in public deliberations.[9]) A
second reason may well have to do with the less explicit, unconscious
motivations of political actors. In a country dominated by poor peasants
belonging either to backward castes or falling altogether outside the caste
structure, a restricted franchise would certainly have meant their
exclusion from the political process. In a numbers-dominated democratic
system, this could have significantly weakened the bargaining power of
Hindus. I remain unpersuaded by this strongly communitarian, almost
communal, argument. A third reason might have to do with the growth
of the idea of the nation. It is more or less integral to the concept of the
nation that members who comprise it are equal. If so, and if the idea of
democracy has been accepted, then no member of the said nation can
be excluded from the exercise of franchise. This response needs further
examination.

In 1916, 19 members of the Imperial Legislative Council, including
Madan Mohan Malaviya, Tej Bahadur Sapru, and Mohammad Ali Jinnah,
sent a signed memorandum to the viceroy, outlining a scheme of self-
government for India which claimed that without self-government,
Indians in India feel that 'though theoretically they are equal subjects of
the king, they hold a very inferior position in the British empire.'[10] The
memorandum continued:

Humiliating as this position of inferiority is to the Indian mind, it is almost
unbearable to the youth of India whose outlook is broadened by education

and travel in foreign parts where they come in contact with other free races. In the face of these grievances and disabilities, what has sustained the people is the hope and the faith inspired by promises and assurances of fair and equal treatment by the sovereign.[11]

The signatories argued that to regain self respect the Indian people needed not merely good government or efficient administration but a government 'that is acceptable to the people because it is responsible to them'.

The memorandum to the viceroy reflects how Western modernity was lived from the inside by the elites of a conquered culture. A traditionalist refusal of Western modernity would have entailed a turning away from popular rule, but Indian elites embraced the idea and complained, in the name of that very idea, that to be denied self-rule is to be demeaned, to be diminished in one's own eyes. Moreover, this loss of self-esteem was a shared experience—the experience of humiliation was irreducibly collective. The emotional power of nationalism is derived from this register of collective pride and humiliation.[12] Therefore, self-respect could only be restored and felt collectively. Self-government had to be a collective matter too.

But how large must this collectivity be? Should it be restricted to the aspiring elite, denied full access but already on the margins of power? It is of course true that a link exists between nationalism and self-governance and the nationalist demand is indistinguishable from the demand for self-governance, but why should the nation include the entire people? Why could it not be restricted to a small elite? Why should everyone govern or why should some govern in the name of everyone? Why have universal franchise? Why must nationalism be almost identical to democracy?

One possible answer to these questions may be that the particular form of community known as a nation is a functional requirement of a distinctively modern society where social ranks, no longer fixed and immutable, are up for grabs; and the smooth operation of which requires flexible, context-free agents who not only move freely across physical and social space but communicate easily with each other. This freedom from social rank and content brings with it the idea of symmetrical (equal) relations as well as a degree of individualization. It follows that ideas of equality and individualism go hand in hand with the idea of a nation. The making of a nation, therefore, is the process of binding together a particular kind of people, those who have begun more or less to see themselves as individuals and relate to each other as equals. The functional tie envisaged by this account assures that no particular temporal sequence need be followed; a nation-state may precede or succeed a modern society of individualized and equalized human beings.

If what is said above is true, then we have at least some explanation for why no one within the social order can really be left out of the nation. If social hierarchy and strongly particularized identities cease to matter, then no reason exists to exclude anyone (or so it appears, because nationalism does bring with it its own forms of strong exclusions). Liah Greenfeld has helpfully drawn our attention to a change in the semantics of the term 'nation'.[13] In the late thirteenth century, the term 'nation' meant a community of opinion where the constituents of the said community were representatives of cultural and political authority. In short, a nation was a group of social elites. In the sixteenth century, however, the meaning of the term 'nation' changed: it began to be applied to the entire population of a country and became synonymous with the word 'people'. This change in meaning signalled the symbolic elevation of the rabble into an elite, its movement from the wings on to centre stage, from irrelevance to relevance. Henceforth, every member of the population could partake of this superior, elite quality. The transformation of a rabble into a people and of a people into an elite presupposes a profound change in the way societies are imagined—from hierarchical communities to networks consisting of free and equal individuals.

This effected yet another change; in the self-understanding of the nation or the people, the nation exists prior to and independent of the political organization of society, which has the power to give itself a constitution. I have already touched upon the background which makes this possible and which includes, among other things, complex constituents such as a particular frame of time and of common action, and I shall therefore not spend much time on it. The important point I want registered is that the idea of the basic rules of society as stemming from the common action of a people, of a nation, is identical with the democratic idea, for which sovereignty is located within a people, each of whom is fundamentally equal to one another. As Greenfeld puts it, 'Nationalism was the form in which democracy appeared in the world, contained in the idea of the nation as a butterfly in a cocoon.'[14]

This is precisely what appears to have happened in India. Once the idea of a nation took root among the elite, a conception of a political order growing out of the will of every single member of society, and eventually the idea of democratic self-government, could not but have followed. The idea of universal franchise lay securely within the heart of nationalism. In the Constitution of India Bill (1895), the first non-official attempt at drafting a constitution for India, the author (probably Tilak) did not contest that the 'sovereign power of India is vested in the sovereign of Great Britain and Ireland, the supreme head of the Indian nation' or challenge the authority of the viceroy as representative of the sovereign. He did, though, declare at the same time that every citizen—that is, anyone born in India—had a right to take part in the affairs of the country and to be admitted to public office, and therefore hoped that 'under the benign government of the British', Indian citizens would 'in future enjoy and use the rights proposed to the greatest advantage of their country and the British government.'[15]

The Motilal Nehru Report (1928) reaffirms this conception of citizenship. Section 9 of the report reiterates that every person of either sex who has attained the age of 21 is entitled to vote for the House of Representatives or Parliament. It defines the word citizen as any person who is born, or whose father is either born or naturalized, within the territorial limits of the commonwealth and has not been nationalized as a citizen of any other country.[16] The Motilal Nehru Report is unequivocal about the powers of government as derived from the people.

In his presidential address to the National Convention of Congress Legislators (1937), Jawaharlal Nehru opposed the Government of India Act (1935) for not representing the will of the nation. He declared that the convention stands for a genuine democratic state in India where political power has been transferred to the people as a whole. Such a state, he said, can only be created by the Indian people themselves, through the medium of the Constituent Assembly elected on the basis of adult suffrage, and having the power to determine finally the constitution of the country.[17] Not much more evidence is required to substantiate my claim that democracy came to India in the guise of nationalism, with universal franchise as the most important and legitimate instrument by which the will of the nation was to be properly expressed.

The second achievement was to reinforce and reinvent forms of liberal individualism implicit in a commitment to civil liberties, once again in a context suffused with communitarian values that are indifferent or hostile to individual autonomy. A commitment to civil liberties flows directly from acceptable norms of dissent and the availability of political liberty within the confines of a liberal state. As early as the beginning of the nineteenth century, Ram Mohan Roy protested against a regulation curtailing the freedom of the press. He argued that a state that is responsive to the needs of *individuals* and ready for intervention on their behalf makes available to them the means by which such needs are communicated, and must therefore permit unrestricted liberty of publication. The demand for a free press and opposition to its gagging persisted throughout British rule, particularly when the press was the principal instrument for the propagation and consolidation of India's nationalist ideology. Consider the fierce opposition to the infamous Rowlatt Act, which gave the colonial state enormous emergency powers, similar to war-time controls. It is true that opposition to this act was not expressed in ways that were obviously liberal, but in its substantive content the protest was fundamentally liberal and individualist. An opposition to arbitrary detention is as classically liberal as you can get, and this liberalism had a pronounced individualist character.

Third, against the background of communalism and despite its manifest incompatibility with individual rights, a commitment to group rights (the right to the expression of cultural particularity) indicates that the framers of the Constitution were more than willing to face up to the challenges of what more than four decades later has come to be known as multiculturalism. The question of group rights needs further scrutiny. The prospect of the breakdown of hierarchical communities—that is, emotional solidarities that are shot through with asymmetrical relations—provoked many responses. One such viewpoint, known in India as 'communalism', legitimizes a full-blooded conflictual relationship between communities that may view each other as equals, but are obsessively self-focussed and intent upon maximizing their own interests at the expense of the other. Distinct from both hierarchical communitarianism and an egalitarian communalism is *individualist egalitarianism*, a view committed to equality among individuals and marked by a drive towards abstract universalism and *communitarian egalitarianism* that forges a relationship of equal *respect* among communities. Two features distinguish the aforementioned views: one has to do with their attitude to difference, and the other with their understanding of the source of this difference. In individualist egalitarianism, differences are due to individual choice or to a culturally neutral, socially generated circumstance that must be ignored or eliminated in order to achieve an egalitarian order. In communitarian egalitarianism, differences are a result of irreducibly diverse cultural backgrounds and need to be properly recognized and affirmed rather than jettisoned from the egalitarian framework.

The strategy of the individualist response is to treat difference as a disadvantage suffered by a group; the removal of disadvantages by working through and eventually dissolving groups into individuals is, therefore, a natural objective of state policy. From the perspective of the collectivist viewpoint, this strategy fails to understand how groups sustain culture and why every cultural difference is not a disadvantage that must be shed; the eradication of difference is undesirable and impossible. Instead, a parity between irreducibly different cultural communities is required. This does not mean that particular cultural communities never disappear or assimilate into other communities; however, it does mean that a culture-neutral, homogeneous society consisting only of radically self-directing individuals is an impossibility. Though both the individualist and the collectivist responses were in the making in the early twentieth century, post-war liberalism articulated and theorized the former at the expense of the latter.

It is important not to read the mind of the political elite in India within the interpretive grid of post-war liberalism, which, to ward off hierarchical communitarianism and communalism, relies exclusively upon the resources of individualist egalitarianism. The Indian political elite may not have made a distinction between hierarchical and egalitarian communities—they frequently failed to keep the idea of communalism distinct from egalitarian communitarianism. But it is difficult to deny that the discourse of mutual respect between cultural communities was always within their reach.[18] To counter the challenge of hierarchical communitarianism and communalism, they relied on and frequently wavered between individualist and non-individualist egalitarianism. The Constituent Assembly Debates reflect this tension. The political elite in India, working with the resources of a ragbag liberalism, was sensitive to both individual and group rights, and wrestled with the tension between them within the context of a forever-threatening anti-liberal conception embedded in the then existing political practice. The Constitution too reflects, and was perhaps even born out of, this turmoil, and uneasily tries to reconcile individual rights with group rights.

In this volume, Rochana Bajpai examines the discussion of preferential provisions for religious minorities in the Constituent Assembly Debates and identifies why political safeguards for them were withdrawn, and why community rights were restricted to the preservation of their cultural identities. She argues that to explain why this happened purely in terms of the logic of Partition is inadequate. This issue of the rights of religious minorities is also dealt with extensively by Gurpreet Mahajan. Although the issue of special provisions for the *Adivasis* of India (Scheduled Tribes) has been dealt with briefly in some essays in this volume (Rochana Bajpai, Ashok Acharya, Christophe Jaffrelot), the failure to deal with their issues separately is admittedly a major weakness of this volume.[19]

Fourth, a constitutional commitment to caste-based affirmative action programmes shows how far ahead India was compared to other nations. Can one forget that affirmative action programmes in the US were begun after the 1964 Civil Rights Movement, almost two decades after they were constitutionally entrenched in India? But how does a commitment to affirmative action programmes sit with liberal values? Here it is important to remember that liberalism must not be viewed only as a doctrine of individual rights; nor was it believed to be so by more articulate members of the Constituent Assembly. For example, take the views of Sardar K.M. Pannikar, who in the Sarojini Naidu Memorial Lecture (1961) argued that Indian liberalism was made up of two streams, each with 'a fairly long history'.[20] For Pannikar, the founder of the first stream was Ram Mohan Roy, who, 'by emphasizing the right of women to freedom and the establishment of casteless society put the Hindu people on the road to liberal transformation and contributed to the growth of liberal thought in India'.[21] The second stream comprised figures like K.C. Sen and M.G. Ranade, but more importantly Swami Vivekananda, who 'introduced into orthodox Hinduism the spirit of social justice'. By disassociating institutions such as caste and prohibitions like widow remarriage from the Hindu religion and by espousing the view that the reform of such practices is a matter essentially of social justice, Vivekananda spurred a movement of reordering Hindu society infused with liberal principles.

Pannikar also argues that Gandhiji's ascendancy within the Congress initiated a programme of political action based on the same ideas for which liberalism stood. The Congress not only advocated political liberalism but emphasized the 'rights of the individuals and the value of essential freedoms, the rule of law, secularism in politics and faith in social justice'. Two features stand out in this account as constitutive of liberalism: equality and social justice. Pannikar's vision of liberalism in general and of Indian liberalism in particular is far more in consonance with the core values of liberalism than the identification of it exclusively with individualistically construed rights. Some of these issues are discussed in this volume with considerable deftness by Gopal Guru, who agrees that by abolishing all feudal titles and upholding the principle of the equal worth of all persons, the Indian Constitution has the potential to bring about a major social revolution.

A concern for liberal justice is nowhere more evident than in constitutional provisions for affirmative action programmes.[22] To tackle the basic inequalities already existing in the Indian social structure, and to make the formal political empowerment of severely disadvantaged groups more effective, the introduction of constitutionally protected preferential treatment of these groups was thought necessary. It was widely recognized that a mere right to vote and to equality of opportunity is insufficient to ensure meaningful, effective social and political equality. Thus, apart from several general provisions to the right of equality, special constitutional measures were taken to protect and advance the interests of the Scheduled Castes and Scheduled Tribes. For example, Article 334 provides for reservations for seats in legislatures for these groups; similarly, under Article 335 the claims of Scheduled Castes and Scheduled Tribes are taken into consideration while making appointments to public services. Here, the makers of the Constitution appealed not only to backward-looking principles justifying compensation to victims of past harm but also to a forward-looking liberal principle that aims at future equality of opportunity. Indeed, it was precisely because past injustice continued to be a source of current injustice that programmes of affirmative action were believed to be necessary.

Two essays in this volume deal specifically with the complex issue of affirmative action in India. Ashok Acharya's essay seeks to track the trajectory of affirmative action policies in India and tries to highlight its distinguishing features by comparing it to the experience of the US. In India, affirmative action programmes are part of the Constitution. They seek to strike a balance between formal and substantive conceptions of equality and in the process recognize specific marginalized groups as beneficiaries of these programmes. Furthermore, policies of affirmative action have taken the form of quotas. In the US, on the other hand, affirmative action programmes were a result of executive orders and remain outside the Constitution, are tied to the framework of liberal individualism and do not take the form of quotas. This comparative perspective enables us to grasp that the present form of affirmative action is neither inevitable nor permanent.

Acharya also identifies and examines various justifications for affirmative action, all of which he subsumes under liberalism. He examines three arguments; the first is the argument from the principle of non-discrimination. The non-discrimination principle fails to tackle continuing discriminatory practices or to offset structural inter-group inequalities. Since affirmative action policies are meant to tackle precisely these problems, they cannot be properly supported by this argument. The equal opportunity argument is ambiguous between a formal approach and a substantial one. One might expect the substantial approach to undergird affirmative action policies, but even this approach has its problems. Affirmative action programmes in India are best defended by the group disadvantage argument, which requires a policy of radical redistribution that brings us to the threshold of equality of results, though it stops well short of it. Along with the idea of compensating for historically disadvantaged groups, this principle nearly justifies quotas in the Indian context.

Acharya is, however, critical of the extension of this argument to cover the Other Backward Classes (OBCs). The implementation of the Mandal Commission Report, he believes, has compromised both the effectiveness of quotas as a policy of compensatory justice as well as the right to equal opportunity. In his contribution to this volume, Christophe Jaffrelot, appears to take the opposite view, arguing that affirmative action policies for the OBCs should or at least could have been initiated earlier. He argues that in the Constituent Assembly there appears to be a general consensus that the term OBC should be left as vague as possible. People and parties with divergent backgrounds all appear to have collaborated to leave this term ambiguous so that no identifiable group could claim the benefits that might accrue from such policies. Jaffrelot also claims that reservation under joint electorates has failed to secure adequate representation for the Scheduled Castes.

Fifth, by introducing the articles concerning Kashmir and the Northeast, the Indian Constitution anticipates the very important concept of asymmetric federalism. Valerian Rodrigues claims that asymmetric federal provisions embody the idea of 'differential citizenship'.[23]

All these are what might be called the substantive achievements of the Constitution. However, there were also some procedural achievements. First, the Indian Constitution reflects a faith in political deliberation. The Constituent Assembly Debates demonstrate a common commitment to the idea that political outcomes will not be only a reflection of the self-interest of currently well-organized groups but will also embody inclusive principles which encompass even the interests of groups that are ill-organized or invisible at that time. This open-endedness indicates the willingness of people to modify their existing preferences— in short, to justify outcomes by reference not to self-interest but to reason. It also shows a willingness to recognize the creative value in difference and disagreement. This point is not adequately mentioned, a grave error in my view, because what is required instead is its elaborate celebration. It shows that the Constitution is more than a combination of rights-based procedures and goal-based outcomes; it is not just an attempt to bring together negative and positive rights but espouses a substance-sensitive, broadly conceived procedure of arriving at acceptable outcomes.

Further, it reflects a spirit of compromise and accommodation. For many, these are terms not of moral commendation but of disapproval and degradation. I am not sure I agree. Not all compromises are bad. If something of value is traded off for mere self-interest or for a morally degrading choice, then we naturally have compromised in the bad sense. However, if one value is partially traded off for another value, especially in an open process of free deliberation among equals, then the compromise arrived in this manner can hardly be objected to. We may lament that we could not have everything, but to be able to secure a bit of all things important cannot be morally blameworthy. This may have something to do with a conjunctive rather than disjunctive mode of thinking, which allows for the conception of separation of spheres or for a Hegelian-type reconciliation. Both were exemplified in different ways in the Indian Constitution.

Finally, a commitment to the idea that decisions on the most important issues must be arrived at consensually rather than by majority vote is equally morally commendable. However, not everyone in this volume considers this to be an achievement and there is some truth in what they say. Upendra Baxi argues that the Constitution-makers were forced to embody subaltern expectations in ways that 'negotiated avoidance of wholesale derangement of dominant expectations. They accomplished this in a whole variety of compromising ways, by a mix of the "symbolic" and "instrumental" strategies'. Similarly, Nigam argues that the Constituent Assembly was not a terrain where different people participated in the Habermasian rational-critical mode of deliberation to arrive eventually at a consensual 'single will'. Rather, the assembly was a site where different groups came together under the compulsion and logic of power to have a negotiated settlement. The compromise was not only fragile but also morally objectionable from the perspective of those who benefit least from it. Thus, for Nigam it is a gross exaggeration to claim that the Constitution is a rationally deliberated moral document.

CRITICISMS

The Indian Constitution can be subjected to many other criticisms of which I will briefly mention four: first, that it is unwieldy; second, that it is unrepresentative; third, that it is fruitlessly ambiguous; and, fourth, that it is an alien document.

The criticism that it is unwieldy is predicated on the assumption that the entire constitution of a country must be found in one compact document. Some countries have a single compact document called the constitution. Others lack a single document and their constitution consists exclusively of several written documents. In India, we have a single document, though it is not as compact as the US Constitution. Nowhere is the Constitution identified *exhaustively* with a single document. If so, the Indian Constitution is unwieldy only if we compare it to, say, the US Constitution, and only on the supposition that the entire US Constitution is contained in that compact text. But that supposition is clearly mistaken. If so, there is nothing particularly unwieldy about the Indian Constitution.

The fact is that a country's constitution lies not only in a compact bounded document but also in other written documents that have constitutional status. In the case of India, these include not only the many amendments to the Constitution made over the years by Parliament but also some key judgements of the Supreme Court. This also underlines the importance of not restricting the understanding of the Constitution in terms of the intentions of the original framers. The nature of the Constitution is at least partly constituted of the way it is made to work by the courts and Parliament. In this volume this point is substantiated in the contributions of Nivedita Menon, Sanjay Palshikar, Pratap Bhanu Mehta, and Peter deSouza; it is also registered in the distinction made by Upendra Baxi between constitutions as texts (C1) and constitutional law (C2), the site of ongoing interpretative practices of authoritative interpretative communities. In my perspective then, every constitution is an amalgam of C1 and C2. Indeed Baxi wishes to go further and interpret C2 even more broadly to include within it not only the interpretations of courts but also of other 'non-authoritative communities', such as those who are part of larger social movements.

The second criticism of the Constitution is that it is unrepresentative. Here we must distinguish two components of representation: one that might be called 'voice' and the other 'opinion'. The voice component of representation is important. People must be recognized in their own language or voice, not in the language of masters. If we look at the Indian Constitution from this dimension, it is indeed unrepresentative because members of the Constituent Assembly were chosen by a restricted franchise, not by universal suffrage. However, if we examine the other dimension, we may not find it altogether lacking in representativeness.

Austin's claim that almost every shade of opinion was represented in the Constituent Assembly may be a trifle exaggerated but may also have something to it. To show what I mean, allow me to conduct a thought experiment. Suppose that members of the Constituent Assembly were elected not by restricted franchise but by universal suffrage, what kind of members would there be? Would they have been substantially different from the ones actually chosen? I doubt if the quality of representativeness would have been substantially different in 1946 than, say, in 1952 when universal suffrage was put into practice. If so, even with universal suffrage, we would have got roughly the same kind of Constituent Assembly. Suppose further that the voice component was fully respected and that the assembly did became truly representative. Would the actual content of the Constitution have been substantially different? My own view is that given the enormous social diversity in India and our procedural commitments, the content of the Constitution may not have been dramatically different from the one we actually have. Anyhow, the embedded textual intention in the Constitution must be seen to provide us an open normative resource rather than supply a rigid normative regime whose contours were fixed once and for all by the framers.

Still one may wonder if am being naively starry-eyed about the past? I do not think so, because it is my belief that societies receive and invent special moments in crucial phases of their collective life history that are replete with great opportunity, and in which individuals and groups try to transcend their particular preferences to arrive at collective judgement about the common good. It is of course true that they cannot succeed fully, but the outcome occasionally has the imprint of that effort. Is it a coincidence that the *nukkad* (crossroads) of every other small town has a statue of Ambedkar with a copy of the Indian Constitution?

Far from being a mere symbolic tribute to him, in my view this expresses the feeling among Dalits that the Constitution reflects many of their aspirations.

A third criticism claims that the Constitution is morally unstable and does not provide an unambiguous criteria in conflicting situations. This charge is predicated on the assumption that a constitution must give us a general criterion to resolve all value-conflicts and yield a clear prescriptive decision. Now it is true that some moral documents embody a theory that provides a general policy for resolving conflicts between an unambiguous good and an equally unambiguous evil. However, between these two extremes on the continuum lie all the values that actually shape our public conduct and which cannot be disambiguated and fixed for all times.

The Constitution of India, or indeed of any other country, does not embody just one value. It attempts to realize multiple values, some mutually related and others not only distinct but following quite different moral trajectories. The Indian Constitution seeks to nurture national unity but also to protect regional autonomy. It grants liberty to individuals but must also seek to limit these liberties to realize the common good. It is committed to freedom of expression but also to civic peace. Although these values do not necessarily come into conflict with one another, they may frequently do so. Value conflict is an endemic feature of any constitution. No constitution is unambiguously committed to only one set of values and it is unreasonable to expect that it will make explicit mention of a general principle by which to lexically order these values. No constitution can mention very precisely what we must do if there is a conflict between individual liberty and the common good. If so, a constitution must remain an internally riven, quite unstable moral document, forever needing fresh interpretation, contextual judgements, and attempts at reconciliation and compromise. The refusal of the framers to give us well-delineated criteria to settle all moral conflicts is the strength, not the weakness, of the Constitution. A sophisticated democratic constitution cannot yield unambiguous general criteria for resolving conflicts.

Now there is a view in political theory that not only is value conflict necessarily present in human affairs but also that it is irreconcilable. On this view, the gain in some moral value must always entail a corresponding loss in some other value. For example, the translation of many of our goals into the language of rights, while consistent with individual dignity, also increases mutual distrust and hostility and undermines social solidarity. Thus we must either sacrifice individual dignity or fraternal love; we cannot have both. We cannot escape being tragically torn between different values, and this conflict frequently surfaces as real-life, tangible moral dilemmas with which we must live. Something must be sacrificed or compromised. As the American economists would say, there simply has to be a trade-off.

None of the two views or strategies mentioned above—one that urges us to tolerate our tragic moral life and the other that bludgeons us into believing that a higher general principle unearthed or invented by ingenious philosophers can resolve moral conflict—is correct. Even so, the first view is infinitely more accurate and sensitive to our real situation. The dilemmas we continually face disappear only if we are blind to important values. We may also make this blindness our own existential condition; we may live as if other values do not matter. But sooner or later these more neglected dimensions of our moral existence catch up with us. Indeed, they strike back with a vengeance, damaging our commitment to even that value which we had mistakenly privileged earlier. It is best not to delude ourselves into embracing simplistic, Manichean solutions. So what is the way out?

For a start, let me defend the strategy of compromise. Not all compromises are bad. They appear so only from the perspective of those who espouse a single general principle or those with a Manichean view of the world, that is, the moral purists or the moral monists. So suppose there is a conflict between freedom of expression and civic peace, and in order to maintain peace we limit freedom. I do not think this is a bad compromise because here a genuine moral value is given up for the sake of another equally significant value. It does not follow from this, of course, that all compromises are good. If a value is given up to satisfy a whim, self-interest or plain greed, then such a trade-off is not morally defensible and must be condemned. But if we strive towards two or more values which cannot all be realized and then trade them off against each other, in that case, provided one value is not overwhelmingly given up in favour of the other, the compromise arrived at cannot be dismissed as morally unworthy. Many such compromises were arrived at by the Constituent Assembly and incorporated in the Constitution. To my mind, only some of these compromises are morally objectionable.

However, I wonder if this tragic view of the world associated with moral pluralism is not linked to what we may call the disjunctive mode of thinking. By disjunctive mode of thinking I mean a manner of thought that is obsessed with a mutually exclusive this or that. This may be contrasted with what one can call a conjunctive mode of thought, in which it is possible to have both this and that. Examples of such conjunctive thinking and being are to be found in the idea of separation of spheres, as when we agree to do something in one sphere but not in the other. We may allow the expression of some preferences in private but not in public, some forms of entertainment in one type of public domain but not in others. Another form of conjunctive thinking places different values at different levels. Things which conflict at the same level live harmoniously when at different levels. A third example of conjunctive thinking comes with the introduction of temporality into our discussion, a feature curiously but remarkably absent in much contemporary political-theoretic discussion of value pluralism. Here you can have both X and Y, but not now. Introducing X now will create the conditions for not only the attainment of Y later but also for the eventual reconciliation of X and Y. Now this is an element found in Hegel's dialectical thinking and in contemporary Hegelians such as Charles Taylor who work with his idea of reconciliation. The attempt to reconcile apparently conflicting moral values is not always a dangerous disaster as many liberals imagine, but a necessary feature of transcendence. In an inspired passage in his famous book on the Indian Constitution, Austin remarks that the principle of accommodation, much the same as reconciliation, is India's original contribution to constitution-making and is possible only by virtue of the supreme Indian ability to think, without dogmatism, at different levels.

The Constitution reflects compromise, accommodation, and, in some measure, Hegelian reconciliation, all of which exemplify the conjunctive mode of thought.

The fourth and final criticism alleges that the Indian Constitution is entirely an alien document, borrowed article by article from Western constitutions, and thus sits uneasily with the cultural ethos of the Indian people. This is what in a different context I have called the cultural inadaptability thesis, one that I associate with vulgar Gandhianism. In this view the Constitution of India is deeply flawed because its cultural and normative vocabulary is totally at odds with the cultural and normative grammar in terms of which the real people of India conduct their life. One member of the assembly claimed that the ideals on which this Draft Constitution was framed have no manifest relation to the fundamental spirit of India. He predicted that such a constitution would prove unsuitable to the Indian context and break down soon after its operationalization. Another member called it a slavish imitation, a surrender to the West. A third put it more sensuously 'we wanted the music of *veena* or sitar but here we have the music of an English band'.[24] How far is this charge true?

The more specific charge against the Indian Constitution is that it reflects a model of Western liberal democracy that might reflect the values and ethos of the tiny Westernized upper caste but is radically different from the cultural system with the help of which the Indian people make sense of their life. As such it can only be imposed on these people from the outside, probably through coercion by the state. I agree that the Indian Constitution is modern and partly Western. But as we shall see, this does make it entirely alien.

First, many Indians made a rational claim to be Western, with hyper-Westernization becoming a form of protest against the problematic areas in their own traditions. Ram Mohan Roy started this and it is continued to this day by Dalits. Indeed, as early as 1841, it was noticed that the Chamars, despised untouchables of northern India, were not afraid to use the newly introduced legal system and bring suits against their landlords. Second, when Western modernity began to interact with local cultural systems, something like a hybrid culture began to emerge, possibly by creative adaptation, for which an analogue can be found neither in Western modernity nor in indigenous tradition. These new phenomena resemble Western modern and traditional entities and can be mistaken one for the other, but they escape the interpretative grid and discourse relating to both. This cluster of newly developed phenomena forged out of Western modern and indigenous traditional cultural systems forged a different, alternative modernity. In non-Western societies, different modernities emerged as non-Western peoples tried to break loose not only from their own past practices but also from the shackles of a particular version of Western modernity imposed on them.

A weaker version of the cultural inadaptablity thesis also exists. This variant does not argue for the impossibility or general difficulty of modernity's entry into India but claims that despite the efforts of early social reformers, the discourse of liberal-democracy could not, entirely for contingent specific historical reasons, be implanted on Indian soil. For example, the discourse of rights was disengaged in India from its original individual moorings and attached to religious communities. This view is found in Kaviraj, Khilnani, and even in Hansen.[25] I am not entirely persuaded by this view. For a start, this perspective fails to account for questions that are crying for explanation. Why did India adopt the constitution that it did? Why were Fundamental Rights accorded a central place within the Constitution? Why adopt a constitution in the first place? Why the scramble to protect the rights of individuals and only a grudging acceptance for group rights? And, in a deeply hierarchical society, why such scant opposition to universal franchise, to the ban on untouchability, and to formal gender equality? I believe it more plausible to argue that at least since Ram Mohan Roy, and well before the radical politicization of the Indian National Congress, a distinct liberal stream existed, which merged with and inherited a diffuse but persistent strain of something akin to a liberal view within local Indian traditions; that Western modernity could make a considerable impact on an aspiring middle strata of Indian society because it genuinely articulated and responded to their needs. Moreover, liberalism came to India not only through the spoken or printed word but as directly embedded in certain practices, as a structural feature of institutions and technologies.

A third version of this criticism, in my view more subtle, is found in Hansen, who proposes that though the language of negative individual rights, defined in opposition to colonial power, existed in India, it was eventually subordinated to the rights of communities. But Hansen merely asserts this claim without citing any evidence to support his claim. True, the language of collective rights had a visible and sometimes overwhelming presence in India but it hardly follows from this that it automatically subsumed the other language of individual rights. In fact, Hansen's claim begs a number of questions. Were the two languages always seen as mutually exclusive? Did one have to necessarily subordinate the other? Could they not complement one another, occupying and responding to different spheres of equally valuable human aspirations? Indeed, his claim sits uncomfortably with his own view that 'the agrarian movements of the 1970s reveal that as commercialization and democratization transform class and status, the language of rights and entitlements—the right to protest, assert oneself, to be heard by the government—has become naturalized in rural India.'[26] This language of political assertion and protest is part precisely of the discourse of 'negative rights defined in opposition to colonial power'. In conclusion, I would concur with Austin's remarks that though non-Indian, the Indian Constitution is not un-Indian and that most Indians have shown little fondness for traditional politics understood as the rule of the many privileged view. At any rate Indians live far more comfortably on the margins between tradition and modernity than most ideologues of modernism or traditionalism are prepared to believe.

LIMITATIONS

Let me now briefly come to the limitations of the Constitution. First, the Indian Constitution has a very centralized idea of national unity. Second, it appears to have glossed over some important issues of gender justice, particularly concerning matters to do with the family. Third, it does not have enough safeguards to ensure a minimal representation of minorities in the legislature; it too easily side-stepped the issue of political representation of minorities. Fourth, some of the restrictions imposed from the very beginning on liberty and rights always had the potential to generate what Baxi calls 'the rightless people'. For Baxi, the Indian Constitution has been frequently 'consistent of the violent translation of the democratically enfranchised citizens into rightless peoples' (p. 109 of this volume). Fifth, I have never been fully convinced why in a poor developing country, certain basic socio-economic rights were relegated to the section on Directive Principles rather than made an integral feature of our Fundamental Rights. Sixth, although it works with a worthwhile conception of social justice, it does not provide adequate institutional mechanisms to realize it. Parekh's essay elaborates this point, as it does the Gandhian point implicit in the seventh critique—that it is insufficiently attentive to rural India. I shall not write in detail about each of these limitations. I focus on two limitations that have been partly addressed by the Supreme Court of India, and then raise a deeper question about the overall character of the Indian Constitution.

One of the fundamental ideas of the Indian Constitution is that all of us, irrespective of caste, religion, language, gender, race, and region have a fundamental interest in leading a decent life. To lead a decent life is to pursue one's freely chosen or endorsed conception of a worthwhile life and, unless physical suffering is a constitutive element in one's idea of a worthy existence, to be free from physical suffering. A modicum of material well-being is essential to our ability to remove physical suffering or the possibility thereof. If this is so, we all have moral rights against others that they do not interfere with the fulfilment of our basic needs and equally a similar moral right against those who have economic or political power to facilitate those conditions under which these needs are fulfilled. In short, all of us have moral rights to a minimum income, to adequate housing, to primary healthcare and, under modern conditions, to primary education. The Indian Constitution recognizes not only the traditional rights to civil and political liberties but also the moral right to an adequate means of livelihood, the right to work, to education, and to public assistance in cases of unemployment, old age, sickness, and disablement. In short there is an explicit recognition of socio-economic rights in the Constitution. However, as in the Irish Constitution, most of the traditional, civil and political rights are made justiciable and socio-economic rights are not. These latter rights, as we all know, were made part of the section entitled the Directive Principles of State Policy. A question worth asking is why were these rights also not constitutionally entrenched? Why, given their importance, particularly in developing countries such as India, are they still subject to the ordinary process of legislation?

Generally there are three arguments made against the constitutionalization of socio-economic rights and, therefore, of privileging civil and political rights for constitutional entrenchment.[27] The most important one is that socio-economic rights make demands on scarce resources, while civil and political rights do not. One assumption guiding this view is that wherever a demand is made on scarce resources, conflict is inevitable. However, no such conflict ensues when the scarcity of resources is not at issue. But how justified is this assumption? Is it true that where scarce resources are not involved, conflict is avoided and that therefore, while conflicts are at the heart of socio-economic rights, civil and political rights are free of such conflicts. This is hardly the case. As my point about the value conflict made clear, the right to freedom of expression may conflict with the right to privacy. Similarly the individual right to freedom of conscience may conflict with the collective right of a religious group to autonomous religious practices. None of these are conflicts over material resources, yet it can hardly be denied that such conflicts exist. If, despite these conflicts, we can constitutionally entrench civil and political rights, why single out socio-economic rights for a non-justiciable status on the ground that they are inherently conflictual?

A second argument against the constitutional entrenchment of socio-economic rights is that unlike civil and political rights these rights demand state action. On this view, civil and political liberties set limits on the power of governments but do not demand that the state do something. However, this argument is specious. It is simply not true to say that civil and political liberties make no demands on the state. Consider, for example, the right to vote, which is a political right. The right to vote requires that the state hold fair and free elections. This entire business of holding and managing election requires that a great deal of resources be spent by the state. The right to vote cannot be exercised without extensive positive action by the state. Then again, take the right to the freedom of expression. This right demands from the state that it creates conditions by which a public sphere is formed and nurtured and within which people can freely express themselves and communicate with one another. The state may need, for example, to set up an independent broadcasting service. This requires positive action by the state. For free expression and communication, the state must also ensure that any interference with such expressions or communications is checked. This too requires extensive action on the part of the state and the expenditure of material resources.

Most of our civil and political rights are protected at considerable expense and with positive help from a large governmental machinery. The view that one set of rights require only that the state abstain from interfering, and that the other set demands that the state act in certain ways is either wrong or utterly simplistic. A third view is that socio-economic rights can be exercised only if the state spends a vast amount of resources, which are simply not available at its disposal. Now this view misreads the content of many of these rights. For example the right in question is not an unlimited right to any type of education or to any type of healthcare or standard of living. The rights in question ensure a minimal level of decent existence—for example, a minimum wage, primary healthcare, or education. The resources needed for this can and should be available to public agencies. No one has a right to higher education or to a heart transplant, but we must all have rights to functional literacy or to basic immunization from some fatal diseases. In short, I am not entirely convinced that such rights should remain non-justiciable. At any rate this is an issue worth exploring, even though the current Zeitgeist is entirely against any thinking of this kind.

A final limitation is addressed forcefully by Gopal Guru. For him, the Indian Constitution must be evaluated not only by invoking the principle of secularism but equally by adequate standards of social justice. Gopal Guru asks if constitutional provisions have succeeded in creating the cultural conditions which enable mutual and equal recognition. Have the state and its institutions 'succeeded in augmenting the moral stamina of civil society so that it could accept the claims for recognition of the untouchables?' For Guru, the Constitution does not empower the state to intervene in market-driven 'humiliations'. Moreover, it fails to penetrate the inner cultural/moral self of the upper castes. This creates a lasting tension between moral and legal rights. For Guru this tension is internal to the constitutional understanding of untouchability, defined exclusively in terms of those castes which were considered as defiling. The experience of untouchability captures the sites where it takes place but not its source—the upper castes. The upper caste person may avoid being touched 'on the ground that he values his atomized self more than any moral commitment to affectionately touch others'. In other words, for Guru the Indian Constitution is not equipped to generate the moral vocabulary of love, care, and concern. Moreover, since the upper castes retain the ritual power to define what is touchable and untouchable, continue to define the purity-pollution line, and retain the right to associate with whoever they wish to, the pervasiveness of untouchability remains entrenched. For Guru, constitutional provisions do not provide sufficient conditions for achieving cultural goods like recognition and dignity.

I would like to end the discussion with a limitation in the Constitution that the framers could not possibly have addressed. One of the most pressing issues before us now is how to continue the project of social revolution ushered in by the Constitution in a more culturally sensitive way—that is, in a way which is far more culturally sensitive to all the diverse groups in our society and specially sensitive to our most marginal groups. Modern constitutionalism came to us from the West and was extremely handy to fight imperialism. Yet, in very subtle, unnoticed, unacknowledged ways, behind our backs it also linked to the exclusion and suppression of indigenous peoples, of women, of linguistic and ethnic minorities, of other backward castes and classes, and, finally, to what we have now come to call 'Dalits'. Moreover, the language of contemporary theories of modern constitutionalism is dominated by certain authoritative traditions which interpret the key evaluative terms within a certain narrow range and which have all been developed by mainstream Western cultural traditions. Therefore, we need to explore the extent to which the language of the Indian Constitution, resistant as it was to imperialism and facilitative as it was to the birth of a new egalitarian social era, is still prone to marginalizing and excluding all those people who have been traditional victims in our society, even as it helps them to lead a decent life with dignity and some self-respect. These people can use this language and yet be troubled by it. We need to explore the precise form and the exact source of this trouble, this tension.

Given these limitations and weaknesses, is there a case for a wholesale change in the Constitution? It can hardly be a reasonable person's position that the Constitution is immutable. The Constitution is a socially constructed document and must change with the times. However, the whole point of a written constitution is lost if it is changed at will. At issue here then is the following problem:

On the one hand, we may feel that there is little reason why decisions made in the past by our forefathers, and embodied in the Constitution, should be binding on us. On the other hand, we could be faced by the chronic myopia of present-day citizens who might shipwreck themselves, and in a moment of drunkenness destroy everything in one fell swoop and affect the ability of a society to consolidate its gains. We cannot be too rigid either way. We cannot treat the Constitution with sanctimonious reverence, too sacred to be touched, nor can we allow frivolous attempts to revise the Constitution every time a political deadlock occurs or there is a new government in power. This middle path is found by allowing for constitutional amendments but making them difficult. By making constitutional amendments difficult, citizens are encouraged to resolve political problems by processes of negotiation, bargaining and mutual learning. Obligatory delays have the same effect: they too give all parties more time for thought. But how long can we proceed with piecemeal constitutional amendments? Why not introduce major constitutional reforms? Is there a need for such reforms? I do not fully know the answer to these questions. Implicit in what I have said so far is that this is not required. However, we can still specify the conditions under which any constitutional reform must take place.

First, there should be free and open debate on constitutional change over a sufficiently long period. Second, something as basic as constitutional reform must pass the test of unanimity. Every group must be fully involved in the process of debate and discussion and a decision on any particular reform should be taken only if different groups coming from different perspectives and background still manage to converge on it. Every decision on reform must have legitimacy, which is to say that no one affected by it should have a reasonable ground for complaint that his best interests have been neglected or subverted. So, my own position on reviewing the Constitution is this: yes, there is nothing immutable about it but, given that the basic structure is sound in that it encourages freedom and equality for everyone, any reform must be undertaken with a great deal of caution and only if it is morally legitimate (where moral legitimacy depends on inclusiveness in debate and consent on reasonable grounds). Any attempt to bring about changes in the Constitution which appears unreasonable to any section of society will lack legitimacy and will in the long run be detrimental to the overall interests of our country.[28]

NOTES

1. Ivor Jennings, *Some Characteristics of the Indian Constitution* (Oxford: Oxford University Press, 1953).
2. C.H. Alexandrawicz, *Constitutional Developments in India* (Oxford: Oxford Unviersity Press, 1957).
3. Granville Austin, *The Indian Constitution: Cornerstone of a Nation* (Oxford: Clarendon Press, 1966).
4. No book dealing with a particular theme can cover all its major ingredients. Although this volume attempts to articulate the major values embodied in the Constitution, it does not always achieve its objective. For example, many of the normative ideals in the Directive Principles of State Policy have been dealt with perfunctorily. No one has dealt adequately with the section on fundamental duties. Needless to say, it has deliberately left out governmental mechanisms and procedural details from its deliberations.
5. See Rajeev Bhargava, 'Liberal, Secular Democracy and Explanations of Hindu Nationalism', in Andrew Wyatt and John Zavos (eds), *Decentering the Indian Nation* (London: Frank Cass, 2003).
6. Rajeev Bhargava, 'Giving Secularism Its Due', *Economic and Political Weekly*, July, 1994; 'Political Secularism', in John Dryzet, B. Honing, and Anne Philips (eds), *A Handbook of Political Theory* (Oxford: Oxford University Press, 2006).
7. Jon Elster and Rune Slagstad (eds), 'Introduction', in *Constitutionalism and Democracy* (Cambridge: Cambridge University Press, 1993), pp. 8–14.
8. Robert Dahl, *Democracy and its Critics* (New Haven and London: Yale University Press, 1989), ch. 9.
9. It is not implausible to claim, however, that for the leaders of the national movement a part of the self could be abstracted from the substantive commitment flowing from one's traditions and customs, from family and community. In short, a domain existed where a person could be legitimately viewed simply as an individual rather than a member of this or that particular community. Significantly, in this domain a person's unequal status within a particular community also had no relevance. The process of individualization went hand in hand with the process of equalization. Once this idea of political equality—equality in the public domain—grew in importance, universal adult franchise was only a small step away.
10. B. Shiva Rao, *The Framing of the Constitution: Select Documents*, vol. I (New Delhi: Indian Institute of Public Administration, 1967), p. 21.

11. Ibid.
12. On this aspect of nationalism, see Charles Taylor, 'Nationalism and Modernity', in Ronald Beiner (ed.), *Theorizing Nationalism* (Albany: State University of New York Press, 1999), pp. 219–46.
13. Liah Greenfield, in 'Introduction', in *Nationalism: Five Roads to Modernity* (Cambridge and London: Harvard University Press, 1992).
14. Ibid., p. 10.
15. Shiva Rao, *The Framing of the Indian Constitution*, vol. I, pp. 5–14.
16. Ibid., p. 59.
17. Ibid., pp. 86–92.
18. On this, see, for example, *The Constituent Assembly Debates*, vol. 8, 16 May–16 June 1949, (New Delhi: Lok Sabha Secretariat, 1999), p. 326.
19. However, an attempt was made in the seminar to compensate for this by looking at the provisions for Maoris in the Constitution of New Zealand. In his presentation, Andrew Sharp deftly analysed the complex and the shifting manner in which Maoris have been treated within the framework of New Zealand's Constitution. Sharp argues that the problems faced by Maoris are due to a large extent because of the absence of a principled reconciliation between the philosophical basis of the Maoris' interpretation of the history of their relationship with the English settlers. The experience of the Adivasis of India is obviously is not identical to that of the Maoris in New Zealand but there is a lesson to be drawn from Sharp's account in that the modernist constitutional worldview may differ sharply from the Adivasi understandings in different parts of India on how their own society and politics must be organized. Even so it cannot be denied that the Indian Constitution partially addresses this problem by provisions in Article 371A. To maintain focus on the Indian Constitution, we have had to unfortunately omit Sharp's paper as well as Rainer Baubock's on federalism. Both very generously offered to withdraw their papers for the sake of the thematic integrity of the volume.
20. K.M. Pannikar, *In Defence of Liberalism* (Bombay: Asia Publishing House, 1962).
21. Ibid.
22. In all fairness, this is recognized by Khilnani. He acknowledges that 'Reservations had been intended to be a temporary expedient to a less just society', in Sunil Khilnani, *The Idea of India* (London: Hamish Hamilton, 1997), p. 37. But my point is that he fails to see it as reflecting liberal principles.
23. In the paper presented at the conference, Rainer Baubock provided a more general theoretical justification for asymmetric federalism and although he does not refer explicitly to India, many of his substantive points have a direct bearing on Indian federalism.
24. On this discussion, see *The Constituent Assembly Debates*, Lok Sabha Secretariat, New Delhi, 1999.
25. Thomas Blom Hansen, *The Saffron Wave: Democracy and Hindu Nationalism in Modern India* (New Delhi: Oxford University Press, 2001); Sudipta Kaviraj, 'The Imaginary Institution in India', in Partha Chatterjee and Gyanendra

Pandey (eds), *Subaltern Studies*, vol. 7 (New Delhi: Oxford University Press, 1992); Sunil Khilnani, *The Idea of India* (London: Hamish Hilton, 1997).

26. Thomas Blom Hansen, *The Saffron Wave: Democracy and Hindu Nationalism in Modern India* (New Delhi: Oxford University Press, 2001), p. 141.

27. For a discussion of these issues, see Cecil Fabre, *Social Rights Under the Constitution* (Oxford: Oxford University Press, 1999).

28. In this respect, it is instructive to look at the report of the Venkatachaliah Commission set up in February 2000 to review the working of the Constitution. From our point of view, it is noteworthy that the commission suggested the expansion of existing rights. For example, it recommended that the Right to Freedom of Expression incorporate the Right to Freedom of Press and that the Right to Life and Liberty include the Right to Compensation in case of unfair deprivation of liberty. It also seeks to include the Right against Torture and recommends further that education be made a Fundamental Right (an amendment which has already been subsequently made).

Section I

1

The Constitution as a Statement
of Indian Identity

Bhikhu Parekh

I

Our sense of identity or who we think we are informs our values, guides our small and large choices, and gives our lives a sense of direction and coherence. It is a product of the conscious and unconscious interaction between the range of alternatives offered by the wider society and our self-understanding. In a traditional society or one that is relatively stable, our self-understanding is generally in harmony with the way our society encourages us to think of ourselves. We grow up with a reasonably clear conception of who we are and how we should structure our lives, and navigate our lives without critically reflecting on or even becoming aware of it.

A new situation arises when our customary self-understanding, including our assumptions about the world, proves inadequate or is jolted. This happens when we come in close contact with other societies and begin to question our own, or when our familiar world undergoes rapid and extensive changes, or when we are confronted with unexpected problems, or can no longer continue to make choices as before. We feel confused and disoriented, and are not quite sure how to organize our lives. We are then led to reflect on ourselves and ask who we really are and what we want to be.

What happens to individuals also happens to societies. They generally rely on their traditions, customs, and historically inherited self-understanding to structure their lives and define their goals. When they undergo rapid industrialization, become part of a globalizing world, face new problems, find strange people living in their midst and cannot rely on unspoken conventions to regulate their relations with them, or are in danger of losing their familiar landmarks, they feel troubled, bewildered, and disorientated, and ask themselves who they are, how they are changing, and what they wish to become.

National identity is about national self-definition, how a society understands and defines itself. It cannot be defined in the abstract but only in the light of the country's history, present circumstances and self-understanding, hopes for the future, and its assessment of the kind of world that is beginning to emerge and with which it has to cope. A country cannot be whatever it wants to be, for it is limited by its history and the way it has been shaped by this history. It needs to explore and critically evaluate its intellectual and moral resources, so that it knows where it needs to change consistently with its grain. Those who ignore their history as well as those who remain trapped in it are condemned to repeat it and pay for it. Like personal identity, national identity involves a delicate and judicious balance of continuity and change.

National self-definition requires and should emerge out of a vigorous national debate. It should be inclusive and take full account of the variety of views to be found in every society. It should obviously be based on a broad consensus, and can only emerge from a public debate. It cannot command widespread loyalty unless ordinary men and women are willing to own and identify with it, which they can do only if they are actively involved in its formulation. The definition of personal or national identity has an inescapable pathos. It becomes necessary when the individual or society feels destabilized, unhinged, disoriented. But that is precisely the time when they are least able to reflect on it with the required degree of detachment and perspective. Furthermore, since they are overwhelmed by a particular set of problems, these problems are likely to dominate their attention and cloud their views. Unless they can summon up a sense of historical balance and powers of critical self-reflection, the way they resolve the problem of identity is likely to prove unsatisfactory and store up problems for the future.

Constitution as a Statement of National Identity

India first faced the agonizing question of national self-definition in the course of its anti-colonial struggle. It was engaged in the great historical task of creating a new India, and naturally its leaders asked what they meant by India and what it referred to. Was it a territorial unit bounded in a certain way? Or a society with a certain kind of structure and set of institutions? Or a people with a certain history and set of intellectual and moral characteristics? Or was it a civilization? The question was extensively debated for nearly a hundred years by some of the country's finest minds, and generated the broad consensus that India basically referred to a civilization and that it was distinguished by a particular view of the world and by a set of values. There were deep disagreements about what this view and values were. Raja Ram Mohan Roy, Vivekananda, Aurobindo, Ranade, Gokhale, Tagore, Gandhi, Nehru, and others articulated them differently in their writings.

By and large, they all agreed that Indian civilization was plural, and included different currents of moral and philosophical thought, ranging from polytheism to atheism and from crude materialism to the highest form of idealism. In spite of their occasional quarrels and periods of intolerance, these bodies of ideas enjoyed considerable freedom of expression, engaged in a critical dialogue, challenged or borrowed each other's ideas, and created over time a distinct and internally differentiated composite culture. Leaders of India's independence struggle acknowledged that India's intellectual and moral life had become static and frozen, that its social structure had become fragmented, rigid, and deeply divided, and that its civilization had lost its creativity and intellectual vitality. They were nevertheless convinced that it still had enough energy and resources left in it to form, after suitable revitalization, the basis of a new India.

The leaders of the Indian freedom struggle felt strongly that India had something unique to offer to the world, and that its age, rich history, size, and talents of its people entitled it to a major role in it. India was not and could not be just a society or a country like any other. It stood for important values and represented a distinct worldview, and owed it to itself and to the world to make its voice heard. Sadly it had been bypassed by history, and that had to be set right once it became independent. The passionate conviction that India was unique, had once contributed greatly to human civilization, and should once again resume its rightful place in the world was widely shared, and has since then remained an integral part of our national self-consciousness.

II

Although this civilizational view of India persisted after Independence, it inescapably went through important changes. India now had a state of its own, the like of which it never had before, and this naturally became the centre of its collective life. The country faced economic, political, and other problems, and only the state was in a position to address them. Indian civilization had to be revitalized, and here too the state had a vital role. For these and other reasons, leaders of independent India under the stewardship of Nehru defined India not as a civilizational entity but as a nation-state. The civilization was certainly there, but as a kind of a background that was to be selectively appropriated.

Defining India as a nation-state meant a number of things. India belonged to its people, who collectively constituted the nation. 'We the people', as the Constitution puts it in its striking opening phrase, own the country, underpin the state, and can alone decide what kind of country we wish to create. The idea of democracy was not an add-on, but was inherent in the idea of India as a nation-state. If Indians were to take charge of their collective destiny, they needed to develop a common sense of belonging and become a reasonably cohesive political community. This required a shared identity, based on a shared conception of what their country stood for.

There was an extensive debate on this in the Constituent Assembly, resulting in the Indian Constitution, which provides the clearest statement of the country's self-given identity. The Preamble commits India to certain basic principles such as justice, which is mentioned first, followed by liberty, equality, fraternity, and the dignity of the individual. Fundamental Rights institutionalize and protect individual dignity, freedom, and the basic equality of rights and status. The Directive Principles, expected to be 'fundamental in the governance of the country', go yet further. They have a strong egalitarian thrust, and as many as half of them relate to social and economic equality in one form or another. They require that every citizen should have an adequate means of livelihood, that wealth and the means of production should not be concentrated in a few hands, that men and women should receive equal pay for equal work, that there should be equality of status and opportunities not only between individuals but also groups, and so on. The architects of the Constitution were convinced that India could not be a cohesive nation so long as it was scarred by vast economic and social inequalities.

This statement of India's national identity was further articulated by Nehru and summed up in what he called the 'national philosophy of India'. It included individual liberty, equality of opportunity, social justice, secularism, the spirit of rational inquiry or what Nehru called a scientific temper, independence of action and judgement in world affairs of which non-alignment was a contingent expression, and so on. India's acute poverty had to be tackled and that required economic development, but the latter was not an end in itself but a means to a democratic, just, egalitarian, and humane society. As in Europe so in India, the idea of the nation-state implied not only democracy but also equality and social justice.

The symbols of the Indian republic were carefully chosen to evoke its plural civilization and to give the new state a historical depth and continuity. The national motto, Satyameva Jayate, is drawn from the Mahabharata, and it reiterates the central importance given to the variously interpreted idea of *satya* (truth) in the Indian tradition, and connects with Gandhiji's emphasis on truth, truthfulness, and satyagraha. The national emblem refers to Ashoka and the confluence of Hindu and Buddhist influences. The colours of the national flag have a historical and cultural resonance symbolizing religious pluralism. The national anthem is a wonderful statement of identity, and could not be more different from those of other countries. It is non-triumphalist, unlike that of France, Britain, and many other countries. It sketches the territorial boundary of the Indian state in such a way that the latter refers both to the country's natural landscape and ethnic diversity. It sacralizes the territorial space by invoking the blessings of the architect (*vidhata*) of the country's destiny. Rather strikingly the reference to vidhata can be read in several different ways, including the secular. It appeals not to *vishwavidhata*, which is clearly religious and refers to a transcendental deity, but to *Bharatbhagyavidhata*, which could be a transcendental deity, an unspecified local deity of the kind that abounds in Hindu mythology, or simply an idealized masculine version of the more familiar figure of *Bharatmata*. Its indeterminacy has led some to suggest that Tagore had King George VI in mind, but that is absurd. None of the subsequent invocations, such as *gaye tava yashgatha*, and *tava shubha ashish mage*, could apply to the British monarch, and Tagore himself thought the interpretation beneath contempt. The fact that such a charge could be levied at all, however, shows that Bharatbhagyavidhata is not necessarily religious and could be read in secular terms.

As India's first prime minister, Nehru threw all his weight behind the vision of India articulated in its Constitution. He toured the country with indefatigable energy, used every conceivable occasion to tell his countrymen what their country stood for, wrote long letters to chief ministers, and symbolized his national philosophy in his actions and way of life. He won all the elections he fought, and each of these tested, reaffirmed, and legitimized his vision. He took a keen interest in Indian culture, especially though not exclusively the classical, and set up several academies. He had a clear vision of the kind of world he wished to see and of India's role in it. He gave India a distinct moral voice on the world stage, and backed it up by the unique moral authority derived from its great anti-colonial struggle and Gandhi's leadership of that struggle.

Nehru's vision had its characteristic strengths and weaknesses. It was inclusive, secular, culturally sensitive, based on the ethnic and cultural plurality of India, and could be owned by all Indians. It gave democratic institutions deep roots in Indian self-consciousness, held the country together during its critical period, nurtured dissent and disagreement, inspired millions, and gave India the distinct international presence that it desperately craved for. Its limitations were just as great. It was statist, elitist, did little to speed up India's economic development and tackle poverty, paid only limited attention to primary education, healthcare, and other basic needs of the masses, and was insufficiently insensitive to rural India and the religious aspirations of its people.

Although Nehru's successors tinkered with his vision and modified it in important respects, none of them provided a well-thought-out alternative that retained its virtues and freed it of its weaknesses. The Hindutva movement claimed to offer one, but its vision was too narrow, religiously and culturally exclusive, casteist, and culturally confused to carry much conviction. It had no coherent response to globalization, which it could not reconcile with the *swadeshi* spirit. It talked of making India great, but had no idea of how to bring this about other than through military power. It had no coherent strategy on tackling poverty, reducing growing economic inequalities, integrating minorities, giving India a distinct international voice, and addressing the long recognized weaknesses of Indian society and civilization. For these and other reasons it could not enjoy the intellectual and political hegemony that Nehru's vision did. Although the frustrated electorate gave the Bharatiya Janata Party (BJP) a chance, they never fully trusted it with political power, and increasingly saw through its contradictions, which became particularly stark after its defeat at the last election.

CRISIS OF IDENTITY

Not surprisingly, India has been experiencing an agonizing crisis of identity for the past few years. The visions of Nehru and the BJP are widely challenged, alternatives are not in sight, and there is an intellectual vacuum. The frustrations of the Indian people are beginning to boil over. Poverty remains, inequalities are increasing, India counts for little in the world except as a huge market, and China—India's point of reference since the 1980s—is by comparison making huge strides on all fronts. It is in this context that a new view of India's identity has begun to be canvassed by an influential body of people cutting across the usual ideological and political divide. This view, tentatively mooted in the late 1980s and gathering momentum since, is assumed to be so self-evident that its criticism is limited to a few 'unpatriotic' fringe groups.

This new view of India's identity is largely a reaction against Nehru's, and holds him responsible for setting off independent India in a wrong direction. We would expect this line of criticism from the Nehruphobic Sangh Parivar, but it is also shared by Nehruphiles and his erstwhile associates and followers who, though less sweeping and self-righteous, nevertheless feel that he was perhaps right for his time but is no longer relevant today. In any case the argument is that Nehru's India was poor, an economic embarrassment, given to moralizing and preaching to the rest of the world while ignoring its vital defence and other interests, isolated by its non-alignment, and counting for little in international affairs. It is time to break with him and concentrate on the two vital economic and military areas that he had ignored.

According to this new view of Indian identity, India should see itself not as a civilization or even as a culturally embedded nation-state, but as a state like any other. It should learn the art of realpolitik, acquire political power (which alone commands the world's respect), and use it to promote national interest. Political power comes from economic and military strength, and India must aim to become a great economic and military power. This is what China is supposed to be doing, and India must follow suit. Poverty must of course be eliminated, but that is expected to come about as a result of the trickle-down effect, limited forms of rural and urban employment schemes, rural industrialization, further extension of reservations, globalization, etc. Inequalities and injustice will remain and even increase, but that should not matter; and in any case it is neither the state's business nor in its power to do anything about them.

It is argued that if India is to become a great economic and military power, it should be integrated into the global economy, open up its markets, liberalize and deregulate its economy, and in general do all that is needed to ensure a free inward flow of capital and goods. It should also forge close ties with great powers, above all the US, with its control of or decisive influence in all major international institutions and its ability to meet our nuclear ambitions. As Condoleezza Rice put it with a shrewd understanding of India's driving ambition, the US will 'make you great'. Some Indian leaders and most of the media enthusiastically welcomed this patronizing and perhaps offensive remark. Hardly any of them bothered to ask how greatness can be given by others, and whether a country that acquires it in this way does not remain perpetually mortgaged to them. It would seem that some Indian leaders see nothing wrong in becoming America's 'poodle' (an expression frequently used to describe Tony Blair's Britain) if that is the price to pay to realize its burning ambition. Others think that if India can play the game of realpolitik smartly, it will get as much out of the US as the US gets out of India, and eventually emerge out of its shadow.

This view of India is propagated by a coalition of different groups. It has the active support of the globalized and cosmopolitan techno-managerial elite. It is supported by large Indian business houses with global markets in sight, and the ambitious middle classes who want foreign consumer goods, benefit from outsourcing, welcome the prospect of working abroad, and feel elated at India's international status. It is also shared by influential sections of the Sangh Parivar who swear by the policy of *dam*, *danda*, and *bheda* and hope that this will inaugurate Hindu India's long-delayed *suvarnayuga*. This vision of India also enjoys great popularity among large sections of the media and almost all the major groups of non-resident Indians (NRIs). The fact that several influential individuals in the government and bureaucracy have worked in international institutions, or were closely associated with them and have a managerial background, ensures that this vision has a receptive audience.

It is important to note how radically this view of India differs from those of Nehru and the leaders of its freedom struggle. Unlike them it places the economy at the centre of national life, promotes military strength and militarization of the Indian psyche, ignores the moral core of Indian civilization, and has neither a sense of history nor much appreciation of India's ability to introduce a note of sanity in a world dominated by new forms of imperialism. Like them it too is born out of a desperate desire to be internationally recognized, but its methods could not be more different. It seeks international recognition by conforming to others' norms, whereas Nehru and others deeply valued India's autonomy and capacity to set its own norms. No wonder advocates of this new view of India's identity directly or indirectly dismiss Gandhi as a maverick who never understood power, Nehru as a moralizing fool, Tagore as a sentimental romantic with little to say about anything other than literature, and so on.

The appeal of this vision of India as a strong, united, and widely respected economic and military power is easy to understand, especially to a proud and talented people who feel undervalued, bitterly resent their centuries of subjugation and marginalization in world affairs, and envy the way their big but equally backward neighbour (China) has managed to turn the corner. However one must ask if this vision is sufficiently inclusive, inspiring, and noble, does justice to our history and contemporary reality, and creates a just and culturally vibrant India. The answer is a qualified 'no'. Global integration is fine if it is of the right kind and serves emancipatory rather than repressive purposes. And India should of course be friends with every country, especially the sole superpower, provided that this does not damage its autonomy, result in its being used as a foil to China, foreclose its options, and prevent it from fighting for a just and non-hegemonic world order.

I feel troubled by this vision for several interrelated reasons. First, it is born out of fear and frustration: the fear of being bypassed by history and overtaken by China; frustration at not being recognized and respected by others. It is other-determined, and does not spring from autonomous choices based on a careful assessment of the available alternatives.

Second, unlike the earlier definitions of India's national identity, this vision has not emerged from a vigorous and extensive public debate. The country is forced—even perhaps frightened and blackmailed—into it by false fears and skilful propaganda. It is striking that it has not been told the full details and implications of the agreement it has recently signed with the US on civilian nuclear energy, and that the experts are deeply divided about its long-term political and military consequences. Not surprisingly, this vision does not enjoy widespread support in the country, and even arouses deep suspicions that are bound to increase as its consequences become clearer. No view of national identity can be built on such a basis.

Consider the recent strong reaction against the appointment of foreign experts on the advisory committees of the Planning Commission. The reaction was understandable because of the widespread feeling that such appointments betrayed a lack of national self-confidence, and were part of the larger project of compromising national autonomy to reassure international institutions. At another level it too betrayed the same lack of self-confidence. Nehru's India had the confidence to ask Mountbatten to stay on and help clear up the mess he had partly created. Sardar Patel asked British ICS officers to stay on to help stabilize the country. In recent years successive governments have asked NRI businessmen and professionals for advice, and there is no reason why brown foreigners should be more acceptable than white. China has been inviting American CEOs and university presidents to run its universities and industries without worrying about the loss of national autonomy or pride. If the country's political establishment were to inspire greater confidence and be more transparent, and if its critics were to be less nationalistic, then the role of foreign experts, advisers, and even managers would hardly deserve to be a subject of agonized discussion. India should import skills and talents it badly needs and lacks, and use foreign experts to promote efficiency and good management. Like China and many advanced Western societies, which freely recruit foreigners, Indian universities and even public enterprises would greatly benefit from such an import.

Third, suppose India did become a great economic and military power by 2020, or at least 2050. So what? Military power is always relative, and cannot guarantee security beyond a certain point. It would eliminate acute poverty, and that is to be warmly welcomed, though poverty is relative and will always emerge in new forms. But if inequalities increase or persist in their current form, as they certainly will, should it be willing to pay that price, especially as they impact unevenly in our religiously, ethnically, linguistically, and socially divided society? In other words, economic development cannot be an end in itself. It is a means, and requires a clear moral vision of what we intend to do with it. The dream of becoming another America with all its economic and social problems that drives many of our middle classes can easily degenerate into a political nightmare.

Fourth, the proposed vision leaves unanswered the question as to the kind of people Indians wish to be. Unlike most Western societies in which the middle classes played a socially and culturally revolutionary role, their Indian counterparts remain intellectually superficial, with limited interest in ideas, culturally dilettante, and politically apathetic to the plight of their underprivileged countrymen. Recent surveys suggest that the reading habits of most of them remain disappointingly shallow. Few read serious literature even in their own languages or patronize the arts, and many of them find even the newspaper editorials and the declining number of serious columnists intellectually challenging. Few display a strong social conscience—the constant complaint of the leaders of the Indian independence struggle—and are embarrassed by the widespread practice of untouchability and the mindless display of wealth.

According to recent surveys of Gujarat and Tamil Nadu, over three quarters of the villages deny Dalits access to wells and temples, and harass them in all conceivable ways. The story in the rest of the country is just as shameful. Dhirubhai Ambani had 450 kilograms of pure sandalwood for his funeral pyre. Crores of rupees were spent on Sharad Pawar's sixtieth birthday. Amitabh Bachchan's birthday celebrations were just as extravagant. Theme weddings with huge canvas replicas of the Sistine Chapel and palaces of Udaipur costing crores are fairly common among the affluent middle classes, in utter contempt of the acute poverty that surrounds them and without the slightest desire to contribute even a fraction of this money to its alleviation.

When President K.R. Narayanan in his Republic Day speech spoke of 'vulgar indulgence in conspicuous consumption' shadowed by 'sullen resentment among the millions', one would have expected a national debate on what has happened to Indians, why they have become so coarse and insensitive, why they are not outraged by poverty and degradation. Instead the *Indian Express* lambasted him for his 'usual lamentations', *The Times of India* dismissed it in six column inches, and most other papers did not even take notice of it. A vision of India that does little to encourage a sense of social justice, compassion, active concern for the less well-off, a vibrant culture, and maturity of taste has little to be said for it.

Finally, this vision of India as marching single-mindedly towards an economic and military superpower is narrow and exclusive. It has no place for large sections of Indians and even sees them as an embarrassment, is consumerist in its orientation, morally uninspiring, and lacks shared values on which to unite all Indians. It is hardly surprising that it relies on the state to ensure unity and order. The poor and the underprivileged can no longer count on the state to redress their heart-rending grievances, nor on their morally insensitive fellow citizens to campaign for them. They either suffer and decay quietly, or direct their fury against the state, which predictably responds with violence. Since the state is widely perceived to be corrupt and in thrall to vested interests, they respond to its violence with their own. The state, urged on by the frightened middle classes, resorts to even greater repressive violence.

Such a vicious cycle of violence, underplayed by some of the complicit media, has been the pattern for the past few years in many parts of India, and augurs ill for stability and democracy.

The idea that India's overarching aim should be to become an economic and military superpower, then, is deeply flawed. India is not as bereft of imagination as this idea assumes, nor as devoid of alternatives as it implies, nor so desperate for international respect and a seat at the top table that it should fall for what a coalition of interested indigenous and foreign groups wants to sell it. The cynical world of great powers does not respect mimics, and it has its own agenda.

AN ALTERNATIVE VISION

India needs a clear vision of the kind of country it wishes to be, and of its place in the world. That vision must have a moral core, and should embody the principles of individual liberty, social justice, equal opportunity, and fraternity or a sense of community that are articulated in the Preamble, the Fundamental Rights, and the Directive Principles of its Constitution. Its economic development should be judged and guided by these goals. This calls for a democratic set-up, not the neoliberal state that India seems to be bent on becoming; carefully monitored global integration; and a regular assessment of the quality of life available to all our citizens, especially the poor. The state must guarantee livelihood, primary healthcare, and education to all its citizens as a right, develop their capacities to take charge of their lives, give them a stake in the country's development and a greater participatory control over their workplaces, and legislate against their increasing exploitation and vulnerability.

While India must be able to defend itself against those who wish it ill and must equip itself accordingly, it needs to make a clear and objective assessment of the likely sources of threat. It needs to appreciate that a sensible and generous foreign policy devoted to cultivation of friends, regional cooperation, and giving voice to the poor and oppressed people of the world is a better form of national defence than military power or dubious global alliances. The way in which it is beginning to internalize the American terms of discourse and way of seeing the world is deeply damaging to its identity; this serves neither its interests nor those of the US and the world at large. India led the greatest anti-imperialist movement in history, and well knows how imperialism strikes roots and harms both its victims and alleged beneficiaries. It should ensure that no country is in a position to dictate to the world, and should work with others to build up powerful global institutions and a system of international balance of power.

India has long been a home to many different peoples and cultures, and has evolved a synthetic, composite, or what I might call a multicultural common culture. Hindu culture is itself a work of many hands and contains with it a large range of unhomogenizable diversity. This is even more true of Indian culture at at large. It includes and is daily nourished by the creative interplay between its Hindu, Buddhist, Jain, Sikh, Muslim, Christian, secular, Western, and many other strands of thought. Being the work of many hands, it has, happily, no single owner—and that is its strength. Since all its communities have contributed to it, they can see their own images in it and can enthusiastically accept it. It therefore provides an ideal framework within which to find their commonalities and enjoy their differences.

To parody Ernst Renan, a nation's culture is a daily plebiscite, and its legitimacy is derived from the daily discourse and practices of its people. An average Indian can hardly speak for five minutes without resorting to his Sanskritized local language, Urdu, and bits of English. Not only is their language plural, their ways of thinking too switch from one traditional idiom to another. They draw on the great Muslim heritage when they want to express romantic love; on the English or Western heritage when they think of civil, economic, and political matters; and on the rich and great Hindu heritage when they express their deepest moral, social, and religious emotions. Like their civilization, their individual identity too is composite and plural at its very core. As the rest of the world turns increasingly multicultural and agonizes about how to live with its plural identity, India has much to offer it. It will only be heard and respected if its voice remains true to its rich and plural civilization.

Indians need to appreciate that there is no single model of a good Indian. Every Indian has a different personal and political biography, and appropriates India in his or her own different way. They are also embedded in their regional cultures and identities, which deeply matter to them and mediate their relations with their Indian identity. They feel at home in India but are inevitably more at home in some parts than in others. Strong regional loyalties nurture national loyalty. One does not need to stop being a proud Bengali or a proud Kashmiri in order to be a proud Indian. Indeed, one is likely to be a more ardent Indian if one is also secure in one's regional identity. We have seen in recent years how regional pride, whether in Andhra Pradesh or in Karnataka, can release great entrepreneurial energy and stimulate new political experiments without undermining the commitment to national unity and well-being.

Indians need to take a just view of the place of minorities in their collective life. India began well after Independence and successfully overcame the trauma of its birth. In recent years it seems to be regressing, especially in relation to the Muslims. Although Muslim leaders have sometimes spoken and behaved insensitively and failed to join the national mainstream as well as they could and should have, they have been loyal to India and have taken great pride in the country. Some years ago there was a small affray between Indian and Pakistani Muslims in a northern British town. The Pakistani Muslim hurled abuses at Indians, calling them, among other things, inauthentic, and *jhoota* (false) or 'Hindu Muslims'. Indian Muslims retorted by calling them 'fundamentalists' and 'backward', and stressing their pride in a secular and democratic India. The atrocities committed after the Godhra train incident did shake the Muslim faith in India. However Muslims well know that the events in Gujarat were not repeated in the rest of India, and that even in Gujarat, the attack on the Akshardham temple a few months later provoked no anti-Muslim violence whatsoever, largely because the religious leaders involved urged calm. With all its obvious limitations, India has much to be proud of in its treatment of minorities.

Much of the anti-Muslim sentiment arises from a widespread but dubious view of the partition of the country. It is argued that since India was partitioned along religious lines, Muslims really belong to Pakistan and that their presence in India is either illegitimate or an expression of Hindu generosity. Nothing could be more mistaken. India was not partitioned along religious lines—rather, Pakistan was sliced off along religious lines with the rest of India remaining what it had always been, a multi-religious and multi-ethnic country. Indian Muslims do not represent the unfinished agenda of the Partition. They are and have always been an integral and valued part of India, a fact whose full political import neither they nor the Hindus have yet fully grasped.

No statement of Indian identity can be complete without a reference to its diaspora. Contrary to the myth that Indians have been reluctant to travel abroad, a good part of their history is enacted outside India. The Buddhist missionaries to South, South East, and Central Asia, Hindu traders in East Africa, West Africa, Southeast Asia, and elsewhere, indentured labourers in different parts of the British empire, and recent Indian immigrants to the West are all examples of this. Thanks to the Indian diaspora of about twenty million people, India is a significant cultural and economic presence in the world. And thanks, among other things, to the diasporic ties to India, the rest of the world is an integral part of Indian self-consciousness. Just as India is being globalized, the globe too is being Indianized. The role of the Indian diaspora in mediating between India and the world and in shaping each other's perceptions needs to be more fully appreciated than is the case at present. The *karmabhumi* of Indians is as much at home as outside it; there are many little and large Indias outside India, and part of India lies outside its territorial boundaries. Its diaspora gives it both a unique vantage point from which to re-examine its past and a bridge to almost every part of the world.

India has a long and inspiring tradition of rajdharma, which has in recent years suffered a lamentable decline. Whether we turn to its epics, its great Hindu, Muslim, and even some British rulers, or to its great classical literature, political power has always been understood as a trust, a means to public service, and requiring such great virtues as selflessness, self-sacrifice, a strong sense of justice, and refusal to arouse base passions for short-term gains. The great leaders of its freedom movement lived up to this ideal and have left behind inspiring examples. Gandhi identified himself with the poor and the humiliated, rejected for himself what they too could not enjoy, and had no personal property. Pandit Nehru was personally and politically incorruptible and drew no salary as prime minister. Sardar Patel rebuked colleagues seeking to curry favour with him by recruiting his daughter to an important position in the Congress party. Rajendra Prasad, Lal Bahadur Shastri, and many others set similar examples. This is India at its best. Its current situation could not be more different. Petty personal and political corruption is bad but excusable. But disregard of vital national interests, corrupting political life by introducing suicidal casteist considerations, sacrificing the country's long-term stability for narrow political gains, cynical misuse of power, and the sheer lack of shame and embarrassment when publicly exposed are wholly inexcusable. India needs to find ways of radically cleaning up its political life if its political system is not to lose its legitimacy in popular eyes.

A country is only as good as its people, and every statement of its identity is as much about its goals and institutions as about the moral character of its people. As a people Indians have great strengths and weaknesses. Their strengths include their openness to the world (as symbolized in *ano bhadra kritavo yantu vishvatah*); their pluralist attitude to life (as symbolized in *ye yatha mam prapadyante tam tathaiva bhajamyaham*); their capacity to take a relaxed view of and live with multiple identities; their composite culture that has resulted from the unplanned dialogue and day-to-day negotiations of the various cultures and religions that came to their land; and their aesthetic, erotic, and philosophical heritage that is so rich that few currents of thought in the world are without analogues in theirs.

Their weaknesses include a relatively rigid social order, weak social conscience, passive tolerance that allows different cultures and religions to co-exist in peace but without much critical engagement, and their inegalitarian and hierarchical self-consciousness that finds it difficult to detach individuals from their social status and nurture the spirit of equality. They need to take a calm and critical look at all this, consolidate and build on their strengths, finds ways of overcoming their weaknesses, and construct a new vision of India on that basis. Indian leaders realized the vital importance of this great cultural task of self-transformation over a century and a half ago, and made some progress in that direction. Sadly they have neglected it in recent decades, and need to return to it with a renewed sense of urgency.

The alternative vision of India that I am advocating cannot be fashioned in seminar rooms, the Prime Minister's Office, the Planning Commission, or this or that advisory body. It can only grow out of a vigorous democratic debate. Democracy is not only about voting in an election or protesting against injustices. It is also about deciding what kind of country its citizens wish to live in. If people are not involved in the process of national self-definition, or if their deliberations are distorted by misinformation and false fears, the very basis of democracy is undermined. Political freedom involves not just a choice between available alternatives, but imaginatively creating new ones.

2

Gandhi and the Constitution
Parliamentary Swaraj and Village Swaraj*

Thomas Pantham

I

In some influential writings on the Indian Constitution, the Gandhian contribution to the contextual construction of its ethical-political values and institutional practices is interpreted in a problematic manner. In those writings, the parliamentary–constitutional philosophy of Jawaharlal Nehru, Vallabhbhai Patel, B.R. Ambedkar, and others, is shown to have differed very sharply from Mohandas Karamchand Gandhi's constitutional vision of democratic government through directly elected panchayats at the village level, and indirectly elected, decentralized governmental structures at the state and national levels. The Indian Constitution, we are told, is a framework of parliamentary–democratic government derived from the Euro-American constitutional tradition and chosen, by the Constituent Assembly, as an 'alternative to a Gandhian constitution'. Such an interpretation can be found, very notably, in Granville Austin's *The Indian Constitution: Cornerstone of a Nation*, which, in many respects, is undoubtedly the best book on the political history of the framing of the Constitution by the Constituent Assembly. 'The Assembly's alternative to a Gandhian constitution', he writes, '...was a constitution in the European and American tradition—a constitutional tradition with, quite evidently, very different principles.'[1] Pointing to those

* The author retains the copyright of this article. It is based on his research as a National Fellow of the Indian Council of Social Science Research. He gratefully acknowledges Bhikhu Parekh's critical comments on an earlier version of this paper.

'very different principles', Austin writes that while a 'Gandhian' Constitution is that of a system of decentralized government with directly elected village panchayats and indirectly elected governmental structures at the provincial/state and national levels, the constitution actually adopted by the Constituent Assembly is that of a centralized, direct, parliamentary–democratic government.

According to Austin, the divergence between a 'Gandhian' and a 'parliamentary' constitution and the non-acceptability of the former to the leadership of the Constituent Assembly were so obvious to its members that even those who, during the discussions of the Draft Constitution, intervened successfully for the addition of Article 40 to the Directive Principles of State Policy (which instructs the state to organize and empower village panchayats as units of self-government) did not see themselves as 'putting forward an alternative, a Gandhian, constitutional philosophy'; they only saw their role as that of trying to accommodate 'the apparently incompatible goals of centralization and decentralization, of rejuvenated panchayats and direct government'.[2] Perceptively, Austin does note that in keeping with its admirable framing or decision-making process through consensus and accommodation, the assembly did eventually avoid an either/or choice between the principles of centralization and decentralization: it decided to apply the former to the relationship of state governments to the Union government and the latter to the government below the state level. 'The inclusion of Article 40', he writes, 'was a conscious device to accommodate apparent incompatibles [namely, centralization and decentralization in government].' The modern state and the panchayat institutions were seen to be not incompatible with, but complementary to, each other.[3]

Yet, even after the incorporation of Article 40 (which provided for village panchayats), the Constitution, says Austin, remains 'surely committed to direct, parliamentary government', rather than to a 'Gandhian' vision of panchayat-based democratic government.[4] According to him, in other words, the 'Constituent Assembly's rejection of a decentralized, indirect constitution was a repudiation' of Gandhi's vision of a village-based democratic republic. Fittingly, Austin points out that Jawaharlal Nehru, Vallabhbhai Patel, B.R. Ambedkar, and others had compelling reasons for the choice of a centralized, parliamentary–democratic state: it was needed not only to foster economic development and technical advancements but also to tackle such problems as famines, communal riots, the Pakistan-supported invasion of Kashmir, the Telengana rebellion, and the defiance of the Nizam of Hyderabad.

It is true, as Austin and several other scholars have pointed out,[5] that the Constituent Assembly chose a centralized, 'direct', parliamentary–democratic government as an alternative to a decentralized, 'indirect', panchayat-based system of democratic government, which Gandhi had desired. This interpretation however is often associated, as seems to be the case with Austin, with some problematic claims or assumptions about the overall bearing of Gandhian thought and practice on the Indian Constitution. It seems to be assumed, for instance, that a system of directly elected village panchayats with decentralized, indirectly elected democratic governmental structures at the state and national levels is almost all that there is to a Gandhian Constitution and that, by rejecting the former, the Constituent Assembly rejected the latter.[6]

Such a sharp contrast between the 'parliamentary' and 'Gandhian' constitutional frameworks deflects our attention from their common, overlapping, or complementary democratic values and principles. It does some semantic violence to the Gandhian term 'parliamentary swaraj', which he repeatedly used to describe what he regarded to be a minimally necessary aspect of India's independence from British imperialistic rule, and to attain and secure which he devoted his 'corporate activity' during the entire duration of his leadership of the Indian freedom movement from 1920 till his assassination in 1948. For instance, in his preface to the 1921 edition of his book, *Hind Swaraj*, he wrote: '...today my corporate activity is undoubtedly devoted to the attainment of Parliamentary Swaraj in accordance with the wishes of the people of India.'[7] Similarly, Gandhi welcomed the Constituent Assembly as 'the logical outcome' of the 'parliamentary programme' which the Congress had been pursuing under his leadership.

No doubt, Gandhi's notion of 'parliamentary swaraj' cannot be equated with the centralized, parliamentary constitution adopted by the Constituent Assembly. Gandhi had maintained that the *ideal* constitutional framework for independent India had to have, as its basic aspect, a plan for an 'oceanic circle' of 'village republics' or 'village swaraj'. But finding that the Congress was not agreeable to such an ideal, he reconciled himself to the fact that a centralized parliamentary–democratic constitution, as favoured by Nehru, Ambedkar, and most other leaders, had become a practical necessity. Gandhi also made many publicly expressed appreciations of the consitution, not only for its democratic–national and liberal–secular character but also as being compatible with his 'constructive programme' for the resuscitation, social reform, and empowerment of villages and their panchayats.

II

Austin does indeed rightly acknowledge that both the 'parliamentary' constitution adopted by the Constituent Assembly and the incompletely formulated 'Gandhian' constitutional vision were 'democratic' in character. He also observes that, although it is mostly of Euro-American origin, 'secular democracy in India...has permitted the existence of such "Indian" forms of politics as satyagraha, the fast, and the Bhoodan movement of Vinoba Bhave.'[8] This is indeed a valid observation. Yet, I would rather stress the point that it was the Gandhi-led nationalist mass-movement through the politics of satyagraha and constructive pro-gramme that played a decisive role in bringing about a post-colonial turn to the trajectory of the Western imperialist/colonialist parliamentary constitutionalism. An irreducible Gandhian element in the genealogy of the post-colonial parliamentary–democratic constitutionalism in India needs to be recognized and emphasized.

Austin's analytical attention, however, remains concentrated on the political history of the choice, made by the Constituent Assembly, of the 'cornerstone' of India's independent nationhood in the form of a centralized, direct, parliamentary–democratic government as *an alternative to* 'a completely Gandhian system of indirect government'. In the preparation and laying of that 'cornerstone' of the independent Indian nation, Austin however sees no significant mark of any touch on it by Gandhi, who, however, was acknowledged, most notably by Nehru, in the Constituent Assembly as its 'architect' and as 'the Father of our Nation'! Moving the Objectives Resolution in the Constituent Assembly on 12 December 1946, Nehru, whom Gandhi designated as his 'political heir', spoke thus:

There is another person who is absent here and must be in the minds of us today—the great leader of our people, the Father of our Nation—who has been the architect of this Assembly and all that has gone before it and possibly of much that will follow...his great spirit hovers over this place and blesses our undertaking.[9]

Verily, when the Constituent Assembly, if we are to follow Austin's metaphor, was laying the 'cornerstone' of the independent Indian nation (in the period 1946–8), Gandhi, if we are to follow Nehru's metaphors, was actually tending, like a 'father' and 'architect', to securing the constitution or, rather, the pre-constitution of the democratic, liberal–

secular identity of the emergent, post-colonial Indian republic, which he saw was threatening to become seriously deformed by the fires of the Partition riots.[10] In that work, there was a *complementarity* between the institutional practices of 'parliamentary–democratic' government (in the formation or pre-constitutionalization of which Gandhi had played no less a role than that played by anyone else) and his politics of satyagraha and 'village-minded' constructive programme, with which he sought to embed 'constitutional swaraj' in the soil of 'organic swaraj'.

In fact, during the entire period of his leadership of the freedom struggle, Gandhi maintained that the struggle for parliamentary–constitutional swaraj should not be dissociated from the struggle for the attainment of village swaraj or organic swaraj. For instance, referring to the success of the 1928 Bardoli satyagraha (which had been preceded by the Champaran and Kheda satyagrahas) and the historic ratification, by an All-Parties Conference at Lucknow in August 1928, of the constitutional proposals of the Motilal Nehru Committee Report, Gandhi wrote:

If the Bardoli victory is part of history, so will be the victory at Lucknow. Bardoli has shown the way to organic swaraj—to *Ramarajya*, while Lucknow has opened the gates of constitutional swaraj. *Both things were essential.* Whereas learned and politically astute leaders were required for the Lucknow swaraj, the ordinary, illiterate masses served the purpose for the Bardoli swaraj. While the intellect played the chief role in the one case, faith did that in the other.[11]

Following the same line of thought, Gandhi, as we shall see below, made, in December 1947, a strong criticism of the omission in the Draft Constitution of any mention of village panchayats—a criticism which eventually resulted in the addition of Article 40 (providing for village panchayats) to the Constitution's Directive Principles of State Policy.

III

Very appropriately, in the opening sentences of his book, Austin traces the origin and justification of the Constituent Assembly to Gandhi's leadership of the Indian national movement. We are reminded of Gandhi's 1922 statement that Swaraj will not come as a gift of the British Parliament but that it had to emerge from 'the wishes of the people of India as expressed through their freely chosen representatives'. Austin also notes that by 1939, Gandhi, unlike in earlier years, had become enamoured of the prospect of a Constituent Assembly. Yet, he gives insufficient attention to Gandhi's world-historic, satyagrahic role in affirming, activating, and instituting in practice, in a post-colonial direction, the basic values and norms of a liberal–democratic republic in India in the teeth of opposition and oppression by the colonial rulers, who, paradoxically, belonged to the mother-country of liberal–parliamentary democracy.

To say, as Austin does, that the 'provisions and principles' of the Indian Constitution are 'almost entirely of non-Indian origin, coming as they had largely from the former colonial power'[12] is to underplay the significance of the 'post-colonial' turns or re-significations and reconfigurations of those very principles for which, Gandhi and Nehru, like many of their illustrious, nationalist predecessors and contemporaries, were severely punished with long jail terms by the colonial power. I submit that we need to emphasize the fact that even though Gandhi and Nehru, like many of their predecessors and contemporaries, were deeply influenced, in different ways, by the liberal–democratic constitutional ideas of the West,[13] they were *original, emancipatory thinkers* of, and heroic fighters for, post-colonial liberal–democratic constitutionalism. They pioneered the process of the resignifying and reconfiguring of the values and principles of the Euro-American liberal–democratic constitutional tradition in a 'post-colonial' direction. In his famous Quit India Speech of 8 August 1942, Gandhi said:

...I do not regard England, or for that matter America, as free countries. They are free after their own fashion, free to hold in bondage the coloured races of the earth. Are England and America fighting for the liberty of these races today? You shall not limit my concept of freedom. The English and American teachers, their history and their magnificent poetry have not said you shall not broaden the interpretation of that freedom. And according to my interpretation of that freedom, I am constrained to say, they are strangers to that freedom which their poets and teachers have described. If they will know the real freedom, they should come to India.[14]

Dissatisfied with the European tendency to reduce freedom/independence to license or mere negative liberty, he experimented with the idea of swaraj, by which he meant both outward freedom and inward freedom. He mobilized and led India's mass-based national movement for *purna swaraj* (full independence), which was to be achieved through non-violent means, including, in particular, the methods of satyagraha.[15]

His notions of swaraj and satyagraha are syncretistic notions, which have both liberal and trans-liberal features. Civil liberties, freedom of speech, freedom of association, etc., are, according to Gandhi, 'the very roots of swaraj'. He, however, differentiates 'liberty' from 'license'. 'Independence,' he writes, 'may mean license to do as you like. Swaraj is positive. Independence is negative...The word swaraj is a sacred word, a Vedic word, meaning self-rule and self-restraint, and not freedom from all restraint which "independence" often means.'[16] Accordingly, satyagraha is conceptualized by Gandhi as 'a method of securing rights by personal suffering'.

In 1931, he influenced, and introduced the motion on, Nehru's famous draft resolution on Fundamental Rights adopted by the Indian National Congress at its Karachi session. Gandhi believed that that resolution could be used by Indians as a 'strong bulwark of freedom'. 'The resolution on fundamental rights', he wrote, 'is the most important resolution of the Congress. It shows what kind of swaraj the Congress wants to achieve.'[17]

In the light of his well-known commitment to civil liberties and democratic rights, he caused some bafflement to his followers when, in 1947, he commented critically on the debate on Fundamental Rights that was then taking place in the Constituent Assembly. In his prayer meeting of 28 June 1947, he said:

The Constituent Assembly is discussing the rights of the citizen....As a matter of fact, the proper question is not what the rights of a citizen are, but rather what constitutes the duties of a citizen. Fundamental rights can only be those rights the exercise of which is not only in the interest of the citizen but that of the whole world. Today everyone wants to know what his rights are, but if a man learns to discharge his duties right from childhood and studies the sacred books of his faith he automatically exercises his rights too. I learnt my duties on my mother's lap. She was an unlettered village woman. . .She knew my *dharma*. Thus if from my childhood we learn what our *dharma* is and try to follow it, our rights look after themselves. . .The beauty of it is that the very performance of a duty secures us our right. Rights cannot be divorced from duties. This is how satyagraha was born, for I was always striving to decide what my duty was.[18]

It must be remembered that Gandhi made this statement in the context of the then surging Partition-related Hindu–Muslim conflagration, which was seriously threatening the very formation or, rather, the constitutionalization of the Indian national political society and its citizenship. He maintained that any citizen, whether Hindu, Muslim, or of any other religion, who 'neglects his duty and cares only to safeguard his rights does not know that rights that do not spring from duties done cannot be safeguarded'. He went on to add:

Whether it is the Hindus living in a place or Muslims or both, they will come to acquire rights if they do their duty....If Hindus consider Muslims their brothers and treat them well, Muslims too will return friendship for friendship...The duty of the Hindus is to share with the Muslims their joys and sorrows.[19]

Given the multi-religious or multicultural composition of the citizenry in India, Gandhi maintained that the liberties and rights of citizenship could be secured only if that citizenship is grounded not only in their civic duty toward the common good of the political community but also in their moral duties, as human beings, towards one another.

IV

In the concluding chapter of his book, Austin attributes the successful working of the Indian Constitution to the fact that 'the Indian tradition and Indian society were congenial to democratic government' or, in other words, to the fact that 'the ideas and spirit of English liberal democracy fell on fertile ground'.[20] Actually, those 'ideas and spirit' did not fall like manna from heaven onto the grounds of a democracy-hungry society. No doubt, Gandhi, like most of his colleagues, was receptive to, and deeply influenced by, the ideas and spirit of English liberal democracy. But he was painfully aware, as he wrote in 1921, that the day was far off when 'Swaraj would descend upon India from heaven'. He, however, unlike any other leader before him, transformed the Indian National Congress from an urban, elite gathering into a democratic–nationalist mass-movement, in which the peasantry came to play a major role. An integral part of that movement was the much-misunderstood and much-resisted Gandhi-led struggle *against* such utterly anti-democratic Indian traditions as untouchability.[21]

Can a constitution which sanctifies adult franchise and abolishes untouchability be said to be 'an alternative' to a 'Gandhian' Constitution? Similarly, since it was Gandhi who, since the infamous Rowlatt Acts (1919), mobilized and led the Indian democratic–nationalist movement till the coming of Independence, the underlying or justificatory political philosophy of India's post-colonial liberal–democratic Constitution cannot be said to be lying mostly outside of the Gandhian political or constitutional philosophy. Civil liberties and democratic rights, which are enshrined in the Indian Constitution, are basic to Gandhi's political philosophy.

V

In his celebrated booklet, *Hind Swaraj* (1909),[22] Gandhi made a severe criticism of modern Western civilization and its major institutions, including, in particular, the modern, 'direct' parliamentary government of imperialist England. He found its parliament to be an institution, which operated according to 'outside pressure' or for the self-interest of its members. He argued that 'Hind Swaraj', if it had to be 'truly Swaraj', could not be had by 'copying' or 'importing' the institutions of 'the Government of England'. For its swaraj, India should, he argued, rely on those institutions of its own civilization, which have remained largely unaffected by the operations of the main institutions of modern Western civilization. Whereas, according to him, the ancient villages of India had been a self-reliant 'congeries of republics', they have become reduced, after the coming of the British colonial system, to 'a state of miserable dependence and idleness'. He said that the building up of the city-based colonial network of trade and governance in India had broken up 'a part of her village system'. He wrote in 1921:

Our cities are not India. India lives in her seven and a half lakhs of villages, and the cities live upon the villages. They do not bring their wealth from other countries. The city people are brokers and commission agents for the big houses of Europe, America and Japan. The cities have cooperated with the latter in the bleeding process that has gone on for the past two hundred years.[23]

In his political approach to, and vision of, independent India, therefore, the resuscitation, social reform, and empowerment of India's villages and their panchayats came to acquire crucial importance. Relatedly, he transformed the Indian National Congress from an urban elite gathering to a mass movement in which the rural masses of India came to play an important role. His 'villageism', however, he said, was not an ideology for 'putting back the hands of the clock of progress'; it was a call to the city-dwellers to give back to the villages what is due to them and to engage in village-oriented constructive programme. He wrote in 1942:

My idea of village swaraj is that it is a complete republic, independent of its neighbours for its own vital wants, and yet interdependent for many others in which dependence is a necessity...As far as possible, every activity will be conducted on the cooperative basis. There will be no castes such as we have today with their graded untouchability...The government of the village will be conducted by a panchayat of five persons annually elected by the adult villagers, male and female, possessing minimum prescribed qualifications. These will have all the authority and jurisdiction required.[24]

The attainment of village swaraj was, however, according to Gandhi, dependent upon, or, rather, associated with, the attainment of 'parliamentary swaraj': without the latter, the British imperialistic rule along with its city-centred, collaborative network would continue indefinitely. That is why he devoted his 'corporate activity' during his leadership of the nationalist movement to the securing of 'parliamentary swaraj'.

At the Second Round Table Conference (1931), Gandhi declared that the National Government of India 'would be engaged in passing legislation in order to raise the down-trodden, and the fallen, from the mire into which they have been sunk by the capitalists, by the landlords, by the so-called higher classes, and, then, subsequently and scientifically, by the British rulers.'[25] In 1946, when the Constituent Assembly was set up, he welcomed it and made the following acknowledgement: 'The labour of the late Deshbandhu Chittaranjan Das and Pandit Motilal Nehru opened my eyes to the fact that the parliamentary programme had a place in the national activity for independence.'[26] Gandhi urged all the parties and the princely states to join the Constituent Assembly. Earlier, on 14 September 1939, when Jawaharlal Nehru introduced a Congress resolution calling for the setting up of the Constituent Assembly, Gandhi wrote:

Pandit Jawaharlal Nehru has compelled me to study, among other things, the implications of a Constitutent Assembly. When he first introduced it in the Congress resolutions, I reconciled myself to it because of my belief in his superior knowledge of the technicalities of democracy. But I was not free from scepticism. Hard facts have, however, made me a convert and, for that reason perhaps, more enthusiastic than Jawaharlal himself. For I seem to see in it a remedy, which Jawaharlal may not, for our communal and other distempers, besides being a vehicle for mass political and other education...[T]he way to democratic *swaraj* lies only through a properly constituted [Constituent] Assembly...[27]

VI

In Gandhi's view, 'parliamentary swaraj' was a necessary but not sufficient condition of the true swaraj of India in terms of its villages. He distinguished a pyramidal, state-centred, top–down model of parliamentary–democratic government from his ideal social order of concentric circles of individual swaraj, village swaraj, parliamentary swaraj, and a worldwide confederation of free and friendly states.

With the approach of Indian independence, he made special efforts to persuade his colleagues to adopt a panchayat-based or 'village-minded' constitutional framework and developmental approach. In October–November 1945, he and Nehru exchanged letters about the 'difference of outlook' between them concerning 'the system of government' and approach to development to be followed in independent India. On 5 October 1945, Gandhi wrote to Nehru that although he still stood by 'the system of government envisaged in *Hind Swaraj*', he felt that it would be 'better for me to draw the picture anew in my own words' so as to convey 'what I feel today'. He stated that 'if India is to attain true freedom', the main focus has to be on the life of the people in the villages. He went on to write:

While I admire modern science, I find that it is the old looked at in the true light of modern science which should be reclothed and refashioned aright. You must not imagine that I am envisaging our village life as it is today. The village of my dreams is still in my mind. After all every man lives in the world of his dreams. My ideal village will contain intelligent human beings. They will not live in dirt and darkness as animals. Men and women will be free and able to hold their own against any one in the world. There will be neither plague, nor cholera nor smallpox; no one will be idle, no one will wallow in luxury. Everyone will have to contribute his quota of manual labour. I do not want to draw a large-scale picture in detail. It is possible to envisage railways, post and telegraph offices etc.[28]

In his reply, dated 9 October 1945, Nehru wrote that 'vast changes have taken place all over the world' since *Hind Swaraj* was written. He pointed out that Gandhi's views on the village were unrealistic and devoid of any appreciation of the good that is present in such modern developments as 'scientific growth', industrialization, modern means of transport, etc.

These, Nehru stated, are inevitable for achieving such minimal requirements as 'sufficiency of food, clothing, housing, education, sanitation, etc'. He pointed out that India's modern-day needs do not 'fit in with a purely village society'. 'I do not understand', he wrote, 'why a village should necessarily embody truth and non-violence. A village, normally speaking, is backward intellectually and culturally and no progress can be made from a backward environment. Narrow-minded people are much more likely to be untruthful and violent.'[29]

On 12 November 1945, Gandhi and Nehru met and discussed their fundamentally different approaches to development. Nehru's firm affirmation of their differences 'involving varying philosophies of life' and his strong criticism of the conservative and unrealistic assumptions and implications of Gandhi's village-based approach had considerable impact on Gandhi. On 5 October 1945, Gandhi had felt concerned about the widening difference between their outlooks and had written that for India's true freedom 'people will have to live in villages', but on 13 November 1945 he wrote to Nehru that he was gladdened by their meeting and that 'there is not much difference in our outlook'. Gandhi felt that they were agreed on the ideals of 'equal right and opportunity for all' and of 'equality between the town-dwellers and the villagers in the standard of food and drink, clothing and other living conditions'.[30]

Following this renewed exchange of ideas with Nehru, Gandhi became more appreciative of the necessary role of the Constituent Assembly and of parliamentary–democratic activity for bringing about order, communal harmony and social justice.[31] While retaining his earlier commitment to the ideal of village swaraj or panchayat raj, he henceforth came around to recognize the practical necessity of viewing his plan of village swaraj as a necessary and salubrious complement to, and check or pull on, the Nehru-favoured parliamentary–democratic government. He made it clear, in word and deed, that parliamentary swaraj and village swaraj were envisaged by him to be critically complementary to, or at least compatible with, each other.

On 28 July 1946, Gandhi said:

Independence must begin at the bottom. Thus, every village will be a republic or panchayat having full powers…Thus, ultimately, it is the individual who is the unit. This does not exclude dependence on and willing help from neighbours or from the world…

…

In this structure composed of innumerable villages, there will be ever widening, never-ascending circles. Life will not be a pyramid with the apex sustained by the bottom. But it will be an oceanic circle whose centre will be the individual always ready to perish for the village, the latter ready to perish for the circle of villages, till at last the whole becomes one life composed of individuals, never aggressive in their arrogance but ever humble, sharing the majesty of the oceanic circle of which they are integral units.[32]

Gandhi clarified that this was not a descriptive account of actual village life in contemporary India but an ideal picture, which, 'though never realizable in its completeness' is worth striving for in independent India.

During a train journey to Calcutta on 30 November 1945, he wrote an endorsing foreword to Shriman Narayan Agarwal's booklet, *A Gandhian Constitution for Free India*, which, in the main, proposed a system of governance through directly elected village panchayats and indirectly elected governmental structures at the provincial/state and national levels. In his foreword, Gandhi wrote that although he found nothing in the book which 'jarred on me as inconsistent with what I would like to stand for', the reader should not take the book as representing 'my view in every detail'. Gandhi noted: 'Perhaps the expression "Gandhian Constitution" is not a fitting title for Principal Agrawal's pages...The framework is really Principal Agrawal's, based on his study of my writings.' Gandhi added that Agrawal's book, as he has himself indicated, is not meant to be taken as a 'complete constitution' but only as a broad indication of 'what a constitution of my conception would be'. Gandhi concluded that he regarded Agrawal's book to be 'a thoughtful contribution to the many attempts at presenting India with constitutions'.[33]

In July 1946, Gandhi acknowledged that he was not very hopeful that 'the India of his dreams', as an oceanic circle of village republics, would be agreed to by the Constituent Assembly or the Congress. 'I know on the contrary', he went on to say, 'that many [Congressmen] would have India become a first-class military power and wish for India to have a strong centre and build the whole structure round it.'[34] As he had by then become more appreciative than before of the instrumentality of the parliamentary–democratic activity for order, communal harmony, and social justice,[35] he gave added emphasis to the idea that the state-centred or parliament-based approach to democracy in independent India had to be *kept in check and complemented* by resuscitated, reformed, and empowered villages and their panchayats. As if in recognition of the merits of Nehru's and Ambedkar's objections to what may be called the ideology of 'villagism', Gandhi placed renewed emphasis on the need for village-level 'constructive programme' or social reform. As we shall see below, in his 'Last Will' he stipulated that the eradication of untouchability and the promotion of communal harmony should be among the primary duties of the village-oriented *Lok Sevaks*.

VII

During 1946–8, both Gandhi and Nehru became increasingly appreciative of the fact that their differing constitutional visions had some significant normative and institutional commonalities or overlappings, and complementarities or compatibilities, which they, in fact, cooperatively relied on to save and secure the integrity of the nascent post-colonial liberal–democratic republic of India.

In a long meeting with the Deccan Princes at Pune on 28 July 1946, the following question was put to Gandhi: 'What would you say if the [Princely] States organized themselves on the basis of village republics first and then formed them into a union?' Gandhi replied: ' That would be excellent, but then you will speak a different language [from that of the Constituent Assembly] and proceed to work in an altogether different way.' When asked how this was to be brought about in the princely states, Gandhi replied that neither the princes nor their ministers are fit, by their tradition and training, to attempt any such task. 'Therefore', he went on to say, 'my advice to you is: Make Pandit Jawaharlal Nehru your Chief Minister, if you are in earnest. Let him present you with an outline. He will naturally consult the people.'[36] He also advised the princes to leave the major political decisions about the future constitutional set-up of the princely states to the Constituent Assembly.

In November 1946, Gandhi consulted Nehru as to whether or not he should go on his peace mission to riot-torn Noakhali. Nehru replied: 'Although we need you so much here [in Delhi], we need you more in Noakhali.' In Noakhali, Gandhi, the satyagrahi, moved about under police and military protection. In June 1947, Gandhi and Nehru together visited the refugee camps at Haridwar. Some three months later, Gandhi was saved by the police when he was seriously wounded by a violent mob in Calcutta. On his return to Delhi from Calcutta, Gandhi, during his satyagrahic fast against communal riots, made repeated appeals to the people that they have to give the newly formed central 'parliamentary' government of independent India a chance 'to set the house in order'.

During the last two days of that fast, incidentally, Prime Minister Jawaharlal Nehru too did not take any food. When Gandhi came to know of this, he wrote in what was to be his last letter to Nehru: 'Give up your fast…May you live long and continue to be the jewel of India.'[37]

These are admittedly instances or episodes of practical-political complementation or supplementation, rather than any theoretical or philosophical reconciliation, between the 'Gandhian' and the Nehruvian/ 'parliamentary' approaches to liberal–constitutional democracy.[38] Those practical-political complementations that were actually pursued are, however, in my view certainly reflective of a common meeting ground or overlapping between the political philosophies underlying or informing the 'Gandhian' and Nehruvian/parliamentary constitutional frameworks. The basic values and principles of a liberal–secular, democratic republic, such as personal freedoms, civil liberties, freedom of conscience and opinion, freedom of speech and association, public reason, adult franchise, democratic rights, representative democracy, minority rights, a liberal–secular state, and social justice are common to both the Gandhian and Nehruvian/parliamentary versions or variants of liberal–constitutional democracy. In adopting those values and institutionalizing them in India, Gandhi and the Gandhians played a far more important role than that played by anyone else.[39]

VIII

In the last few months of his life, Gandhi made renewed interventions to secure a constitutional status for village panchayats and to affirm and ensure the relative autonomy—from the state—of the Gandhian organizations engaged in the village-based or village-minded constructive programme.

In December 1947, his attention was drawn to the fact that the Draft Constitution contained no mention of village panchayats. Reacting to it in a meeting of the Constructive Works Committee of the Congress on 11/12 December 1947, Gandhi said:

Shriman Narayan Agrawal has written to me that in the Constitution that is being framed now, there is no mention of gram panchayat, whereas the Congressmen have always said that the gram panchayat must be the foundation of our future polity. We have to resuscitate the village, make it prosperous and give it more education and more power. What good will the Constitution be if the village does not find its due place in it?[40]

Just four days before his death at the hands of his assassin on 30 January 1948, Gandhi, in an interview given to Vincent Sheean, reiterated his commitment to the critical-complementary relationship between parliamentary–democratic government and village-based or 'village-minded' constructive work. Sheean asked Gandhi how the existing government can be transformed if those engaged in the Gandhian 'Constructive Programme' were to keep away from it, as Gandhi wanted them to. Gandhi replied: "There are about half a dozen constructive work organizations. I do not send them to the parliament. I want them to keep parliament in check by educating and guiding the voters.'[41]

On the eve of the day of his death, Gandhi drafted a new resolution-cum-constitution for the Indian National Congress. (He had presented a somewhat similar earlier draft resolution in 1946.) In the new draft, which has come to be known as his 'Last Will and Testament', he proposed that as India has 'attained political independence through means devised by the Indian National Congress', the latter should now disband its existing organization and flower into a Lok Sevak Sangh to work for India's attainment of 'social, moral and economic independence in terms of its seven hundred thousand villages as distinguished from its cities and towns'.[42] In the document, the composition and organization of the Lok Sevak Sangh is indicated briefly. 'Every panchayat of five adult men or women being villagers or village-minded shall form a unit.' Two such contiguous units are to elect a first-grade leader. Fifty first-grade leaders will then elect a second-grade leader. All second-grade leaders so elected 'shall serve jointly for the whole of India and severally for their respective areas'. They may elect, whenever they may deem necessary, a chief to regulate and command all the groups.

Gandhi did not spell out the specific nature of the inter-relationship between the basic units of the Lok Sevak Sangh and the village panchayats. He may however be taken to have envisaged both village panchayats and the Lok Sevak Sangh to exist and function in a relatively autonomous, complementary, and 'constructive' relationship with the parliamentary–democratic government, which, as he knew, the Constituent Assembly was then in the process of adopting.[43] Gandhi, as perceptively noted by Bhikhu Parekh,

...pleaded for a polity articulated in terms of the complementary and mutually regulating institutions of the state and the Lok Sevak Sangh. The new polity was to be a partnership between them in the massive task of regenerating

India. The state was to draw on the Sangh's grassroots experiences and expertise in formulating its policies and enact facilitating legislation. For its part the Sangh was to take over much of the nation-building work of the state and help implement its policies.[44]

As Parekh goes on to add, Gandhi was 'most anxious that the state and the Sangh must retain their distance and respect each other's autonomy'.

By working in and/or for the villages, the Lok Sevak Sangh, Gandhi wrote, can contribute to 'India's progress towards its democratic goal'. He listed ten sets of duties for the Lok Sevaks. Included in the first set was their duty to work for untouchability eradication and communal harmony. 'If a Hindu', Gandhi wrote, 'he [i.e. the Lok Sevak] must have abjured untouchability in any shape or form in his own person or in his own family and must be a believer in the ideal of inter-communal unity, equal respect and regard for all religions and equality of opportunity and status for all irrespective of race, creed or sex.' Another task assigned to the Lok Sevak was to assist the villagers to secure the right of franchise.

By way of a conclusion, I would say that the Indian parliamentary–constitutional philosophy is not dichotomous with, or exclusionary towards, the Gandhian constitutional philosophy. They have a considerable range of overlapping and complementary or compatible democratic values and institutions: for example, individual freedoms, civil liberties, democratic rights, social justice, a liberal–democratic–secular state, village panchayats, a value-commitment to peace and justice in the world at large, and a commitment or openness to the values and principles of civil disobedience and satyagraha. I feel that we need to recognize and emphasize those democratic overlappings and complementarities or compatibilities if we are to appreciate the normative originality and resourcefulness and the institutional vitality and suppleness of the Indian post-colonial constitutional democracy, which might not without them have come into existence or survived its post-Independence crises of identity and hope.[45]

NOTES

1. Granville Austin, *The Indian Constitution: Cornerstone of a Nation* (New Delhi: Oxford University Press, [1966] 1999), pp. 31–2.
2. Ibid., pp. 37–8.
3. Ibid., pp. 49, 319.
4. Ibid., p. 38.

5. See, for instance, Dilip Kumar Chatterjee, *Gandhi and Constitution Making in India* (New Delhi: Associated Publishing House, 1984); R. Sudarshan, 'The Political Consequences of Constitutional Discourse', in T.V. Satyamurthy (ed.), *Social Change and Political Discourse in India*, vol. I (New Delhi: Oxford University Press, 1994); and Upendra Baxi, 'The (Im)possibility of Constitutional Justice: Seismographic Notes on Indian Constitutionalism', in Z. Hasan, E. Sridharan, and R. Sudarshan (eds), *India's Living Constitution* (New Delhi: Permanent Black, 2002).

6. Interestingly, Austin, *The Indian Constitution*, p. 37, points out that a 'Gandhian governmental system' would have amounted to a negation of centralized planning, great-power status for India, the development of heavy industry, etc.

7. M.K. Gandhi, *Hind Swaraj or Indian Home Rule*, revised new edition, 7th Reprint (Ahmedabad: Navajivan, 1989), p. 16.

8. Austin, *The Indian Constitution*, p. 326.

9. *Constituent Assembly Debates (CAD)* (New Delhi: Publications Division, Government of India, Reprint 1966), vol. I, p. 60.

10. For a valuable discussion of Gandhi's satyagrahic activities in Kolkata (from 9 August to 7 September 1947), including a three-day fast for bringing about communal harmony, see Dennis Dalton, *Gandhi's Power: Nonviolence in Action* (New Delhi: Oxford University Press, [1993] 1999), ch. 5: 'The Calcutta Fast'.

11. M.K. Gandhi, *Collected Works of Mahatma Gandhi* (New Delhi: Publications Division, Government of India, Print Version in 100 vols., 1958–1994), vol. 37, pp. 249–50, emphasis added.

12. Austin, *The Indian Constitution*, p. 308.

13. See Anthony Parel, 'A Gandhian Liberalism?' in A. Copley and G. Paxton (eds), *Gandhi and the Contemporary World* (Chennai: Indo-British Historical Society, 1997).

14. *Collected Works of Mahatma Gandhi* (CD-ROM version) (Publications Division, Government of India, New Delhi, 1999), vol. 83, p. 203.

15. See Bhikhu Parekh, *Colonialism, Tradition and Reform* (New Delhi: Sage, 1989); Anthony Parel, 'The Doctrine of Swaraj in Gandhi's Philosophy', in Upendra Baxi and Bhikhu Parekh (eds), *Crisis and Change in Contemporary India* (New Delhi: Sage, 1995); Thomas Pantham, 'Beyond Liberal Democracy: Thinking with Mahatama Gandhi', in T. Pantham and K.L. Deutsch (eds), *Political Thought in Modern India* (New Delhi: Sage, 1996); Thomas Pantham, 'Postrelativism in Emancipatory Thought: Gandhi's Swaraj and Satyagraha', in D.L. Sheth and Ashis Nandy (eds), *The Multiverse of Democracy* (New Delhi: Sage, 1996); and Dennis Dalton, 'Gandhi on Freedom, Rights, and Responsibility', *Gandhi Marg*, July–September 1998, pp. 133–54.

16. Gandhi, *Collected Works* (Print Version), vol. 45, p. 264.

17. Ibid., vol. 46, p. 166.

18. Ibid., vol. 88, p. 230.

19. Ibid., vol. 88, pp. 236–8.

20. Austin, *The Indian Constitution*, p. 330.
21. For a valuable analysis of the Gandhian movement for the abolition of untouchability, see Bhikhu Parekh, *Colonialism, Tradition and Reform: An Analysis of Gandhi's Political Discourse* (New Delhi: Sage, 1989), ch. 7. That Gandhi's anti-untouchability movement formed an integral part of his conception of the national movement for constitutional democracy in independent India is insightfully analysed in Ravinder Kumar, 'Gandhi, Ambedkar and the Poona Pact, 1932', in Jim Masselos (ed.), *Struggling and Ruling: The Indian National Congress, 1885–1985* (New Delhi: Sterling Publishers Pvt. Ltd., 1987).
22. See Anthony J. Parel (ed.), *Gandhi: Hind Swaraj and Other Writings* (Cambridge: Cambridge University Press, 1997). This book contains a long and instructive introduction by Parel.
23. Gandhi, *Collected Works* (Print Version), vol. 21, pp. 288–9.
24. *The Harijan*, 26 July 1942.
25. Gandhi, *Collected Works* (Print Version), vol. 32, p. 150.
26. *The Harijan*, 28 July 1946.
27. *The Harijan*, 29 November 1939.
28. From the Gandhi–Nehru Letters, as reproduced in Parel (ed.), *Gandhi: Hind Swaraj and Other Writings*, pp. 149–50.
29. From Parel (ed.), *Gandhi: Hind Swaraj and Other Writings*, p. 152. In this context, it may be noted that B.R. Ambedkar too was opposed to the idealized picture of India's 'village republics'; in them, he saw the evils of localism, ignorance, narrow-mindedness, communalism, and 'a kind of colonialism of the Hindus designed to exploit the untouchables'. 'I hold', he said in the Constituent Assembly, 'that these village republics have been the ruination of India....I am glad that the Draft Constitution has discarded the village and adopted the individual as its unit.' *CAD*, vol. VII, pp. 38–9. For insightful discussions of the Gandhi–Ambedkar differences on the village and panchayati raj, see Peter Ronald deSouza's contribution in this volume and Surinder S. Jodhka, 'Nation and Village', *Economic and Political Weekly*, 10 August 2002.
30. As in Parel (ed.), *Gandhi: Hind Swaraj and Other Writings*, p. 155.
31. On this Nehru-influenced change in Gandhi's political thinking, see Thomas Pantham, 'Gandhi, Nehru and Modernity', in Upendra Baxi and Bhikhu Parekh (eds), *Crisis and Change in Contemporary India* (New Delhi: Sage, 1995).
32. As in Parel (ed.), *Gandhi: Hind Swaraj and Other Writings*, p. 188.
33. Raghavan Iyer (ed.), *The Moral and Political Writings of Mahatma Gandhi* (New Delhi: Oxford University Press, 1987), vol. III, p. 311.
34. As in Parel (ed.), *Gandhi: Hind Swaraj and Other Writings*, p. 190.
35. In *The Harijan*, 28 July 1946, Gandhi wrote: 'I am free to confess that a Constituent Assembly is the logical outcome of parliamentary activity. The labour of the late Deshbandhu Chittaranjan Das and Pandit Motilal Nehru opened my eyes to the fact that the parliamentary programme had a place in the national activity for independence.'
36. *The Harijan*, 4 August 1946.

37. Jawaharlal Nehru, *A Bunch of Old Letters* (Bombay: Asia Publishing House, [1958] 1960), p. 515.

38. As perceptively noted by Bhikhu Parekh, Gandhi's theory of the state, like his theories of ahimsa and satyagraha, 'lagged behind his practice'. See Bhikhu Parekh, *Gandhi's Political Philosophy* (London: Macmillan Press, 1989), p. 120.

39. For some recent discussions of these aspects of Gandhi's political thought, see Thomas Pantham, 'Gandhi, Nehru, and the Democratic-Secular State', in Bindu Puri (ed.), *Gandhi and his Contemporaries* (Shimla: Indian Institute of Advanced Studies, 2002); and Thomas Pantham, 'Religious Diversity and National Unity: The Gandhian and Hindutva Visions', in V.R. Mehta and Thomas Pantham (eds), *Political Ideas in Modern India* (New Delhi: Sage, 2006).

40. Gandhi, *Collected Works* (CD-ROM version), vol. 98, pp. 36–7.

41. See D.G. Tendulkar, *Mahatma: The Life of Mohandas Karamchand Gandhi* (Publications Division, Government of India, 1963), vol. 8, p. 283.

42. As in Parel (ed.), *Gandhi: Hind Swaraj and Other Writings*, pp. 191–3.

43. As was to be expected, Gandhi's proposal for disbanding the organization was not accepted by the Congress, which however decided, in line with his suggestions, to establish its basic organizational units at the panchayat level with indirect elections to many party organizational positions at the higher levels.

44. Bhikhu Parekh, *Gandhi's Political Philosophy*, p. 122.

45. The identity crises of constitutional democracy in India have occurred not only during Partition but also during the Emergency and the horrible spates of communal violence. As pointed out by Upendra Baxi, Jayaprakash Narayan and Vinoba Bhave have 'revitalized the Gandhian tradition' by seeking, in their distinctive ways, 'to approximate Mohandas Gandhi's Swaraj within the contexts of Indian parliamentary democracy'. Jayaprakash Narayan's movement for Total Revolution, says Baxi, was a 'neo-Gandhian' movement, which laid the foundations of 'a new Indian constitutionalism'. See Upendra Baxi, 'The (Im)possibility of Constitutional Justice'. See also R. Sudarshan, '"Stateness" and Democracy in India's Constitution', in Z. Hasan, E. Sridharan, and R. Sudarshan (eds), *India's Living Constitution* (New Delhi: Permanent Black, 2002); and Ashutosh Varshney, *Ethnic Conflict and Civic Life* (New Delhi: Oxford University Press, 2002).

    By 'institutional vitality and suppleness' of India's post-colonial constitutional democracy, I mean, among other things, the promising developments that are taking place in 'democratic decentralization' through panchayati raj in several states. For a valuable discussion of the largely Gandhi-inspired village-oriented articles of the Indian Constitution and of some post-1950 developments in democratic decentralization, see Marc Galanter with Upendra Baxi, 'Panchayat Justice: An Indian Experiment in Legal Access', in Marc Galanter, *Law and Society in Modern India*, edited with an introduction by Rajeev Dhavan (Delhi: Oxford University Press, [1989] 1997), pp. 54–91. See also George Mathew, *Panchayati Raj: From Legislation to Movement* (New Delhi: Concept Publishing Co., 1994).

3

Institutional Visions and Sociological Imaginations
The Debate on Panchayati Raj

Peter Ronald deSouza

If there was a moment, however feeble, during the Constituent Assembly Debates when the constitutional order being fashioned stood 'threatened' by an alternative order, it was when the article concerning panchayati raj was being considered. The foregoing statement may, I concede, seem a bit dramatic, since the 'threat' was never really significant. It was just an ephemeral moment, when the idealism of the Gandhian vision got an audience in the face of the overwhelming realism of the Nehruvian–Ambedkarite vision. It was just one of those 'perhaps' moments in history which makes a fleeting appearance and then vanishes before it can be given a chance. It did not get its chance. Most members of the Constituent Assembly implicitly concurred with Ambedkar when, while presenting the Draft Constitution, he replied to the charge that the Draft had borrowed heavily from other constitutions by stating that:

What the scope of a Constitution should be has long been settled. Similarly what are the fundamentals of a Constitution are recognized all over the world. Given these facts all Constitutions in their main provisions must look similar. The only new things, if there can be any, in a Constitution framed so late in the day are the variations made to remove the faults and to accommodate it to the needs of the country.[1]

Where then was the 'threat'? In the spirit of Gandhi, it hung over the assembly like a mist. Less than a year had passed since his assassination, and his absence must therefore have been very palpable for the men and women entrusted with the task of building a new nation from the dreams of the freedom struggle—and from the trauma of Partition. Theirs was the special responsibility of giving this new nation its founding document.[2] Against this backdrop the followers of Gandhi felt that the deliberations had grievously erred in not attempting to design a constitution along Gandhian lines. Their remorse referred to the historic opportunity to build a new society and polity, which they felt they had and were not taking. It seemed like a denial of the Mahatma.

Sir, a very serious situation was created by not making the village republic or the village unit as the real basis of the Constitution. It must be acknowledged on all hands that this is a construction which is begun at the top and which is going down to the bottom. What is suggested in this direction by Dr Rajendra Prasad himself was that the structure must begin from the foundations and it must go up. That, Sir, is the Constitution which the departed Mahatma Gandhi indicated and tried to work up for nearly thirty years. Under the circumstances, it is very fortunate that this should come in at this stage, that this should be introduced and worked in a proper way.[3]

The above statement by T. Prakasam, who spoke at length when Article 31-A (Article 40 in the Constitution) was being discussed, echoed the views of most of the other members who intervened in the debate on the article on panchayati raj. In fact Surendra Mohan Ghose went so far as to say that in his opinion 'the meaning of the Constitution would have been nothing so far as crores and crores of Indian people are concerned unless there was some provision like this in our constitution.'[4] These are strong sentiments and need to be analysed, because a few years earlier, in November 1945, the outline of such a Gandhian Constitution, titled 'Gandhian Constitution for a Free India', had, in fact, been prepared by Shriman Narayan Agarwal, Principal of Commerce College, Wardha. Gandhi wrote a foreword to it, wherein he said, 'I regard Principal Agarwal's to be a thoughtful contribution to the many attempts at presenting India with constitutions. The merit of his attempt consists in the fact that he has done what, for want of time, I have failed to do…There is nothing in it which has jarred on me as inconsistent with what I would like to stand for.'[5]

The fuzziness that emerges from these comments—on whether the Gandhian requirement can be accommodated within a conventional constitution or whether it will require a radically new constitution—now needs to be addressed, a half century later. What is at stake is the validity of Gandhi's vision. This is to be assessed both in moral and in social terms. I shall attempt such an assessment by interrogating the statements on panchayati raj of the members of the Constituent Assembly who, in their earnestness to pay obeisance to the spirit of Gandhi, felt that the inclusion of the article satisfied the requirements of the Gandhian vision. Should one read these statements as mere hyperbole, something we have come to expect from our political class today; or is it just their inability to comprehend, under the pressure of consensus-making, that the two orders are perhaps incompatible? Or, more philosophically, should one see in these statements the impact of an overwhelming moral authority on critical debate, the Mahatma, present in spirit during the discussions? Or in a different vein, is this the start of our *'jugar'* political culture of, at best, well-intentioned compromise? Is this the beginning of the make-the-adjustment-now-we'll-see-later syndrome which has become the dominant feature of our political culture? In this essay I shall try and address some of these issues that came up during the debate in the Constituent Assembly on panchayati raj, especially those that are of relevance today.

Three issues, in particular, will be discussed. The first is the idea of the compatibility between a Gandhian order and a constitutional order. This is an issue that has rarely been examined, yet it needs to be brought out more fully since it allows us to offer at least some reflections on the questions listed above. The second concerns the conflict between Ambedkar and Gandhi, a conflict which is more than just a clash of personalities, for it signifies fundamentally different readings of India. These are perhaps rooted in their experience of the different life-worlds to which they belonged.[6] Most of the discussions on panchayati raj that comment on the Constituent Assembly Debates refer to this clash. All the speakers in the debate took Gandhi's side. They saw the acceptance of Article 31–A (Article 40 in the Constitution) as a compromise offered by Ambedkar. Third, we look at the whole debate, especially now, in the light of the Seventy-third Constitutional Amendment Act which has been passed with the express purpose of creating such institutions of 'self-government'.

Two themes for reflection can be drawn out of this suggestion of the possibility of a 'Gandhian Constitution'. The first suggests that the idea of a 'Gandhian Constitution' is itself a contradiction in terms since it cannot be constructed from either of the two ends—the constitutional or the Gandhian. From the constitutional end, there is no place for

Gandhian aspirations if one begins with the three principles that are fundamental to constitution making: (i) external rules are necessary to govern behaviour, (ii) such rules are especially necessary for creating a situation of limited government, placing constraints on public authority which in the absence of such constraints would behave tyrannically, and (iii) one of the most effective set of such constraints is a 'Bill of Rights', or something equivalent, through which the citizen is guaranteed the enjoyment of certain rights which protect her/him from the arbitrary exercise of power. Gandhi saw little value in external rules.[7] For him satya and ahimsa were the key to constraining behaviour,[8] and these were essentially internal and personal to the individual. Swaraj, read as both self-rule (as in control over the self) and self-government, emerged from an 'internal moral transformation of the individual'[9] through this commitment to satya and ahimsa.

When we are slaves, we think that the whole universe is enslaved. Because we are in an abject condition, we think that the whole of India is in that condition. As a matter of fact, it is not so, but it is as well to impute our slavery to the whole of India. But if we bear in mind the above fact, we can see that, if we become free, India is free. And in this thought you have a definition of swaraj. It is swaraj when we learn to rule ourselves...But such swaraj has to be experienced each man for himself.[10]

So, seen analytically, the idea of a 'Gandhian Constitution' appears to be an oxymoron. But there is a charitable reading of this suggestion as well. This draws on the idea of the importance of 'constitutional morality' for any constitution. This is an idea put forward by Grote, the historian of classical Greece, and quoted by Ambedkar in his motion on the Draft Constitution. 'The diffusion of constitutional morality, not merely among the majority of any community but throughout the whole, is the indispensable condition of government at once free and peaceable.'[11] If the idea of a 'Gandhian Constitution' is then seen more as a symbolic gesture—to present and develop a 'constitutional morality' based on the Gandhian philosophy of satya and ahimsa, as an attempt to define the moral high ground, rather than a call to construct a legal document based on Gandhian principles—then the attempt of talking about a 'Gandhian Constitution' is valid. This perhaps explains why the article on panchayati raj is in the chapter on Directive Principles. It seems to have less to do with the issue of justiciability and more to do with the ideals that are to govern free India. Article 31-A, moved by K. Santhanam, stated: 'The

State shall take steps to organize village panchayats and endow them with such powers and authority as may be necessary to enable them to function as units of self-government.'[12]

In keeping with this spirit of Gandhian 'constitutional morality', there was an interesting discussion on the words 'self-government'. K. Santhanam had stated when moving his amendment that he had dropped the condition of 'self-sufficiency' from his amendment, which some members had suggested because he, along with other members, did not 'consider it desirable to be put into the directives'. L. Krishnaswami Bharathi countered by saying that he thought that one should not 'fight shy of "self-sufficiency"'. For him, 'political independence apart from economic independence has no meaning.' He felt that since 'the idea behind the Directive Principles is to emphasize the way in which we want the country to function, and for that we must make it quite clear to the whole world that economic democracy is important and for that decentralization of economic power is important. It is that aspect of the matter which Gandhiji emphasized.'[13] In reply did K. Santhanam just spin the ball when he said that 'self government is not merely political it may be economic and spiritual'[14] as well?

Curiously, throughout this debate on the article relating to panchayati raj, Ambedkar spoke only twice and that too very briefly. In the beginning, after K. Santhanam had introduced his amendment, Ambedkar merely said, 'Sir, I accept the amendment.' At the end of the discussion he again said, 'Sir, as I accept the amendment, I have nothing more to add.'[15] That was the sum total of his intervention. I say that this is curious because implicit in all the interventions was the feeling that Ambedkar would not accept the amendment. T. Prakasam confirmed the general feeling when he said, 'I did not accept Dr Ambedkar as Chairman of the Drafting Committee to be good enough to accept this.'[16] Their anxiety was caused by a statement Ambedkar had made earlier when moving his motion regarding the Draft Constitution. It was here that the conflict between the two visions, the Ambedkarite and the Gandhian, took place.[17]

Gandhi believed he represented the whole of India including the Dalits, who were close to his heart.[18] Ambedkar was not willing to buy this claim for he believed that he alone represented the Dalits, and that the Gandhian vision had nothing to offer them.[19] Independent India, therefore, had to be built on a different morality. Gandhi's vision romanticized the village, the centrepiece of panchayati raj. For

Ambedkar this Gandhian world did not exist. The two Indias seemed to be in irreconcilable conflict.

Village swaraj was the centrepiece of Gandhi's vision of an independent India. This followed from his fundamental opposition to the parliamentary order, which he saw as producing only domination. For him the village was the locus of genuine freedom. The order that emerged with the village at the centre should, according to Gandhi, be based on a philosophy of limited wants. Its economy must be designed in such a way that the structure of production, consumption, and distribution is locality-centred. It must use technologies that are simple and not alienating. Relationships must essentially be face-to-face. Gandhi developed these ideas at several places. He very eloquently described this vision of the village republic in the issue of *The Harijan* of 26 July 1942. Let me quote it at some length.

My idea of village swaraj is that it is a complete republic, independent of its neighbours for its vital wants, and yet interdependent for many others in which dependence is a necessity. Thus the village's first concern will be to grow its own food crops and cotton for its cloth. It should have a reserve for its cattle, recreation and playground for adults and children...The village will maintain a village theatre, school, and public hall. It will have its own waterworks ensuring a clean water supply. This can be done through controlled wells or tanks. Education will be compulsory up to the final basic course. As far as possible every activity will be conducted on a co-operative basis. There will be no caste such as we have today with their graded untouchability. Non-violence with its technique of satyagraha and non-cooperation will be the sanction of the village community...The government of the village will be conducted by the Panchayat of five persons annually elected by the adult villagers, male and female, possessing minimum prescribed qualifications. These will have all the authority and jurisdiction required. Since there will be no system of punishments in the accepted sense, this Panchayat will be legislature, judiciary, and executive combined to operate for its year in office. Any village can become such a republic without much interference.

[Such village republics would be interlinked in a set of] ever widening, never ascending circles. Life will not be a pyramid with the apex sustained by the bottom. But it will be an oceanic circle whose centre will be the individual always ready to perish for the village, the latter ready to perish for the circle of villages, till at last the whole becomes one life composed of individuals, never aggressive in their arrogance but ever humble, sharing the majesty of their oceanic circle of which they are integral units...[20]

These are stirring words. They belong to an intellectual tradition which sees the world as essentially harmonious once the impediments to such harmony are removed. They see human beings as capable of building a community based on cooperation and sharing, on altruism, and on the denial of greed. It is the world of *sarvodaya*. Gandhi accepted that the world outlined above did not describe village India, although most commentaries present him as thinking so. While such a picture of harmonious and well-organized village life may not be the case today— 'instead of graceful hamlets dotting the land, we have dung-heaps'[21]— he certainly thought that such a future, based on village swaraj, was possible. He admitted this in a letter to Nehru:

You must not imagine that I am envisaging our village life as it is today. The village of my dreams is still in my mind. After all every man lives in the world of his dreams...(he then sets out this dream and concludes rather wistfully...) For me it is material to obtain the real article and the rest will fit into the picture afterwards. If I let go the real thing, all else goes.[22]

The real thing was 'the village', as it could be in potential.

Ambedkar did not see this potential. For him the village was the embodiment of repression. No freedom could emanate from there. Having had to endure this oppression in his youth,

a young boy, who with his brother, was denied on his way home in a bullock cart a drop of water from evening till midnight; a young boy who was made to know that the razor of the barber would be defiled by contact with his hair while it could be used without fear of pollution in shaving buffaloes; a young schoolboy whose teachers would not touch his notebooks.[23]

and having had to endure the eulogies to the village in the Constituent Assembly Debates, as a genuflexion to Gandhi vision, Ambedkar snapped.

It is said that the new constitution should have been drafted on the ancient Hindu model of a state and that instead of incorporating Western theories the new Constitution should have been built upon village panchayats and District panchayats...They just want India to contain so many village governments. The love of the intellectual Indian for the village community is of course infinite if not pathetic...I hold that the village republic have been the ruination of India. I am therefore surprised that those who condemn provincialism and communalism should come forwards as champions of the village. What is the village but a sink of localism, a den of ignorance, narrow-mindedness and communalism? I am glad that the draft Constitution has discarded the village and adopted the individual as he unit.[24]

It is these words which stung the members of the Constituent Assembly. They read it as being not just hostile to the Gandhian vision but disrespectful of the Mahatma himself. Seth Govind Das recorded this anguish when he said that Ambedkar's remarks on the village had 'caused me and, I believe, a great majority of the members of this house great pain'.[25] It was the words 'sink of localism, den of ignorance, narrow-mindedness and communalism' that was the source of their dismay. In the Gandhian spirit they felt that the village republic would end 'food famines', 'cloth famines', black-marketing'. It would bring 'peace'.[26] In their view Ambedkar was going against the current. And against the Mahatma.

The two visions of free India outlined above seem to have irreconcilable differences. Three in particular need to be noted. The first is the contrasting views on the 'good society' of Gandhi and Ambedkar. For the former the 'good society' was constituted around the principle of 'harmony', a harmony that would emerge when satya and ahimsa were practised. Love was the cement of such a polity and society. External constraints were not necessary where people followed the path of satya and ahimsa. For Gandhi, therefore, it was necessary to create conditions where people could live their lives based on these values. His discussions on bread labour, education, machinery, satyagraha, swaraj, and sarvodaya seek to set out these conditions. For the latter, in contrast, the 'good society' was based not on love but on law. It was constituted upon a body of rights that had both protective and developmental features. The Gandhian promise was just so much wishful thinking, for the particular oppressions that the Dalits experienced every day of their lives could not be accommodated by Gandhian piety. It was this abuse that had to be contained not by love but by law.

This brings one to the second irreconcilable difference between them: on the constitutional order. I have discussed this in some detail earlier. For Ambedkar it must be based on 'Western theories' of a separation of powers, a federal structure, citizenship, Fundamental Rights, safeguards for minorities, stability of the executive, amendatory clauses, etc.[27] For him a constitutional government was one that was limited by such rules and one that was accountable to the citizens. For Gandhi, as stated earlier, it was the 'structure composed of innumerable villages'...producing an 'oceanic circle' based on truth and ahimsa. For Ambedkar the basic unit of politics, the repository of rights, was the individual. For Gandhi too it was the individual, but one who was 'always ready to perish for the village', and therefore one who was the repository of duties. The needs of the village overrode the rights of the individual.

This brings us to the third irreconcilable difference between them: on the potential of the village. For Gandhi, independence must begin at the bottom—that is, from the village which has therefore to be 'self-contained and capable of managing its affairs even to the extent of defending itself against the whole world'.[28] For Ambedkar there was no hope or scope in the village. It was the site of unspeakable repression. A different site for the reconstruction of a free India was therefore necessary.[29] Paradoxically both Gandhi and Ambedkar seemed to base their understanding of the village on an implicit acceptance of the orientalist picture of the self-sufficient, unchanging village.[30] While for Gandhi it contained the seeds of an idyllic village, for Ambedkar it was the embodiment of repression. The compromise that was forged in the two views resulted in a constitution that largely belongs to he Ambedkarite worldview that 'all Constitutions in their main provisions must look similar.' Panchayati raj, the concession to Gandhi, entered the Constitution as Article 40 in the Directive Principles.

Keeping this debate in mind, it is important to note that in the 50 years since the Constitution was framed, the situation of the poor and oppressed has not improved very much. The situation in 2001—when the Supreme Court, recognizing the irony of a 50-million-ton food mountain while millions of people starve in India, was compelled to direct the Union government to distribute food, even give it away free— is an example of the depravity to which governance in India has sunk.

Neither of the two institutional paths—that of the developmental state of the Nehru–Ambedkar mindset, nor that of the panchayati raj model of Gandhi—has done much for the poor. The problems of landlessness, rural indebtedness, displacement, migration, high female and child malnutrition, illiteracy, inadequate health and educational facilities, violence against women, caste oppression, plundering of rural resources, especially of forest and mineral wealth, and so on can all be linked to the inability of the rural poor to benefit from the opportunities created by the developmental state.[31] The failure of this state to deliver arises from two broad causes: (i) from the insensitivity, casualness, lack of accountability, and inertia in the delivery process,[32] and (ii) from the manipulation, for their benefit, by the rural elite of the state structure, as a result of which the various opportunities created by the developmental state do not reach the poor.[33] Freedom has bypassed the poor.

Building an independent India remains an unfinished project. There are few options available today. They require departures from both Ambedkar and Gandhi. One of them involves the strengthening of panchayati raj institutions. Indian intellectuals[34] have spent the last 50 years trying to discover ways by which this can be done. From the Balwantrai Mehta Committee of 1957, to the Ashoka Mehta Committee of 1978, to the L.M. Singhvi Committee of 1986, and finally to the Seventy-third Constitutional Amendment Act, they have sought to understand the problem of panchayati raj.[35]

Five problems in particular plagued the earlier experiments of panchayati raj. These are: (i) irregular elections and supersession, (ii) insufficient devolution of powers, (iii) bureaucratic resistance, (iv) domination by rural elites, and (v) unsatisfactory working of the Gram Sabha. The Seventy-third Amendment has tried to address these lacunae by reserving one-third of the seats for women and for Dalits and Adivasis in proportion to their population, by creating a State Election Commission and State Finance Commission, by keeping terms fixed by conducting regular elections, etc. But much still remains to be done. The rural elites seem to have an infinite capacity to manipulate the new system. Take the case of reservation for women.

The study of the Panchayats suggests that reservation for women has only led to a membership or even pradhanship by proxy. For the *pradhan*, the statutory female quota appears best filled by selecting socially vulnerable women: divorcees, widows, and spouses of migrant husbands fit the bill. Their bargaining power is usually non-existent. Their knowledge of the world outside the village and of opinion within he village on important developments in that world is abysmally low.[36]

Reading the above makes one realize that building an egalitarian society in India is a Hanumanian task, as neither the constitutional order of Ambedkar nor the village swaraj of Gandhi seem to offer satisfactory solutions. The new Panchayati Raj Amendment is the required hybrid: Gandhian in its focus on the village, Ambedkarite in its emphasis on constitutionalism. It takes the structure of representative government one step lower, to the third tier of the Gram Panchayat, while keeping an important place for the village assembly (Gram Sabha). This has introduced a new dynamic in the transformation process and, in spite of the manipulations described above, still represents the best opportunity to push India further toward the goal of equal citizenship.

NOTES

1. B.R. Ambedkar, 'Motion Regarding Draft Constitution', in *Constituent Assembly Debates: Official Report* [henceforth CAD], vol. VII, p. 37.
2. The day's session, in fact, began with a homage 'to the Father of the Nation who breathed life into our dead flesh and bones, who lifted us out of darkness of despondency and despair to the light and sunshine of hope and achievement and who led us from slavery to freedom. May his spirit continue to guide us. May his life and teaching be the torchlight to take us further to our goal'. Opening Statement by Rajendra Prasad, ibid. p. 1.
3. Ibid., p. 521.
4. Ibid., p. 523.
5. H.D. Malaviya, *Village Panchayats in India* (New Delhi: Economic and Political Research Department, AICC, 1956), p. 246.
6. The intensity of this conflict precedes the Constituent Assembly Debates and can be seen in their discussions on the Poona Pact. Gandhi wrote: '...with all my due regard for Dr Ambedkar and for his desire to see the Untouchables uplifted, with all my regard for his ability, I must say in all humility that here the great wrong under which he has laboured, and perhaps the bitter experiences that he has undergone have for the moment warped his judgement. It hurts me to have to say this, but I would be untrue to the cause of the Untouchables, which is as dear to me as life itself, if I did not say it. I will not bargain away their rights for the kingdom of the whole world...Those who speak of the political rights of Untouchables do not know their India, do not know how Indian society is constructed, and therefore I want to say with all the emphasis I can command that if I was the only person to resist this thing I would resist it with my life.' Quoted from Gail Omvedt, *Dalits and the Democratic Revolution: Dr Ambedkar and the Dalit Movement in Colonial India* (New Delhi: Sage, 1994), p. 171.
7. I am grateful to Adi H. Doctor for helping me understand the place of rules in Gandhi's thought.
8. Raghavan N. Iyer, *The Moral and Political Thought of Mahatma Gandhi* (Delhi: Oxford University Press, 2000), ch. 9.
9. A. Parel (ed.), *Gandhi: Hind Swaraj and Other Writings*, Cambridge Texts in Modern Politics (New Delhi: Cambridge University Press, 1997), p. 73, fn. 144.
10. Ibid., p. 73.
11. Ambedkar, *CAD*, p. 38.
12. *CAD*, p. 502.

13. Ibid., p. 525.
14. Ibid., p. 526.
15. Ibid., p. 527.
16. Ibid., p. 521.
17. The struggle that Ambedkar had to wage with the legacy of Gandhi—and to compromise with, becoming thereby a little less Ambedkarite—is brilliantly brought out by Upendra Baxi in his typology of seven Ambedkars. Upendra Baxi, 'Emancipation as Justice: Babasaheb Ambedkar's legacy and Vision', in Upendra Baxi and Bhikhu Parekh (eds), *Crises and Change in Contemporary India* (New Delhi: Sage, 1995), pp. 122–49.
18. See n. 6.
19. 'There have been many Mahatmas in India whose sole object was to remove Untouchability and to elevate and absorb the Depressed Classes, but every one of them has failed in his mission. Mahatmas have come, Mahatmas have gone. But the untouchables have remained as Untouchables.' B.R. Ambedkar, *What the Congress and Gandhi Have Done to the Untouchables* (Bombay: Thacker and Co., 1945), p. 326, quoted in Upendra Baxi, 'Emancipation as Justice', pp. 133–4.
20. Gandhi, quoted in H.D. Malaviya, *Village Panchayats*, p. 250.
21. 'Constructive Programme: Its meaning and Place' in Parel (ed.), *Gandhi: Hind Swaraj*, p. 174.
22. Letter to Nehru, 5 October 1945, in Parel (ed.), *Gandhi: Hind Swaraj*, pp. 150–1.
23. Upendra Baxi, 'Emancipation as Justice', pp. 124–5.
24. *CAD*, 4 November 1948, pp. 38–9.
25. Ibid., 22 November 1948, p. 523.
26. Speech by T. Prakasam, ibid., 22 November 1948, p. 522.
27. Ibid., Ambedkar's Motion on the Draft Constitution.
28. Parel (ed.), *Gandhi: Hind Swaraj*, p. 189.
29. Ambedkar's views on the village are similar to Nehru's: 'I do not understand why a village should necessarily embody the truth and non-violence. A village, normally speaking, is backward intellectually and culturally and no progress can be made from a backward environment. Narrow-minded people are much more likely to be untruthful and violent.' Nehru's reply to Gandhi on 9 October 1945, in Parel (ed.), *Gandhi: Hind Swaraj*, p. 152.
30. The works of Thomas Munro and Charles Metcalfe seem to be the basis of this picture of the unchanging village. Even Ambedkar quotes Metcalfe in his address: 'Dynasty after dynasty tumbles down. Revolution succeeds to revolution. Hindoo, Pathan, Mogul, Maharatta, Sikh, English are all masters in turn but the village communities remain the same. In times of trouble they arm and fortify themselves. A hostile army passes through the country. The village communities collect their little cattle with their walls and let the enemy pass unprovoked.' *CAD*, 4 November 1948, p. 39.

31. Peter Ronald deSouza, 'Multi-State Study of Panchayati Raj Legislation and Administrative Reform', unpublished Report to the World Bank, New Delhi, 29 February 2000.

32. This failure to deliver is noted in chapter 5, on 'Implementation, Delivery Mechanism and Institutional Development', of the Ninth Five-Year Plan (1997–2000), of the Planning Commission of India, New Delhi. The deficits are (i) inadequate analysis of available information during the programme formulation, (ii) top down and target oriented rather than a bottom up approach, (iii) lack of accountability of the implementing agencies either to the government or to the people, (iv) social sector programmes formulated without addressing the question of sustainability of benefits, (v) failure to ensure timely and adequate flow of funds to implementing agencies, etc.

33. The *Indian Rural Development Report: Regional Disparities in Development and Poverty* (Hyderabad: NIRD, 1999), recognizes this nexus between dominant castes, land, and the state. It sees 'land and agrarian reforms [as the] unfinished agenda of the last five decades. Even if its scope is severely restricted in the present day due to demographic pressure, access to land, its optimal use, investment and cooperation are possible only if such reforms are put in place. Land reforms is not just distribution of land. Its aims are to break the land-caste based political controls, guarantee access to technology and credit, and create conditions for maximum production and marketable surplus, all so necessary for rural transformation', p. 121.

34. The fascination of 'the village' for the Indian intellectual that Ambedkar thought pathetic has however continued in Independent India. Jan Breman sees the discussion as passing through four moments: (i) the village colonized, of Munro and Metcalfe, (ii) the village nationalized, of the national movement, (iii) the village developmentalized, of the community development plans, and (iv) the village anthropologized, of M.N. Srinivas. Jan Breman et al., *The Village in Asia Revisited* (Delhi: Oxford University Press, 1997).

35. Peter Ronald deSouza, 'Decentralization and Local Government: The "second wind" of Democracy in India', in Zoya Hasan *et al.*, *India's Living Constitution: Ideas, Practices, Controversies* (Delhi: Permanent Black, 2002).

36. G.K. Leiten and R. Srivastava, *Unequal Partners: Power Relations, Devolution and Development in Uttar Pradesh*, Indo-Dutch Programme on Alternatives in Development no. 23 (New Delhi: Sage, 1999), p. 203.

4

Outline of a 'Theory of Practice' of Indian Constitutionalism

Upendra Baxi

INTRODUCTION: SITUATING THE 'SEMI-LEARNED PRODUCTION'

This essay explores the tasks of social theory and philosophy of Indian constitutionalism at work. But these presuppose a stable discourse concerning the notions of constitutions and constitutionalisms, which is only partially.

A discourse addressed to 'the' philosophy of the Indian Constitution makes several assumptions, the most crucial being that there is a genre called 'philosophy' even in this post-modernist and post-Derridean world.[1] It assumes a 'universal' called 'political philosophy'. Admittedly, the singular here altogether misleads; all we have are genres of social and political theories/philosophies. I merely straddle this philosophical biodiversity here.

To begin with the North 'liberal' theory/philosophy genres, the distinctive foundational concerns[2] address normative issues of what makes prescriptively at least, a 'good' constitution, in ideal and less than, or sub-/second best, 'ideal' (and in some senses 'non-ideal') circumstances.[3] Social theorists remain, in contrast, more interested/ concerned with the problem of the 'constitution' of constitutions, that is, the assorted social, symbolic as well as material labours of power/ governance.

In its elementary social sense, a constitution is something that stands 'constituted' by the labours of some peoples and processes. What these 'peoples' and 'processes' are at any given historic moment, how they may be named, how their labours acquire some degree of 'legality', and social legitimation, how these fatefully configure power and resistance, and with what social futures, are some issues that eminently pre-occupy social theorists of constitutions. They remain concerned with the modes of constituting or reconstituting the 'unconstituted', and the ways of interplay and interwar between the 'constituted' and 'unconstituted', or the 'pre-constituted.'

Even assuming/hypothesizing the constitutive moment, the 'constitutive' and the 'constituted' stand in a dialectical relation. Does the constitutive limit the horizons of the constituted? How, and in what ways, that which is constituted acts back upon the agency of the constitutive? Does the constitutive agency, power, force, as it were, exhaust itself once a thing, state of affairs, or a phenomenon is constituted or does it remain alive as active residue? How does one narrate the histories of the constitutive and the constituted powers? In relation to life under actually existing political/juridical constitutions, these questions assume grave importance in terms of legitimation of power and resistance; for example, in the distinction between the 'legal' and the 'popular' sovereign, the latter attributed the plenitude of constituent power.

Second, which 'givens' (structures) are assumed in constitution-talk, and which 'givens' remain subject to the play of construction (agency)? How may social consciousness and prior histories of power and struggle shape the project of writing a constitution and the specific modes of governance and production of juridical norms? This particular question is of grave importance for constitution-making in the post-colonial, post-Cold War, and the transitional post-socialist societies.

Third, what notions of historic timespace inhere the notion of a constitution, that is, how do we construct spatial distribution of rights, the geographies of (in)justice? The construction of imperial spaces for nation-states entails a great deal of violence and social exclusion; it destroys many a plural life-worlds and worldviews. Constitutions, in their founding and developmental moments, destroy timeplaces by 'geopolitical combination, a form of articulation centred on the internal distribution of rhetoric, bureaucracy, and violence in a given legal field'.[4] How much of this violence is jurisgenerative always remains an open question.

Fourth, is the idea of constitutional chaos at all sensible, given the notion that constitutions always enact a principle of order (of knowledge/power)? How may we describe this principle in terms other than those Nietzsche once so sharply proclaimed: 'Only where the state ends, there begins a human being who is then not superfluous'? What principle of ordering ('consensus') do constitutions translate as principles of order ('principled' repression between 'dissent' and singular 'treason')?

Fifth is the notion, in terms of history of ideas or ideas of history, a distinctively Euroamerican heritage? Put another way: are all South constitutions pre-eminently mimetic? And must (as a matter of necessity laced by 'choice') this so always remain? This qualifier 'always' is crucial, given the Fukuyama-type dogma of the 'End of History and the Last Man.'

Sixth, even when we situate the understanding of constitutions in terms of structures of governance and rights, are state constitutional orderings conceivable outside the framing notions about ideology (Marx), episteme (Foucault), and habitus (Bourdieu)? Each offers a startling critique of the 'Western' rationality; each, however, remains enclosed in contexts of progressive Eurocentric paradigm . These have no use for a Mahatma or a Mandela, or for Ambedkar, the 'Aristotle' of Dalits.

Seventh, understanding the theory and practice of constitutionalism as an assemblage of state formative practices raises issues concerning the relationship between constitutionalism and the province of state theory. How may acts of constitution-making and constitutional change affect the reproduction of state power? Is the case that various constitutions at work introduce a variety of 'stateness' (for example, the rule of law at the national level and microfascism at the level of the 'local' state)? How may one relate state formation to constitution-making practices?

Furthermore, constitutions furnish arenas of contested relationships between state and civil society. Since state formative practices are ongoing, and indeterminate, it is necessary to differentiate, at least, between three interactive meanings of constitutions as texts, constitutional law, and theory/ideology ('constitutionalism'). I have named these, not too elegantly, as C1, C2, C3,[5] a theme I revert to later in the essay.

Eighth, in what ways may we distinguish the positive morality of constitutions by the standards furnished by critical morality? Outside some few clear examples where the positive morality is indeed ethically obnoxious (as in the case of the Nazi and apartheid constitutions) most constitutions themselves furnish some new elements of critical morality by which the very constitutional legitimacy of the operations of power-structures and political representation may be adjudged (thus for example, constitutions containing enunciation of fundamental rights, directive principles of state or social policy, and fundamental duties of all citizens, not here further to instance the sonorous perambulatory constitutional value enunciations). Further, articulations of shared standards of critical morality by which we adjudge constitutional morality remain a contested site. Now we may fail to note what clearly is the case: indeed, many a salient feature of modern constitutions seem to remain ethically neutral: for example, the choice between unitary and federal structure, the principle and detail of the distribution of legislative and administrative powers, the presidential or Cabinet form of structuring executive power, methods and scope of amending power, and first-past-the post or proportional electoral systems. Both Habermas and Rawls[6] address this issue in discursive terms of post-metaphysical liberal or libertarian theory. This discourse, of course, presupposes visions of the rational and the reasonable social/dialogical cooperation to produce and reproduce quest for justice in human societies but even so does not reclaim within the province of critical morality the above-mentioned issues. It also remains clear that in the approaches towards enunciation of ethical standards for judging the moarlity of constitutions, the non-Euroamerican other remain singularly inconspicuous in these labours, suggesting that any normative constitutionalism theory must either be 'Western' or forfeit its claims to existence.

These, and related, issues at least direct movement from the 'Constitution', an unexamined notion of a constitutional formation, a mass of heterogeneous constitution generative, sustaining, defying and denying practices, and the order of expectations and experiences. Constitutional formations are at once 'tradition-constituted' and 'tradition-constitutive'.[7] But the MacIntyre 'constituted' tradition' here only refers to the Enlightenment and its derivatives and active residues. Important as all this is, it ignores the role of the 'traditions' of non-European Enlightenment in Asian and African constitutional formations.

The circumstance of globality[8] named by Lenin as 'juridical world outlook'[9] of course shapes constitution-making practices; that outlook was thought to be exhausted by bourgeoisie and socialist models of constitutionalism. This is no longer the case as manifest in the first contemporary post-colonial Indian Constitution enacted in the middle of the twentieth century CE, and as the South African Constitution towards its end now fully remind us. Further, we also ought to acknowledge that theocratic constitutionalism becomes problematic when it occurs outside Christendom, as has been the case with Ayatollah Khomeini's shari'a-based Constitution of Iran, which inaugurated the shari'a as containing the potential for the development of Islamic public law. This innovation is scarcely exhausted by name—calling such as 'fundamentalist' or 'revivalist' constitutionalism, which does not in the dominant discourse somehow extend to the Israeli Basic Law. Comparative constitutional studies need to practice the virtue of humility in understanding juridical world outlooks thus constituted outside the Euroamerican 'Enlightenment traditions. The former far from constituting eclectic and mimetic constitutional borrowals from the latter traditions often constitute an epistemological break from these, which surely deserve the dignity of reasoned discourse.

It remains, of course true that a new emergent form of global economic constitutionalism now enforces a new mimetic reproduction of innovative constitutionalisms. We note this dimension a little later, as globalization, now defines 'democracy', 'good governance', 'rights' and 'development' not so much with a solicitude for the nation-peoples as for the community of foreign investors. The South State is increasingly conceived of as a host state, held hostage by movement of global capital. Contemporary globalization then offers constitutional narratives of hostage states.

SITUATING CONSTITUTIONALISMS AMONG THE KABYLE

Pierre Bourdieu was fortunate in finding the Kabyle who helped him to contribute, germinally, to the renewal of much of contemporary social theory.[10] The emergent traditions of comparative constitutional studies are not so privileged. Ethnographical approaches to the understanding of the making, working, and unmaking of constitutions are still not in sight. The hegemonic traditions[11] of constitutional studies, at their very best, address histories of comparable normativity, that is, the hermeneutics of constitutional law, and at their worst prescribe universalistic approaches to constitutional interpretation.[12]

The Kabyle–Bourdieu perspective, in its potential extension to constitutionalism,[13] entails at least two kinds of epistemological breaks: first, the break 'with native experience, and the native representation of that experience' and second a break that 'calls into question the presuppositions inherent in the practice of an "objective observer..."'[14] This requires an entirely fresh approach to tasks of understanding constitutions at work or put to sleep.

The first 'break' invites many-sided social theoretical understanding of the inaugural practices of constitution-making, through which some epistemic communities represent themselves as invested somehow (by force of circumstance) with the power to enunciate a constitution. Almost all constitutions carry historic burdens of democratic deficit at the point of origin. Never directly elected and usually constituting an enunciative oligarchy, constitution-makers legitimate their narrative monopoly as the voice of whole people. Rarely made with peoples' participation (the only major exception being the post-apartheid South African Constitution), the career of constitutions stands deeply affected by the original constitutional choices already made. Constitutions usually archive basic decisions made by elderly, homophobic, non-tribal, gender-biased, metropolitan, professional, political, and propertied males; their practices necessarily reflect special interests and specific constellations of power and ideology.

Broadly, democratic (including erstwhile socialist)[15] constitutions thus remain historically burdened by the need to transcend the basic legitimation (democratic) deficit. What is of interest is not so much the overall unity of original intendment but its deeply conflicted character. The hegemonic logic of constitution-forming practices that attempts the representation of militant particularisms (to evoke David Harvey's notion from another context) into a universal norm is never free of contention. Yet the histories of politics of desire that sculpt the constitutions remain usually well-kept secrets.

The second break entails interrogation of the 'living' constitution beyond the presuppositions and postulates of those practising constitutional theory, which elaborates standards for evaluation of native practices of constitutions, whether in the languages of 'constitutional essentials'[16] or ways of production of 'legitimate law'.[17] In this universe, self-sufficient epistemic communities that articulate normative constitutional theory assume 'god'-like functions; to borrow the language of Bruno Latour, from another context, 'they even produce natures and societies they need only themselves' by 'strange bootstrapping operations' that 'produce references internal to their discourse and to the speakers installed in within discourse...'[18] The daily practices of lawpersons[19] and the everyday experience of life under actually existing constitutions count for little or nothing in the production of understanding of constitutions at work, or preferred universalistic prescriptions mandating how these ought to work; it is not surprising that much of normative constitutional theory, and much of comparative constitutionalism, is South-annihilating.[20]

In contrast, and to begin with, philosophical anthropological understanding of constitutions directs attention to the internal logics of the practices of lawpersons—adjudicators pre-eminent among these. How may one outline the 'theory' of practice of constitutions at work? Is the labour of locating the 'logic of practice' of constitutionalism at all worthwhile? Are contemporary lawpersons (legislators, justices, jurists, and legal administrators) capable of providing insights as theoretically profound as the Kabyle of Algeria? And, if so, is the heritage of contexts in which law is thought (jurisprudence/legal theory) sufficiently self reflexive to harness this learning? Or, rather, is it the case that much of constitutional theory/discourse is no more than a '"semi-learned" production', a 'theoretical artefact totally alien to practice?'[21] How then may one, if this feat is at all possible, seek to overcome the 'theory effect'[22] of varieties of normative constitutionalism discourses?

The 'theory effect' not only fails to archive the plurality and multiplicity of practices of representation generated by a whole variety of lawpersons, but also more importantly, obscures from view the perspectives of non-lawpersons, people bearing the cumulative weight of the constitutional practices that they often seek to shed, even overthrow. How may we grasp different types of citizen interpretive practices that insist on a redirection of ways of production of constitutional meanings? May we include within this range militarized forms of insurgent citizen interpretation? How may we grasp forms of meaning that strategize confrontation between expectations and experience of constitutionality against the constitution itself ? How may we observe and relate the impact of citizen interpretive practices with native official ones? May one, then, with appropriate caution, speak of the 'dominant' and the 'subaltern' practices of constitutional theory?[23]

In all its protean senses, ethnography of constitutionalism has still to emerge. This is a mixed blessing, for its belated birth helps us avoid wholly state-centric and heavily globalized approaches to understanding of the theory of constitutional practice. Constitutions are, all said and done, codifications of heterogeneous dominant practices of state power, but never wholly so unitedly a success story because they do not quite 'tame' the jurisgenerative constituent power of people's insurgent practices. How else, may one ask, do we grasp the passive revolution of the post-Marcos Philippines or the more recent critical events in Indonesia?[24]

This essay explores issues relating to construction of an Indian constitutional anthropology, in the hope that this may have some relevance for comparative constitutional theory. It endeavours to do so by recoursing the shades of distinction between the expectation and experience of Indian constitutionalism. This insufficient Bourdieu-like way of articulating the habitus and the hiatus guides us, however, to an interlocution that generates a whole crowd of distinctions.

The first set invites us to make general and necessary distinctions between constitutions, constitutional law, and constitutionalism; the second pertains to the notions of expectation and experience; the third invites close attention to the practices of citizen constitutional interpretation. The fourth (without being exhaustive) impels some concern about career and future of constitutional practices in a globalizing/glocalizing world. (For reasons of space, this last aspect is not directly addressed in this essay.)

CONSTITUTIONAL FORMATIONS:
GENERAL AND NECESSARY DISTINCTIONS

I have distinguished indeterminate and ongoing state formative practices as compelling differentiation, at least, between three interactive meanings of constitutions as texts, constitutional law, and theory/ideology ('constitutionalism'). I have named these, not too elegantly, as C1, C2, C3.[25]

C1 names the corpus of texts, historically inaugural inscriptions of 'original intention' that seek to fashion a unified semiotic description of a new political formation, usually described as a 'nation-state'. The prime function of C1 is to 'rightfully "write society" through law', to present the state as provider of social cohesion, mystifying 'its...secrets, sources of violence, and evil', its 'hidden resources, designs and immense power'.[26] C1 is a corpus, containing diverse genres of texts. Most C1, even extreme situations of 'constitutions without constitutionalism'[27] and military constitutionalism, contain governance as well as rights/justice texts. Some convey a sense of constitutionally desired future social orderings; preambles furnish a standard genre of apsirational overreach. A few texts emerge as justice and rights texts; slender in comparison with the governance texts, in practice these often avenge them.

C1 is, however, never wholly written; indeed, the unwritten all too often animates that which stands codified. Thus, and summarily put, C1 is always a conflicted site, a battlefield, marking struggles for ascendancy between, first, the texts of governance and rights and justice texts and, second, between the written constitution at play and war with the unwritten. The unwritten often cancels the written texts; and often enhances the apsirational aspects of the written.

But this comforting general proposition masks the ferocity of the struggle between unwritten. To experience this, one has to go beyond from Their Lordship's fancy prose, their eloquence about the rule of law to literature, to Mahasweta Devi's *Bashai Tudu*[28] and to Saddat Hasan Manto's epigrammatic story of a rickshaw puller who elated by the news of the new Indian Constitution had to learn in the police station that it was still the old one: the uncomprehending police exclaimed:

What rubbish are you talking? What new constitution? It is the same old constitution, you fool!

Then they locked him up.[29]

C2 offers sites of ongoing and endless interpretive practices of variegated authoritative interpretive communities, resulting in what is commonly called constitutional law. Authoritative interpretive practices deploy different means, methods, and modes of interpretation, practices that overall create stable orders/networks of meanings. Of these, the adjudicatory practice have received the most attention, even though in life under actually existing constitutions the executive and the legislative practices often determine dominant configurations of meaning.

C3 designates the practices of reflexive understanding of C1 and C2. In its dominant liberal theoretical forms, it stands expressed in the practices that enunciate standard narratives concerning the rule of law, both in its normative and institutional senses.[30] The contemporary (post-Cold War) constitutional theory and practice that dismisses as 'pathological' all alien forms (socialist, Islamic, and related constitutionalism) invites anthropological gaze, especially on the site that self-constitutes the 'normal'.[31]

This apart, C3 also opens itself to view as 'cultural software'[32] programming performative acts of power as well as resistance. C3, as cultural software, is programmed both by practices of national (and subnational) politics as by differing circumstances of globality. Understanding of patterns of global politics, in the unitary foundational as well as many a diverse developmental, moment remains central to a nuanced grasp of C3. The term 'post-colonial', as well as the 'transitional', emerges in this context as somewhat hegemonic, as it reduces diverse circumstances of globality to a somewhat flattened perception of historic time that give birth to C3.[33]

The notion of C2 is severely impoverished when it ignores interpretive practices of non-authoritative communities. Social movements, including human rights movements as social movements,[34] remain anchored in citizen interpretations of texts of C1 and contexts of alternate C3, often deeply at variance with C2. The power these movements gather often result in the change, not just in but also of both C1 and C2.[35] If we were to view all constitutional formations as so many recombinations of the rule of law and the reign of terror inherent in the social reproduction of the power to rule, these manifest different forms of the Gulag statenesses. Catastrophic politics of cruelty inhere all forms of state power; only in some constitutional formats are these writ large.

At the same time, we may note that the relationship between C3 and C1, C2 remains not linear but dialectical. If C3 is a forming practice (in the sense that Georg Simmel describes[36] enclosing practices in the domain of C1 and C2, it is also the case that C3 is often shaped by the latter practices. In Bourdeian terms, C3 provides the habitus outside of which the juridical constitutional practices remain wholly insensible.

These distinctions provide no final vocabularies for constitutions put to work or to sleep. But these provide registers of practices, and ledgers of logic 'sustaining' these practices, even if in complex and contradictory modes of understanding.

EXPECTATIONS

The making of a constitution heralds, to use a cliché, 'the revolution of rising expectations'. But we lack analysis that situates the making and interpretation of constitutions to the dialectics between the law, as politics of state desire, and the law as articulating insurgent orders of social expectations.

Jeremy Bentham offered an inaugural understanding—in *The Theory of Legislation*—of all law as an endeavour to negotiate a 'multitude of expectations', the law even when providing systems of 'conciliation and concession' also modulated and rearranged these, at times by the process of creation of new expectations.[37] He described expectations as a 'presentiment', which endows human beings with the power of forming 'a general plan of conduct', such that 'successive instants which compose the duration of life are not isolated and independent points, but become continuous parts of the whole'.[38] Bentham, of course, counselled that the legislator follow, on the whole, the general course of social expectations; laws rooted in common expectations carried greater prospect of willing compliance and the legitimation of the legal order in general. But he also realized that legally induced social change entailed 'shocking', 'deranging', and 'disappointing' common (dominant?) expectations. He counselled gradualism:

Men who are rendered free by gradations, will be much more capable of being so than if you had taught them to tread justice under foot, for the sake of introducing a new social order.[39]

Violent 'deranging' of a general course of common expectations, on this view, produces a disproportionate sum of evil. From a Benthamite perspective, then, revolutionary constitutionalism remains problematic; all violent reconstructions of state and society entail the loss of capacity, even capabilities, to exercise freedom as well as signal erosion of languages of justice. This is an attractive proposition, until we begin to realize that all constitutions are orders of violence in that they entail 'shocking', 'disappointing', and 'deranging' expectations of large classes of people who remain progressively disenfranchised (though formally possessed of rights) by structures and practices of lawless governance.

I may here add that Niklas Luhmann's fascinating (though unself-conscious) renovation of Bentham invites us to think of law's role to expectations in contexts of its radical complexity and contingency, where conduct has to orient itself not just to one's own expectations but also to the 'expectation of other people's expectation'.[40] He guides us to a germinal distinction between 'cognitive' and 'normative, expectations.' The former promote social learning from disappointments; the latter, in contrast, signify 'the determination not to learn from disappointments'.[41] For, when people begin to respond to failures in constitutional governance as an experience to which they must somehow adjust, constitutions in losing all normative efficacy also tend to reaffirm legitimate expectations. The existential loss of human capabilities to exercise control over governance practices paradoxically renews the power of political hope still arising Phoenix-like from the ashes of disappointed/disestablished normative expectations. Refusal to learn from disappointment of existential expectations defines the very struggle for recovery of the rule of law and human rights.

Constitutions respect social expectations differentially; they endow only *some* people, here and now, with the power of forming a 'general plan of conduct,' in ways that creates *fate* for others. In this, both Bentham and Luhmann lead us to the understanding the time–dimension of

constitutionalisms. People living under actually existing constitutionalisms that orient legitimation of state conduct towards popular
expectations, they differentially suggest, are better off across generations
than those living under regimes not concerned *at all* with these. Non-
revolutionary constitutions accomplish, to invoke a phrase of Bourdieu,
'the work of time'. There is then no way that helps avoid the enormous
human violation and tragedy in the acts of *making* and *reading*
constitutions that mark the passage from normative constitutional
expectations to lived constitutional *experience*. In what follows, I trace in
the Indian contexts the dialectics of expectation and experience. While I
essay the first in the next two sections, I must here leave the notion of
'experience' somewhat inarticulate.[42]

THE FORMATION OF ANTERIOR EXPECTATIONS: THE FLAWED INVENTION OF CITIZENSHIP?

The habitus[43] that shaped Indian Constitution-making was the product
of the highly diverse national independence movement. Already, the
tyranny of the singular is in place; we totalize the independence
movement, an extraordinary series of formation of experience (a protean
shaping practice may not be exhaustively codified and whose readings
may never be exhausted). Axiomatic constitutional enunciations already,
on this description, cancel the plurality and multiplicity of movements.
We run this narrative risk every time when we talk about the formative
histories that bring constitutions into being.

The makers of the first Indian Constitution[44] were all, even if
unselfconscious, Benthamites. The nationalist/self-determination
movement had created a mass of 'anterior expectations', not all of which
could be fulfilled by modes of instituting non-revolutionary constitutionalism. The movement raised a whole lot of diffuse expectations
concerning stability and change in Indian society. The constitution-
makers had then to embody 'subaltern' expectations in ways that
negotiated avoidance of wholesale derangement of dominant
expectations. They accomplished this in a whole variety of compromistic
ways, by a mix of the 'symbolic' and 'instrumental' strategies.

Most crucial for the Indian C3 was the notion that free India would be
constituted as a republic, enunciating the equal worth of all citizens.
The idea of a republic was not entirely unknown to ancient/classical

political theory but the idea of citizenship was. That idea was constructed by serious political practice during the freedom struggle; Indians were no longer to be subjects of an imperial power but were constituted as beings with a range of powers in relation to state and civil society. The Indian Constitution remarkably extends the idea of citizenship beyond operations of governance to everyday transactions and interactions in society and economy. Anterior expectations determined this construction in ways that had few parallels in the history of modern C3.

The invention of republican citizenship is indeed momentous; it defines arenas of struggles to de-symbolize ritual hierarchy, based on notions of purity and pollution. The social bases of a radically heterogeneous freedom movement, generating a mass of anterior expectations, creates the necessary bases for the proclamation of the constitutional outlawry of the practice of untouchability (as a fundamental human right: Article 17), forms of agrestic serfdom (Article 23), and discrimination of the grounds of sex (Articles 14, 15).

The invention of 'citizenship', in the traumatic events of the partition of India, also generates a special regime of solicitude for minority rights (Articles 25–30). Constitutional secularism that mandates radical reform of the 'majority' Hindu religious traditions also results now in a cautious, piecemeal charter, based on communitarian-oriented, consensual bases for reform of the 'personal law' system of minority communities. The social constitution of Indian citizenry stands constructed, with fateful impact, along 'communal/communitarian' bright lines, providing the very sites for the eventual gender—respecting constructions of citizenship. So do, though with much ambivalence, concerns for the plight of the non-Bharat/Indian indigenous communities; falling short of radical self-determination, autonomous governance (the Fifth and the Sixth Schedules of the Constitution) recognizes civilizational, not just cultural, pluralism, thus going beyond the contemporary yet wholly conventional disputations concerning 'multiculturalism'.[45]

All this having been acknowledged in fullness, we now proceed to the recognition that the Indian C1 constructs citizenship variously. First, citizenship is defined in state-centric ways; the state determines who is (by birth or descent) to count as an Indian citizen.[46] Second, the right to adult suffrage constructs citizenship via assurances of constitutional rights, though not declared as 'fundamental' in Part III of the

Constitution. In a sense, this right relates more to the legitimation needs of governance than to active agency of citizens. Citizens, as individuals, have the right to contest and vote regardless of their socio-economic position but do not have, collectively, any constitutional right to a system of free and fair elections.

Third, not all citizens have an equal right to contest elections. Initially a decade-long, but by now almost irreversible system of legislative reservations for Scheduled Castes and Scheduled Tribes differentiates the right to adult franchise; Indian citizens not belonging to these categories may not offer themselves as candidates in reserved seats. This limitation has now acquired self-evident legitimacy, although the political and social cost–benefit analyses suggest cause for concern.[47]

Fourth, while all Indian citizens have access to the same normative order of rights, the division of rights through the device of parts III and IV of the Constitution ensures that enjoyment and achievement of fundamental rights stands differentially distributed among Indian citizens. This original distinction in India's first Constitution has been subsequently, though perhaps not substantially, mutated principally in the domain of Indian C2.

Fifth, citizens do not enjoy any collective right, outside the representation constituted by electoral verdicts, to shape national policy thorough referenda, plebiscites, and related devices (for example, recall of elected representatives); legislative majorities without any popular participation can accomplish even changes in, and of, the Constitution. This suggests an impoverished understanding of the idea of a republic.

The Indian C3 is also somewhat incoherent concerning the relationship between the idea of a republic and the idea of citizenship. The Preamble of course proclaims all the five values of a republic: equality, liberty, justice (social, economic, and political), dignity, and fraternity. Yet, the C1 as it emerged and in the long history of the Indian C2, retained structured innocence concerning the values of dignity and fraternity in terms of relationship between the governors and the governed. Structures and processes of governance remain least constitutionally obligated to respect individual or associational dignity of Indian citizens.[48] In their dealings with governments, the bulk and generality of Indian citizens stand reconstituted as subjects all over again. The idea of respect for fellow-citizens constitutes (as I understand it) the very notion of republic. In a republic, as Aristotle taught us very long ago, citizens emerge as beings that know how to rule and how to be ruled, an assemblage of virtues that at least entail equal respect for all co-citizens.[49] Do we understand the insufficiency of the grasp of these republican virtues as a failure of decolonization or as an integral part of anterior expectations that led to the very making of the Constitution of India or even as genetically coded in the conceptions of republic in classical Indian political thought?

C3 has been somewhat more assured in the elaboration of the value fraternity finds through the anti-untouchability provisions of C1. Legal and constitutional enforcement of fraternity, in this context has, however, comprehensively failed, when measured in association with the value of dignity.[50] The Indian C1, C2, and C3 put together, have failed to create an authentic practice of the idea of republican citizenship.

HUMAN RIGHTS IN THE SHADOW OF GOVERNANCE: STATE SECURITY AND CIRCUMSTANCES OF RIGHTLESSNESS

The practices of the Indian freedom struggle shaped, in many ways, the logics and languages of contemporary human rights, the most stunning being the fashioning of the human rights to self-determination. Neither classical nor modern political theory/discourse fully anticipated such a world historic practice of enunciation of this kind of human right.[51] The Gandhian practices of shaping the protean notion of Swaraj were exercises in practical reason par excellence. There is simply no way of grasping Indian C3 outside these practices, even though these till today remain un-theorized. Its constitutive elements did not mimetically spring forth from the Euroamerican Enlightenment discursive traditions; nor were these grounded in the extant traditions of 'Indian' political theory or practice. This formation of autonomous, originary fields of political praxis generates a new episteme, whose national and global significance is far from exhausted.

If the practices of swaraj in colonial India, charismatically instituted but mass practised, constituted the 'point of departure', the tasks of governance of an independent nation, 'the point of arrival',[52] provide a register of practices of dissipation. Swaraj notions now get re-constructed in the idiom and grammar of the 'unity and integrity' of the new Indian state. The birth of the Indian Constitution also signals the end of potent practices of swaraj. The right to self-determination now gets scattered in intricacies of the difficult practices of the so-called Indian federation.

The constituted 'Indian' self permits no derogation by way of secession, even when it furnishes space for relatively autonomous practices forming sub-national regional identity politics. The enforcement of 'constitutional patriotism' (to borrow a notion now so dear to Habermas) sets boundaries to the Indian post-swaraj languages and logics of human rights; the right to free speech and expression, conscience and belief, movement and association must be held within the bounds of sedition/treason, and draconian security legislations routinely and tragically sustained by the Supreme Court of India.

The creeping militarization of the Indian state and polity begins simultaneously with enunciation of basic rights. The Indian C1 enshrines in Article 21 the rights of all persons against predatory practices of power that invade life and liberty; the very next article provides for constitutionality of the preventive detention system! The Indian C2 provides an extraordinary narrative of 'detention jurisprudence' (unparalleled in the annals of modern constitutionalism) but judicial valour stops short of invalidation of draconian security laws. The union home minister, even as I write, makes a strong plea for constitutional immunity for manifest, ongoing, and massive violations of human rights in national 'security' operations, even when they configure citizens as vermin: as in the languages of law and order that speak to us of 'Naxalite/ terrorist/ 'dacoit'-infested arenas of law enforcement. The militarized practices of governance continuously reproduce patterns of confiscation of Indian citizenship; those whom the Indian state apparatus can successfully stigmatize as constitutional outlaws stand thus wholly denied of their rights as citizens and as human beings.

All this raises the question of what meaning may we give to notions of the rule of law in the context of what Hannah Arendt termed, in a different context the 'rightless peoples'.[53] The constitution of rightless peoples does not speak to the limits of rights; rather, it is one of the impossibility, or the intelligibility, of human rights assertions under situations where state officials monopolistically determine threats to the life of the 'state'. Indian constitutional theory and practice urges us to examine the notion that human rights remain intelligible only within contexts of creation of conditions of rightlessness. In this, it comes closest to Carl Schmidt's notion that the power to determine the exceptional gives legibility to the normal. 'Sovereignty' here manifests itself as excess, within which alone may we meaningfully situate the three Cs.

'Subaltern' perspectives (in the nature of things there cannot be the subaltern perspective), however, question the sovereign monopoly over constructions of security and integrity of a 'nation'-state. Its complex notions about 'state terrorism' seek to delegitimate state monopoly over violence and deconstruct its logic, clothed in the languages of national unity and integrity by alternate conceptions, even visions, of these. Even pacific subaltern perspectives urge that human rights may not be silenced amidst the clash of arms. Constitutional policing of 'excesses' of peoples' human rights praxes must remain just that—constitutional policing— and no more. Subaltern critiques also insist on practices of state differentiation, practices providing scope for reflexive concerns involving the reproduction of forms of statenesses and rightlessness. It demands, thus, that the adjudicatory form of state power (through C2) inveigh against creation of circumstance of rightlessness, created singly or in combination by executive and legislative power. The 'subaltern' perspective contests Althusserian rendering of the bourgeois consti-tutionalism doctrine of separation of powers as a mask for the centralized unity of state power by its insistence on differentiation of state powers and purposes.

No known genre of contemporary constitutional theory takes this contestation seriously. I believe, though, that understanding of Indian constitutional practice holds potential for making a beginning in this direction.

DEVELOPMENTALISM AND REPRODUCTION OF RIGHTLESSNESS

The situation gets complicated, however, as we move from the 'security, integrity, and unity' of Indian discourse to theologies of 'development'. Practices of development programmes, policies, and priorities remain paranoiac, to a lesser degree, than state security policies although, from time to time, 'anti-developmental' citizen activism gets constructed, even decreed, as 'anti-national'. Developmentalism, as state ideology, con-stitutes the very 'being' of South constitutionalisms. Non-participatory developmental practices of politics also create circumstance of right-lessness, celebrating the power of the few as the destiny of millions of human beings.

Ideological practices of development entail hard constitutional or political labour, producing 'symbolic capital' and well as material conditions of ongoing human deprivation. A chief characteristic of these practices is that these create, almost constantly, circumstance of rightlessness. A subaltern outline of constitutional theory will necessarily read into the original Indian C1's division of rights, reinforced by fifty years' long constitutional practice, into Part III and Part IV. The fulfilment of conditions and capabilities that in practice affirm the equal worth of all citizens stands here eternally deferred.

Yet this distribution of rights into those judicially enforceable and those casting a paramount obligation on the legislature or executive in the making of law and policy (Article 37) was not informed at all by Indian C3. The practices of the freedom movement do not, on any responsible reading of it, warrant this structure of postponement; nor does any reading of developmental economics suggest logics other than those of intense engagement in the pursuit of social and economic rights. I have seen no argument in the Constituent Assembly Debates, and in the varieties of state planning discourses that followed, stating the case for the Indian state's disability to pursue the only time bound Directive Principle contained in Article 45, providing free and compulsory education for children below the age of fourteen;[54] nor is any exorbitance argument available for non-implementation of the sensible Directive Principle urging, inter alia, for maternity relief (provision for which is made only, and in wayward ways, in 1961 Parliamentary Act, requiring as late as the year 2000 the Supreme Court to direct that casual/daily wage labouring women were entitled to such benefits under that Act).[55] At least we had a national asset, not historically replicable, for the implementation of Article 45 in the charismatic figure of Jawaharlal Nehru, fondly called by the children of India as Chacha Nehru, who loved them as much as he did; yet, this grand constitutional avuncular presence did not move the cause even by a historic centimetre! I need not here multiply instances of constitutional immiseration of the large mass of Indian citizens[56] beyond an utterance in Mahasweta Devi's *Bashai Tudu*:

The Indian Constitution respected every citizen's fundamental right to become whatever he could becomes by the dint of his guts. The poor therefore had the right to become poorer still.[57]

The experience of development planning results in whole varieties of 'democratization of disempowerment'.[58] Large irrigation projects (from Bhakra Nangal to Narmada and Tehri), projects of urban development and siting of heavy industries, Green Revolution of which Bhopal catastrophe is the archetype, and related 'developmental' programmes, have created simultaneously infrastructures for Indian development as well excess in social reproduction of rightless peoples. It is this economy of excess, confiscating constitutionally enshrined human futures of large masses of Indian citizens, which defines practices of developmentalism, now contested (through social action litigation), with depressing turns of Fortuna, before the Supreme Court of India and the high courts. Judicial activism is sensible only as codifying archives of the 'logic' of reconstruction of Indian C3, responsive to human rights denying political practices of Indian 'development'.

Judicial activism (C2 in its postures of contemporary restlessness) sites itself at a point of protean contestation concerning constitutional conceptions of 'development'. What the dominant discourse construes as the economy of scarcity, the subaltern discourse knows as the economy of excess. The practice of Indian Constitution consists of this violent translation of the democratically enfranchised citizens into rightless peoples. Judicial activism inaugurates a new constitutional register, archiving transactional discourse between state practices that forever create classes of rightless peoples and state-adjudicatory practices that seek to limit the range of disenfranchised Indian citizens. In its variegated accomplishments,[59] judicial activism remains sensitive to the problem of transaction costs in accomplishing the reversal of the phenomenon of reproduction of rightlessness. In so doing, it constantly risks its (now notoriously Arundhati Roy induced) legitimacy with activist as well as state managers constituencies. In its manifold negotiation of this legitimation contingency,[60] the Supreme Court of India remains insecure, parlous, and at times schizo-paranoid. So does the involuted elite discourse concerning the nature, future, and range of judicial activism. Amidst all thee forms of intra-state/elite conversations, unsurprisingly, rightlessness grows apace.

PRACTICES OF CITIZEN INTERPRETATION

The power of practices of citizen interpretation lies un-theorized in constitutionalist discourse in India. Unlike the events of May 1968, or campus anti-Vietnam protests in the 1970s, which catalysed political thought in Euroamerican societies, 'critical events' (in a Lyotardian sense) have left no trace in the doing of constitutional and political theory in India. Movements of profound social significance bearing pivotally on constitutional experience and development remain at best on the margins of theory. I have traced elsewhere, in some detail, the Gandhian/neo-Gandhian, parliamentary communist and the Naxalite, communal and communitarian, and the subaltern citizen interpretive approaches to Indian constitutionalism.[61] Yet, these bear the burden of additional reflection in the context of this essay.

First, (and so far noted) the very notion of citizen interpretation pluralizes the notion of interpretive communities. Constitutions are not arenas of practices of state power; they also provide registers of interpretive practices of active citizenry. Second, citizen interpretations often remain contradictory to the canonical state interpretive performances. Third, to deploy Stanford Levinson's germinal distinction between 'Catholic' and 'Protestant' approaches to reading constitutions,[62] citizen interpretation is typically Protestant, in which the privilege of reading the sacred text belongs to each and every member of the community of belief. The Protestant mode questions the production of constitutional meaning as narrative monopolies of the privileged few. Fourth, by definition such interpretive mode produces very different ways of reading. Women citizens read constitutions in ways different than men. Ecocitizens read constitutions differently from the class of 'developmentalists'. Capitalists read C1 differently than trade unionists. So do indigenous peoples and related communities of *atisudras*. The diversity of patterns of citizen interpretation remains bewildering in comparison with whatever embarrassment de riches authoritative interpretive communities, the gourmet diet of constitutional theorists, may have to offer. Fifth, in sum, practices of citizen interpretation offer a chaos to the ordered universe of authorized interpretive/epistemic communities. The latter, however special interests driven, in all their moments of contingency/expediency, do end up with constructions of 'common' or the 'public' good or interest. Citizen interpretive practices remain irredeemably diverse, conflicted, and contradictory. Thus, active citizenry interrogates judicial activist postures on environmental protection at the bar of the rights of livelihood of ordinary citizens; antidam activists (and those cause-lawyering the plight of the urban impoverished) protest state 'logic' concerning 'developmental' decisions; feminist interpretive strategies interlocute the hidden patriarchy in the languages of law reform movements; the lesibgay movements question the homophobic state/law, and at times the logics and languages of human rights oriented social movements. This astonishing diversity ambushes, at vital moments, the fragile legitimacy of state/law social reproduction. Sixth, these establishment and insurgent modes of interpretation, in turn produce, moments of constitutional stupidity and tragedy.[63]

Overviewing practices of citizen interpretation runs large narrative risks. Not all citizen interpretation stands possessed of an equal power of social articulation; constitutionally 'valid laws'[64] and conflicted notions of political correctness[65] set effective boundaries. Not all citizen interpretation marshals the power of social movement and in turn social movements often define frameworks for citizen interpretation, for example, as is the case with the feminist and ecological movements. Citizen interpretation, initially free of practices of party politics, may be co-opted by power brokers. What matters in the Indian constitutional experience is the regime-sponsored appropriation of modes of citizen interpretive practices. Dominant structures of interpretation often convert the poetry of apsirational contest over production of constitutional meanings into the prose of governance.

Finally, without being exhaustive, the bases of judgement concerning the progressive/regressive character of citizen interpretation remain always deeply contested. Thus, we have no agreement, even among activist communities, concerning the progressive nature of violent citizen interpretation such as provided by an assortment of 'Naxalite' movements; even non-revolutionary, at least in their modality as pacific civil disobedience, interpretive movements like the Total Revolution movement, remain exposed to inconclusive contention when they (as Jayaprakash Narayan did in the early 1970s) urge security and armed forces to disobey unconstitutional orders. The *kar sevaks* who wantonly destroyed Babri Masjid even today do not see the 'counter-revolutionary', even reactionary, potential of citizen interpretation; for them the shaking of the foundations of Indian constitutional secularism, in profound human rights violative modes, emerges as constitutional necessity! And what shall we say of the elite citizen interpretation in the 1990s, which so volubly begrudged the legislation of reservations for backward classes in federal public services?

The allied question of impact of citizen interpretation on the structures of production of authoritative meanings of constitution stands partially answered by the fact that the its power, for weal or woe, is most remarkably resilient in the domain of the Indian C2; the histories of its impact in grasping transformations in C3 still await the birth of its raconteurs.

NOTES

1. See, for example, within the traditions of liberal political discourse, Bhikhu Parekh, *Rethinking Multiculturalism* (London: Macmillan, 2000).
2. Such as justifications for political authority and obligation; the aporias of rights and justice; notions of citizenship; fidelity to constitutional values, standards, and norms; and constitutional conceptions of individual, associational, and political good life.
3. See J. Rawls, *Political Liberalism* (New York: Columbia University Press, 1993).
4. See Bouaventura de Sousa Santos, *Towards a New Commonsense: Law, Science, and Politics in the Paradigmatic Transition* (London: Routledge, 1995), p. 113.
5. Upendra Baxi, 'The Avatars of Indian Judicial Activism: Explorations in the Geographies of (In) justice', in S.K. Verma and Kusum (eds), *Fifty Years of the Indian Supreme Court: Its Grasp and Reach* (Delhi: Oxford University Press & Indian Law Institute, 2000), pp. 156–209.
6. Jürgen Habermas, *Between Facts and Norms: Contributions Towards a Discourse Theory of Ethics* (Cambridge: MIT Press, W. Rehg, trans., 1995). Also see Rawls, *Political Liberalism*.
7. To borrow the phrase regime of A. MacIntyre, *Whose Justice? Which Rationality?* (Oxford: Oxford University Press, 1988).
8. By this phrase, I signify ways in which unequal international power relations and structures, including the modes of production of knowledge, which shape the national practices of enunciation of constitutions. Leading (or misleading?) terms of comparative constitutional discourse that refer us to post-colonial constitutional formations and more contemporaneously of the so-called 'transitional constitutions' are insensible outside fields of play of world hegemonic state actors.
9. V.A. Tumanov, *Bourgeois Legal Thought: Marxist Evaluation of Basic Concepts* (Moscow: Progress Publishers, 1974).
10. Pierre Bourdieu, *Outline of a Theory of Practice* (Cambridge: Cambridge University Press; R. Nice, trans., 1977); also see Bourdieu, *The Logic of Practice* (Stanford: Stanford University Press; R. Nice trans., 1980).
11. I name these as 'hegemonic' because traditions of doing comparative constitutional studies remains, even today, irredeemably Eurocentric. One looks in vain, for example, in the corpus of Ronald Dworkin, Jürgen Habermas, and even Antonio Negri for even the remotest understanding of the constitutional jurisprudence of the South.
12. Notions concerning activist judicial role responsibilities, an issue of traumatic importance for South justices, stand prescribed (even proselytized) in terms of democratic deficit of judicial review power. South justices must always stand in mimetic relationship with the high discourse on what North justices may or may not legitimately accomplish from the judgement seat.
13. Three notions need careful distinction: C1 (the text that make the constitution), C2 (interpretation of texts), and C3 (constitutionalism, the theory or ideology

underlying, as well as shaped by forms of C1 and C2). For further elaboration, see Section II of this essay.

14. See Bourdieu, *The Logic of Practice*, p. 27.
15. These too represented themselves as manifestations of alternative conceptions of democracy.
16. See Rawls, *Political Liberalism* and *A Law of Peoples* (Cambridge: Harvard University Press, 1999).
17. Habermas, *Between Facts and Norms*.
18. Bruno Latour, *We Have Never Been Modern* (London: Prentice Hall; C. Porter trans., 1993).
19. By this term, I designate the wielders of constitution-making powers, and those upon whose creative energies the development of constitutions mostly depends. These include justices, jurists, and self-authorizing interpreters of constitution, people possessed, mainly, of the executive power of the state. This dominant frame of reference excludes citizen, and dissident/subaltern, interpretive communities, which at least count in my understanding of 'lawpersons'.
20. The celebrated corpus of Rawls, Habermas, and Dworkin, for example, carries not a single reference to South constitutionalism from India to South Africa.
21. To adopt the phrase regime in Bourdieu, *The Logic of Practice*, p.103.
22. Pierre Bourdieu and L.J.D. Wacquant, *An Invitation to Reflexive Sociology* (Chicago: University of Chicago Press, 1992), pp. 235–53.
23. If we were momentarily to elevate justices to the privileged status of 'local informants' to the constitutional ethnographer, how then may we deal with the problem of 'the true nature of their practical mastery as learned ignorance, *docta ignorantia*, that is a mode of practical knowledge that does not contain knowledge of its own principles?' See Bourdieu, *The Logic of Practice*, p. 102. Put another way, how may we unravel constitution-making, and interpretation, as a 'kind of acquired mastery, functioning with the automatic reliability of an instinct' that makes it possible to 'respond instantaneously to all the uncertain and ambiguous situations of practice?' See Bourdieu, *The Logic of Practice*, p. 104. Indeed, the nascent 'theory' of comparative constitutionalism, or more precisely comparative constitutional adjudication, such as it is, does not quite guide us to understanding of the distinction between 'the objectivist model and the habitus, between the theoretical schema and the scheme of practical sense...shadowed by practical rules, partial and imperfect statement of principles'. See Bourdieu, *The Logic of Practice*, p. 107. Normative constitutional theories about adjudication do not leave much room for contingency of practical reason, which offers unlimited scope for strategies exploiting the opportunities for manipulating the peace of action—holding back or putting off, maintaining suspense or expectancy, or on the other hand, hurrying, hustling, surprising, stealing of a march, not to mention the art of ostensibly giving time...or withholding it (ibid.).
24. I must here clarify that my use of the term 'practice' is derived more from Louis Althusser than from Pierre Bourdieu (although a closer study may reveal

a kinship between the two discourses). For Althusser, practices, as material labour, assume primacy: 'all levels of social existence are sites of practices.' Practices are distinct and relatively autonomous and stand possessed of an 'element of knowledge' of prior practices; all types of practices (economic, political, ideological, technical, scientific/theoretical) constitute 'a complex unity...of a determinate human society.' In this sense, Althusserian notions of practice are as egalitarian as Bourdieu's. The parting of ways occurs when Althusser insists that the different internal structures of a whole variety of practices relate, in the last instance (howsoever one may chose to regard this lonely hour of the last instance) to 'the structure of production'. See Louis Althusser, *For Ma*, Ben Brewster (trans.) (London: Allen Lane, 1977), pp. 166–7. Although Bourdieu's notion of 'structuring structures' (partly, the *habitus*) deftly avoids traces of 'determination', for both thinkers practices are at once symbolic and material. Constitutions are then sites of (in the Althusserian sense) both ideological and repressive practices or apparatuses of power; Bourdieu will not accept this characterization but there is much in his discourse that, at the end of the day, reworks this categorization, at least in my reading of him. In any case, Althusser speaks more readily to concerns of constitutional theory and practice.

25. Upendra Baxi, 'The Avatars of Indian Judicial Activism'.
26. See pp. 34–5 of T.B. Hansen, 'Governance and the Myths of State in Mumbai', in C.J. Fuller and V. Benei (eds), *The Everyday State & Society in Modern India* (New Delhi: Social Science Press, 2000), pp. 31–67.
27. Oketh-Ogando, 'Constitutions without Constitutionalism:Reflections on an African Paradox', in Shivji G. Issa (ed.), *State and Constitutionalism: An African Debate on Democracy* (Harare: Southern Africa Political Economy Series, 1991).
28. Mahasweta Devi, *Bashai Tudu* (Calcutta: Thelma Publication, 1990).
29. Saddat Hasan Manto, *The Mottled Dawn*, Khalid Hassan (trans.) (Delhi: Penguin Books, 1997), p. 175.
30. The normative dimension, in liberal constitutionalism includes elaboration of 'values' that ought to inform both C1 and C2, such as equality before the law, due process of law, basic human rights; the institutional dimension includes the doctrine of separation of powers, autonomy for judicial independence, and powers of judicial review over executive and legislative action, free and fair elections. The ways in which these dimensions are elaborated offer the angst of contemporary forms of normative constitutional theory, as readers of Rawls and Habermas well know.
31. If we were to view all constitutional formations as so many recombinations of the rule of law and the reign of terror inherent in the social reproduction of the power to rule, all constitutional orderings manifest different forms of the Gulag statenesses. Catastrophic politics of cruelty inhere all forms of state power; only in some constitutional formats these become writ large.
32. In the sense in which Balkin views all law, see J.M. Balkin, *Cultural Software* (New Haven: Yale University Press, 1998).

33. Thus, one needs to decompose the term 'post-colonial' into different historical moments. The Indian Constitution of 1950 is 'post-colonial' in a very different temporal register than, for example, Asian and African constitutions enwombed in the practices of the Cold War; post-Cold War constitutions, the so-called transitional 'constitutions' of the former Soviet Union led state orderings may be described as post-colonial in a wholly different, if at all appropriate, sense.

34. Upendra Baxi, *The Future of Human Rights* (Delhi: Oxford University Press, 2008), 3rd edn.

35. It is impossible to understand developments in American constitutional development, outside the framing power the civil rights movements and to grasp Indian development outside the Total Revolution movement. Every activist Indian justice is a lineal descendent of Jayaprakash Narayan; so are leading American activist justices heirs of Martin Luther King Jr.

36. George Simmel, *Essays on Sociology, Philosophy and Aesthetics*, Kurt H.E. Wolff (ed.) (New York: Harper Row, 1959), p. 33. Also see Baxi, 'The Avatars of Indian Judicial Activism'.

37. Jeremy Bentham, *Theory of Legislation*, Bombay: N.M. Tripathi, 1975, pp. xvii–xxii, 90.

38. See Bentham, *Theory of Legislation*, p. 68.

39. Bentham, *Theory of Legislation*, p. 75.

40. Niklas Luhmann, *A Sociological Theory of Law*, Elizabeth King-Utz and Martin Albrow (trans.) (London: Routledge, 1985), p. 108.

41. Ibid., p. 33.

42. I leave to the interested Reader of this essay the obscurity of the concept of experience that Hans Georg Gadamer insightfully invites us to consider in his *Truth and Method* (New York: Crossroads, 1989), pp. 55–87, 347–79. Obviously, what I present as lived constitutional experience straddles several aspects of *Erlebnis\Ergebnis*, that which is 'positively experienced' and that which is the result of experiencing, oscillating between the 'permanent content of what is experienced' and 'transience of what is experienced' or the way in which this yields 'lasting result' (ibid., pp. 61, 64.)

43. Systems 'of durable, transposable dispositions, structured structures, predisposed to function as structuring structures...principles which generate and organize practices and representations that can be objectively adapted to their outcomes without presupposing a conscious aiming of ends or an express mastery of the operations in order to attain them', see Bourdieu, *The Logic of Practice*, p. 53.

44. When we attend seriously to the internal logic of dominant constitutional practices, we destroy the nominalist regimes of representing the Indian Constitution. Even from that perspective, India has at least five constitutions:
    - The original text of 1950;
    - The Ninth Schedule Constitutionalism: 1950–1964 Nehruvian Constitution elevating executive understanding over judicial interpretation;

- The State Finance Capitalist Constitution (marked by Bank Nationalization Case);
- The 1975–1976 Emergency Constitutionalism;
- The Basic Structure Constitutionalism (from Golak Nath, and Kesavananda Bharathi to Bommai and beyond);
- The globalization (WTO/post-WTO) Constitutionalism.

45. Bhikhu Parekh, *Rethinking Multiculturalism* (London: Macmillan, 2000).
46. Upendra Baxi, 'Conflicts of Laws', 8 Annual Survey of India Law 146, 1972.
47. Marc Galanter, *Competing Equalities* (Delhi: Oxford University Press, 1984); Upendra Baxi, 'Legislative Reservations for Social Justice', in R.B. Goldman and J. Wilson (eds), *From Independence to Statehood: Managing Ethnic Conflicts in Five African and Asian States* (London: Pinter, 1984), pp. 210–24. See also Upendra Baxi, 'Justice as Emancipation: The Legacy of Babasaheb Ambedkar', in Upendra Baxi and Bhikhu Parekh (eds), *Crisis and Change in Contemporary India* (New Delhi: Sage, 1995), pp. 122–49.
48. The various oaths of offices that the Constitution prescribes remain singularly innocent of enunciation of the duty to respect citizens. At less symbolic, but no less important, levels civil service codes of conduct entail no acknowledgement of treating fellow-citizens with respect.
49. I do not here invoke the more complex association of the idea of republic with notions of popular sovereignty.
50. Large numbers of Indian citizens remain officially and socially treated as subhuman as any reader of Rohinton Mistry's *A Fine Balance* (London: Faber and Faber, 1995) surely knows. Fifty years, and more, of Indian constitutionalism at work have not improved in the least bit the plight of scavengers and sweepers, the real Dalits. Much the same may be said concerning the atisudras (as Babasaheb Ambedkar used to designate the social and economic proletariat)—the bonded and attached labourers, sex-workers, people in state and private custodial institutions, 'beggars' and street children, the 'dammed' peoples, the disabled, and those violated by political catastrophes ('communal' violence, people affected by the Bhopal gas tragedy).
51. In the era of colonialism, it remained more concerned with the elaboration of a Divine Right to Empire than with ideas of a human right to self-determination. See P. Fitzpatrick, *Modernism and the Grounds of Law* (Cambridge: Cambridge University Press, 2000); Bhikhu Parekh, 'Liberalism and Colonialism: A Critique of Locke and Mill', in *The Decolonisation of Imagination* (Delhi: Oxford University Press, 1997); U. Mehta, *Liberalism and Empire* (Chicago: University of Chicago Press, 1998).
52. Partha Chatterjee, *Nationalist Thought and the Colonial World* (Princeton: Princeton University Press, 1986).
53. See Hannah Arendt, *The Origins of Totalitarianism* (New York: Harcourt Bruce, 1950) and Baxi, *The Future of Human Rights*.
54. The Supreme Court rendered this provision into a judicially enforceable right as late as 1993: see *Unnikrishnann v. State of Andhra Pradesh* (1993) 1 SCC 645.

55. *Municipal Corporation of Delhi* v. *Female Workers* (Muster Rolls) AIR 2000 SC 1278.

56. Even as regards republican rights, enshrined in Part III, affirming fraternity and dignity of all citizens political practices respecting state obligations corresponding to the fundamental right against exploitation (Articles 23 and 24) remain marginal to the practices of constitutional development.

57. Mahasweta Devi, *Bashai Tudu*, p. 87.

58. C. Ake, 'The Democratisation of Disempowerment in Africa', in *The Democratisation of Disempowerment: The Problem of Democracy in the Third World* (London: Pluto Press, 1995), pp. 70–89.

59. Baxi, 'The Avatars of Indian Judicial Activism'; S.P. Sathe, *Judicial Activism in India* (Delhi: Oxford Universty Press, 2001).

60. Upendra Baxi, *Judicial Activism, Legal Research and Legal Education in India* (Delhi: Capital Foundation of India, 1996).

61. Upendra Baxi, 'The (Im)possibility of Constitutional Justice: Seismographic Notes on Indian Constitutionalism', in Sridharan et al. (eds), *India's Living Constitution: Ideas, Practices, Controversies*, Delhi: Permanent Black, 2002.

62. Stanford Levinson, *Constitutional Faith* (Princeton: Princeton University Press, 1987).

63. See the interesting anthology by Levinson, *Constitutional Faith*, p. 19.

64. Laws that penalize free articulation of conscientious opinions such as the Official Secrets Act, the security legislation, contempt of court, law of parliamentary privileges, and offences against the state in the Indian Penal Code mainly, sedition.

65. Illustrated vividly by the current controversy over the revelation that the intrepid journalists of tehelka.com allowed the services of commercial sex workers being made available to army officers in a sting operation, which also recorded live the acts of intimate sexual relations.

5
A Text Without Author
Locating the Constituent Assembly as Event

Aditya Nigam

Perhaps the fault lies with the composition of the Drafting Committee, among the members of which no one, with the sole exception of Sriyut Munshi, has taken an active part in the struggle for our country's freedom. None of them is capable of entering into the spirit of our struggle, the spirit that animated us; they cannot comprehend with their hearts—I am not talking of the head, it is comparatively easy to understand with the head—the turmoiled birth of our nation after years of travail and tribulation.

– H.V. Kamath[1]

Now Sir, we have inherited a tradition. People always keep on saying to me: oh, you are the maker of the Constitution. My answer is I was a hack. What I was asked to do, I did much against my will.

– B.R. Ambedkar[2]

INTRODUCTION

In a sense, all constitutions can be said to be texts without authors—or at any rate, texts with many authors, such that no singular authorial voice can be attributed to them. Constitutions are normally written, or one may say, they write themselves, in the course of major upheavals and transformations in the lives of societies. Be it the American Civil War or the French Revolution, the Russian Revolution or the Chinese, the Indian nationalist struggle or the innumerable other national liberation struggles around the world, constitution-making represents in some sense a crystallization and codification of the aspirations that have dominated these movements. Yet, constitutions are rarely about change; they are codes that are meant to legitimize the new dispensation that emerges from the historical conflicts and struggles that bring them forth. They seek to provide a quasi-permanent shape to the new regime ushered in by these struggles. Against the old power they establish and institute the power of the new. They are, therefore, already there in a sense, even before they are formally written—and we know that they need not ever be written.

However, the Indian Constitution can be said to be a text without author in a more profound sense. This can be understood by dislocating the document from the authorized location within which it is supposedly produced, namely the Constituent Assembly. It is no doubt important to understand the serious debates that went on in the Constituent Assembly and which provide an important window into the nationalist struggle itself and into the concerns that animated the framers of the Constitution. Yet, it seems to me that by exclusively focusing on what went on *inside* the Constituent Assembly, we might be missing out on some of the more interesting and critical developments that went into the formation of the assembly itself. Locating the Constituent Assembly as an event, on the other hand, affords us the possibility of looking at the ways in which the different currents and different voices came together in the forming of the conjuncture within which the assembly took the shape it did.

By 'event' I mean two things: first, that it is an occurrence that institutes a break in the logic of the situation that existed till then and, second, that this occurrence itself is produced by the coming together of different logics into a kind of unity that then governs for some time the actions of different players. In a sense, the meaning of 'event' here is close to what Marc Auge, for instance, says, drawing on Francois Furet's discussion of the French Revolution. Auge says that 'the event or occurrence has always been a problem to those historians who wished to submerge it in the grand sweep of history, who saw it as a pure pleonasm between a before and an after conceived as the development of that before.' What Furet's discussion of the French Revolution says, he points out, is that, from the day the revolution breaks out, the revolutionary event 'institutes a new modality of historic action, one that is not inscribed in the inventory of the situation.'[3] Alternatively, we might refer to Bakhtin's discussions of Dostoevsky's novels, where he counterposes the idea of the polyphonic novel, marked by a 'plurality of independent and unmerged voices', to the logic of the event. What unfolds in Dostoevsky's works, says Bakhtin, is 'not a multitude of characters and fates in a single and objective world, illuminated by a single authorial consciousness; rather a plurality of consciousnesses with equal rights and each with its own world' which 'combine but are not merged in the unity of the event'.[4]

In other words, what I read in this description of the polyphonic novel and its dissimilarity with the idea of an 'event' is that the latter, in Bakhtin's view, requires a certain merging of the different worlds, of the 'different consciousnesses with equal rights', such that they inaugurate a new, unitary logic. And such a merger does not leave the 'different consciousnesses' untouched, for they must now become part of a common, larger logic that is not their own. I see a resonance here with the phenomenon of nationalism.

In one sense, ever since the advent of nationalism, these different consciousnesses were subject to conditions not entirely within their control. Often, they were forced to act in specific ways because of such conditions. We might, for example, see the activities of Ambedkar or the Muslim League, around the Round Table Conference, as in some way dictated by such extraneous logic. However, it is still possible to see in the period preceding the formation of the Constituent Assembly a certain 'polyphony' insofar as these different voices/consciousnesses have not yet been forced to merge their being within a larger entity. That begins to happen around the time of the formation of the Constituent Assembly. Thereafter, all of them had to become a part of a common national territory, tradition, and history.[5] The political logic that this inaugurates, as we will see, is such that it forces all the actors in the drama to make their choices in particular ways—and those who cannot do so must decide to part ways.

THE BACKDROP

It is tempting to read a liberal intent in the Indian Constitution, given the fact that so much of the phraseology and the terms used, are manifestly liberal in appearance. However, if we read the text of the Constitution and the Constituent Assembly Debates, in the context of their specific historicity, we can see a very different set of meanings emerge.

It may be useful to begin by underlining the three great absences that haunted the Constituent Assembly as it began its first session amidst tremendous uncertainty: the Muslim League (ML), the representatives of the so-called Indian States and the 'Father of the Nation', Mahatma Gandhi. The absence of the Muslim League members was, of course, an absence that was commented upon by the first speaker S. Radhakrishnan, who spoke to greet the new chairman, Rajendra Prasad, who himself referred to the abstention with a considerable sense of responsibility: 'Our brethren of the Muslim League are not with us and their absence increases our responsibility.' He went on to observe that '(w)e shall have to think at each step what they would have done if they were here' and that 'if unfortunately their seats were to remain unoccupied, it will be our duty to frame a Constitution which will leave no room for complaint from anybody.'

But the Muslim League was not the only absence. The prime minister-in-waiting Jawaharlal Nehru began his speech, moving the 'Aims and Objectives' resolution, haunted by the absence of the ML and the States' representatives and, above all, of Mahatma Gandhi, who was away on his trek for communal amity in Bengal.[6] As the preparations for transfer of power began, the new nation-to-be appeared at the very moment of its birth as a threatened entity. It was in such a precarious situation that the Constituent Assembly began its work and, needless to say, it marked the direction and substance of its proceedings throughout.

Also worth registering at the outset is the logic of the process that saw, in the penultimate year of the nationalist struggle, the ironic reversal of fate between Gandhi, the acknowledged 'Father of the Nation', now outcaste, and Ambedkar, the representative of the nation's outcastes, now in his final hour of glory as one of the key architects of the Constitution. There is, as a matter of fact, a double irony here in this reversal of fate. For Ambedkar was elected to the assembly with the support of the Muslim League, as a member from the Bengal Legislative Assembly, which had a Muslim League ministry in office in these fateful years. This was the period when the Muslim League and Ambedkar's Scheduled Castes Federation (SCF) were in alliance, and the situation was fast moving into a different plane where it would be governed by the logic of state- and nation-building. The imperatives of state- and nation-building were lodged in a very different temporality, marked by an urgency of the here-and-now, and were to determine the course of all future events: there was no time here for the Gandhian project of communal amity or for his periodic withdrawals into the realm of social reforms, marked by the temporality of the everyday.

One might, in fact, argue, against the grain of much accepted Marxist common sense that this Gandhian tendency of withdrawal was itself lodged within a deeper understanding of the processes of inter-community relations. It has often been argued that these withdrawals were attempts at reigning in mass movements whenever they seemed to transgress the limits of the permissible from the standpoint of the bourgeoisie. It seems to me that this completely misses the point of the Gandhian logic. Gandhi, in my opinion, worked with an understanding that was fundamentally at variance with the dominant understanding of his colleagues and comrades in the Indian National Congress (INC), which saw the nation-state as the precondition of the forging of a homogeneous national culture. This was an understanding that was most clearly articulated, with some variations, by Nehru and Patel, but was generally shared by the other leaders of the INC. Gandhi, on the other hand, simply reversed this logic. To him amiable relations between different communities, particularly Hindus and Muslims, was the precondition of India's freedom. And this bond could only be forged outside the domain of the state and its nation-building project.

Reading Gandhi's life itself as a text, one might suggest that his wariness of rushing headlong towards the goal of 'complete independence' was born out of his fear that the logic of the nation-state would tear the different communities apart from their temporality of the everyday and insert them into that of the political—one where the slow work of forging amiable inter-community relations would have to be given up. To Gandhi it seemed quite clear that 'truth lay outside the nation-state' and more, outside history. Drawing on Tolstoy's adage that 'happy families have no history', Gandhi on occasion argued that history only recorded conflicts and struggles.[7] Truth, on the other hand, lay in universal love and non-violence: love that lies unspoken and unspectacular, in the everyday practices of popular existence. It is to this realm that one had to periodically come back to nurture the love that was being lost in the mutual injuries that communities inflicted on each other once they entered the realm of the political.

There is no doubt that there is a utopian quality to the way in which Gandhi saw the future of India and I will suggest that it is this utopian vision that was responsible for his rapid marginalization. For, once the 'kingdom of freedom' was at hand and the logic of the nation-state completely colonized the domains of the everyday, there was no room left for Gandhi. Nehru writes in his autobiography that they often joked that 'after swaraj' Gandhi's 'fads must not be encouraged'.[8] 1946 and the logic of the nation-state saw to it that Gandhi—and his fads—were taken care of. Towards the end of July 1946 (21 July), Gandhi wrote to Patel in despair that 'a great many things seem to slipping out of the hands of the Congress'.[9] He was referring to the postal strike in Bombay, the communal riots in Ahmedabad, and the general distrust of the Congress among the 'Harijans and Muslims'. However, more than anything else, I think, this despair reflected Gandhi's own sense of marginality, rather than that of the Congress as a whole, which was preparing to take power in the near future.

THE ROAD TO POWER

Writing of the difficulties faced in the business of taking power, Nehru wrote to his Congress colleagues:

The Indian states offered some difficulties...It has been suggested that the door should be left open for them to enter the Constituent Assembly...*We should rely on the compulsion of events* which is bound to be considerable, and...a large number would join, if the British government's attitude was clear and they could get no help from it...I felt sure that *the creation of the Constituent Assembly would give rise to such power in India that no one would be able to withstand it.*[10]

In writing of this 'compulsion of events' and the irresistible power that the very constitution of the Constituent Assembly would generate, Nehru was actually pointing to the unfolding logic of the new temporality of power, which would force people to choose. It is noteworthy that what he says of the Indian states applies equally to the ML and the Muslims more generally; it applies also to Ambedkar and his SCF. Equally importantly, it applies to Gandhi too. He too would have to choose, and history would show that he chose wrongly from the standpoint of the new dispensation of power. This led to his rapid marginalization in these penultimate years of colonial subjugation. Gandhi, it needs to be remembered, had scripted one important chapter of the Constitution-to-be through his moral blackmail—his fast-unto-death—after the announcement of the Communal Award. The Poona Pact that was agreed upon at the end of his fast took away forever the possibility of separate electorates from the Dalits and thus laid the foundations of the 'liberal constitution'.

A joint electorate would thenceforth become an article of faith for the writers and commentators of the Indian Constitution. As a matter of fact, when Lord Wavell called the Simla Conference in June–July 1946, this was the basis of his discussions. Scheduled Caste leaders were not invited to the Conference; nor were they granted separate representation.

And none but Gandhi could have accomplished this feat, for no one had the moral stature to do so. Yet, we might do well to remember that Gandhi's move in 1932 was dictated by his own, utterly misplaced, logic of communitarian well-being, which was then, 14 years later, incorporated into the logic of the nation-state. His decision in 1932 was governed less by the logic of electoral politics and the nation-state-to-be and more by the desire to maintain the 'unity of Hindu society', which he saw as the basis of Hindu–Muslim unity and a future India that would represent his cherished 'unity in diversity'. However, the Gandhi of 1946 was consistent with the Gandhi of 1932, when he made the 'wrong choice' of opting out of the logic of power—for in both situations, his actions were governed by the logic of community being and not those of state.

In this context, it might be useful to recall the actual development of events preceding the formation of the Constituent Assembly and the transfer of power. As the Cabinet Mission announced its plan of 16 May for a three-tiered federation, Gandhi reacted with a fair degree of resignation. He told Louis Fischer, 'My instinct rebels against my reason', and therefore he had advised his colleagues to 'follow their own reason'.[11] His resignation was alarmingly inward-looking: 'If India is destined to go through a blood-bath, it will do so.'[12]

In the meanwhile, Nehru's will to power was playing itself out to the fullest. Two days after his election as Congress president, on 10 July, he made the fateful statement to the press that 'the Congress had made no commitment to the Cabinet Mission or the viceroy concerning the Constituent Assembly'.[13] While the overt thrust of this statement was directed at British power, Nehru was clearly targeting the ML and Jinnah, whom he was now forcing to choose under the 'compulsion of events'. And sure enough, this move was read as a 'signal of the possibility that there would be "no grouping", since the majority of the elected members in the Constituent Assembly would be Congress members'.[14]

Nine days later, Ambedkar was elected to the Constituent Assembly as an independent candidate, supported by the ML, from Bengal. An alliance between the ML and the SCF was being forged. The threat of a Hindu upper caste rule being instituted in the name of swaraj was now as real as ever—at least to the two biggest minorities. From late August onwards, this alliance took the shape of ML leaders addressing SCF protest meetings against the Cabinet Mission decision to deprive them of separate representation.[15] On 29 July, the ML Council unanimously voted to empower Jinnah to 'resort to Direct Action to achieve Pakistan'.

For the Congress and the nationalists, though, the problem was the ML–SCF alliance. If the Muslim League and the Muslims were to be singled out as the anti-national forces that were bent upon partition, then this alliance had to be broken. More than anything else, it was a question of the legitimacy of nationalism's claims to represent the nation that was at the root of their discomfort. It is therefore around this time that leaders like Sardar Patel proposed to 'negotiate with Ambedkar out of fear of the League' (these words are Gandhi's).[16] Patel had in fact been requesting Gandhi to meet Ambedkar in order to negotiate with him. Gandhi's answer was matter of fact: 'I have said that I will see Bhimrao if he comes to Poona or Sewagram.' Clearly, unlike Patel he did not see the need to make any move on this count on his own. When Patel pressed on the need to win over Ambedkar, Gandhi wrote:

I see a risk in coming to any sort of understanding with him, for he has told me in so many words that for him there is no distinction between truth and untruth, or between violence and non-violence. He follows one single principle, viz., to adopt any means which will serve his purpose. One has to be very careful indeed when dealing with a man who can become Christian, Muslims or Sikh and then be reconverted according to his convenience…To my mind it is all a snare.[17]

Gandhi's refusal of the logic of power had now taken another perverse turn. Probably, he still had confidence that he would win over the Dalits, despite Ambedkar, by returning to his favoured site of everyday existence. He simply refused to bow before the urgency of the situation. For the likes of Patel, on the other hand, it was crucial that the SCF alliance with the ML be broken. To do this Patel was prepared to give Ambedkar a place of honour in the new dispensation. In the event, he would even forsake Gandhi, his teacher and leader. And Nehru would later, in April 1948, appoint Ambedkar his law minister, not for the sake of the untouchables, but in keeping with the logic of power. In between, as events rapidly played themselves out, Ambedkar lost his seat in the Constituent Assembly due to Partition, and the Congress made the important gesture of nominating him as Congress candidate from the Bombay Legislative Council. While the Congress was under some compulsions in making these overtures to Ambedkar, the latter too had to choose his moves in a rapidly changing and uncertain situation. There were clearly pressures on him too. Once it became clear that the partition was now inevitable, he had to make the best of a bad deal. Ambedkar's statement given in the epigraph to this essay should be read in that light.

This then was the context in which the Constituent Assembly began drafting the new constitution. This was the situation in which the programme of forging the new Indian nation was undertaken. But the Constituent Assembly did not begin writing on a clean slate. If Gandhi had already written one crucial chapter for it, so had the last three-and-a-half decades of intense struggle within the incipient nation/s since the Morley–Minto Reforms of 1909. These reforms—implemented through the Indian Councils Act of 1909, which had for the first time provided separate representation to the Muslims—have been routinely represented in nationalist historiography as having 'sowed the seeds of separatism'.[18] Right from Nehru—undoubtedly the most secular of the nationalists—to people like K.M. Munshi and Patel, all nationalist leaders have shared this reading of 'Muslim separatism'.[19]

This is an issue that I shall return to later. For the present, it is relevant to note that though the complex processes of the quest for selfhood in the late colonial period were irrevocably shaped by the activities of the colonial state and its census operations, it is only by denying any agency to the other subordinate social groups and communities that nationalism could represent other assertions of selfhood as 'creations of colonial divide and rule policies'. Nationalism's reading in this respect is relatively straightforward and unaware of the extent to which its own self-understandings were shaped by colonial knowledge. Whatever be the case, once certain notions of selfhood were in place, acute contestations among them, particularly for political representation, mark the entire course of the anti-colonial struggle.

In fact, I would argue that the whole history of the anti-colonial struggle can be read as an intricate process of the writing of the Constitution. The various landmarks of the freedom struggle—starting with the struggles against the initiatives of the colonial government like the Morley–Minto Reforms, the Montague–Chelmsford Report, and the Government of India Act 1919, to the proceedings of the Simon Commission and the Round Table Conferences—are episodes in the writing of the text that emerged, with significant embellishments, of course, from the Constituent Assembly.

It has been widely acknowledged, even in the Constituent Assembly Debates, that the final draft of the Constitution owed not a little to the Government of India Act of 1935. Nationalism, represented by the Congress, did not always find itself at ease with the way in which these developments took shape. Nationalist initiatives were thus marked from their founding moment itself with a deep split within, which was represented by various assertions of selfhood by various subordinate social groups and communities. It is through a continuous play and tension between these different impulses that we see the different positions of the Constitution formulated.

THE MODERNIZING AGENDA OF THE POST-COLONIAL ELITE

By the time the Constituent Assembly assembled for its fourth session on 14 July 1947, Pakistan had been, in principle, formed. Twenty-two ML members signed the register to take their place in the assembly. K.M. Munshi, while moving the motion on the Report of Order of Business Committee, declared that now that the British parliament was about to adopt the resolution 'setting India free', 'we' could go ahead with the agenda of constitution-making in absolute freedom. 'The plan of May 16', he said, 'had one motive—to maintain the unity of the country at all costs. A strong Central Government was sacrificed by the May 16 plan at the altar of preserving unity which many of us, after close examination, found to be an attenuated unity...'[20] Munshi went on to thank God that now, 'we have no sections and groups to go into, no elaborate procedure...no double majority clause, nor more provinces with residuary powers, no opting out, no revision after ten years...We have now a homogeneous country, though our frontiers have shrunk...'[21]

Munshi's relief, of course, was not shared by everyone. M. Ananthasayanam Ayyangar expressed surprise that 'my friend Mr Munshi, who stood for Akhand Hindustan' is now 'supporting this solution'. He went on to add that he personally thought that the 16 May solution was the best and was 'sorry that solution has been given up'.[22] However, on a close reading of the Constituent Assembly Debates, it seems that Munshi represented the dominant sentiment. There was a feeling that now that all the constraints were out of the way, federalism could also be given short shrift and a centralized state could go about its modernizing agenda in real earnest.

One can get a sense of this from the major conflict around Clause 12 of the Principles of a Model Provincial Constitution. This clause said: 'The Governor's Ministers shall be chosen and summoned by him and shall hold office during his pleasure.' Amendments were moved to this clause by Aziz Ahmed Khan, Begum Aijaz Rasul and others, and were supported by practically all ML members, defending the elective principle, proportional representation, and calling for a term for the ministry that would be co-terminus with that of the assembly. This amendment was opposed by practically all non-Muslim members.[23] A similar scene was enacted in relation to the amendment moved by Mahboob Ali Baig Sahib Bahadur regarding the constitution of the council of ministers at the Centre. His amendment too, called for a council of ministers, elected by both Houses of Parliament and on the basis of proportional representation, based on a single transferable vote. This innocuous, and one might say democratic, amendment was moved by Mahboob Ali Baig amidst heckling from nationalists like Algu Rai Shastri, Mahavir Tyagi, and Pandit Thakur Dass Bhargava. While Shastri accused him of propounding a 'narrow minded party-politics view',[24] Tyagi went on to remind the house that the country had had to face Partition because of a mixed-bag cabinet and that Baig's insistence on a proportionately represented cabinet was in effect a demand to revive the portent of partition.[25] Baig had to in fact repeatedly state that he should not be misunderstood because he is a Muslim.[26]

This kind of heckling occurs repeatedly in the course of the proceedings of the Constituent Assembly and we might see from the ways in which questions are formulated by respective members that the words themselves often appear quite innocent. I will return to this question later in the essay. For the time being I am concerned with something quite different.

There appears to be, in the dominant majority of the Constituent Assembly members, a desire for a centralized state. This appears both in relation to the question of residuary powers for the provinces/states, as well as in relation to the composition of cabinets, in the provinces as well as in the Centre. In the case of the provinces, this is expressed in the attempts to keep the council of ministers under the governor's thumb, and therefore under central control. It is also significant that Nehru, while moving the Aims and Objects Resolution, spends some time explaining the absence of the word 'democratic' in the resolution. 'It is possible', he says, 'that a republic may not be democratic, but the whole of our past is witness to the fact that we stand for democratic institutions'. He went on to add that 'we' were aiming at nothing less than a democracy, but added that the shape that it would take was uncertain.[27]

This roundabout way of explaining the absence of the word 'democracy' reveals clearly that it was not an inadvertent error but a well thought-out decision. Why, we may ask? One of the fears was, of course, expressed in Tyagi's speech about the possible consequences of a 'mixed-bag cabinet'. However, another great fear of the nationalist mind becomes evident here. With 570 states out of the purview of the emergent nation-state's jurisdiction, with the 'unresolved' Muslim question hanging fire, and with the host of other issues that they might have had to deal with, the constitution had to be framed in such a way that kept open all options for the future. It seems that the impulse towards centralization here was not simply born out of a drive towards an authoritarian state. On the contrary, it seems to me that Nehru was being quite truthful in suggesting that the new ruling elite wanted some form of democracy. Granville Austin, one of the most serious scholars of the Indian Constitution, also concurs when he argues that 'the belief in parliamentary government seemed in fact to be nearly universal'. In support of this contention, Austin says that the draft constitutions published by groups of the Left, Centre, and the Right—those of the Marxist M.N. Roy, of the Socialist Party and of the communal Hindu Mahasabha—were also all parliamentary, centralized constitutions.[28] In fact, Austin goes further to suggest that 'nearly everyone in the Assembly was Fabian and Laski-ite enough to believe that 'socialism is everyday politics for social regeneration' and that 'democratic constitutions are...inseparably associated with the drive towards economic equality'.[29]

I would argue, therefore, that the desire for a centralized state expressed by a majority of the nationalists was not so much a 'communal' one to keep the ML out of power, as the glimpse into the debate above might suggest, but, on the contrary, it was a desire for a modern and homogeneous nation-state that moved them into taking such a position. This is also evident in the nationalism's representation of itself as the modernizing force, continuously at odds with the 'backward' and 'separatist' minorities acting at the behest of the colonial rulers. K.M. Munshi's relief at the formation of Pakistan is in fact symptomatic of a wider feeling shared by the nationalist elite that now, with all obstructions—notably the ML—out of the way, the task of building a homogeneous nation could be seriously addressed. The theme of building a modern India, where no differences on account of religion and caste would be recognized, is a recurrent one in the debates in the Constituent Assembly.

Yet it needs to be underlined that this desire for a homogeneous, modern nation-state was not always democratic. Its liberal language and justifications very often performed another function in nationalist discourse. I have argued elsewhere that the resort to certain liberal notions of abstract, unmarked citizenship, for instance, worked against the interests of the minorities because they drove the community to the realm of the unspeakable. Any articulation of community-based discrimination was deemed illegitimate in this framework.[30] It might be worthwhile to return briefly here to the problem of the innocence of the words, not only in the language in which matters are articulated in the Constituent Assembly but more generally in nationalist discourse. Scholars have often referred to Govind Ballabh Pant's celebrated diatribe against 'community'—upholding the sovereignty of the individual citizen—as an indication of the liberal impulses behind constitution-making in India.[31] In this oft-quoted passage, Pant says:

I cannot however refrain from referring to *a morbid tendency which has gripped this country* for the last many years. The *individual citizen* who is really the backbone of the state, the cardinal centre of all social activity, and whose happiness and satisfaction should be the goal of every social mechanism, *has been lost here in that indiscriminate body known as the community.* We have forgotten that a citizen exists as such. There is the unwholesome, and to some extent degrading habit of thinking always in terms of communities and never in terms of citizens.[32]

This passage is impeccably liberal in its advocacy of the individual citizen's direct relationship to the state—unmediated by any community markers, we might say. Yet, this passage would make a very different kind of sense within the structure of nationalist discourse. How such an advocacy of the erasure of community markers functions within that discourse is evident from the following episode in the Constituent Assembly. Z.H. Lari, Muslim member from the United Provinces, moved an amendment to the Draft Constitution, proposing the inclusion of an additional clause to the effect that any section of the citizens of India, residing in any part of the country and having a distinct language and script, shall be entitled to education in the mother tongue. Lari invoked the Motilal Nehru Committee Report and a recent Resolution of the Government of India (GoI), published in the Gazette, to support his contention. Lari then went on to argue that students from Urdu-speaking families should be imparted education in Urdu. As it happens, Lari's six-year-old son had been told by his teacher that he should use Hindi and Hindi alone to do his mathematics. Lari claimed that on making inquiries he found that a similar situation prevailed in most schools.[33]

The same Pandit Govind Ballabh Pant, in his response to Lari stated: '(T)here is no particular language attached to the followers of any particular religion, [therefore] the question of language with reference to or *vis-a-vis* any minority, does not arise at all.' 'No language is the language of the Hindus and no language is the language of the Muslims,' he went on to add, amidst cheers from like-minded members in the House.[34] He continued, saying that 'boys' are taught in their mother tongues in primary schools and that 'the mother tongue of Hindus and Muslims and all boys [sic] is more or less the same. *There is no difference whatsoever.*' And then, once again amidst cheers, he went on to add: 'Those who in the olden [sic] days, were obsessed by the idea of separatism have not been able to shed it off even now and the ghost of "Two Nations" seems to be lingering somewhere, even within the precincts of this very august Chamber.'[35]

In nationalist discourse, the emphasis on the individual, then, was not really a straightforward expression of the liberal ethos. The demand for the erasure of community markers, the placing of the individual citizen at the centre, in Pant's mind—as in nationalist discourse more generally—then represents the desire for a homogeneous national culture. In asserting this, however, I am not asserting that Pant's or the nationalists' advocacy of the liberal creed was hypocritical. What I am suggesting is that to them the only way the liberal dream of the abstract citizen could be achieved was through erasure of difference and the production of a homogeneous national culture. To be sure, this discourse was not averse to acknowledging the contribution of Islam to composite Indian culture—but it did require, in the manner of the only models of nationalism it sought to emulate, the erasure of the separate existence of 'religious' communities. The new nation-state would be the agent that would, through its network of educational institutions, produce that culture.

Partha Chatterjee has argued that the nationalist elite had, through the anti-colonial struggle, been resisting the reformist-modernist intervention of the colonial state in the 'inner' spiritual/cultural affairs of the nation—not because it was opposed to reforms but because it considered that realm its own sovereign realm. He has persuasively suggested that for this reason, while it continued to oppose all such colonial initiatives, its desire for internal reform accumulated over time and exploded in the immediate post-colonial period, through a host of legislations that sought to introduce major changes within the Hindu community. He also suggests that much of this intervention of the independent nation-state in the affairs of the community became possible precisely because of the formation of Pakistan and the migration of large sections of the Muslim elite there. With regard to the Muslim community that remained here, the situation was now pretty much the same as it had been with the Hindu community in the colonial period— even though during the periods of ML ministries, there had been similar interventions of reform within them.[36] Our reading of the Constituent Assembly Debates seems to affirm Chatterjee's understanding about internal reform, at least in the majority community. Much of the resistance of the nationalist elite to the idea of minority or community rights seems to be directly related to this desire for a new homogeneous, modern nation. Yet, it was the very logic of events that constituted the Constituent Assembly, the manner in which alliances were shaped and reshaped during this period, that made it impossible for the new Constitution to avoid the question of minority rights altogether.

It is also interesting here to note that the debate on minority rights generated a lot of heat in the Constituent Assembly even before the Muslim members joined the proceedings. The debate here was primarily with the Christian members of the assembly. In the course of the debate, K.M. Munshi moved that one part of that clause (Clause 18) be referred back to the Advisory Committee, while Mohanlal Saksena and Mahavir Tyagi wanted the entire clause to be referred back to it. No reasons were, however, given for this proposal. An inkling to the machinations going on behind the scenes is, of course, provided by an astute observation by Ambedkar. He pointed out that the only reason one could sense was the rights of minorities would be decided after seeing what the Pakistan Assembly decided. He argued forcefully against such relativity of rights. Minority rights, he held, should be absolute.[37]

Insofar as the dominant leadership of the new nation-state was concerned, it was perfectly possible for them to enact legislations for the abolition of untouchability and leave the matter at that. They—and here I include the more Right-wing Hindu Mahasabhaite leaders— undoubtedly considered the practice of untouchability to be the bane of Hindu society. The entire logic of nationalism was predicated upon the decades of introspection about the internal divisions and weaknesses of Hindu society that had made it prey to repeated external invasions. It had, therefore, internalized the idea that at least the worst features of caste society must go. What they did not consider was that for somebody like Ambedkar the mere abolition of untouchability was not enough. What was required was the political recognition of the demands of the Dalits, their demands for separate representation. In the case of the Muslims, however, the case was different. Speech after speech in the Constituent Assembly emphasized that now that we are making a new beginning, now that the new nation is about to be born, the idea of separate recognition of communities in politics must be given up. And this repeated assertion was often backed up by not-so-subtle threats.

The reason I narrate this drama inside the Constituent Assembly in some detail is precisely to highlight that the Constituent Assembly was actually functioning within a certain code, the language of which was forged largely outside the precincts of the assembly itself. Within this code, words changed their meanings and performed very different functions. The narration also shows that the Constituent Assembly was not exactly a Habermasian terrain of rational–critical discourse, and that members of the minorities, particularly the Muslims, were under tremendous pressure to act according to these codes. Their repeated heckling and booing, accompanied by the continuous insinuation that they were still nursing their separatist desires and that everything that they suggested was to be attributed to their continued allegiance to the two-nation theory, is evidence enough of this attitude. Reading the Constituent Assembly Debates in their very literal meanings can therefore be quite misleading. There is certainly no doubt that there are strong liberal elements in the provisions of the Constitution, and the debates themselves reveal much of these concerns. What is not so evident is the way in which what was speakable and what not was shaped in an altogether different arena.

A question that one might then legitimately ask here is whether this means that the leaders of the Indian republic were being dishonest? Was there no ethical ground on which they based their positions? Did they act merely out of considerations of the logic of power? Did they act purely out of self-interest? I think this will be a misleading conclusion to draw from the above discussion. In the first place, such a poser assumes a certain dichotomy or antagonism between ethical action and self-interest which does not always hold. In fact, it is possible to argue that even the most anti-democratic, fascistic political programmes are usually grounded in some ethical vision of the future, like the 'regeneration of the German nation', which are seen as the precondition for the attainment of yet larger goals. What the discussion above shows, in my view, is that there are conflicting ethical visions in continuous tension and contestation throughout the nationalist movement and in the Constituent Assembly. When mainstream nationalism advocates a strong centralized state along with an insistence on the value of individual citizenship, it does so out of a vision of a particular kind of modern nation-state where, eventually, individual citizenship will be the sole relevant criterion regulating the state's dealings with its people. It possibly genuinely believes that markers of community need to be erased for a truly democratic future to be realized. On the other hand, when representatives of the Muslim minority strike a different posture, they do so out of the belief—as the exchange between Lari and Pant so graphically illustrates—that, being dis- criminated against as a community, all their problems cannot be articulated in the language of individual rights, and, given that they have lost the possibility of separate political representation, they will need separate safeguards. The best that is possible in that case is a federal structure where all powers are not concentrated in one centre.

It is also interesting that Ambedkar, who generally shared the nationalist position on the need for a strong, centralized state, did so for entirely different reasons. To him such a state was necessary in order to be able to ensure compliance of society with regard to the rights of Dalits. Nevertheless, he was not prepared to go along with the nationalists on the question of minority rights and took a fairly uncompromising position on the issue. In other words, what we see here is that there is no transcendental ethical ground on which justifications of specific measures in the Constitution can be based, such that they will be acceptable to all. What is important, it seems to me, is that both the specific provisions as well as the ethical justifications for them become meaningful within the specific life-contexts and from the locations of different players. It is from these locations that justifications are either advanced or contested. In other words, the ethical visions involved are themselves *situated* visions.

THE NATION AND ITS FRAGMENTS?

In concluding this discussion, I would like to suggest that much of the scholarship that seeks to concentrate its sight on the inside of the Constituent Assembly, as a window to the philosophy of the Indian Constitution, proceeds with a kind of unstated assumption of a nation already in existence, whose representatives, after deliberations, wrote the Constitution. Even when we take note of the diverse currents and the diverse sections and groups, there is somewhere an underlying assumption of the prior existence of the nation. Such, for instance, is also the assumption underlying the introductory note by Rajeev Bhargava outlining the concerns of the conference in which this paper was presented. So when it talks of uncovering the 'structure of ideals embedded in the Indian Constitution', it assumes a kind of unitary structure that is arranged according to some particular logic. That is why it is possible for it to ask: 'When *the framers of the constitution* chose to guide Indian society and polity by *a particular set of values rather than others*, they could not have done without a set of reasons, many of which remain implicit, unarticulated.' My submission here will be that even a cursory reading of the Constituent Assembly Debates suggests that there was no such thing as 'a particular set of values' that was given preference over others, precisely because their was no single authorial voice, as assumed in the expression 'the framers of the constitution *chose...*' There is in the statement an assumption of a singular will which 'chose' one, rather than another, set of values and with a kind of coherent justificatory framework.

My general problem with this way of posing the problem of the political theory of the Indian Constitution can thus be stated in the following manner: first, the assumption of a single will underlying the Constitution can be understood in either of the two ways. One way would be to posit a prior community of interests upon which a 'general will', as it were, arises. As we have seen, this is a problematic assumption to make, given that there were such vastly different interests at play here. Another way of understanding it is to argue, for instance, that even though there were fundamental differences of opinion between different players, they were all basically reasonable people operating within a generally Habermasian terrain of rational–critical discourse, coming up in the end with a consensual 'single will'. This means that their disagreements were fundamentally intellectual in nature and, as such, they were prepared to convince and be convinced by the others. In other words, there is an implicit positing here of a kind of 'disengaged subject' freed of all existential and community attachments. Only on such as assumption can we really posit an ethical subject that is devoid of interests, passion, and power.

A notion of an embedded subject, on the other hand, will require us to consider the fundamental relationship between thought/consciousness/ethical vision on the one hand, and social being on the other. It will require us to recognize that for such an embedded subject,

existential and community attachments are constitutive of ethical being—
and therefore of all intellectual positions that such a subject might hold.
It is from this standpoint that the self-understandings of different
communities become crucial to our discussion of the constitution-
making process, since, broadly speaking, they reveal such embedded
subjects. Their articulations of their own notions of the future are
inextricably linked to their position in terms of power and subordination,
and voiced in terms of cultural autonomy and difference.

Therefore, if we consider the fact that the different communities that
assert their selfhood throughout the anti-colonial struggle in ways that
significantly diverge from the nationalists' do so often in direct liaison
with colonial rule; if we consider that even at the time of Independence,
570 Indian states, comprising a fourth of the population of the nation-
to-be were almost totally outside the process of nation formation, then
we might need to understand the process of the formation of the
Constitution itself very differently. It might be more realistic and
productive to see the Constituent Assembly itself as the site where
different currents and diverse groups come together, under the
compulsion of the logic of power, to hammer out a negotiated
settlement—a settlement that aspires to nationhood no doubt, but which
remains nevertheless an articulated totality whose very being is always
threatened by the very fragility of the settlement. In other words, I am
suggesting that we see 'Indian society' not as a given pre-existing totality,
evolving according to some evolutionary logic into a nation, but rather
as different entities, having different histories, that have come together
into an articulated whole. The terrain on which these different histories—
and therefore different temporalities of the everyday—come together is
the accelerated temporality of the Indian state. It is here—in the
harmonization of different temporalities, through what Althusser
describes as torsion, displacement, and fusion of different times—that
the nation-state emerges.

As Poulantzas has suggested, it is on the terrain of the state that the
different pasts of different social groups are fused into a whole and the
nation acquires its past—moving then to a common future, a common
destiny. It is the state that constitutes the 'national tradition' 'by making
it the moment of a becoming designated by itself'. The modern nation-
state, he argues, 'also involves eradication of the traditions, histories and
memories of dominated nations'. He suggests that 'the state establishes
the modern nation by eliminating other national pasts and turning them

into variations of their own history'.[38] My reading of the Constituent Assembly as event and the Indian Constitution as an outcome of negotiations that brought forth the 'Indian nation' seems to affirm this relationship—the Constituent Assembly being the intellectual core of the emerging state.

NOTES

1. *Constituent Assembly Debates (CAD)*, vol. 7, p. 219.
2. *Proceedings of the Council of States*, 2 September 1953, columns 864–80 and 3 September 1953, columns 997–1003. I thank Ajay Dandekar for bringing this reference to my notice.
3. Marc Auge, *Non-places: Introduction to an Anthropology of Supermodernity* (London & New York: Verso, 1995), p. 27.
4. Mikhail Bakhtin, *Problems of Dostoevsky's Poetics* (UK: Manchester University Press, 1984), p. 6.
5. I will discuss this point at greater length in the last section.
6. See *CAD* Official Report, reprinted by the Lok Sabha Secretariat, New Delhi, vols. 1–13. For this part, see vol. 1.
7. In *Hind Swaraj*, Gandhi records his critique of history: 'History, as we know it, is a record of the wars of the world, and so there is a proverb among Englishmen that a nation which has no history, that is, no wars, is a happy nation.' M.K. Gandhi, *Hind Swaraj and Other Writings*, Anthony J. Parel (ed.), (New Delhi: Cambridge University Press and Foundation Books, 1997), p. 89. And again: 'History is really a record of every interruption of the working of the force of love or of the soul.' (ibid., p. 90) He, of course, continues to speak in the name of 'the nation', which he does not directly critique. For instance: 'Hundreds of nations live in peace. History does not and cannot take note of this fact.' But to Gandhi, this 'nation' has a kind of universal existence outside of the state and statehood. This is not the place for a detailed discussion of this issue but it can be shown that to him the idea of a nation is quite distinct from that of the state and of nation as generally understood.
8. Jawaharlal Nehru, *An Autobiography* (JLN Memorial Fund and Oxford University Press, 1998), p. 73.
9. *Mahatma Gandhi, Collected Works* (henceforth, *CWMG*), vol. LXXXV (The Publications Division, Ministry of Information and Broadcasting, Government of India, 1982), p. 35.
10. Stanley Wolpert, *Nehru: A Tryst With Destiny* (New York: Oxford University Press, 1996), p. 240, emphasis added.
11. *CWMG*, vol. LXXXV, p. 17.
12. Ibid.
13. Wolpert, *Nehru*, p. 370.
14. Ibid.
15. See Ramnarayan Singh Rawat, 'Partition Politics and Achhut Identity: A Study of the Scheduled Castes Federation and Dalit Politics in UP, 1946–48', in Suvir

Kaul (ed.), *The Partitions of Memory: The Afterlife of the Division of India* (Delhi: Permanent Black, 2001), pp. 119–23.

16. *CWMG*, vol. LXXXV, p. 102.
17. Ibid.
18. D.D. Basu, *Introduction to the Constitution of India*, 18th edition (New Delhi: Prentice-Hall of India Pvt. Ltd., 1998), p. 5.
19. *CAD*, vol. 3. See especially, the interventions of Rajendra Prasad and Purushottamdas Tandon.
20. *CAD*, vol. 4, p. 546.
21. Ibid.
22. Ibid., p. 551.
23. Ibid., pp. 628–48.
24. *CAD*, vol. 7, p. 1142.
25. Ibid., p. 1150.
26. Ibid.
27. *CAD*, vol. 1, p. 62.
28. Granville Austin, *The Indian Constitution: Cornerstone of a Nation* (Oxford: Clarendon Press, 1966), p. 40.
29. Ibid., p. 41
30. Aditya Nigam, *The Insurrection of Little Selves: The Crisis of Secular Nationalism in India* (Delhi: Oxford University Press, 2006), see esp. ch. 5, pp. 222–57.
31. Gurpreet Mahajan, *Identities and Rights: Aspects of Liberal Democracy in India*, (Delhi: Oxford University Press, 1998), p. 82.
32. *CAD*, vol. 2, p. 332, emphasis added.
33. *CAD*, vol. 7, pp. 901–2.
34. Ibid., p. 914.
35. Ibid., p. 915.
36. This rendering of Chatterjee summarizes his arguments in the following three texts: Partha Chatterjee, 'Secularism and Toleration' *Economic and Political Weekly*, vol. XXIX, no. 28, 9 July 1994; Partha Chatterjee, *Nation and its Fragments* (Delhi: Oxford University Press, 1994); Partha Chatterjee (ed.), *Wages of Freedom: Fifty Years of the Nation-State*, 'Introduction' (Delhi: Oxford University Press, 1998).
37. *CAD*, vol. 3, p. 507.
38. See Nicos Poulantzas, *State, Power, Socialism* (London: New Left Books, 1978), esp. pp. 112–13. Of course, Poulantzas' discussion of nations suffer from some of the residues of orthodox Marxism that see nations and nationalisms as 'objective entities' embodied in certain kinds of cultural communities. However that is a separate matter and does not concern us here.

Section II

6

The Indian State
Constitution and Beyond

Suhas Palshikar

Ever since the Indian state was put in place, it has evoked a number of different assessments. The initial period was marked by an enthusiastic welcome for the welfare state apparatus evolved by the Constitution, which was seen as the document for social revolution. An air of expectancy surrounded the Indian state. Soon came the days of scepticism and the loud murmurs against the 'license-permit-quota raj' that allegedly emerged during the prime ministership of Indira Gandhi. The Indian state looked like a bureaucratic leviathan to its critics. In this backdrop there arrived the phase of 'liberalization' of the economy. It soon became fashionable even among academic circles to take potshots against the 'Nehruvian' state. Glib ideologies of the state as a facilitator gained currency in the 1990s. At the same time, the supporters of the old welfare state complained about the retreat of the state or its withdrawal. Obviously, the alleged withdrawal referred to the retreat of the state from social welfare policies. The Indian state, however, continued to be actively engaged in advancing the new economic policies.

Here was an irony: the state was active but not active in areas where it was expected to act. The golden jubilee of the Indian Constitution too had its own share of ironies. The Constitution completed 50 years of its existence when a commission was already deliberating upon the need to review that document. The main ruling party happened to be the inheritor of the ideology opposed to this Constitution. Apart from these ironies emanating from political contingencies, one further irony of an intellectual nature needs to be mentioned. As the Constitution came under attack from Rashtriya Swayamsewak Sangh (RSS) and threat from the review exercise, a defence of the Constitution was put forth by intellectuals, activists, and academicians, who included many critics of the Indian state.

These ironies give rise to many questions. Is there, as alleged by some scholars, a tension between 'state and democracy' in the Indian Constitution? Or, has the Indian state deviated from the conception of state as enshrined in the Constitution? If the Indian state is guilty of various 'sins'—as alleged by its critics—to what extent do these sins originate in the Constitution? In the following pages, an attempt is made to discuss these questions. We try to construct the conception of state as implicit in the Indian Constitution. Then we look at the criticism of the Indian state mainly flowing from the experience of the state as it evolved, and, finally, we attempt to problematize the constitutional conception of state and suggest the need for radicalizing the constitutional discourse.

I

FROM COLONIAL TO MODERN STATE

The post-Independence Indian state is the product of three factors: colonial state, the Constitution, and post-Independence practices. While the Constitution was being prepared, a transition from colonial state to independent Indian nation-state had already taken place. Constitutional conceptions of state were themselves influenced and conditioned by both colonial state practices and this new nation-state. The new nation-state was led by Nehru and Patel, who also tried to formalize the practices adopted by them through incorporating these practices in the Constitution.

The constitutional conceptions of state and the practices of new nation-state both derived three aspects from the colonial state. First, the logic of state intervention implicit in the colonial state was inherited by the constitutional discourse as also by post-Independence practices. This logic, according to Sudipta Kaviraj, included (a) introduction of new categories which would govern public discourse, (b) assertion of the principle that state had authority to interfere in social order, and (c) promotion and justification of new identities.[1] Second, the structural aspects of the colonial state were adopted by the Indian state. These included the many provisions of the Government of India Act of 1935, notably the emergency powers, and, more generally, the predominant character of the state as a 'law-and-order' apparatus. Many such provisions (constitutional and legal) are problematic. Baxi has pointed out many such 'anti-democratic' aspects.[2] Third, following in the footsteps of the colonial state, the Indian state too took up the responsibility of expanding capitalist production relations and providing a basis for capital accumulation. The bias in favour of the industrial sector and the rhetoric of development, both mentioned earlier, need to be seen in the context of this aspect of the state, as continuation of the role of the colonial state.

But the Indian state has equally been a product of national imagination and the resilience of democratic aspirations. In this sense, it is the outcome of the struggle for independence. It is not merely the ideological component of the freedom movement that informed the process of state formation. The freedom movement brought forth two things above all else. Democracy as an idea gained its meaning through the movement. As such, democracy, in the Indian imagination, did not remain confined to the form of government; instead, it referred to the content of government. Concerns of public good became incorporated in the rhetoric of democracy. Second, the freedom movement established a norm of contestability with respect to competing claims over ideological and material resources. This had the effect of extending the scope of political competition beyond electoral competition. The repressive apparatus of the state notwithstanding, the 'practice' of politics continued to place a high value on struggles by different sections of society. These two inheritances played a very important role in the evolution of the state's practices (and resistance to them) in the post-Independence period.

STATE IN THE INDIAN CONSTITUTION

Let us first look at what type of state emerges from the Constitution. A well-knit theory of state may not exist in the document since the Indian Constitution engages itself in the details of governance within the framework of broad ideological concerns. State is implicit in both these areas. Second, the founding fathers very rarely discussed theoretical issues or rarely approached the questions before them in a specifically theoretical manner. It is true that there was considerable interest in comparative arrangements existing in different countries. But these were seen in experiential light rather than from a theoretical viewpoint. The expert advice tendered by B.N. Rau often followed this trend too. Perhaps, the legal training of most members made them more sensitive to institutional details than to the theoretical implications of those details. In any case, the debates in the Constituent Assembly are only indicative. This bestows a certain amount of tentativeness upon our construction of the conception of state in the Indian Constitution.

Further, discussions in the Constituent Assembly show that most members were overwhelmed by the fact that they were writing the constitution of free India. The sense of fulfilment and expectation resulted sometimes in the relegation of controversy to a secondary place. Writing a foreword to the Socialist Party's draft constitution in 1948, Jayaprakash Narayan commented upon this by complaining that debates in the Constituent Assembly lacked revolutionary mood. He pointed out that there were rarely any fights over ideologies and interests.[3] A spirit of sedate compromise predominated in the assembly. Nehru himself echoed this sentiment while moving the objectives resolution. His speech on that occasion is full of sentiment but somewhat short on substance. Explaining the absence of 'socialist state' as a goal, Nehru had this to say: This goal may be '...agreeable to many and may not be agreeable to some and *we wanted this resolution not to be controversial...*' Thus, the urge to avoid controversy and strike a compromise meant that the assembly did not enter into serious debate on many occasions. Nehru further explains, rather candidly, '... We have laid down, *not theoretical words and formulae*, but rather the content of the thing we desire.'[4] Going by this rule, we may overlook 'labels' and look at the contents to understand what kind of state emerges from the Constitution.

OVERLAPPING CONCEPTIONS OF STATE

As far as labels are concerned, two surpass any other label in terms of popularity among the assembly members: democracy and welfare. The Indian state was to be a democratic state and a welfare state. As Ambedkar pointed out, these labels scarcely required repetition because it was a foregone conclusion that India ought to establish a state that was not short on democracy and welfare.[5] However, there is room to doubt whether all members did read the same meaning in the terms democracy and welfare. The struggle for independence always saw 'swaraj' (self-government) as a precondition of '*surajya*' (good government). This implied that democracy could come about only by ensuring the welfare of all. Yet, there were hardcore 'liberal democrats' who would see democracy only in the classical sense of the term as protecting individuality and individual freedom. Minoo Masani, then a socialist, spoke about the 'democratic' nature of the state as against the 'police state', 'totalitarian state' or 'party state'. He welcomed the objectives resolution for avoiding a state 'where an individual is made a robot or...reduced to "a small screw" in the big machine of state'.[6] He saw the objectives resolution as a refutation of the thesis that socio-economic change cannot take place without an all-powerful state.[7] It is evident that Masani is speaking here from a liberal–socialist position. His goal is social good but his paradigm is liberal. Therefore, he believes that it is necessary and possible to change society without endangering the liberal notion of individuality. Implicit in his comment is also the belief that the state's power needs to be carefully restricted lest it go out of control.

In contrast, Ambedkar wanted the state to function as an instrument of change and justice. In his constitutional proposals contained in 'States and Minorities', the state is supposed to 'secure the blessings both of self-government and good government'.[8] He did not actively pursue these proposals once he became chairman of the drafting committee. Nevertheless, Ambedkar remained committed to this basic idea that the Indian state must take the responsibility of changing society. He wanted the state to be strengthened so that state power would be exercised to implement social and economic justice.[9] And although Ambedkar was not a supporter of the Congress, it would not be a mistake to suggest that many Congress members too looked toward the state for addressing many ills of the Indian society. The result was that the Constitution vacillates between the liberal–democratic conception of state and a more active, welfarist conception of state. In a sense, the different positions adopted by Masani and Ambedkar symbolize the then prevalent differences in the Constituent Assembly. While Masani approaches the issue of social change and the role of the state in a doctrinaire liberal manner, Ambedkar, as is evident from 'States and Minorities', adopts a creative liberal position which allows him to shift towards socialism. Ambedkar's pragmatism and creativity were both rooted in his critical assessment of the civil society in which the new state was to operate. Thus, the positional difference between Ambedkar and Masani was not merely one of intellectual creativity but of perceptions of civil society.

One very common impression of the Indian Constitution is that it is an 'interventionist' document. Thus, one ex-judge of a high court (Allahabad High Court), and later Rajya Sabha member, forcefully argues, 'It is apparent from directive principles that the founding fathers were no believers in the *laissez faire* state. Clearly they were visualizing an interventionist state...For them the state was an organization which should help its citizens to be free, rational and happy with well-marked zones of privacy...'[10] We shall deal with this 'interventionist' feature of the state later. But it needs to be mentioned that an enthusiastic reading of Directive Principles prompts the 'interventionist' interpretation. If we were to go back to Masani's concerns mentioned above, the result appears to be more in the form of a compromise where extremes are avoided and a golden mean struck. The assembly, deliberating during the middle of the century, was influenced both by political thinking of the previous century and the more radical ideas of more contemporary origin:

Essentially the Indian constitution is an individualist document. Its prophets are Burke, Mill and Dicey: yet some at least of the members of the Constituent Assembly thought in collectivist terms. On the one hand the individualism of the nineteenth century sought to limit the powers of government in the interest of liberty, on the other hand the collectivism of the twentieth century has sought to expand the powers of government in order that the state may regulate economic life and incidentally restrict liberty. In such conditions, compromise and complexity were inevitable.[11]

In order to better understand the nature of this 'compromise and complexity', we need to remember that there were no clear-cut factions of individualists and collectivists. For many members, it was a question of striking a balance between these two. Members were unable to resolve this tension by making a firm choice. Instead, they allowed themselves to be pulled in both these directions.

The complexity of the result lies in the fact that although many members were not convinced of the need to give primacy to inter-ventionism, they nevertheless accepted the need to vest the state with impressive powers. The most common justification for this was the desire that India should be able to handle internal tensions. Partition and the pre-Partition deliberations regarding provincial autonomy were indicative of the dangers which a newly created state might face. The Constituent Assembly wanted a strong state, capable of sustaining itself against all odds. Leaving aside the role of state in shaping society, the assembly visualized a strong state. This near-instinctive support for the strong state was justified by Nehru's belief that a strong state was necessary for planned development. Ambedkar, while supportive of planned development as the goal of the state, placed equal emphasis on removal of social and economic injustices. Combined, these arguments provided a more respectable purpose for the creation of a strong state. Even when members of the Constituent Assembly spoke of development and welfare, the link between state-initiated development and a powerful state apparatus was lost upon them. But unwittingly, many were supporting an active state deriving its justification from welfare programmes. Thus, liberal democratic concerns, inclination towards a strong national state and welfare ideology interacted to produce the state under the Indian Constitution.

The main inconsistency among the somewhat overlapping notions of state emerging from these three influences may be located between liberal democratic state and welfare state. At this stage, it is possible to argue that the welfare state was in fact a Western liberal democratic response to the Marxist ideology. As such, there need be no conflict between liberal democracy and welfare state. However, if we look at the constitution-making process, we find that many of the founding fathers perceived a tension between these two. In fact, the constitutional advisor, B.N. Rau, gave expression to the then prevailing wisdom on this subject. While vigorously pursuing the idea that some rights depended upon 'positive action' by the state, Rau proposed that there may be a mention of fundamental principles of state policy.[12] In November 1947 Rau wrote from Washington saying that provision should be made to give precedence to 'fundamental principles' over individual rights because, '...the general welfare should prevail over the individual right'.[13]

If Rau's proposal had found acceptance in the assembly, it would have provided a radically different foundation for the Indian state. But the assembly chose to leave a certain amount of ambiguity in this respect, while strengthening the 'liberal democratic' dimension of the state. Ambedkar was forced to defend this by arguing that '...whoever captures power will not be free to do what he likes with it. In the exercise of it, he will have to respect these instruments of instructions, which are called Directive Principles.'[14] This arrangement implied that liberal democracy would be the legal basis of the state, while welfare would supply the 'non-justiciable' politico-ideological basis for the state. The state was allowed and enabled to take 'positive action' but it was left to the state itself to define the scope of such positive action. It was believed that no one could ignore the Directive Principles because the electorate would insist on their implementation. This belief indicates that the Constitution wanted the state to be sensitive to public opinion. In any case, this arrangement is curious and awkward. Curious, because the state is handed down with a mandate which is optional as far as its implementation goes; and awkward because, in the ultimate analysis, this arrangement provides a legitimating ideology to the state on the one hand and on the other a space for curtailing individual rights in the name of welfare policies, something that happened during the mid-1970s. The state could get away with delegitimation of these rights without bringing about substantive welfare.

INTERVENTIONIST STATE

Let us return to the issue of the interventionist state. In a sense, this issue is redundant in the contemporary context when the free market states are at least, if not more, interventionist as the previous 'socialist' states. And yet, in the Indian context a specific meaning is attached to the notion of interventionist state. Three issues appear to be central to the debate about the interventionist state in the Indian context. First, there is a clear realization of the tension between the state and what is contemporarily called 'civil society'. Inviting the displeasure of many members, Ambedkar mentioned this in his speech while moving the Draft Constitution in the assembly. Condemning India's village society in no uncertain terms, Ambedkar dubbed Indian society as 'essentially undemocratic' and opined that 'In these circumstances it is wise not to trust the legislature...'[15] According to this viewpoint, an in-built mechanism to enable the state to intervene in social matters was required. Indian society needed to be restructured. There were not enough forces from within the society working in this direction. Hence state intervention was seen as necessary. The state had to be suitably empowered to intervene and carefully protected from getting contaminated by the afflictions ailing the society. This implies a state not only superior to civil society but 'autonomous' of civil society.

This position leads us to an important problematique: can a state realistically be autonomous of civil society institutions? And, if yes, will not an 'insulated' state produce only superficial democracy? The Indian Constitution attempts to grapple with this problematique. Formal legal mechanisms ensure some autonomy of the state from civil society institutions. In fact, the state is infused with powers to reform civil society institutions and, wherever necessary, build a new social order altogether. The edifice of formal power is armed with the ideology of social reform deriving sustenance from a number of sources: Western welfarism,

Gandhian ideas, modern conceptions of equality and justice, and the like. The Constitution in fact imbues the state with these ideological sources. This entire exercise is predicated on the assumption that the state can be founded independently of the society, and that the state can act independent of the interests operating in the society.

Following from the above assumption, the second issue involved in the conception of an interventionist state is how to protect the state from being an instrument of established interests. 'Law...should not be allowed to become an instrument of...preserving the privileges of classes and vested interests...The founding fathers were not looking upon democracy as an instrument in the hands of private monopolists...'[16] Probably, very few members of the Constituent Assembly were aware of this issue. For most of them, the state constituted public power exercised on the basis of public reason. Therefore, the state was capable of acting impartially. In the context of India, Ambedkar was doubtful whether the state could be impartial. But, on the whole, he too believed in the capacity of the state to rise above sectional interests and act as a natural arbiter.

It may be safely argued that the founding fathers did not consider the theoretical implication of positing neutrality in the state. The only worry which some entertained was about the state being hijacked by established interests. Like Ambedkar, K.T. Shah was also concerned with this aspect. In 1946 he sent a detailed note to the president of the Constituent Assembly on the topic of Fundamental Rights. Therein, he mused about the possibility of vested interests overwhelming the Congress. He pointed out that the Congress was a 'creature' of capitalists and landowners. Once the goal of independence is achieved, these classes will force the Congress to 'pay them back'. Shah felt that by putting 'obligations of state' in the Fundamental Rights, the masses can be protected from this danger.[17]

The state as repository of power was expected to intervene on behalf of the masses. This intervention was to be guided by public reason. However, few realized that the interventionist powers of the state would be an arena of contestation among various classes. This was true in the case of social change as much as in the case of economic reorganization. Therefore, while the Constitution conceptualized the interventionist state, efforts were made to assert public reason by committing the state to a broad framework of socio-economic change within which its interventionism was to operate. The ability of the state to rise above class interests, its neutrality, and the scope of state intervention are all disputable aspects. Yet the founders of the new Indian state as well as some important ringside observers of that exercise were agreed on the basics. Notwithstanding Ambedkar's and Shah's doubts (with which the socialists tended to agree), it was felt that the Indian state would be above class interests. This was premised on a theoretical mix between a liberal democratic conception of state and a Fabian socialist conception of state. Besides, the new Indian state was seen as an outcome of a mass democratic struggle. Therefore, it was supposed to be suffused with a democratic character, enabling it simultaneously to remain 'pro-people' and escape the manipulation of vested interests.

The third issue involving the interventionist state has been the scope of intervention. Having settled the problem of class interests and convinced of neutrality, the founders of the state set about defining the scope of intervention. Again, although Ambedkar ('States and Minorities') and socialists would have wanted a stricter commitment, the interventionist programme was based on the minimum agreed principles. The Socialist Party published a 'Draft Constitution' in 1948, wherein it complained that the Indian Constitution was only bringing about 'controlled capitalism' and demanded extension of public ownership.[18] Needless to say, it agreed on the principles that the state should take initiative in restructuring the society and economy. Similarly, Kishorilal Mashruwala argued that state should adopt 'a policy calculated to (a) remove caste...spirit and social inequality, (b) prevent exploitation of masses, (c) end minority problems...'[19] Shriman Narayan Agarwal, putting forth a 'Gandhian' constitutional proposal said, 'All land shall belong to the state', 'key industries will be owned by the Nation', property may be acquired by the state if necessary, and 'Every citizen shall avoid, check and if necessary, resist exploitation of man by man...'[20] Gandhi, in his characteristically non-committal foreword to Agarwal's tract, says 'There is nothing in it...inconsistent with what I would like to stand for.'[21]

It seems that there were three areas of broad consensus among the main political actors. First, most of them agreed on the need to put into place a welfare state, which will be authorized to regulate the growth of capitalism and thereby keep a check on capitalism. This may be seen as a consensus on rejecting the laissez faire notion of state. Second, a general agreement existed about the need to empower the state to remove caste inequalities. This stemmed from the assumption that caste, being inconsistent with democracy, needed to be removed, but that the civil social context was not likely to do this. Therefore the state had to work as a modernizing force and intervene in this regard. Third, many, if not all, political actors were sceptical about feudal landlordism and wanted the state to preside over the decline of landlordism. It is curious that in spite of such a broad consensus, state intervention was applied to areas of social justice, equality, and standard of living in a somewhat ambiguous and platitudinal manner. More than actual legal provisions, the Constitution relied on supplying the state with an ideological base, which exemplifies the consensus mentioned above.

Our contention is that the reformist or social revolutionary conception of state was based on the ideology of the Constitution, while more substantial provisions enabling state intervention were made with a view to making the state an instrument of the vision of development. As already noted, Ambedkar wanted the state to be interventionist so that the state could effectively handle the caste question. Nehru, on the other hand, looked forward to the state as instrument of a modern society. Thus, side by side with the reformist state, another conception of state has been operative that is inclined more to instrumentality than to the interventionist role of the state. Therein lies the tension between the two overlapping yet somewhat different conceptions of state as an instrument of social reform and an instrument of economic development.

THE NEHRUVIAN STATE

Although this conception is described as 'Nehruvian state', it had a fairly large support both in the Constituent Assembly and outside of it. It is called 'Nehruvian' only because Nehru presided over this state apparatus and guided the course of its activity. As for the essential principles of this state, there was broad agreement between Nehru, Patel, and Ambedkar. This conception of state does rely upon the state's ability to intervene although from a slightly different ideological standpoint. Social reform or restructuring of the society is not emphasized. The emphasis is on the creation of a modern nation-state, which will be an instrument of modernity. Even democratic government is seen as flowing from the principle of rationality and modernism. Many aspects of the Indian state can, thus, be traced to the conception of modern state. Secularism, rule of law, equal opportunity, dignity of the individual, a strong and united nation-state, a regime of rights, provision for minority rights: all these are part of this conception of a modern state. The state was also responsible for the economic development of the society. Therefore, it was equipped with 'directives' or guidelines. The impressive list of subjects included in the union list, and the overall bias in favour of the

Union government, partly emanate from the idea that the Indian state was to promote vigorous economic development through a process of planning and state control of the economy. In other words, the state had to assume the role of an active agent of progress and development.

A modern state, thus conceived, takes the shape of a bourgeois state. The Indian state is no exception to this. It adopted rapid industrialization as the main objective and relied on a bourgeois strategy for the realization of the objective. The competing claims of landed interests and the bourgeoisie were engaged in an ongoing battle even during the making of the Constitution. Many leading members of the Constituent Assembly wanted to abolish feudal agrarian relations and put an end to the zamindari system. However, at the same time, expropriation of private property was not acceptable to many members. The general sentiment was anti-zamindari;[22] rather than against the propertied classes in general. In fact, the then Government of India was quick to make a distinction between landlordism and matters pertaining to the industrial sector. While many were ready to provide for expropriation of landed property only with nominal compensation, the Union government assured that 'fair and equitable' compensation would be paid when industrial undertakings were acquired. Besides, the Ministry of Works, Mines and Power and the Ministry of Industry and Supplies busied themselves by proposing that 'just' or 'reasonable' compensation should be made payable when any property is taken over by the state.[23] It was also feared that in the absence of appropriate compensation clause, foreign capital would not be forthcoming. To this, Nehru's response was that foreign capital would be dealt with by special agreements.[24] Thus, the Indian state was to apply separate standards of intervention to the agricultural sector and the industrial sector. As conceived by the Constitution, the state was to intervene strongly in the former, in order to pave the way for the emergence of a different basis for India's socio-economic development.

II

The Indian state embodies the various different, often overlapping conceptions of state discussed above. These conceptions shape the character of the state both in terms of its ideology and in terms of its practices. The behaviour of the state in response to concrete social situations is mediated by these different conceptions of state. Since the introduction of the structural adjustment programme, 'statism' has become the chief target of the neo-classical critics of the Indian state.

But even before these became influential, the Indian state was criticized by Rajni Kothari on the grounds of its anti-people practice[25] and by Ashis Nandy on grounds of its modernist pretensions that subordinated everything else.[26] While Kothari's criticism focuses on repressive 'interventions' by the state, Nandy disapproves of the 'reformist interventions' by the state. However, in both cases the interventionist character of the state comes under criticism. One critic even goes to the extent of characterizing the Indian state as ' imperial bureaucratic state'.[27]

Although most critics of the Indian state would also underline the momentous changes in the state's practices brought about during the regime of Indira Gandhi, the issue here is not about the deviations and distortions that crept in during the later years but the conception of state as enshrined in the Constitution itself. This is echoed by the Rudolphs in their characterization of Indian state as a weak-strong state.[28] Sethi lays the blame squarely at the doors of the makers of the Indian Constitution when he says that the 'model of strong state was "sold" to the people of India in 1949 through a new constitution by a popular leadership'.[29] The Rudolphs have contextualized the Indian state by suggesting that it is 'constrained' by organized social forces besides being constrained by legitimacy requirements.[30]

Thus, debates about the post-Independence Indian state and its practices implicate the conceptual foundations of that state. What we mean to suggest is that arguments of 'deviations' from the 'original' may not close the debate. Surely, the Indian state has, on occasions, deviated from the expected or ideal position. But rather than the deviations, the conceptions of state need to be problematized. This point becomes all the more relevant in the context of the policies adopted since the 1990s under the rubric of economic liberalization. Since then, the opponents of the new economic policies have repeatedly invoked the spirit underlying the Constitution. What these arguments ignore is that economic liberalization is in fact seen as a pragmatic corrective to the excessively interventionist conception of the state adopted by the Constitution. Therefore, it is essential to probe the foundations of the constitutional conceptions of the Indian state.

NEUTRALITY–INSTRUMENTALITY

The state is posited as possessing neutrality on the basis of the idea that state is an agency outside of and external to the society. It is not a party to the conflicts within the society; rather, it is in a position to adjudicate these conflicts. The state does not share, advance, or oppose any of the interests existent in society; it constitutes 'universal' interest and therefore embodies public good. It can rationally weigh the competing interests, arbitrate, and enforce the 'common' good. Rationality and universality are the corollaries of neutrality.

In the Indian context, there is yet other additional route to neutrality. The state is seen as the creation of a long, democratic struggle. It is believed that 'people' have created this state. Since 'people' are the source of the state, the state becomes only a representative of popular will. In this sense, the state is the expression of public good. The category of nation intervenes here. The state is a nation-state. It expresses the 'nation'. Therefore, it takes care of all interests. The democratic and nationalist underpinnings of this argument make theoretical allowance to the assumptions both that rulers (those who run the state) can rise above their sectional interests and that the state possesses a (democratic) correctional ability if it is driven away from universality. Finally, the neutrality argument, both via the route of externality and the route of democracy, looks upon the bureaucratic machine as a neutral, rational, and universal expression on behalf of the state.

The instrumentality argument is derived from the neutrality of the state. Once the state is conceived as a power independent of the rulers and the ruled, it becomes possible to posit instrumentality in it. The state is seen as an instrument of effecting development, welfare, and/or social reform. In this argument, a high value is placed on certain objectives, and state power is employed to bring about these objectives. It is also implicitly accepted that there may be some opposition to these objectives. Thus, development may be seen as industrialization or, worse, Western modernity or reform may be seen as interference with established social practices. The state can provide the necessary ideological force or impetus for overcoming such opposition. Also, the change and methods used to bring about change are legitimated by the state.

One may look at the role of the state as instrument of change/ development in a slightly different manner. Society may be seen as having inadequate capacity to generate development and related requirements. Thus, typically when industrial development is the objective, the state may be required to act for igniting processes of accumulation and capital formation. The 'power' of the state will be used for extraction and capital formation. For this purpose, the state will be allowed to employ mechanisms for resource generation and to assign those resources for specific developmental purposes. It is not impossible to find such a view among India's early planners, who saw the state as an instrument for rapid industrialization. In this role, if the state gave differential treatment to industry from that given the agricultural sector, it would be seen as a neutral act based on rational choice for furthering universal interest— that is, common national interest.

The constitutional conceptions of state follow these twin principles of neutrality and instrumentality. The state is seen as an instrument for realizing liberty, equality, and justice, along with fraternity and unity. The tasks of economic uplift, eradication of poverty and of inequality, raising the standard of living, etc., are assigned to the state. Besides, the state is also seen as an instrument of social justice and social change. Along with these responsibilities, the state is entrusted with the responsibility of protecting individual liberties. However, a major problem can arise if the state has to become the 'instrument' of social change and social justice. Ever since the goal of 'social revolution' was popularized by Austin,[31] it has been rather unquestioningly assumed that the constitution is a document for social change. The state, under such a document, has to be partisan; it has to shake off its neutrality.

Does the constitution actually surrender neutrality of the state? It may be argued that, the constitution, realizing the tension between neutrality and instrumentality, seeks to strike a balance. The state is conceptualized by the constitution on the basis of neutrality. Instrumentality follows from neutrality. Because the state is going to be neutral, some tasks are entrusted to it. Social revolutionary readings notwithstanding, the constitution visualizes a primarily neutral state. For instance, the famous social justice clauses (15–3, 15–4, and 16–4) come as 'permissions' or enabling provisions for the state to act in certain manner. 'Nothing...shall prevent the state' from making special provisions for women, children, backward classes, or from providing reservations. Because the state is neutral and capable of rational choices, it is empowered to decide what is backwardness and who are backward; and it can provide for reservations without jeopardizing efficiency of administration (Art. 335). Similarly the state is 'permitted' to legislate for purpose of social reform.

These provisions are rightly known as 'enabling' provisions, and yet, it must be noted that they are not obligatory provisions. The point here is simply this: certain 'interventionist' power is vested in the state but the mainstay is supposed to be neutrality. Even social change which is to be brought about has to follow from the neutral state. And because the neutrality of state is assured, it is not expected to act hastily, or in a biased manner, in matters of social change. This same neutrality and rationality of state comes into play in the case of 'reasonable' restrictions on various rights of the individual. The state is further vested with power of preventive detention and suspension of Fundamental Rights (during national emergency) because rationality and neutrality are the foundations of state.

STATE AS FIELD OF CONTESTATION

We have already noted the issue of tension between the state and civil society in the Indian context. The neutrality–instrumentality arrangement partly addresses this tension. In a sense, the issue is not quite unique only to the Indian context. Apart from caste, the institutions and practices emanating from feudal relations and inequalities of a class society would also pose similar problems. By positing neutrality, the state is elevated above the distortions of civil society. This is an attempt to conceptualize a notion of public power which will not possess those characteristics of society that are undemocratic. On the other hand, the neutral state is posited with 'instrumentality' in order to reorganize civil society, from which the state is somewhat distanced.

The empirical reality called the 'Indian state' is only partly a product of the conceptions visualized by the Constitution. An assessment of state practices over the last half-century is not intended here. But we need to note here that the principles of neutrality and instrumentality did not fully govern the practices of the Indian state. On the one hand this suggests the weakness of grounding the state on these principles; on the other, this tells us about the 'character' of the Indian state.

In the field of rhetoric, the state always took the position that its 'instrumental' role is more significant than its neutral role because the state must 'change' the society and bring about development. Very often, neutrality was lost, because the state, in the ongoing tussle between agrarian interests and industrial interests, firmly sided with the latter. On issues of 'social reform' and restructuring of the social order, the state chose to adopt neutrality instead of actively pursuing the goal of social change. Thus, when neutrality was necessary, the state invoked its instrumental role and when intervention was required, the state took shelter behind neutrality.

At the time of Independence, Indian society was undergoing a number of processes, which were pulling the society in different directions. Apart from the pressures generated by Partition, a debate was going on—and still continues—about the role of minorities and the meaning of a plural society. Similarly, within the context of Hindu society, the question of untouchability and related distortions had dominated ever since the 1930s. This had generated a heated debate about 'separate' representation. More broadly, the caste issue too was a contentious one. While generally agreeing upon the point that caste needed to be removed, controversies arose over the methods. The issue of social reform—particularly that of reforming Hindu (and Muslim) personal laws—attracted much attention in the 1950s. This list can be expanded to include economic issues. The post-Independence state evolved through these contestations. Not only was the state pulled in different direction by the contending forces, the state—through its various organs—even responded differently on the same issue. Land reform is probably the most famous example of this, where different state governments would take different positions; the Centre would insist on land reforms and states would prevaricate; etc. The gap between rhetoric and actual policy would also signify the inability of the state to arrive at a firm decision.

Immediately after Independence, two issues—land reforms and the Hindu Code bill—challenged the neutrality and instrumentality of the state. As is well known, opinion was divided on both these issues, among Congressmen and between the Union and many state governments. The state officially took a position in favour of land reforms (even by amending the Constitution) and trying to push the Hindu Code bill (though the state subsequently temporarily retreated).

Two points need to be emphasized here: first, the state did not and could not act as an interventionist monolith or reformist giant. Second, the state's positions—its prevarications, rhetoric, subterfuge, heroic intervention—were not in isolation from the contestations taking place in the reality of civil society. In fact, state practices were shaped to a considerable extent by these developments taking place in civil social relations. In this sense, state was *not* acting as an independent repository of power. It would equally be an exaggeration to suggest that state was acting *only* as an extension of civil social contestations. State practices emerged through a combination of factors: constitutional conceptions, civil society contestations, perceptions of the leadership, democratic compulsions and limitations, and the composition of ruling classes who presided over both the state and civil society. Often, competing forces realized that they needed to gain control over the state. Therefore, the state became engulfed in the ongoing contestations.

In other words, we may come across multiple images of the state. First we have the idealized image grounded in the Constitution, according to which the state is independent of civil society but intervenes in civil society. Second, we confront the actual state practices, which are a mix of policies and actions, pushing ahead capitalist development but also directed at 'poverty alleviation'. Third, we have the image of state based on its rhetoric. This state is interventionist, welfarist, and even socialist. But we also need to appreciate that the state is always a battleground for the struggles going on in the realm of civil society.[32] The policies, actions, and ideology of the state are responses to these struggles. In the Indian context, the aforementioned struggles—class, caste, communal—were, and continue to be, fought in the field called state. The state is thus both a battleground and a product of these struggles. Rather than conceptualizing the state as a mere extension of civil society, this view implies a more dynamic and integrated relationship between the state and civil society.

The empirical reality in India too supports such a formulation. The Indian state is embedded in a multitude of social divisions, which have competing and even conflicting interests. A fierce competition often takes place among different sections of society to gain control over public authority. This situation results in the existence of multiple interpretations of 'public' interests. These give rise to the politics of privileging certain interpretations of public interest as more universal. All these factors underline the fact that the state is itself the terrain of contestations. The earlier controversies regarding the interpretation of constitutional provisions and the contemporary controversy regarding the review of the Constitution need to be seen in this context. If the state is the field of contestations, it is obvious that different meanings would be attached to the constitutional conceptions of state too. How does one then explore the radical potential in the constitutional discourse?

RADICAL POSSIBILITIES

By positing neutrality and instrumentality, the Constitution has provided a framework for critically responding to state practices. In the first place, the overlapping conceptions of state imply that there is no final and 'authorized' conception of state in the Constitution. To that extent, the Constitution too recognizes the role of social contestations in shaping the state. It is therefore very natural that state practices would also operate in the framework of both neutrality and instrumentality. In order to critique the practices of the state, it is necessary that we re-read neutrality and instrumentality. Neutrality may be seen as insurance against the tendency of the state to incline towards the privileged sections.

Instrumentality, on the other hand, gives us the basis for critiquing the state on the grounds of its policy contents. Ambedkar, for instance, hoped that Directive Principles and policies of the government would be major election issues dominating popular choices.[33]

If such a critique is not evolved—as indeed it was not—then the same framework of neutrality and instrumentality is far removed from concrete issues and democratic struggles. The constitutional discourse in post-Independence India is mostly an example of this phenomenon. One has only to recall the debates about Fundamental Rights, parliamentary supremacy, judicial review, and the like, revolving around the First, Twenty-fourth and Twenty-fifth amendments and judicial pronounce-ments of the period from 1951 to 1967 (for example, the *Golak Nath* ruling of the Supreme Court). These debates often revolved around falsely ideological issues. For instance, they sought to project the judiciary as the anti-poor villain or the executive as power-hungry leadership. A critique of the Indian state can be evolved if the post-Independence constitutional discourse is seen simultaneously as an instance of contestations and as exemplifying the tension between neutrality and instrumentality. The Congress of Nehru–Indira Gandhi correctly realized that the Constitution was much too inclined towards a neutral state and that this could be an impediment to their conceptions of capitalist development. Therefore, instrumentality of the state was over-emphasized through the major amendments of this period (1951–76).

In this background, what we witness in the 1970s is consolidation of the instrumentalist conception of state *along with* the abrasiveness of the state in casting off the ideological basis of instrumentality. Since the 1980s the state has been strengthening itself and its coercive powers, but it does not show any inclination to use these powers for 'the people'. Therefore, state practices can be critiqued both on grounds of tilting in favour of the privileged and on the grounds of not doing enough for the underprivileged.

Such a twofold critique is possible only when the key source of the authority of the Indian state is redefined. The Indian state is supposed to derive its authority from 'the people'. The category of 'people' is often taken up quite unproblematically. In a sense, this is a legacy of the nationalist struggle where 'the people' as one Indian nation needed to be juxtaposed before the colonial rulers. But even during the freedom movement, and more so in post-Independence practice, the unmediated conception of 'people' gave rise to discomfort. Different 'people' have different claims on the state and the state also responds differently to them. When the state adopts an instrumental stance, it is directed at one set of people and when it remains neutral, the neutrality is directed to another set of people. This contrast is more visible in the context of policies of liberalization but it is by no means new. This practice of the state renders the claims about 'the people' rhetorical.

And yet, in identifying the state as anti-people, or opposed to civil liberties, the category of 'people' is equally unproblematically posited. In the case of both—the constitutional conception of people and the contemporary anti-state constructions of people—there is a tendency to avoid a class-caste-based definition of people. The argument that the notion of people should be seen in terms of claims by different sections of society for recognition as the people is only consistent with our earlier argument that the state is a field of contestations. When we reject a simplistic view that 'the people' constitute the source of public authority, it becomes possible to posit a more radical meaning to the term 'people'. The Congress under Mahatma Gandhi symbolically identified 'people' with the starved and destitute: 'the *daridranarayan*'. While disputing the claims of the Congress and Gandhi, Ambedkar sought to identify, more sharply, 'the people' as oppressed castes.

These are only two instances of the ways in which 'people' can be understood. The main point is that publicness of authority does not rest on an undifferentiated mass of all citizens as people, but on 'people' for whom authority is supposed to function. Such a construction of 'people' would itself be part of the social contestations. The empirical reality called the state unfolds through and as contestations over material and intellectual resources. The constitutional notion of state is only one moment in this ongoing contestation.

NOTES

1. Sudipta Kaviraj, 'The Modern State in India', in Zoya Hasan (ed.), *Politics and the State in India* (New Delhi: Sage, 2000), pp. 43–4.
2. Upendra Baxi, 'Saint Granville's Gospel: Reflections', *Economic and Political Weekly*, vol. 36, no. 11, 2001, p. 926.
3. Socialist Party, *Draft Constitution of Indian Republic* (Bombay: Socialist Party, 1948), p. 5.
4. *Constituent Assembly Debates* (CAD) (New Delhi: Government of India, 1950), vol. I, p. 60, emphasis added.
5. *CAD*, vol. I, p. 97.
6. *CAD*, vol. I, p. 91.

7. *CAD*, vol. I, p. 92.
8. Babasaheb Ambedkar, *Dr. Babasaheb Ambedkar: Writings and Speeches*, vol. I, (Bombay: Government of Maharashtra, 1979), p. 387.
9. *CAD*, vol. I, p. 98.
10. P.N. Sapru, *The Relation of the Individual to the State under the Indian Constitution* (Calcutta: University of Calcutta, 1959), p. 13.
11. Ivor Jennings, *Some Characteristics of the Indian Constitution* (London: Oxford University Press, 1953), pp. 22–3.
12. B.N. Rau, 'Notes on Fundamental Rights', 2 September 1946, in B. Shiva Rao (ed.), *The Framing of India's Constitution: Select Documents*, vol. II (New Delhi: Indian Institute of Public Administration, 1967), pp. 33–4.
13. Rao, *The Framing of India's Constitution*, vol. III, p. 226.
14. *CAD*, vol. VII, p. 41.
15. *CAD*, vol. VII, p. 38.
16. Sapru, *The Relation of the Individual*, pp. 15–16.
17. Rao, *The Framing of India's Constitution*, vol. II, pp. 39–40.
18. Socialist Party, *Draft Constitution of Indian Republic*, pp. 41–5.
19. K.G. Mashruwala, *Some Particular Suggestions for the Constitution of Free India* (Bombay: Hamara Hindostan Publications, 1946), p. 4.
20. Sriman Narayan Agarwal, *Gandhian Constitution for Free India* (Allahabad: Kitabistan, 1946), pp. 79, 126.
21. Ibid, p. 3.
22. *CAD*, vol. III, pp. 506–18.
23. Granville Austin, *The Indian Constitution: Cornerstone of a Nation*, Indian edition (Bombay: Oxford University Press, 1972), pp. 90–1.
24. Austin, *The Indian Constitution*, p. 95.
25. Rajni Kothari, *State Against Democracy* (New Delhi: Ajanta Publications, 1989).
26. Ashis Nandy, 'The Political Culture of the Indian State', *Daedalus*, Fall, vol. 118, no. 4 (1989), pp. 1–26.
27. J.D. Sethi, *Character of the Indian State: A Non-Marxist View* (Shimla and New Delhi: IIAS and Manohar, 1992), p. 29.
28. Ibid.
29. Sethi, *Character of the Indian State*, p. 1.
30. Lloyd I. Rudolph and Susanne Hoeber Rudolph, *In Pursuit of Lakshmi: The Political Economy of the Indian State* (New Delhi: Orient Longman, 1987), p. 61.
31. Austin, *The Indian Constitution*.
32. Nicos Poulantzas, *Classes in Contemporary Capitalism* (London: New Left Books, 1975); Nicos Poulantzas, *State, Power and Socialism* (London: New Left Books, 1978).
33. *CAD*, vol. VII, p. 41.

7

Citizenship and the Indian Constitution*

Valerian Rodrigues

Demarcation of citizens from non-citizens and the principles that should inform this distinction have posed major challenges before political communities always, and particularly so in modern national political communities. The very constitutive basis of the latter lies in the way they characterize their citizens and such characterization does not preclude the self-definitions of citizens, who they are and wish to be. Colonial domination in India stressed the deep diversities and separatedness of its communities as its hallmark. In such contexts, imagining a common citizenship and making it the foundation of a free national community was a daunting challenge. Such a task was further complicated by the demand for Pakistan and the imagination of the national community that it advanced, and the desire of the Indian national movement to propose a different conception of nationhood wherein the kind of exclusiveness, cultural chauvinism, and domination of the colonizing imagination can be put to rest. When India became free, there were also communities worldwide that stressed their ethnic ties with India and such ties needed to be taken into account in the definition of citizenship. There was the huge problem created by Partition and since India did not accept the basis of the demand for Pakistan, it had to make place for those who accepted its own understanding of nationhood with all the responsibility of territoriality and culture. Further, citizenship remained a deeply debated issue in post-independent India given the

* An earlier version of this paper was published in Rajeev Bhargava and Helmut Reifeld (eds), *Civil Society, Public Sphere and Citizenship: Dialogue and Perceptions*, New Delhi: Sage, 2005, pp. 209–35.

contestations in which the nature of the national community was embroiled in and the existence of ethnic communities outside India that identified with it in the context of the growing ethnicization of nationalist imagination in the host societies. Citizenship, therefore, has been quite central to India's nationalist imagination and it has continued to remain so even in the present.

While the national movement as a whole in India could be credited for formulating a conception of citizenship—differentiated and contested—the central platform and concentrated expression of such formulation was the Constituent Assembly. Its avowed rationale was to authoritatively formulate the moral and political basis of India and institute a normative order for public life. Interestingly citizenship became a pronounced theme in its debates and it was seen as the anchor of the envisaged good polity. Citizenship was conceived both as the constitutive basis and the rationale of the polity.[1] Citizens formed the polity and defined its pursuits and orientations through their associational bonds and liberties.

The Indian Constitution or subsequent legislation in this regard nowhere defines the word 'citizen' except in Part III of the Constitution which makes a distinction between Fundamental Rights available to a person and those guaranteed to a citizen. Lawyers and judges have taken recourse to Black's Law Dictionary whenever clarity had to be sought regarding its conceptual dimensions. It defines citizen 'as a member of a free city or jural society (civitas) possessing all the rights and privileges which can be enjoyed by any person under its constitution and government and subject to the corresponding duties'.[2] The Constitution as a text highlights three issues regarding citizenship, the first two being the immediate concern of this essay:

1. The first, demarcates persons entitled to be recognized as citizens and consequently to the rights, privileges, and obligations of citizens. The latter are dealt in detail following the demarcation of citizens. The text orders these concerns sequentially.

2. The second recognizes different kinds of citizens on the basis of their group-affiliation and cultural belonging. All citizens are not alike although all are citizens. In consideration it proposes differential treatment to citizens over and above equal rights. It is, however, possible to argue that only some differential belongings are marked at the expense of others. Further even when differences

are recognized the weightage given to them may markedly vary. There is heightened presence of certain differences and some of them are bountifully endowed. Besides, considerations of democracy and power closely monitor differential considerations.

3. The third proposes the composition of public institutions and normative consequences for public policy arising from the recognition of equal but differential citizenship.

In this essay we will explore three questions that are interwined with one another on this issue:

1. Who should be included and excluded as citizens of India and what should be the basis of such inclusion and exclusion?
2. How did different conceptions of nationhood affect understanding of citizenship?
3. How did diversity and difference, characteristic of several communities and social strata in India, affect conception of citizenship?

WHO ARE ENTITLED TO BE CITIZENS?

THE EXCLUDED AND THE INCLUDED: CONSTITUTIONAL PROVISIONS

An early response to this query was formulated in Articles 5 to 11 of the Indian Constitution. Subsequently, the Citizenship Act of 1955 specified some of these provisions and prescribed others in accordance with the powers conferred by Article 11.[3] The Constitution and the Act of 1955 together with subsequent amendments exhaustively circumscribe the boundaries of citizenship in India and they have to be read together.[4]

1. As per the constitutional provisions included within, citizens were persons who at the time of the commencement of the Constitution had their domicile in India and
   (a) Were born in the territory of India, or
   (b) Either of whose parents were born in the territory of India, or
   (c) Who have been ordinarily resident in the territory of India for not less than five years immediately preceding the commencement of the Constitution.

As is obvious, the above provisions adopted an inclusive and generous approach towards citizenship qualifying territorial location and stressing on associational belonging.

2. It extended citizenship to a set of people arriving from Pakistan in the wake of the Partition. Accordingly, citizenship was extended to those

   (a) Who or whose parents or grandparents were born in India as defined by the India Act 1935 and were migrants to independent India before 19 July 1948[5] and continued to ordinarily reside in India after such migration.

   (b) Who migrated after 19 July 1948 but before the commencement of the Constitution and registered themselves as citizens of India before the concerned authority.

   (c) Who having gone to Pakistan returned to the territory of India under a permit for resettlement or permanent return issued by competent authority. However, those who left India after 1 March 1947, to settle in the territory of Pakistan, were not entitled to Indian citizenship under any of the above provisions.

These provisions upheld the non-denominational character of Indian citizenship while taking peoples' choices seriously. While the ascriptive identity of a person in terms of territory and culture was seen as important for citizenship, a person was not reduced to his/her ascriptive location but was perceived as someone who in important respects had the ability to make choices concerning himself/herself and his/her future, and a free and fair society had to consider such choices with the necessary weight for the entitlements due to him/her.

3. The Constitution entitled a set of people of Indian origin residing outside India to citizenship if they fulfilled certain conditions:

   (a) They or their parents or grandparents should have been born in India as defined in the India Act, 1935 and

   (b) They should have been registered as citizens of India before the diplomatic or consular authority, before or after the commencement of the Constitution of India in the form and manner prescribed.

It, however, excluded from citizenship those who had voluntarily acquired citizenship of other countries.[6]

These provisions related citizenship to ethnic and associational ties unless the concerned chose otherwise. Therefore citizenship was not confined to the progeny of people found within the territorial bounds of India alone. This was a bold and generous provision in 1948 as the vast majority of people to whom such recognition was accorded were indentured labourers and poor emigrants.

The draft articles as they were initially proposed, and in their final version too, had some pronounced features which could be termed secular, understood as non-preference to any and inclusion of members of all relevant communities or groups. As per this perspective, the Indian nation would be composed of all those born in the territory of India or whose ancestry lay there in the appreciable past. There were differences regarding how far that past should go. Thereby the basis of Indian nation was clearly suggested as non-preference to any community and inclusive of all communities. The fact of Partition, which was deeply felt and swayed several other provisions of the Constitution, was not allowed to affect the understanding and demarcation of citizenship. If anything, it made the Constituent Assembly deeply sensitive to issues of group affiliation. Formally, all those who were found in Pakistan could be citizens of India if they made such an option before the relevant provisions were enacted by the Constituent Assembly. Members of all communities and other entitled members, including Muslims, living in the Pakistan side could move into India and claim citizenship. Such provisions were looked on apprehensively by many, particularly by representatives of Assam, in the assembly. But such fears alluding to immediate demographic and social composition were not allowed to vitiate this secular perspective.

Generally when people opted for another country, such options could be considered free. The mainstream secular stance, however, felt that profound political instability, communal passions, and civil disturbances might make such options coercive and compelling. The events surrounding the Partition were clearly perceived by this stance as characterized by such conditions. Therefore, the Constitution made provision for the return of Muslims, who had migrated to Pakistan in the wake of Partition, back to India within a specified period.

Persons of Indian origin living outside India were given the option to retain Indian citizenship for an indefinite future by fulfilling certain formalities. Considerations of caste and community were not invoked for the purpose.

Foreigners were given the choice of becoming Indian citizens by demonstrating their interest to be part of the national community. Such demonstration could be marriage or residence in India. Children born to them could pass on their citizenship to their progeny, like other Indians hailing from the ethnic stock even if they shifted their domicile outside India. Further, the Government of India was left free to confer citizenship on deserving persons who in its opinion would enrich the national community, economically and culturally.

It was a grand vision of the nation, rooted, but open to the world and towards the future. It accepted the fact that people were embedded in identities but citizenship was grounded on principles irreducible to them but at the same time took cognizance of them. It allowed individuals to make choices and even to re-evaluate their decisions, to opt for and opt out of Indian citizenship. It felt that there were certain higher values that India should highlight by keeping its citizenship open to outstanding personalities.

THE CITIZENSHIP ACT, 1955

The Constitution while upholding the continuation of citizenship to all groups mentioned above did not, however, make any provision with respect to the acquisition of citizenship after its commencement, nor did it provide for the termination of citizenship. It was the Citizenship Act, 1955 which dwelt on these issues. This act identified five types of citizens: by birth, descent, registration, naturalization, and incorporation of territory. In the wake of the Assam agitation, a memorandum of agreement was signed by the central government with the leadership of the agitation. As per this agreement, an amendment was made to this act in 1985, adding Article 6A, making way for a sixth type of citizenship.

By Birth

i) Everyone born in India after the enactment of the Constitution but before the amendment to the Act in 1986, unless excluded (that is, those whose father possessed immunity from suits and legal processes accorded to an envoy of foreign power and is not a citizen of India and whose father is an enemy alien[7] and the birth occurs in a place under enemy occupation) is considered a citizen of India.

ii) After the amendment of 1986, everyone born in India and either of whose parents is a citizen of India at the time of his/her birth, unless excluded, as per (i) above, is an Indian citizen.[8]

The successive amendments to this act narrowly circumscribed birth as entitling one to citizenship. Birth came to be emphatically qualified by ethnic belonging. The open and inclusive approach to citizenship reflected in the Constitution gave way to a pronounced sense of insularity. Such a narrowing down of the boundaries was reflected in several judicial decisions particularly with respect to people who had associated themselves with Pakistan.[9]

By Descent

i)   A person born outside India after 26 January 1950 but before the commencement of the Citizenship (amendment) Act, 1992 could be a citizen of India by descent if his/her father is a citizen of India by birth.

ii) On or after the Citizenship(amendment) Act, 1992,[10] a person could be a citizen of India by descent if either of his parents is a citizen of India at the time of his/her birth.

If the father of the person, referred to in (i) above, is a citizen by descent, then such a person should have been registered as so in an Indian consulate within one year of the commencement of the Citizenship Act, 1955 or within one year of his/her birth, whichever was later. If, in addition to being citizen by descent, he/she was in the service of Government of India such registration was not required.

After the Citizen (amendment) Act, 1992, the fact of either of the parents of a person being an Indian citizen by descent was not enough to entitle him or her to be a citizen of India. Under the section, his or her birth has to be registered at an Indian consulate within one year of its occurrence or the commencement of the act, whichever is later or the permission of the central government has to be obtained for the purpose after such a period of expiry. Such registration is not, however, required if either of the parents of the person concerned is a citizen by descent and is in the service of the Government of India at the time of his/her birth. The act empowers the central government to accord further extension in the period of registration. By descent, citizenship can be extended generation after generation. Those born outside undivided India at the time of the commencement of the Constitution could enroll themselves as citizens by descent only.

It is clear from the above provisions that gender discrimination that prevailed hitherto was given up by the 1992 amendment act with respect to the parentage of the aspirants to citizenship. But provisions of registration, apart from conferring a great deal of discretion on the executive, reinforced the tendency of exclusion rather than inclusion so eloquently expressed in the Indian Constitution.

By Registration

i)   A person of Indian origin[11] and ordinarily resident in India for five years, before applying for citizenship, is entitled to be an Indian citizen by registration. Similarly, the following categories of persons can seek citizenship under this type: (a) Persons of Indian origin resident in any country by following a set of procedures, (b) A person married to a citizen of India[12] and has been resident in the country for five years immediately before making an application, (c) Minor children of persons who are Indian citizens, and (d) Persons of full age and capacity of a country specified in Schedule I[13] of the Citizenship Act, 1955.

While registering, an oath of allegiance needs to be taken. Those who have renounced or have been deprived from citizenship can obtain the same only with the permission of the Government of India. The courts have consistently upheld the exclusive jurisdiction of the central government in deciding issues falling within these provisions.[14]

By Naturalization

i)   The person opting for Indian citizenship under naturalization should not be a citizen of any country where citizens are prevented by law or practice from becoming subjects or citizens of that country by naturalization, and

ii)   If he is a citizen of another country he has renounced such citizenship, and

iii) Resided in India continuously for twelve months; for seven years[15] preceding the twelve months the person has stayed in India amounting in the aggregate to not less than five years,[16] and

iv)   He has adequate knowledge of a language specified in the Eighth Schedule of the Indian Constitution, and

v)   He intends to reside in India or serve in government service or an international organization of which India is a member.

As is clear, by naturalization, the process of obtaining Indian citizenship was made extremely difficult.

By Incorporating a Territory into India

In such instances the Government of India will specify the persons who shall be citizens of India by reason of their connection with that territory.[17]

Under the Assam Accord[18]

i)   All the persons of Indian origin who came to Assam before 1 January 1966 from a specified territory (meaning territories included in Bangladesh) and have been ordinarily resident in Assam are considered citizens of India from the date unless they choose not to be.

ii)   a) Persons of Indian origin from the specified territory who came on or after 1 January 1966 but before 25 March 1971 and have been resident in Assam since and b) have been detected in accordance with the provisions of the Foreigners Act, 1946 and Foreigners (Tribunals) orders, 1964; c) upon registration, will be considered as citizens of India, from the date of expiry of a period of ten years from the date of detection as a foreigner. In the interim period they will enjoy all facilities including passports but they will not have the right to vote.[19]

TERMINATION OF CITIZENSHIP

The 1955 act provides for the renouncing of citizenship voluntarily. For the purpose, a person, who is also a citizen, of full age and capacity has to make a declaration renouncing his/her Indian citizenship before the prescribed authority in the prescribed manner. Once such a declaration is registered he/she ceases to be a citizen. If such a declaration is made during wartime, a war in which India is engaged, registration of such declaration could be withheld until central government directs otherwise.

When a person ceases to be a citizen of India every minor child of that person thereupon ceases to be a citizen of India. However, such children, within a year of attaining full age can become citizens of India after making a declaration to that effect.

If a citizen of India acquires the citizenship of another country voluntarily by naturalization or registration, he ceases to be a citizen of India. The act however, provides discretion to central government in this regard if such a step is resorted to during wartime.

The authority to decide whether an Indian citizen has acquired the citizenship of another country or not, is not the court, but the central government. However, courts can decide on all facts concerning the issue.

Both the Constitution and the law reject dual citizenship.[20] However, under certain circumstances, courts have held that the central government can let a minor to acquire or retain citizenship different from that of the parent.[21]

DEPRIVATION OF CITIZENSHIP

A citizen of India who is such by naturalization or by virtue only of clause (c) of Article 5 of the Constitution (concerned with the duration of residence) or by registration otherwise than under clause b (ii) of Article 6 of the Constitution (concerned with migration from the territory now included in Pakistan on or after 19 July 1948 but before the commencement of the Constitution with the concerned person having registered himself before the competent authority) or clause (a) of subsection (1) of section 5 of the Citizenship Act 1955 (regarding people of Indian origin who have applied for registration after five years of stay in India) will cease to be a citizen of India if he/she is deprived of that citizenship by an order of central government under the relevant sections.

The central government may deprive persons of citizenship for

1. fraud and false representations or concealment of material facts while registration or seeking certificate of naturalization;
2. disloyalty or disaffection towards the Constitution of India;
3. being associated with an enemy that India is at war with;
4. being imprisoned for a term not less than two years after registration or naturalization; and
5. being ordinarily resident out of India for a continuous period of seven years and if the central government decides that it is not conducive to public good.

We can identify certain pronounced tendencies with respect to demarcation of Indian citizenship over the years. It came to be increasingly confined to people born to Indian citizens or parents of Indian origin and who did not opt out of its rights and privileges. It was effectively closed to people born to parents who were not of Indian origin and who desired to make their permanent domicile in India, unless they had a claim to make on other grounds. Ethnic bond continued to be an important consideration.[22] From a relatively inclusive approach to citizenship, India had moved towards an overtly ethnic conception of citizenship where descent from parentage of Indian origin became an overriding consideration. Given the prevalence of endogamy, caste, and community ties in India, the demarcation and recognition of citizenship primarily on grounds of birth came in support of the prevalent social structure in India. While justifications for such a slide were drawn by pointing out at the measures adopted by other countries, the distinctive path India wanted to chart in this regard, as highlighted in the Constitution, was ignored. Further, there were marked differences in the social structures of India, on one hand and the other countries it cited in justification, leading to deeply differential implications.

In spite of the overriding significance accorded to ethnic ties, judicial pronouncements, by and large, were unfavourable to Muslims with divided families in India and Pakistan. The closure of citizenship in other societies, such as the UK following the agitation launched by Enoch Powell and directed against Asian migrants, had their immediate repercussions in India in not only reinforcing the ethnic slide in considerations of citizenship, but also in fuelling the ethnic divide, particularly between Hindus and Muslims. The Hindus were ascribed a superior claim on citizenship as compared to other communities as reflected in the pronouncements and slogans of the rising tide of the Hindutva wave of the period. Such a tendency went along with the greatly enhanced role of central government in shaping citizenship provisions as reflected in the various amendments that were carried out to the Citizenship Act and the Citizen Rules and Orders. Overall, India attempted to construct a uniform national identity through its intervention in the demarcation of citizens. Such a national identity was identified with the good polity that India envisaged. Citizenship provisions became a tool to construct a pan-Indian identity. The changes brought to the Citizenship Act in the wake of the Assam Accord deviated from this logic to an extent. But the agitation that preceded the accord and the opposition that was mounted against it were indications of the tilt that had already taken place. Any kind of claim to citizenship that deviated from a standardized conception of national identity was looked down upon with suspicion. Further, the Assam Accord did not affect the overall process of consolidation of national identity that was taking place. A citizenship that was deeply marked by ethnic and majoritarian ascriptions was becoming the order of the day and the central government authorized to arbitrate on this issue was increasingly conceding the ground towards such an end.[23]

CONCEPTIONS OF CITIZENSHIP

THE CONSTITUENT ASSEMBLY DEBATES ON CITIZENSHIP

A closer look at the Constituent Assembly Debates on citizenship shows that there was little unanimity on the normative grounds that should govern citizenship in India. A set of substantial considerations were invoked by the different parties in contention on this issue which reflected, in turn, the kind of nationalism they invoked, the rights and privileges of citizens they upheld, and the role, purpose, and design of political power. Therefore, many in the assembly felt that this was the most important issue that they needed to sort out in practice. Differences on the issue necessitated several revised versions of the concerned articles. Ambedkar, the chairman of the drafting committee of the Constitution, stated that it has given the drafting committee a headache in framing these articles.[24] Prime Minister Nehru, in his intervention in the debate on these articles felt, 'All these articles relating to citizenship have probably received far more thought and consideration during the last few months than any article contained in the constitution.'[25]

While one can speak of a mainstream position which eventually prevailed and came to be enshrined in the Constitution, there were profound differences, at least initially, on what the mainstream was. Ambedkar, for instance, was not very enthusiastic about investing the right of citizenship on those who migrated to Pakistan in the wake of Partition and subsequently wished to return to India. He felt that the coercive element in this context was far too exaggerated to permit return of migrants to Pakistan back to India. Those who highlighted the coercive position did not have an adequate understanding of the complex historical and cultural factors that shaped nationalist affiliations: In his book on the factors and tendencies fomenting partition of India, using the work of Renan, Ambedkar had argued that nations are constituted and imagined rather than given.[26] He made a specific kind of human agency central not merely for the precipitation of nationalism but also to uphold its reasonable expression. He felt that a specific process had led to the formation of Pakistan which enjoyed fairly widespread mass-base by reaching out to the variegated imagery of the mass-mind, a process that was very much within collective control at one stage but once it has stepped outside it, instead of wishing it away, everyone's individual collective responsibility needs to be emphasized in the changed context. Otherwise, one does not take one's own responsibility as citizen seriously. Ambedkar was also quite receptive to specific fears of some members of the assembly, such as as Renuka Choudhury of Assam, who thought that a provision such as keeping open Indian citizenship to those who have continued to stay in the Pakistan side of the land might precipitate widespread migration from East Pakistan into relatively sparsely populated Assam.[27] Ambedkar was also apprehensive of the implications of such an understanding of citizenship for the consolidation of a viable and strong polity in India. However, while the mainstream position differed on such and other details, it was clear with regard to certain basic principles: citizenship is not linked to one's denominational belonging, confessional stand, or cultural stance; the rights and obligations of citizens are irrespective of the contexts of their belonging although contexts themselves need not be seen as inimical to subserve the former; however, there may be some contexts which may not be enabling and be made to do so; citizenship need not necessarily come in the way of one's belonging and affiliations; and it is important to foster a culture of rights, dignity, and equality of the human person with the requisite public institutions to shore them up to nurture citizenship in the long run.

We can demarcate another perception on citizenship which, although was not consolidated enough conceptually and in terms of a demarcated constituency, enjoyed extensive public sympathy. Although this conception did not enjoy widespread support in the Constituent Assembly, it had a few articulate spokespersons such as P.S. Deshmukh. He suggested the following amendment to Article 5 on citizenship in Constituent Assembly Debates.

i)   Every person residing in India
      (a) who was born of Indian parents or
      (b) who is naturalized under the law of naturalization and
ii)   Every person who is a Hindu or Sikh by religion and is not a citizen
      of any other state, wherever he resides, shall be entitled to be a citizen
      of India.

In this conception, there is a definite privileging of Hindu and Sikh identities alongside common citizenship. This conception, expressed in several interventions in the debates on this issue, stressed on descent and requirement of longer stay in India to be eligible for citizenship. It emphasized kinship and cultural identity rather than territorial belonging. Deshmukh wanted 12 years of residence in India, instead of five, to be eligible to apply for Indian citizenship. He wanted to substitute 'of Indian Parents', the phrase 'born in territory of India' in the draft.

A specific interventionist role for the Indian state on behalf of its citizens and a stronger bond between the citizen and state was stressed by Deshmukh. He suggested addition of the following section 5B to Article 5 of the Draft Constitution:

Every citizen shall

(a) Enjoy the protection of the Indian state in foreign countries.
(b) Be bound to obey the laws of India, serve the interests of Indian communities, defend his country, and pay all taxes.[28]

It is obvious that if this section was incorporated in the Constitution, it would have conferred extraordinary powers on the state and greatly compromised the rights and sense of belonging of some citizens. Apart from adopting the above normative and institutional stance, this conception favoured specific control and regulation over Muslims. The provision to permit return of migrants to Pakistan back to India was strongly opposed by this strand of thought, for reasons other than those of Ambedkar outlined above. In fact, Deshmukh criticized Ambedkar for making 'Indian citizenship the cheapest on earth'.[29] He posited the threat of 'air-born baby boom',[30] if accident of birth determines citizenship. He accused the 'the specious, oft-repeated and nauseating principle of secularity of the state' for throwing open 'our citizenship so indiscriminately'.[31] Another adherent of this position, Pandit Thakur Das Bhargava, felt that the generosity displayed by the proposal on citizenship is not followed up with adequate responsibility: 'If a country is so poor and so weak as not even to be able to protect the ladies or citizens of this country, what right it has got to extend it so wide'.[32] There was a strong avowal of ethnic belonging in this conception bordering on race. As mentioned earlier, P.S. Deshmukh wanted to replace the phrase 'born in territory of India' with 'of Indian Parents'. When Deshmukh was asked to define who were Indian parents he said that an Indian 'is a very easily recognisable person'. Subtly he suggested, 'colour and complexion', as their mark of identity.[33]

One can identify a third conception of citizenship in the Constituent Assembly Debates which could be termed as hard conception of citizenship, contrasted against the mainstream position, which it termed as soft. The hard position defended itself on pragmatic considerations against the mainstream position, which it felt was overtly idealistic. This position wanted to make Indian citizenship dear by specifications and qualifications. It was against granting citizenship to those who emigrated to Pakistan on the eve of Partition as the votaries of this position considered it desertion in an hour that demanded fidelity. They wanted the naturalization of citizenship to be made rigorous and demanded a quid pro quo consideration for extending citizenship to persons of foreign origin. It was a different matter that such pragmatic considerations, sometimes unconsciously but often consciously, were tilted towards positions which they would not have defended otherwise.

A votary of this position, K.T. Shah, put forward certain interesting proposals on this issue. He felt that if a country allowed Indian citizenship to be retained while granting its own citizenship, there should be no objection to the same. If a country demanded that Indian citizenship should be renounced to obtain its own then India should bear with it. But if discrimination is practised by another country, as prevailed in the then South Africa, then its citizens too may not be extended equality of treatment in India.

This tendency, over the years, was to slide into the mainstream position. Such a slide was possible as the mainstream position itself veered round to the hard conception on citizenship. Such convergence saw citizenship as self-same everywhere differing only in terms of their respective allegiances to states, although it was deeply marked by majoritarianism and a homogeneous invocation of nationalism. The body of citizenry was aggregated together on the basis of a shared national identity which was conceived as both uniform and different. This conception was abstract, interventionist, and called for greater monitoring. It reinforced bureaucratization and centralization. These tendencies of nationalistic reductionism and majoritarianism were also the arms of the state-sponsored project. This project, however, had little capacity to wield a uniform national identity, even if it was desirable and possible. It identified the different and the other as threatening national identity and attempted to streamline them to the image and likeness of the majority. In the process, it was to exacerbate differences rather than evolve ways by which diversity can be made to cohabit in a shared national bond.

It is important to note that the Constituent Assembly Debates which constituted the discursive terrain of the Constitution of India marked a range of perspectives, not necessarily coeval in appeal, unlike the definitive articles of the Constitution on citizenship. The legal provisions on citizenship, eventually, however, came to be deeply influenced by these contentious perspectives. The normative stances adopted by these perspectives on culture, rights, liberties, power, the province of the state and their mutual relations were not merely reflected in the political market-place but even in judicial pronouncements as well. The mainstream position on citizenship was not a compromise among contending versions but was a principled stance. But it was a stance subject to the continued scrutiny of the citizen community which itself was wielded into the body-politic of India by such a stance.

CITIZENSHIP AND GROUP AFFILIATION

There was no overt disagreement in the Constituent Assembly on extending equality of citizenship to all those entitled to be citizens. In fact, those who subscribed to inequality presented themselves as supporters of equality of treatment. The battle for equality was to be waged against versions that masqueraded themselves as expressions of equality rather than against a value or system of values diametrically opposed to it. No one, for instance, came forward to justify the principles of gradation and ranking sustaining the caste system. However, there were many defenders of the uniform application of the principle of equality of treatment to all citizens.

In the Constituent Assembly Debates we find a vertical division between two different viewpoints. The first favoured a uniform set of rights extended to all citizens and defended in the name of equality of rights, equality of treatment, and a single national identity. Citizenship was to be unmarked except for universally shared claims and obligations and a common national identity. It should not be encumbered with any particular markings. This viewpoint contrasted the British rule, as diametrically opposed to such ideals. It often perceived the ghost of colonialism looming large around any differentiated conception of citizenship.[34] A characteristic statement in this regard is that of Babu Ramnarayan Singh who participating in the discussion on the Schedule V pertaining to granting of autonomy to tribal areas, said,

What is our aspiration for the future? Our aspiration is this. Unfortunately, this country has been divided into so many classes and communities. We should proceed in such a way that all the different communities may vanish and we may have one nation, the Indian Nation. If we proceed with this area and that, we shall fail in the future.[35]

There were several others who concurred with this viewpoint. Referring to the proposed measures of autonomy to tribal districts under Schedule VI, Rohini Kumar Choudhary, a representative from Assam, said,

This autonomous district is a weapon whereby steps are taken to keep the tribal people perpetually away from the non-tribals...During the British days, we were not allowed to introduce our culture among those people. Even after the British have gone, we find the same conditions in the New Constitution of Dr Ambedkar.[36]

Broad concurrence with this viewpoint was widespread in the Constituent Assembly in spite of shades of differences and differences with regard to the appropriate strategy to realize this point of view. Many suggested accommodation to differential identities on pragmatic grounds and as a short-time measure and not on the basis of any principle.

The second viewpoint argued, although not always consistently, that there are different identities in India. If these different identities are not recognized and measures adopted to protect their distinct interests, then equality of rights and equality of treatment would effectively reinforce the dominance of the majority. A characteristic stand in this regard is that of Sardar Hukum Singh who strongly pleaded for reservation for minorities in public employment in the context of Art 296 of the Draft Constitution, saying, that if it was not done, 'The aggressiveness of the majority would pass off as nationalism while the helplessness of the minority might be dubbed as communalism.'[37] While there were disagreements with regard to the kind of differences to be recognized and the specific measures needed to sustain differences, the mainstream position in the Constituent Assembly Debates favoured recognition of several differences which had unequivocally asserted themselves during the national movement. This was also the considered position of Ambedkar.

Eventually, the Indian Constitution came to terms with certain significant expressions of group differences and reached out to accommodate them to the overall satisfaction of their representatives.[38] In several instances, the specific nature of the difference came to be reflectively worked out during the course of Constituent Assembly

Debates itself. In such cases where a group showed intense dissatisfaction, some of its demands were conceded while adducing good reasons for the non-consideration of other demands.[39] Some groups came to voluntarily renounce certain claims which they felt were not conducive to attain certain other ends they had in view.[40]

Taking into account such complex considerations, the Indian Constitution was to put together a notion of citizenship informed by group differences and assigning a differential system of rights and obligations to citizens recognized on that basis.

We can identify the following major patterns of recognition of such group-differentiated citizenship in the Constitution.

Differential Treatment Extended to Disadvantaged Groups

Differential treatment in this respect is a corollary to equality of treatment. Without extending such differential treatment which is preferential in relation to the non-disadvantaged there is no level playing field. The Constitution itself in several parts, particularly in chapters III & IV spells out different kinds of disadvantaged citizens. Disadvantage could be based on untouchability, caste community, gender, age, lack of productive resources, physical disabilities, conditions of study and work, lack of skills or even regional disparity. While some of these disadvantages are individual-centred, a large number of people are subjected to group-affiliated disadvantages. Most of these disabilities are socially engendered as constitutive of oneself through one's group affinity, which Iris Marion Young illustrates by making use of Heideggar's concept of 'thrownness'.[41] Even where physical disabilities exist, preferential consideration extended towards those suffering can lead to a greatly satisfied existence to many. Depending upon the kind of disability, the Constitution suggests the kind of differential treatment called for. The Constitution, however, focuses on untouchables and Adivasis for such preferential treatment. Given the kind of disabilities that was their lot, their vast numbers and the kind of mobilization they went through alongside the national movement, this was not surprising. The two social groups which immensely deserved preferential considerations and were largely ignored were women and the disabled.[42]

Differential Treatment Extended to Groups and Communities

This applies to groups who are different with respect to religion, language, and ethnicity. These are primarily group specific rights. Some of these groups may suffer disadvantages such as the Adivasis/Scheduled Tribes, but the reason for conferring these rights are not on account of them but for letting them live and define themselves in their distinctive ways and in relevant respects. Schedules V and VI which confer special powers and responsibilities on scheduled areas, autonomous districts, and autonomous regions make this concern abundantly clear. Given the fact that the distinctive identity of Adivasis was enmeshed in deeply embedded disadvantages, there is the possibility of reading one kind of difference for the other in several parts of the constitutional provisions for them. The deference to differences based on religious professions and linguistic belonging,[43] however, drives home the issue that preferences need not be necessarily bound up with disadvantage.

The nature of the differential rights conferred in instances of disadvantage and in instances of difference significantly varies. In cases of difference of autonomous expression, the relevant difference is ensured and support of the state is extended through a policy of non-discrimination. Preferential assistance, if any, is extended to ensure non-discrimination and non-preference. But where differential rights are a response to disadvantage, the state is called upon to provide enabling resources to offset the disadvantage.

While non-discrimination may involve investment of public resources in favour of a cultural minority, such investment is also available to the rest of citizens through other ways such as state assistance to educational institutions which tend to reproduce the majoritarian culture. But where differential rights based on disadvantage are involved, the state is expected to make investments in addition to what is available ordinarily to the rest. In certain glaring cases of disadvantages suffered by groups such as the Scheduled Castes and Scheduled Tribes, one of the major purposes of political reservation is to ensure that state pursues such objectives through effective representation.

Entitlement based on differences is attempted to be highly circumscribed by the Constitution, while allowing a great deal of elasticity to considerations of disadvantage.

This is obvious when we consider the Directive Principles of State Policy. Such provisions as the uniform civil code look at differences suspiciously. There are obvious attempts in the Constituent Assembly to rein in differences and make them amenable to the susceptibilities of the majority. Deference to difference beyond a limit is perceived as a threat to national unity. Several clauses dealing on autonomy to ethnic groups highlight such a tendency.

Differential Treatment as Deference to Privilege

There are certain provisions of the Constitution where the privileges enjoyed by a group are attempted to be protected lest the group feels a sense of loss, disenchantment, and marginalization. This is particularly the case with respect to the Anglo-Indian community.[44] The language in which such privilege is defended and opposed in the Constituent Assembly does not measure up to the nature of the privilege conferred and sounds like the language of preferential treatment extended to the disadvantaged. However, here was a consideration of respect and acceptance extended towards a community without which it would not have been able to adjust itself to the demands of the new situation. It was characteristically an issue of culture and identity.

But privilege is much strongly guarded by silence on many issues: The dominant strata are protected by ignoring any reference to dominant classes except a set of highly generalized maxims directing the state towards certain desirable ends in the Directive Principles of State Policy.[45] In a way, it shows the farthest limits that even a complex conception of citizenship can reach out to without raising the basic issue of the relations of production.

Differential Treatment by Way of Federal Arrangement

One of the major ways that difference is handled by the Indian Constitution is through the federal organization of power. Organization of states on a linguistic basis was an oft-repeated statement of policy of the Indian National Congress for many years even prior to Independence. Although such a stance suffered a major setback in the wake of Partition including such terminological jugglery as 'Union of States' to describe Indian federation, a vast majority of the states came to be based on linguistic majoritarianism. They accommodated differences within a federal arrangement. Language is also the basis of a distinct identity. Therefore, deference to linguistic identity was also a deference to ethnic pluralism.

The relation of states to the Indian Union is not uniform, even in a formal sense, but different in many cases.[46] The well-known case is that of Jammu and Kashmir, stated in Article 370 of the Indian Constitution. However, diverse provisions exist with respect to many states to safeguard their distinct identity, culture, and distribution of powers. Within states, the Constitution makes further provisions to attend to specific needs and requirements of certain distinct regions such as Vidarbha and

Marathwada in Maharashtra, Saurashtra and Kutch in Gujarat, Tuensang district in Nagaland, etc.

The federal principle does not merely subscribe to differential cultural identity but differential treatment of citizens as well. While equality of treatment in public employment for all the citizens is upheld in certain instances, it is qualified by the provision that Parliament can make a law assigning preference with regard to certain types of employment. There were spokespersons who demanded absolute equality of opportunity in public employment throughout the country and often justification for the same was drawn on the basis of national unity. Jaspat Roy Kapoor argued in respect of equality of provisions:

Every citizen of the country, wherever he might be living, should have equal opportunity of employment under the state. Every citizen, irrespective of his place of residence should be eligible for employment under the state anywhere in the country. [47]

He spoke of the unfettered right and privilege of employment in any part and in every nook and corner of the country based on the idea of a single citizenship.

With regard to all the three issues on citizenship highlighted in this chapter, that is, inclusion–exclusion, normative considerations, and differential entitlement, there was intense contestation in the Constituent Assembly and subsequently in the body-politic of India. Several constitutional provisions which embody these issues while reflecting the considered judgement of the majority in the assembly leave room for alternative considerations and prioritization. This has been amply reflected in the legislative elaboration of some of these provisions and the decisions of the judiciary. While the space these provisions offer for the creative intervention of the political community is welcome, often the interventions have favoured a narrow, ascriptive, abstract, and formal stipulation of citizenship. In spite of such limitations, the understanding of citizenship that the Indian Constitution advances is breathtakingly new and unparalleled in the literature on the subject.

NOTES

1. The Indian Constitution opens with the preamble: 'We the people of India, having solemnly resolved to constitute India into a Sovereign, Socialist Secular Democratic Republic and to secure to all its *citizens* (italics mine): Justice, social, economic and political...'. 'We the people of India' , forming the citizen

body, was to become one of the most vexed issues before the Constituent Assembly. Wider agreements on principles did not preclude deep disagreements on specifics even among those who deferred to those principles.

Incidentally, it might be worth mentioning that constitutional deliberations are foregrounded by a political philosophy. As the nationalist elite gathered in the Constituent Assembly did not subscribe to any consistent political philosophy, the constitutional text had to suggest it, albeit, in an operational way. The Indian Constitution had to take an overt normative role on a wide range of issues. Consequently, the assembly debates and the constitutional text are infused with political philosophical concepts in a practical state.

2. Cited in V.K. Dewan, *Law of Citizenship, Foreigners and Passports* (New Delhi: Orient Law House, 3rd edn, 2000), p. 37.

3. The Citizenship Act has been subsequently amended to make space for several issues including the response of the Government of India to developments in Assam.

4. AIR 1961 March Pr 110 (113, 114 etc.).

5. On 19 July 1948, an ordinance was passed that no person shall come into India from Pakistan unless he has a permit and certain rules were framed by the Government of India under it mandating a permit for persons coming from Pakistan to India.

6. These provisions of law came into force on 26 November 1949 all over India except in the state of Jammu and Kashmir where they were made effective from 26 January 1950.

7. The British nationality Act, 1948 used the term 'alien enemy' but did not define it. According to it, 'an alien enemy is one whose sovereign or state is at war with the sovereign of England. The terms "alien enemy" is also used to denote a person of whatever nationality, including British who is carrying on business or is voluntarily resident in the enemy's country or country occupied by the enemy' (V.K. Dewan, *Law of Citizenship*, p. 52).

8. The amendment of 1986 was effected suspecting the clandestine entry of a large number of persons of Indian origin from Bangladesh, Sri Lanka, and some African countries.

9. See *State of A.P.* v. *Abdul Khader*, AIR 1961 SC 1467 (1962)1SCJ 100; *State of M.P.* v. *Peer Mohammed* (1963) 2SCJ 655; AIR 1963 SC 645; *Mubarak Ali* v. *State of Bombay*, AIR 1957 SC 857: 1957; Cr. LJ 1346: 1958 SCJ 111 etc.

10. Gender equality was highlighted by this amendment.

11. For the purpose of this act, a person will be regarded as of Indian origin if he or either of his parents were born in undivided India.

12. Before the amendment of 1986, citizenship by marriage under this category was confined only to women.

13. Schedule I enumerates the list of Commonwealth countries whose members are offered facility of acquiring citizenship by registration.

14. See *Shamin Bano* v. *Union of India* AIR 1980 Raj 98 and *Deen Mohd.* v. *State* AIR 1960 MP 381.

15. As amended in 1986; earlier it was 12 years.

16. Earlier it used to be nine years.

17. Goa, Daman, and Diu was incorporated by virtue of the Goa, Daman, and Diu Citizenship Order, 1962; similarly Dadar and Nagar Haveli (Citizenship) order, 1962 was published in the gazette of India, dated 29.3.1962; Citizenship (Pondicherry) order, 1962 was published in the gazette dated 8.12.1962, and after incorporation Sikkim (Citizenship) order, 1975 was published in the gazette dated 16.5.1975.

18. Dated 15.8.1985, Assam has been witnessing a continuous influx of land hungry peasants from Bengal from the nineteenth century which precipitated periodic hostile reactions from the local population. In the early 1980s, widespread mass agitation bursting out into intermittent violence started in Assam against refugees from Bangladesh. This movement was led by the All Assam Students Union and the Assam People's Front. The agitation threatened to turn sour India's relations with Bangladesh. The Assam Accord was signed in this background.

19. Recently, the Government of India has proposed extension of dual citizenship to persons of Indian origin who are citizens of certain specified countries. This issue has not been discussed in this article.

20. See note 19 regarding recent changes.

21. See AIR 1963 A11 260, 1963(1) CrLJ 724.

22. This has been reflected on the issue of extending dual citizenship too, with added considerations of status and affluence brought into it. See note 19.

23. The reaction Sonia Gandhi's citizenship evoked in 1990s is a reflection of this 'nationalist' mood.

24. *CAD*, vol. IX, p. 386.

25. *CAD*, vol. IX, p. 398.

26. See B.R. Ambedkar, *Pakistan or Partition of India* in Babasaheb Ambekdar Writings and Speeches, vol. 8, Mumbai (Government of Maharashtra: Department of Education, 1992), pp. 29–39.

27. See, *CAD*, vol. IX, pp. 422–3.

28. *CAD*, vol. IX, pp. 352–3.

29. Ibid.

30. Ibid. p. 354.

31. Ibid.

32. *CAD*, vol. IX, p. 386.

33. Ibid., p. 356.

34. A differentiated conception of citizenship in addition to extending citizenship to everyone carries at least two more meanings: First, particularity is irreducible into universality. It draws attention to how citizens differ from one another rather than merely point at their commonness. Second, there cannot be the same laws and rules for all which are blind to individual and group differences (For its other, the ideal of universal citizenship, See Iris Marion Young, 'Polity

and Group Difference: A Critique of the Ideal of Universal Citizenship', *Ethics*, 99, 1989, pp. 250–1.

35. *CAD*, vol. IX, p. 987.

36. *CAD*, vol. IX, p. 1017.

37. *CAD*, vol. X, p. 232.

38. It is not possible to elaborate here the complex set of reasons that led to the formulation of a differentiated set of rights under the Constitution. Representatives of groups and communities strongly pleaded for them: the earlier constitutional reforms had created extensive precedents for them which was not possible to dismantle without provoking resistance; there were significant strands in the national movements which were sensitive to the different and the other; the fear of fragmentation loomed large in the background of Partition if minorities were not accommodated etc., were important reasons to be taken into account.

39. In this context, mention might be made of the religious minorities renouncing their right to separate electorate: See Report of Minorities Advisory Committee, *CAD*, vol. X, pp. 265–6.

40. One of the most vociferous group in the Constituent Assembly was made of those who saw themselves as representing Sikh interests. In the context of the recommendations of the Cabinet Mission and Partition the interests of the Sikhs had emerged to the fore. While several of these demands could not be conceded as it would have fragmented the kind of nationalist project that was being built. However, one of the interesting demand that was conceded was extending reservation in employment to four Scheduled Castes—Mazhabis, Ramdasis, Kabirpanthis, and Sikligars—among Sikhs, a facility which was not extended towards other religious minorities. Vallabhbhai Patel has the following observation to make in this regard, 'Sikh representatives of the Punjab came to me and they said that so far as the Scheduled Caste Sikhs are concerned, they should be treated separately and given the same advantage that was being given to the Hindu Scheduled Castes. The Scheduled Castes objected to a man that these are not Scheduled Castes, and if they are Scheduled Castes, then they are not Sikhs...Now it was against our conviction to recognize as separate Sikh caste as untouchables or Scheduled Castes, because untouchability is not recognized in the Sikh religion. A Scheduled Caste Sikh Community has never been in the past recognized. But as the Sikhs began to make a grievance continuously against the Congress and against us, I persuaded the Scheduled Caste people with great difficulty to agree to this for the sake of peace' (*CAD*, vol. X, p. 247).

41. Thrownness refers to a form of group affinity where, 'One finds oneself as a member of a group whose existence and relations are experienced as always already having been. For a person's identity is defined in relation to how others identify him or her and others do so in terms of groups which already have specific attributes, stereotypes, and norms associated with them, in reference

to which a person's identity will be formed' (Iris Marion Young, 'Polity and Group Difference', p. 258).

42. The Constitution does extend some preferential considerations to them: For women, See Article 15 (3), 39(e) and 42 and for the disabled, see Articles 41 and 46 of the Constitution.

43. See Articles 29 and 30 in particular.

44. See Articles 336 and 337. In the constitutional debate opposing such privilege, Shibban Lal Saksena was to say, ' I would like to utter a word of warning. I feel that these concessions are based on the principle which has not been followed anywhere else in the constitution...I do wish this community to become one with the rest of the people' (CAD, vol. VIII, pp. 938–9). Even when support came to be extended to the cause it is on grounds of generosity rather than difference. K. M. Munshi appeals to 'generous gesture of the majority community' (CAD, vol. VIII, p. 941).

45. See in particular Article 39. Right to Property which was a Fundamental Right in the Constitution was to be abolished eventually as a Fundamental Right. However, Right to Property is buttressed by a whole system of constitutional and legal provisions.

46. See Articles 370 and 371.

47. CAD, vol. VII, p. 57.

8

Citizenship and the Passive Revolution
Interpreting the First Amendment

Nivedita Menon

READING THE CONSTITUTION/WRITING THE CONSTITUTION

If we ever understood 'reading' as an innocent journey to the meaning of a text,[1] that time is long past. It has been nearly three decades since Barthes wrote that celebrated passage:

…the text is not a line of words releasing a single 'theological' meaning (the message of an Author-God) but a multi-dimensional space in which a variety of writings, none of them original, blend and clash. The text is a tissue of quotations drawn from the innumerable centres of culture.[2]

It is in the act of reading that these 'innumerable centres' derive a unity:

…there is one place where this multiplicity is focused and that place is the reader, not, as was hitherto said, the author. The reader is the space on which all the quotations that make up a reading are inscribed…A text's unity lies not in its origin but in its destination.[3]

In this understanding, of course, neither author nor reader are individual persons, but processes, criss-crossing networks of meaning.

Drawing on this account, there are two aspects of reading that I would like to draw attention to: first, that the meaning of a text is available to us—the readers—only in the present, at the moment of reading, and it is futile to attempt to uncover the 'real' meaning intended by the author; and, second, that meanings emerge from a text and have consequences independently of the intention of the author, since every text is embedded in an interrelated network of other texts whose boundaries are porous. These two aspects—the inescapability of the present and the impossibility of controlling meaning—are both key to a third understanding: namely, that all reading is situated, and is possible only from some location or the other. Location is spatially and temporally specific, and specific in terms of gender, caste, race, class, and a host of other identifications, not all at once, but some of which would emerge as relevant in some contexts and others at other times. If 'reading' is always in this sense an act that is differentially located in relations of power, then 'writing' is all the more so. Indeed, I would argue that every act of reading is in turn an act of writing. Every act of interpretation demarcates and populates a terrain afresh towards a particular end.

What does it mean, then, to read the Constitution today? The overwhelming sense about the Constitution at this moment is that it is under attack from the Hindu Right, that the moral and ethical vision underlying it is threatened—the vision which enabled a multi-religious and multicultural society with a substantial Hindu majority to survive as a democracy. This perception is not unfounded, given the systematic attacks on minorities and minority rights ever since the coalition led by the Hindu Right-wing BJP came to power, and the initiative this government has taken to set up a Constitutional Review Committee. In this climate it is not surprising that there has been a closing of Left-democratic ranks and a reassertion of faith in the values under attack. I too believe that India cannot survive except as a multicultural democracy, but in this essay I attempt to demonstrate that reading and assessing the Constitution simply as if it were a blueprint to construct such a society might be misleading.

The kind of reading that I refer to above is very recent, emerging in the 1990s, in many ways as a response to the attacks referred to earlier. In this trend, several writers have assessed the Indian Constitution and political structures in terms of their liberal–democratic values. The questions that have interested these scholars are primarily whether secularism of one kind or another has been successful, and whether community and individual rights have eroded each other or reinforced one another.[4] Prior to this, there have either been legalistic, technical, ostensibly value-neutral readings of the Constitution,[5] or Marxist interpretations in which the primary purpose of the Constitution was seen to be that of protecting a certain order of bourgeois property rights.[6]

Both the 'Marxist' as well as the 'Liberal' interpretations are limited in their own ways. Each isolates a specific aspect of the Constitution, making for conceptual clarity, but at the cost of richness and complexity. Values such as 'secularism' cannot be understood in isolation from political economy imperatives, any more than 'bourgeois property rights' can be understood in isolation from liberal–democratic concerns. Looking back on the Constitution at the beginning of the twenty-first century, after fifty years of its functioning, it seems to me that we would better understand the current conjuncture in Indian politics if we understood that document as part of a larger story—as a crucial landmark in the story of modernity in India. Telling the story in this way enables a better understanding, both of the specific form that democracy took in India as well as of constitutionalism itself as a process.

I will frame this story within Sudipta Kaviraj's formulation on 'modernity' as a set of processes that can follow different sequences in different societies and at different historical conjunctures. He argues that modernity is not the name of a single process, but 'a time in history in which several processes of social change tend to occur in combination. These processes are…the increasing centrality of the modern state and its forms of governmentality and discipline, social individuation, capitalist industrialization, the rise of nationalism and democracy.' These processes differ from one society to another in the sequence in which they appear as well as in their 'internal sequences (like the sequence between consumer and capital goods industries within the processes of industrialization)'. In addition, modern processes transform traditional structures which differ from one society to another; modernity, therefore, takes differentiated forms in different societies.[7]

In some earlier writings, Kaviraj has argued that while in the West the processes of modernity stabilized themselves before the pressures for democracy began, in India the two processes emerged almost simultaneously. The logic of one therefore, can 'seriously affect, hinder, or alter the logic' of the other.[8] However, the architects of institution-making in India read the evidence of European history simply as reflecting an earlier stage at which India could now be assumed to be. Thus, since 'a functional relationship could be discerned between democracy and capitalism in the developed stages of capitalist society', it was assumed that India could make 'the unworried choice' of a capitalist economy and liberal–democratic constitution. But as Kaviraj suggests, it is equally plausible to contend that in the West there was 'a strictly sequential relationship between capitalist industrialization and political democracy. Initial disciplining of the working class in a regime of capitalist production was achieved only because no democratic obstructions could be placed in its path.'[9]

This essay will explore the dilemmas created by, in Kaviraj's terms, the differences in sequentiality here, by focusing on one revealing moment—the first Act amending the Constitution in 1951. The act was passed by the Provisional Parliament, (228 votes to 20), soon after the Constitution came into effect, and just before the first general elections in 1952—it was, in this sense, both too late and too soon. That is, the amendments reopened crucial issues in Parliament that the same body had, as the Constituent Assembly, considered settled just over a year ago. But at the same time, Nehru insisted that the amendments could not wait for the elections to put in place the first Parliament elected by universal suffrage. 'Far from changing this constitution', he said, 'these amendments give full effect to the constitution as we wanted it to be'. These were not new ideas, he insisted: 'We have only sought to bring out what is implicit.'[10]

I suggest that if we interpret the Constitution as a landmark in the story of modernity in India, 'secularism' must be seen as the central value animating it. However, secularism in this reading goes much further than the state–community relationship. As I have suggested elsewhere, extending the arguments of Partha Chatterjee and of others like Ashis Nandy,[11] 'secularism' mediates three aspects of the modernizing project of the Indian anti-imperialist elites. These are: (a) bourgeois democracy, (which here is about the interrelations among communities, individual citizens, and the state at different levels), (b) the capitalist transformation of the economy, through the creation of the mobile and unmarked citizen, and (c) social justice, to the extent that formal legal equality (for example, through the abolition of untouchability and caste discrimination) was necessary for the project of capitalist transformation.[12]

The First Amendment can be seen as limiting individual rights in three significant areas: (a) Article 15 on the individual's right to equality was circumscribed by strengthening the government's ability to make special provisions 'for backward classes of citizens', (b) Article 19 on the individual's right to freedom of expression was limited in the interests of state security, and (c) Article 31 on the individual's right to property was made subject to the state's right to acquire property to resolve 'the land problem'.[13] In fact, during the debate, some members indignantly reminded the house that while the first amendment to the American Constitution had been to extend 'individual and social rights', our first amendment did the opposite, and curtailed individual freedoms.[14] I will briefly suggest here that the three particular changes sought by the amendment are concerned less with individual freedoms as such; rather, they reflect the imperatives of the project of the modernizing elites that I have outlined above. That is, the First Amendment can be read as an attempt by the national movement-turned-nation-state both to control and ride the forces of democracy in the drive to modernity. 'A curious mixture of revolution and reaction', a member termed it during the debate in Parliament, referring to the amendment to Article 31 as the former and the amendment to Article 19 as the latter.[15] The point I would make here is, of course, that the parameters of 'revolution and reaction' (while readily available in that political context, and even today) are inadequate to comprehend what was happening at that point. The abolition of zamindari, the end of caste discrimination, and limitations on freedom of speech and expression—these three achievements were critical for a nation-state in the process of establishing a capitalist economy through a passive revolution.

THE DEBATE ON WHETHER THE CONSTITUTION IS LIBERAL

Each restriction of individual rights in this amendment sought to empower a different subject: first, a cultural community; second, the state; and third, a class. Clearly, if the individual is understood to be the cornerstone of modern liberal democracies, then the first amendment can be understood to have further disabled what Sunil Khilnani calls 'Indian liberalism'. Even during the Congress' 'most strongly liberal phase', he notes, liberty was understood not as an individual right but as a nation's collective right to self-determination. Thus, 'individuality as a way of social being was a precarious undertaking.' It was because of this that Indian liberalism, in his view, was 'crippled from its origins'.[16] Democracy itself 'stood in a lonely corner' amidst the 'intellectual festivities'[17] of the early twentieth century: it was not debated or thought through, it simply arrived, 'in a fit of absent-mindedness'.[18] The Constituent Assembly Debates, rich and lengthy as they were, 'carry little trace of the classic fears that haunted both advocates and critics of democracy in nineteenth-century Europe: what would happen if the vote was given to the poor, the uneducated, the dispossessed?'[19] Further, the establishment of community rights through affirmative action 'weakened the pressure to accord universal rights' and 'encouraged demands for special dispensations for selected groups'.[20]

Khilnani's understanding is thus predicated on the notion of a universal model of democracy that has already been achieved in the West, in comparison to which post-colonial democracy will always be in deficit. Faced with a political philosophy and practice in another century and another place, which looks as unlike Europe's liberal democracy as he can imagine, he still terms it 'liberalism'—but a liberalism crippled by its inability to give priority to what European liberalism privileged, to fear what European liberalism feared. Perhaps, one is constrained to point out, it isn't liberalism then?

Other scholars would disagree, both with Khilnani as well as with my question to him. Rajeev Bhargava and Gurpreet Mahajan, for instance, argue that liberal–democracy need not look the way Khilnani wants it to look. Bhargava holds that it is a myth that modern conditions destroy every collective formation and unleash different forms of individualism. Rather, while some kinds of groups are undermined by modernity, others are generated by it—for example, the nation. So while there is a functional tie between a nation-state and a modern society of individualized and equalized human beings, no particular temporal sequence is necessitated—a nation-state may precede or succeed a modern society. Thus, Bhargava argues, contra Khilnani, that liberalism understood as the nation's collective right to self-determination does not necessarily preclude individual rights: the two are not mutually exclusive. Indeed, democracy came to India as nationalism, so arguments for nationalism are in fact conterminous with arguments for democracy. For the Indian political elite, a rights-based liberalism construed individualistically was crucial, and hence the emphasis on civil liberties. However, liberalism was also for them associated with social justice. In this context, Bhargava quotes K.M. Panikkar, member of the Constituent Assembly, as interpreting Vivekananda as a liberal, for whom reforming Hinduism was a way of infusing it with liberal principles.[21] In this argument, then, India happened to develop another version of liberalism, one that respected group identities and rights as well as individual rights.

Gurpreet Mahajan makes a somewhat different argument in defence of Indian liberalism against arguments such as Khilnani's, though she does not directly address his work. She too, like Bhargava, holds that the individual is not the only legitimate subject of democratic discourse, and that almost all welfare democracies recognize communities in policy and law. Therefore, the presence of community rights in the Indian Constitution does not mark a radical departure from liberal–democratic practices.[22] But the more interesting argument that Mahajan makes is that the time the Constitution was framed was at a historical moment when the liberal framework did not recognize community rights. Thus, at that point, the Indian Constitution did 'deviate' from liberal principles. Later on, the liberal perspective itself changed, and then the primary concerns of the Indian Constitution conformed with the new liberal agendas and perspectives.[23] The questions that emerges for us here is this: should not the 'deviation' in the first instance have provoked a very different kind of inquiry into the nature of both Indian democracy and liberalism? Why does Mahajan instead take such pains to establish that as a result of *later* changes in the liberal perspective, it was the Indian Constitution that returned to the liberal fold? It would seem that despite their differences, all three scholars discussed above continue in one way or the other to legitimize the expectation that Indian democracy should justify itself in terms of 'liberalism' as an a-priori value.

Sumit Sarkar offers a reading of Indian democracy that, while not engaging directly with the debate outlined above, also focuses on what could be termed the liberal features of the Indian state. He lists these 'five key features of postcolonial[24] Indian state structure' as 'a framework of basic bourgeois-liberal civil rights; parliamentary democracy grounded in universal suffrage; safeguards for "backward" or "depressed" groups through a balancing of "freedom" and "equality" with "justice"; federalism (though eventually with an unusually strong Centre); and secularism (in one or several of its many possible meanings).'[25] Highlighting the interconnections, 'maybe even the inseparability' of democracy, secularism, and federalism in the Indian context, Sarkar urges recognition of the fact that the emergence of India as a democracy was not inevitable. It is a 'major political and human achievement' that we cannot afford to take for granted.[26] In making this argument, he is positioning himself against both 'liberal–imperialist narratives' of constitutional continuity with colonial legislations, as well as against 'colonial discourse analysis', which he attributes to Partha Chatterjee, where the post-colonial state 'is seen as fundamentally an outgrowth of the colonial regime, since both are bound up with the post-Enlightenment

modern nation-state project'.[27] Instead, he suggests that it would be more
fruitful to explore 'the roots of the "liberal" civil rights aspects of the
constitution' through a deployment of Habermas's notion of public
spheres, where private people could come together to constitute publics.
Of course, he concedes, the differences (from the European experience)
are striking, but the point 'lies in multiple appropraitions'.[28]

Sarkar notes that unlike in Western Europe, the public spheres here
were not primarily grounded in the autonomous development of an
indigenous bourgeois civil society. Further, he recognizes that the origins
of individuation 'clearly lay in colonial administrative-cum-
hegemonic...initiatives,' that is, not in an internal dynamic, nor with
individuation here becoming a mass pehenomenon.[29] However, such
'striking' differences are too easily glossed over. It is precisely these
differences that make 'multiple appropriations' a fraught and
unpredictable exercise, and the emergence of public spheres a limited
and fragmented process in India, with profound implications for the very
nature of democracy.[30]

CONSTITUTIONALISM AND POWER

This is where we must go back to Sarkar's characterization of Partha
Chatterjee's position on the post-colonial state, referred to above, as 'an
outgrowth of the colonial regime, since both are bound up with the
post-Enlightenment modern nation-state project.' This reading of
Chatterjee's argument rather misses the point, for it is concerned really
with recalling to memory the manner of entry of modernity into our
societies. The fact that this encounter with modernity occurred through
a political system that was violent at its core distinguishes 'our' modernity
(to use Chatterjee's evocative phrase)[31] from modernity as it emerged in
Europe. On the one hand there was the despotic colonial state strategic-
ally making adjustments at various levels with different sections of the
subject population, and on the other, here were the differing investments
these sections had in the modern norms and institutions brought in by
colonialism. The dislocation caused by modernity in Europe four
centuries ago was equally brutal, but in Asia and Africa there was a double
violence involved: the simultaneous disruption caused by modernity and
colonialism. It is this encounter that is suggested by the term 'post-
colonial' as I use it in this essay. Post-colonialism thus begins from the
very first moment of colonial contact. As one set of scholars puts it, 'it is
the discourse of oppositionality which colonialism brings into being.'[32]

I would like to introduce here a distinction Chatterjee makes, between civil society and political society, that I find key to reconceptualizing democratic politics today.[33] 'Civil society', according to Chatterjee, is constituted by the institutions of modern associational life, while 'political society' is a domain of mediating institutions between civil society and state. The mark of non-Western modernity is the hiatus between civil society (composed of a small section of 'citizens') and political society (composed of 'population'). Population groups, unlike citizens, are not the product of rational contractual association, but are rather the target of the 'policy' of the legal-bureaucratic apparatus of the state. The civil society of citizens, shaped by the normative ideals of Western modernity, excludes the vast mass of the population, towards whom it assumes a 'pedagogical mission' of enlightenment.

On the other hand, in order to understand the principles that govern political society, we must begin with the relationship of the 'development state' to population, which it attempts to regulate through the governmental form of 'welfare'. Political society—parties, movements, non-party political formations—channelizes popular demands on the state through a form of mobilization we call democracy. 'The point is that the practices that activate the forms and methods of mobilization and participation in political society are not always consistent with the principles of association in civil society.' This distinction, it may be noted, is more usefully understood as a conceptual distinction than as representing two distinct spheres. In other words, democratic aspirations, often violate institutional norms of liberal civil society.

It is in this context that we need to understand the rethinking of constitutionalism as a self-evidently democratic exercise. By 'constitutionalism' I refer here to a specific method adopted by modern democracies of safeguarding the autonomy of the self, whether conceived in terms of the individual or the community. By historicizing this method, we remind ourselves, to use Upendra Baxi's words, that 'much of the business of "modern" constitutionalism was transacted during the early halcyon days of colonialism/imperialism. That historical timespace marks a combined and uneven development of the world in the processes of early modernity...[C]onstitutionalism inherits the propensity for violent social exclusion from the "modern".'[34]

It is this aspect of constitutionalism that I find missing in the accounts of Indian democracy discussed earlier. Sumit Sarkar's account of the emergence of democracy in India does acknowledge conflict, but his focus is on anti-liberals—the Hindu Right-wing—who are recognized as significant adversaries. So the conflict is seen as that between the traditional elites, bent on preserving privilege, and the modern elites, using the resources of modernity to build a new order. Sarkar gives two examples of colonial education in Bengal, for example, in which women and lower castes were able to use education to challenge patriarchal and Brahminical social hierarchies.[35] However, the operation of power, the exclusions set in place in the process of constitution-making, go far beyond a simple tradition/modernity or even a liberal/anti-liberal conflict. I am pointing to the possibility that what are considered the 'liberal' features of the Constitution could serve a purpose other than ensuring democracy, if we take seriously my suggestion that the Constitution marks one moment in the arrival of 'modernity' in India. Secularism has not always even been even 'democratic'—Sarkar goes so far as to concede that in India secularism's close association with the 'nation-building' project has strengthened its assimilation with 'statist endeavours', and to this extent, arguments denouncing secularism for being authoritarian and centralist do have a point. However, this was not inevitable, he argues, for secularism can also be democratic. We could concede that possibility—the point is that in India it took the form it did.[36]

The other accounts we have discussed here avoid any acknowledge-ment of power and conflict whatsoever. How accurate is it to see the Constitution as a document emerging from reasoned debate among adversaries, representing different, even conflicting, points of view, in which a balance was reached, or sought to be reached, between individual and community rights, between Centre and states? Let me suggest in advance that what we will find when we look at the debate over the First Amendment Bill is that, rather than people trying to understand one another, there are people talking past one another, that opposing motivations come together to produce apparent agreement. These varying motivations and values come to fall into an apparent consensus that we tend to recognize in terms of existing codes—'liberal democratic', 'bourgeois', 'Hindu Right', and so on. If we remove this familiar grid, however, we may be able to tell a different story. As Chantal Mouffe points out, 'To envisage politics as a rational process of negotiation among individuals is to obliterate the whole dimension of power and antagonism'—that is to say, it is to obliterate the 'political' itself. However, 'to negate the political does not make it disappear, it only leads to bewilderment in the face of its manifestations and to impotence in dealing with them.'[37]

Let us turn now, in order to explore the questions I have raised, to the First Amendment and to the circumstances in which it was thought to be necessary.

Debating the First Amendment

Once the Constitution came into effect, the courts came up with a series of judgements that held up constitutional provisions on both property and special provisions for disadvantaged citizens, and struck down state government actions curbing freedom of speech as unconstitutional.[38] The First Amendment bill was introduced in May 1951, and the three significant changes it proposed were: (a) the addition of Clause 4 to Article 15, by which the government was enabled to make special provisions for backward classes of citizens; (b) the insertion of Articles 31a and 31b, by which government acquisition of land could not be challenged on grounds of inadequate compensation, and the Ninth Schedule was created, in which land reform legislation was to be placed, protecting it from judicial review; and (c) Clause c was added to Article 19, by which the government could limit freedom of speech 'in the interests of the security of the state'. This latter was a wider formulation than the earlier 'overthrow of the state'.

The amendment was introduced in a parliament that was both unicameral (the Rajya Sabha not having yet been constituted) and provisional, for the first general elections were yet to take place. In response to those who argued that the provisional Parliament was not competent to amend the Constitution, Nehru argued, in the characteristic style of one with a 'pedagogical mission of enlightenment' (to use Partha Chatterjee's phrase referred to earlier), that surely those who had framed the Constitution were competent to amend it.[39]

In this section we will look at the debate over these amendments in the Lok Sabha, tracing the network of interconnections between the three articles.

Article 31: Property and the Bourgeois State

Let us begin with Article 31, and the logic of the passive revolution. I refer here, of course, to Sudipta Kaviraj's well-known development of the Gramscian notion to explain the pattern of development adopted by the Indian state. That is, for a thoroughgoing bourgeois revolution to be effected for industrialization to take place, a domestic market must be built up by reducing poverty in the countryside. This can only be done by effective land reforms, which have been legislated but never effectively implemented because of the influence of landed interests in the coalition of ruling classes. The entire planning process until the 1980s has therefore been an exercise in trying to promote industrialization without the radical transformation of agriculture.[40]

Sudipta Kaviraj characterizes the Indian state as bourgeois in three senses.[41] First, it has a bourgeois legal system, property structure, and institutions of governance revealed in the Constitution. Second, the institutions of planning explicitly acknowledge the state in the reproduction of capital and in setting economic targets in a way compatible with bourgeois developmental perspectives. Third, the bourgeoisie exercises leadership function in the coalition of classes which controls the state.[42]

As we have seen, the courts had been holding up many of the land reform legislations. In the Lok Sabha debates, there were many who used the language of justice and equality when supporting the amendment to Article 31. Thus Renuka Ray spoke of economic and social equality[43] and Pandit Kunzru agreed with Nehru's introductory remarks that property was not an absolute right but was subject to the rights of the community which were greater than the rights of the individual.[44] Kala Venkatarao asked of those who claimed high compensation: 'Who compensated the poor *ryot* when feudalism became the law of the land and when free farming was replaced?'[45]

But Nehru's statement, while using the rhetoric of justice too, best captures the real imperatives behind the need to abolish Zamindari: political stability and the need to end feudal relations in land. He pointed out that in those countries of Asia where the 'land problem' had been resolved rapidly, 'a new stability' had been produced. He urged, 'We have to think in terms of large schemes of social engineering...not petty reforms...'[46] Referring to the differing opinions of different high courts, he said, 'While we wait for this confusion gradually to resolve itself, powerful agrarian movements may grow up...Long arguments and repeated appeals to the courts are dangerous to the state, from the security point of view, from the food production point of view and from the individual point of view, whether it is that of the zamindar or the tenant...'[47]

Others too saw land reforms as a means of preventing dangerous revolutionary movements. Rev. D'Souza, for example, said that he did not see the amendment to Article 31 as 'expropriatory or purely socialistic'; rather, the right to property is guaranteed and compensation given. That is why he supports the amendment—'middle fortunes are a true protection of individual liberty.'[48] That these reforms were not meant to weaken property rights as such was spelt out by T.T. Krishnamachari in a letter to Nehru during discussions on the Fourth Amendment later in 1954—'We have to move to the left on agricultural land, but moving left in industry will prevent expansion.'[49] This was what was clear to Hussain Imam too, a zamindar Member of Parliament (MP) from Bihar protesting the lack of fairness and uniformity in compensation: 'Whatever the law you may pass, it must not be for zamindari alone but for all kinds of property. Property must not be sacrosanct when it is held by blackmarketeers and industrialists and taken without compensation when held by simple zamindars of villages.'[50] In a sharp retort reflecting modern capitalist notions of property, Pandit Krishna Chandra Sharma puts Hussain Imam in his place—'The other property a man creates. Land you have not created.'[51]

It is significant that no one in Parliament explicitly opposed the abolition of zamindari. The debate was over whether compensation should be 'just' and 'adequate'. Here was the fledgeling bourgeois state putting in place the notions of legitimate and illegitimate property.

Article 19: Freedom of Expression and the Nation-state

The debate over this amendment reflects most clearly both the disjuncture between civil and political society as well as the concretizing of the national movement into the nation-state. Nehru, while introducing the bill and in his other interventions, repeatedly laid stress on two factors necessitating the need for greater curbs on freedom of speech. The first was the 'moral problem' posed by irresponsible journalism: 'Less responsible news-sheets are full of vulgarity and indecency and falsehood...poisoning the mind of the younger generation, degrading their mental integrity and moral standards. It is for me not a political problem but a moral problem.'[52] More significantly, such newspapers 'peddling filth' are specifically identified as 'small sheets' in Hindi and Urdu 'that do not require much capital'.[53] Others supporting the amendment also refer to 'various language papers' that contain material of which 'any decent journalist would be ashamed'.[54] There are several references to 'the vernacular press' as being full of 'fifth' and 'venom'. The civil society elite with their pedagogical mission are here displayed in all their civilized horror at what goes on in political society in the name of free speech.

The second reason offered is 'great peril and danger to the state'. Nehru makes mysterious references to 'a time of grave danger...', '...a kind of pre-war state of deep crisis', 'a challenge comparable to the challenge of war'. Of course the background is Telengana, where the armed peasant insurrection led by the Communist Party of India (CPI) was in full force. However Nehru makes only a fleeting reference to this—'whether it was in Telengana or wherever in may be.'[55] Later he is more explicit: 'Every state must have the right of…"police power"…Every state has to defend itself against an external enemy or an internal enemy, and freedom is limited for that purpose.'[56]

An impeccably liberal argument opposing these restrictions is made by the Hindu Right-wing leader, S.P. Mookerjee, perhaps because the Hindu Right was so thoroughly crushed and marginalized by the Indian state at the time. 'No country can be governed by force or by coercion,' he argued, pointing out that existing provisions of preventive detention and the exceptions to Article 19(2), as well as the criminal law, were sufficient to handle the situation described by Nehru. Referring to the new provision of restrictions on freedom of expression in the interest of 'friendly relations with foreign countries', Mookerjee demanded to know if this would preclude criticism of foreign countries. More importantly, he declared: 'If I hold that this Partition has been a mistake and has to be annulled some day or the other, why should I not have the right to agitate for it?'[57] In response, Pandit Krishna Chandra Sharma tells him that 'the Constitution is based on the old India being partitioned. So to rise in revolt against Pakistan is to rise in revolt against the Constitution itself.'[58]

A number of members defend the restrictions on the grounds that our 'ignorant and illiterate' population is 'easy to mislead', unlike in other countries where 'long exercise of freedom' has instilled discipline and restraint;[59] that the 'phlegmatic English character' does not 'respond to incitement' as easily as Indians do, so it is not useful to follow the English precedent;[60] that unlike in America, 'our people…are living, some in the 16th century, some in the 17th…'[61]

At the same time, the elite represented in Parliament is suspicious too of the state governments, another manifestation of political society in Partha Chatterjee's sense. Frank Anthony fears that state legislatures might use such power to crush political opposition,[62] and Durgabai that state governments may be influenced by local considerations or by 'the will of the majority party there'.[63] Nehru agrees that he too would have liked such a limitation, both in the interest of uniformity as well as because, as he disarmingly confided, '…it is possible for a State assembly sometime to do something which you and I might not approve of.'[64]

It is left to B.R. Ambedkar to point out that since 'public order' is covered by this amendment, which is under state legislative jurisdiction, either this amendment must give powers equally to Centre and states, or the amendment itself would have to be ratified by state legislatures, which would delay the amendment considerably.[65] Thus he refuses to participate in the debate on the terms that have been set, that is, whether or not state governments can be trusted not to misuse the amendment. Again, it is instructive to look at the reasons why Ambedkar supported these restrictions on the freedom of expression. He makes no reference at all either to immorality or to the need to protect state security. Rather, he focuses on 'public order' and 'incitement to offence'. Specifically, he gives instances and 'concrete cases': social boycott of Scheduled Castes by caste Hindus in a particular village and the prevention of a Scheduled Caste person from using a well. He asked if the definition of incitement to violence should be extended to cover situations 'where one community does something in order to harm or injure another community'.[66]

There are then, at least three positions on freedom of speech during the debate on the First Amendment, none of which is easily amenable to a simple recuperation along democratic/anti-democratic or liberal/anti-liberal lines. The three positions are Nehru's authoritarian statism, Mookerjee's classic liberalism, and Ambedkar's severe distrust of unrestricted freedom of expression in a society marked by extreme inequality and inhuman oppression. Nevertheless, Ambedkar is not unproblematically seduced by the statist argument, as is clear from his refusal to back Nehru's reasons for the amendment. What we see here is a playing out of our post-colonial dilemma at a historical moment when the nation-state is still imbued with the legitimacy of the anti-imperialist struggle, but is in the process of consolidating itself along lines that show a sharp break with its earlier radical agenda.

Article 15: The State and Community

Here lies the root of our post-colonial misery: not in our inability to think out new forms of the modern community but in our surrender to the old forms of the modern state. If the nation is an imagined community and if nations must also take the form of states, then our theoretical language must allow us to talk about community and state at the same time. I do not think our present theoretical language allows us to do this.[67]

Ambedkar was one of those who did attempt the task of talking about community and state at the same time. In a study of Ambedkar's turn to Buddhism, Martin Fuchs says, 'He pursued what one might term a counter-modern modernist project.' In other words, in the modernist style he thought of religions as representing competing interpretations of the world, and used the yardstick of universalist reason to subject them to a test. However, he did this not in order to disown religion but to develop what Fuchs calls a 'civic religion'. Buddhist *dhamma* was for him a way of replacing religion with an ethics of social action. Dhamma becomes a 'post-religious religion' in a search for 'a community religion of self-respect'.[68] For Ambedkar, then, the Dalit identity was borne not by individual citizens but by a community, and mass conversion to Buddhism was the way to offer Hinduism an irrefutable challenge.

The rights of this community had to be protected by the state, for society was corrupt and violent. Thus, as Upendra Baxi points out, Ambedkar departed from the contemporary liberal paradigm of rights and justice. That is, rights borne by the community are not constraints on the power of the state; rather, they are legal entitlements protected by the state that constrain other members of society. The state, therefore, had the power to redefine the cultural practices of society. In developing this understanding Ambedkar anticipated later developments in theories of rights.[69]

It is this understanding that animates the amendment to Article 15 that would enable the government to make special provisions for backward classes. Nehru outlined a complex understanding of group rights as defensible in a democracy

The whole conception of the Fundamental Rights is the protection of individual liberty and freedom...That might be said to be the dominating idea of the 19th century...Nevertheless...other additional ideas came into the field that are represented by our Directive Principles of State Policy. If in the protection of individual liberty you protect also individual or group inequality, then you come into conflict [with the Directive Principles].

In an interesting definition, he characterizes Directive Principles as 'representing a dynamic movement towards a certain objective', while

Fundamental Rights represent 'something static, to preserve certain rights which exist'.[70]

Nehru took pains during the debate to establish that enacting special provisions for backward classes is not 'communalism',[71] a charge made by several members.[72] Nevertheless, in a revealing aside, he says, 'I do not particularly like the words "backward class of citizens". What I mean is this: it is the backward individual citizen that we should help. Why should we brand groups and classes into backward and forward?' At this, several MPs interject, 'That is the point.'[73] K. T. Shah argues that by using the phrase backward 'classes', 'citizens' retreat to the background.[74] Nevertheless, uncomfortable though he and others were with relinquishing the language of individual citizenship rights—in this context, in effect a mask for privilege—the nature of participation in the anti-imperialist struggles and the pressures from political society ensured that community identity had a central place in the Constitution.

Ambedkar spells it out when he responds to arguments complaining that special provisions for backward classes will discriminate against those from other castes. Syamnandan Sahaya for example, argues that the amendment, by making special arrangements for backward classes, violates Article 29 (2), which prohibits discrimination on grounds of castes.[75] Ambedkar states categorically, '...it is impossible to make any reservation which would not result in excluding somebody who has a caste...[T]here is no Hindu who has not a caste...'[76]

It is interesting that while the politics of the anti-imperialist movement never centred around the individual and individual rights, there is a continuous discomfort expressed in Parliament at the marginalizing of individual rights and individual identity. In these debates there is an implied model of democracy at work, which 'we' must try to match, or at least offer reasons for not matching. For instance, Nehru says, referring to the Madras High Court order which struck down the government Order reserving seats on the basis of caste, that from one point of view it was a valid judgement because '...if communities as such are brought into the picture, it does go against certain explicit or implied provisions of the constitution'. I have emphasized the words 'or implied' here because Nehru seems to be suggesting that if an individualistic bias is not immediately visible in the Constitution, it must be implicit, because constitutions are supposed to centre on the individual citizen. Nevertheless, he continues, despite this implied provision 'we have to deal with the situation where for a variety of causes for which the present generation is not to blame...there are groups, classes, individual, communities... who are backward.' Even more telling is the hope he expresses, that eventually, every individual will think, not of his group or caste but of the 'larger community'. That is, his ideal situation ultimately, is not one where individual citizens are actors, but where they form another community that transcends smaller groupings, building the community of the nation.[77]

CONCLUSION

In this interpretation of the First Amendment Act, I have tried to demonstrate that the three main amendments that it made to the Constitution are intrinsically linked, and reveal three different aspects of the nation-building project of India's modernizing elites. I have suggested that we would find it difficult to locate the fault-lines very clearly across liberal/anti-liberal, secular/communal, or democratic/anti-democratic lines. For the logic that operates is the logic of 'our' modernity, of the post-colonial bourgeois state—caught in the throes of the passive revolution, emerging as *nation-state* from the *national movement*, and trying to work out the tension between the liberal theory of the individual and the post-colonial experience of 'incomplete' individuation and lived community identity, all this within a democratic framework which interweaves modernization, industrialization and secularism into one strand.

How do we understand the disjuncture between the Supreme Court's continuous attempts to prioritize individual rights and Parliament's insistence on other bearers of rights—the community, the larger society, the nation-state? It seems to me that the judges of the Supreme Court, being unconstrained by democratic accountability, remained untouched by the pressures of 'political society'. The Supreme Court could therefore continue to uphold an impeccably 'liberal' version of rights such as it imagined to be prevalent in the 'civil society' of the West. Parliament, on the contrary, had both to be directed by political society as well as to control it. What we see in the First Amendment Act is the logic of this situation.

NOTES

1. I understand 'text' to mean simply any delimited space that we may set out to examine and interpret—this could be an event, a social or political process; or a cultural phenomenon, written words, a film.

2. Roland Barthes, *Image, Music, Text* (New York: Hill and Wang, 1977), p. 146.

3. Ibid., p. 148.

4. Rajeev Bhargava, *Secularism and Its Critics* (Delhi: Oxford University Press, 2005); Neera Chandhoke, *Beyond Secularism: The Rights of Religious Minorities,* (Delhi: Oxford University Press, 2000); Sarah Joseph, *Interrogating Culture: Critical Perspectives on Contemporary Social Theory* (New Delhi: Sage Publications, 1998).

5. D.D. Basu, *Introduction to the Constitution of India* (New Delhi: Prentice-Hall of India Pvt. Ltd, 1998).

6. Shibanikinkar Chaube, *Constitutent Assembly of India: Springboard of Revolution* (New Delhi: People's Publishing House, 1973); Sobhanlal Datta Gupta, *Justice and the Political Order in India* (Calcutta: K.P. Bagchi and Company, 1979).

7. Sudipta Kaviraj, 'Democracy and Social Equality', in Francine Frankel, Zoya Hasan, Rajeev Bhargava, and Balveer Arora (eds), *Transforming India* (Delhi: Oxford University Press 2000), pp. 90–1.

8. Sudipta Kaviraj, 'Dilemmas of Democratic Development in India', in Adrian Leftwich (ed.), *Democracy and Development: Theory and Practice* (Cambridge: Polity Press, 1996), p. 132.

9. Sudipta Kaviraj, 'Democracy and Development in India', in Amiya Bagchi (ed.), *Democracy and Development* (London: St Martin's Press, 1995), p. 99.

10. *Lok Sabha Debates,* Part II, vol. XII, 18 May 1951, columns 9070–1, 9074.

11. Ashis Nandy, 'The Politics of Secularism and the Recovery of Religious Tolerance', in Veena Das (ed.), *Mirrors of Violence: Communities, Riots and Survivors* (Delhi: Oxford University Press, 1990).

12. Nivedita Menon, 'Women and Citizenship', in Partha Chatterjee (ed.), *Wages of Freedom* (Delhi: Oxford University Press, 1998).

13. Jawaharlal Nehru, introducing the first amendment bill. *Lok Sabha Debates,* Part II, vol. XII, column 8830, 16 May 1951.

14. S.P. Mookerjee, *Lok Sabha Debates,* Part II, vol. XII, 16 May 1951, column 8838; Kamath, column 8916.

15. Shri Kamath, *Lok Sabha Debates,* 17 May 1951, Part II, vol. XII, columns 8912–13.

16. Sunil Khilnani, *The Idea of India* (London: Hamish Hamilton, 1997), p. 26.

17. Ibid., p. 28.

18. Ibid., p. 34.

19. Ibid. Sumit Sarkar and Rajeev Bhargava offer an alternative reading of Indian democracy's emphasis on universal adult franchise which they see as remarkable, both for its break with colonial practice as well as with Europe in general, where class and gender limitations to suffrage took over a century of struggles to end. Bhargava emphasizes the nationalist acceptance of universal suffrage as a significant break both from colonial rule and from traditional Indian society. Both attribute this largely to 'the sheer sweep of mass movements' and to 'the growth of the idea of the nation'. Sumit Sarkar, 'Indian Democracy: The Historical Inheritance', in Atul Kohli (ed.), *The Success of*

India's Democracy (Cambridge: Cambridge University Press, 2001), p. 30; Rajeev Bhargava, 'Democratic Vision of a New Republic: India 1950' in Frankel et al. (eds), *Transforming India*, p. 51. Thus what Khilnani understands as arising from lack of informed understanding—that is, the inability of the Indian elites to comprehend the fear of the masses that characterized the European bourgeoisie—is seen by Sarkar and Bhargava, correctly, in my opinion, to be a feature of the particular configuration of democracy in India—that is, the anti-imperialist impulse of Indian moves towards democracy.

20. Khilnani, *The Idea of India*, p. 36.
21. Rajeev Bhargava, 'Democratic Vision of a New Republic'.
22. Gurpreet Mahajan, *Identities and Rights: Aspects of Liberal Democracy in India* (Delhi: Oxford University Press, 1998), pp. 155–8.
23. Ibid., pp. 4–6.
24. Here Sarkar seems to be using 'postcolonial' simply in the sense of 'after' colonialism. I use post-colonial in a different, more specific sense later.
25. Sarkar, 'Indian Democracy', p. 25.
26. Ibid., pp. 23, 46.
27. Ibid., p. 24.
28. Ibid., pp. 26–7.
29. Ibid., p. 26.
30. We may note in passing that even in Europe there may have been just 'one blissful moment in the long history of capitalist development', after 1689 in the 'unique historical constellation in Great Britain', that the public sphere was actually practised. Jürgen Habermas, *The Structural Transformation of the Public Sphere* (Cambridge, MA: MIT Press, 1989), p. 79. Otherwise, Habermas's outlining of conditions for the survival of a public sphere that can only be met by advanced capitalist countries has come in for critical attention, for in this understanding both the growth of monopolies as well as of the labour movement threaten the public sphere. In this context, Habermas's assertion that 'Laws passed under the "pressure of the street" could hardly be understood any longer as embodying the reasonable consensus of publicly debating private persons' is telling. Cited by Warren Montag from *Strukturwandel der Offenlichkeit* (Neuwided: Hermann Luchterhand Verlag, 1962), p. 147. See Warren Montag, 'The Pressure of the Street: Habermas's Fear of the Masses', in Mike Hill and Warren Montag (eds), *Masses, Classes and the Public Sphere* (London: Verso, 2000).
31. From the title of chapter 11 of Partha Chatterjee, *A Possible India: Essays in Political Criticism* (Delhi: Oxford University Press, 1997).
32. Editorial note by Bill Ashcroft, Gareth Griffiths, and Helen Tiffin in *The Postcolonial Studies Reader* (London: Routledge, 1999), p. 117.
33. The following discussion is based on Partha Chatterjee, 'Beyond the Nation? Or Within?', *Economic and Political Weekly*, 4–11 January 1997, pp. 30–4, where Chatterjee initially worked out this distinction.
34. Upendra Baxi, 'Constitutionalism as a Site of State Formative Practices', *Cardozo Law Review*, vol. 21, February 2000, no. 4, pp. 1184–5.

35. Sarkar, 'Indian Democracy' pp. 27–8.
36. The example of a democratic secularism that Sarkar gives is of sixteenth-century France, which does not help us address the Indian dilemma. Ibid., p. 33.
37. Chantal Moufee, 'Politics and the Limits of Liberalism', in Chantal Moufee, *The Return of the Political* (London: Verso, 1993), p. 140.
38. For details, see Granville Austin's scholarly yet lively account in Granville Austin, *Working a Democratic Constitution: The Indian Experience* (Delhi: Oxford University Press, 1999), pp. 40–2, 69–86.
39. *Lok Sabha Debates*, Part II, vol. XII, 16 May 1951, columns 8815–16.
40. Sudipta Kaviraj, 'A Critique of the Passive Revolution', *Economic and Political Weekly*, Annual Number, 1988. Since the 1980s the economic policy has changed dramatically, but in this essay we focus on the earlier moment.
41. In Kaviraj, 'Critique of the Passive Revolution', written in 1988. Fundamental changes in economic policy since the 1980s reflect developments in the nature of the bourgeoisie, which is it not possible to go into here.
42. Ibid., pp. 48–55.
43. *Lok Sabha Debates*, Part II, vol. XII, 17 May 1951, column 8906.
44. Ibid., column 8901.
45. Ibid., column 8952.
46. Ibid., 16 May 1951, columns 8830–1.
47. Ibid., 18 May 1951 columns 9083–4.
48. Ibid., 30 May 1951, columns 9685, 9687.
49. Cited in Austin, *Working a Democratic Constitution*, p. 104.
50. *Lok Sabha Debates*, Part II, vol. XII, 17 May 1951, column 8965.
51. Ibid., column 8996.
52. Ibid., 16 May 1951, column 8823.
53. Ibid., 31 May 1951, column 9797.
54. T.N. Singh, Ibid., 2 June 1951, column 10070.
55. Ibid., columns 8823–9.
56. Ibid., 18 May 1951, column 9073.
57. Ibid., 16 May 1951, columns 8840–2, 8846.
58. Ibid., 17 May 1951, columns 8894–5.
59. Pandit Thakur Das Bhargava, ibid., 30 May 1951, column 9717.
60. Rev D'Souza, ibid., column 9692.
61. Mirza, Ibid., 2 June 1951, column 10064.
62. Ibid., 31 May 1951, column 9790.
63. Ibid., 1 June 1951, column 9844–5.
64. Ibid., 31 May 1951, column 9790.
65. Ibid., 1 June 1951, column 9861–2.
66. Ibid., 9867–8.
67. Partha Chatterjee, 'Whose Imagined Community', in Partha Chattejee, *The Nation and its Fragments* (Delhi: Oxford University Press, 1995), p. 11.
68. Martin Fuchs, 'A Religion for Civil Society? Ambedkar's Buddhism, the Dalit Issue and the Imagination of Emergent Possibilities', in Vasudha Dalmia,

Angelika Malinar and Martin Christof (eds), *Charisma and Canon: Essays on the Religious History of the Indian Subcontinent* (Delhi: Oxford University Press, 2001), pp. 252–60.

69. Upendra Baxi, 'Emancipation as Justice', in Upendra Baxi and Bhikhu Parekh (eds), *Crisis and Change in Contemporary India* (Delhi: Sage Publications, 1995), pp. 143–4.

70. *Lok Sabha Debates*, Part II, vol. XII, columns 8820–1.

71. Ibid., 16 May 1951, column 8821.

72. Thakur Das Bhargava, ibid., 17 May 1951, column 8894; Syamnandan Sahaya, ibid., column 8929.

73. Ibid., 18 May 1951, column 9084.

74. Ibid., 29 May 1951, column 9642.

75. Ibid., 17 May 1951, column 8929.

76. Ibid., 18 May 1951, columns 9006–7.

77. Ibid., 29 May 1951, columns 9616–7.

9

Democracy and Constitutionalism*

Sanjay Palshikar

On 17 September 1949, after more than two years of deliberations on what eventually was to be the Constitution of free and independent India, the members of the Constituent Assembly took up for consideration Article 368 (Article 304 of the Draft Constitution) which dealt with amendment procedure.[1] It was late in the day and the speeches had to be short, and yet, given the importance of the article, members could not have simply moved on to the next item without some of them expressing their reservations about making the Constitution too rigid. If we can change our mind so often during the relatively short span of constitution-making, why not leave similar latitude to the future parliament, H.V. Kamath asked. P.S. Deshmukh had a similar view. He said that for all the time we have spent on the exercise, there are still some defects in the Constitution and many more will become apparent once it becomes operational. Unless we make it easy enough for the future parliaments to make suitable changes, they might discard the whole Constitution. Brajeshwar Prasad agreed and said that unless the Constitution is flexible enough to allow for progressive legislation, there might be revolution or anarchy in the country. A moral dimension was added by Mahavir Tyagi. Citing the maxim that 'the earth belongs to all the living equally, and the dead have neither the power nor the rights over it', he asserted that it is morally indefensible for one generation to bind the next. An unalterable Constitution is 'practically a violence committed on the coming generation'.

* I would like to thank Upendra Baxi, and the late Satyaranjan Sathe for their suggestions and G. Sandhya for her help in making available to me some of the material used in this article.

There were also challenges to the presumed representativeness of the assembly. Given that its members were elected on a restricted and indirect franchise, could it claim superiority over any future parliament, H.V. Kamath wondered. Mahavir Tyagi went to the extent of saying that the Constitution they were giving finishing touches to was essentially a Constitution given by the Congress party. In fairness to future non-Congress governments, should we not make it flexible? Several members referred to the suggestion Nehru had made earlier that an initial period of five years of flexibility should be provided. In spite of all these points raised and fears expressed, the Draft Article got approved after Ambedkar's clarifications. He pointed out that there were different degrees of rigidity/flexibility applicable to different parts of the Constitution, depending on the nature of the provisions. This was eminently wise and prudent. But he also said something which, on another day, could have generated controversy. Accepting that the assembly was perhaps not representative owing to the limited suffrage on which it was based, he stressed that it was not for that reason lacking in wisdom. In fact in this respect it might prove to be better than future parliament. 'Power and knowledge do not go together', he said.

Even this brief exchange makes it clear that the relationship between democracy (variously defined as self-rule, majority rule, etc.) and constitutionalism (limited government) is complex and open to many competing constructions. Is there a necessary opposition between the two? There is, by definition, if, following Elster,[2] we take democracy to mean majority rule and constitutionalism to be a set of counter-majoritarian devices. That, however, will be too simple a resolution. In the Anglo-American legal-political tradition, several fascinating arguments and counter-arguments have been made and we need to take note of that debate, if only because of the debt that our 'founding fathers' owed to that thinking. After having looked at the relationship between constitutionalism and democracy in abstract terms, we need to move on to a specific case. This is necessary because we need to be sensitive to what a given democratic rule is about, what is its nature, what it is seeking to do. Constitutionalism, understood as the theory and practice of procedural and substantive curbs on government, cannot be fully comprehended unless we go into the details of these constraints in a given, concrete case, unless we ask what these curbs are. In the next section I will first take up the rather abstract discussions, and then move on to the Indian case in the section after that.

I

A whole range of arguments have been made against the constitutionalist ideal of a basic or founding legal document that will be regarded as binding for its polity not only by the present generation but by the future ones as well.[3] To start with, there is an argument of a purely conceptual kind, made by Hobbes. Assuming that constitutionalism refers to self-imposed limits, the question is whether self-binding is possible. 'A binding promise requires two parties and cannot be performed by one party alone.' Explaining why 'no man can be obliged to himself', Hobbes says: '...he can release himself at his own pleasure, and he that can do this is already actually free. Whence it is plain, that the city is not tied to...[its own] civil laws.'[4] Clearly, Hobbes is taking a non-moral sense of 'binding', and arguing why self-binding is impossible. But if morality is possible at all, then pre-commitment is also possible.

But is it fair for one generation to give a commitment not just on its own behalf but also on behalf of future generations? There is an argument in Locke and Hume of the 'no-father-can-bind-his-son' variety. Further, Tom Paine was essentially following his illustrious predecessors when he said that every generation must be free to act for itself. His reason was that not doing so will amount to shirking the responsibility to make important and at times difficult choices. Thomas Jefferson denied there was any historical continuity across generations: 'by the law of nature, one generation is to another as one independent nation is to another'.[5]

Rousseau's rejection of pre-commitment is different, but given the context of his social contract philosophy, it is also quite understandable. For Rousseau, the individual's participation in the making and adoption of a 'regime-founding constitution' (Holmes's words) has deep moral and psychological significance. The individual will be deprived of this ritualistic experience if he were to simply follow a constitution inherited from his ancestors.

In Paine and Jefferson we also find ideas of change and progress invoked to argue that it is important that each generation looks at its situation, and, in the light of its knowledge, makes its choices without remaining shackled by a possibly outdated constitution.

Some of these points can be readily countered, and they have been, with some plausibility. On the alleged injustice of the father binding the son, it has been pointed out that Locke himself argued that if you inherit

assets from the earlier generation, then you also inherit obligations or
liabilities. Moreover it is important to bear in mind that the idea of one
generation being followed by the next in some neat and orderly succession
is empirically untenable. Generations overlap, the young and the old co-
exist, and therefore, 'the living have no right to repeal, at set intervals,
the legacy of the past.'[6] There is also the argument, to be found in Locke,
that constraints (here, constraints of the constitutionalist kind), don't
simply bind; they make freedom possible by giving it a direction. Apart
from such philosophical arguments, there are pragmatic or prudential
defences of constitutionalism, mainly to be found in James Madison. He
suggests a kind of an inter-generational division of labour: if a
constitution has already been made by our forefathers, we can profitably
spend our energies on doing something else. 'Because it is relatively hard
to change, a constitution can disencumber...the present generation'.[7] If
the hard job of laying down procedures and establishing institutions has
already been done (and presumably in not too unsatisfactory a manner),
then we can better achieve 'our present goals'. Frequent constitution-
making (or plebiscites) can be disruptive and can threaten democracy
itself. On the other hand, if we decide that we are not going to tinker
with the 'rules of the game', then we will be forced to learn the
democratic art of bargaining.

It is often argued that being tied down to a document amounts to
compromising the popular sovereignty which the legislature represents.
There are two different ideas being yoked together here, and both need
to be scrutinized. One is the idea of the absoluteness of sovereignty which
brooks no limits on itself, some sort of an agency free from all external
constraints whatsoever. Much depends here on what is to count as
external. As for internal constraints, the whole tradition of conceptualizing freedom from Locke to Kant has stressed that to be free is
to be self-legislating. There is also a late medieval theological argument,
mentioned by Holmes, that God's capacity to bind Himself is 'an
expression of His awesome freedom and power'. Omnipotence would
be a strange thing indeed if it were helpless against its own power. Nor is
omnipotence truly manifested by the omnipotent power exercising itself
all the time without any reserve. Bodin echoes the theological argument
when he argues that by committing himself to certain basic norms and
rules the sovereign is not diminishing his sovereignty, but that this is rather
the strategy by which he asserts his will 'most effectively'.[8]

That sovereignty is absolute is a modern idea. In the Middle Ages, 'sovereign' simply meant 'superior', which was also its etymological meaning. Any superior was, in relation to his dependents, a 'sovereign'. And the superior too had a...sovereign. In this way society appeared as "a great chain of duties".[9] Even those who believed that the king's sovereignty was absolute held that it was subject to the laws of God, the natural law, and the fundamental laws of the state. de Jouvenel says that in modern times secularization, legal positivism, and democratic ideals have removed those shackles and made it look literally absolute.[10] Unless we accept that will to be free, must have principles governing it (principles derived philosophically or historically)—the dilemma of how a sovereign can be prevented from willing what he ought not to will—will remain unresolved.

The other idea implicit in the notion of sovereignty is that of a single unitary will. Holmes[11] is right in distinguishing between 'voluntaristic democracy' and 'deliberative democracy', because this distinction helps us ask whether the will we are talking about is pre-existing or something which has been 'arrived at'. If the will is already there, all that needs to be done is to have representatives as delegates of the people who will translate people's will into decisions. A constitution which lays down procedural and substantive prohibitions will then indeed be 'anti-democratic'. But if democracy is a deliberative process and representatives are more than just the agents of the people carrying out their wishes, then the constitutional requirements of freedoms, rights, and procedures will in fact make crystallization of that will possible in the first place.

Taking a cue from Holmes, one can question the very idea of 'the people' and argue that it is the constitutionally secured political processes (like canvassing, elections, debates in the public sphere, etc.) which bring into existence the entity called 'the people', the plain empirical existence of which is far from unproblematic. Of course revolutionary upsurges and plebiscites also arguably manifest people in their corporate mode, but whether these are 'genuinely' democratic manifestations of 'the people' is a matter circularly related to (or better perhaps, already presupposed by) the conception of democracy we prefer.

If these arguments are persuasive (and I think they are), then we can accept Holmes's suggestion that 'constitutionalism and democracy are mutually supportive'.[12] The problem with this assertion, however, is that it comes in the form of a strong generalization. I would, therefore, like to proceed with a qualified version of the suggestion—namely, that constitutionalism can have consequences that are positive for democracy. With this orientation guiding my enquiry, I would now like to proceed to discuss the changes in the constitutional status of the right to property in the Indian case. Protection of this cardinal liberal right has been central to liberal constitutionalism and therefore its weakening in the Indian case can be read either as the triumph of majoritarianism or, alternatively, as an assertion of the will of the people untrammelled by the Constitution and by the intrusive judiciary. Avoiding both the readings and the respective prescriptions that would follow from them, I would like to suggest the possibility of a different kind of constitutionalism, one that institutionalizes concerns and anxieties regarding the strategies of development and growth being followed in India (and indeed elsewhere). For convenience's sake we can call it environmental constitutionalism. That there can be such a constitutionalism is not hard to show. What is crucial for the position taken here is to show that it can be harmonious with democracy. Demonstrating that requires recourse to abstract arguments again—something that I will attempt briefly in the last section of this article.

II

In the legal history of modern India, constitutional-legal provisions regarding the right to property have gone through many changes. But all these changes have proceeded in one direction—namely, that of a steady weakening of the constitutional status of that right. The Government of India Act, 1935, had provided that 'no person could be deprived of his property except by authority of law and that no legislature could authorize the compulsory acquisition of property unless the law provided for the payment of compensation or the principles on which it was to be paid.'[13] It may be noted that the formulation of the right here is significantly different from the Fifth Amendment of the American Constitution which says that no person shall be 'deprived of life, liberty, or property without due process of law; nor shall private property be taken for public use without just compensation.'[14]

In the years immediately preceding the drafting of the Constitution and within the Constituent Assembly, all attempts to borrow expressions like 'due process' and 'just compensation' were discouraged or defeated and the state's legitimate powers to take citizens' property were sought to be secured from the judiciary. The First Amendment (1951) was brought in partly to protect the land reform acts of various states, while the Fourth Amendment (1955) sought to make the adequacy of compensation to be paid in the event of confiscation non-justiciable. The Twenty-fifth Amendment (1971) substituted the word 'compensation' by the word 'amount', because the Supreme Court had held that 'compensation' amounted to 'just compensation'. And finally the Forty-fourth Amendment (1978) made the right to property an ordinary, that is, non-fundamental legal right.

Before going into some of the details of this history and drawing implications from it, it might be helpful to take a quick look at what is called the Doctrine of Eminent Domain, which the Right to Property that the original, unamended Indian Constitution implicitly relied on. No modern state is conceivable without the doctrine of eminent domain, whatever the qualifications introduced by judicial interpretations of it. 'The right to take private property for public use does not depend on constitutional provisions, but is an attribute of sovereignty.'[15] So that is what the doctrine asserts: 'The right of every government to appropriate otherwise than by taxation and its police powers, private property for public use.'[16] Grotius, who may have invented the very term 'eminent domain', has this to say: 'the property of the subjects is under the eminent domain of the state; so that the state...may use, and even alienate and destroy such property; not only in the case of external necessity...but for ends of public utility, to which end those who founded civil society must be supposed to have intended that private ends should give way.'[17]

But the eminent domain powers of the state are to be distinguished from those where it can take or destroy property without compensation. 'Making good the loss' is what is distinctive about it. The English law, most of the American constitutions, and most of the judicial decisions in those countries insist on compensation. The necessity of compensation is 'firmly imbedded in American constituional law' and courts generally declare as unconstitutional the statute which 'fails to provide for compensation'.[18]

The 'taking' involved in compulsory acquisition is of course for the common good. *American Jurisprudence* spells it out clearly: 'The law of eminent domain is fashioned out of the conflict between people's interest in public projects and the principle of indemnity to the landowner...It means nothing more or less than an inherent political right, founded on common necessity and interest, of appropriating the property of individual members of the community to the great necessities of the whole community.'[19] The Supreme Court of India in *Ram Chand* v. *Union of India* (1994)[20] makes a similar statement:

The power to acquire private property for public use is an attribute of sovereignty and is essential to the existence of a government. The power of eminent domain was recognized on the principle that the sovereign state can always acquire the property of a citizen without the owner's consent...the right to acquire an interest in land compulsorily has assumed increasing importance as a result of requirement of such land more and more every day, for different public purposes and to implement the promises made by the framers of the Constitution to the people of India.

So what distinguishes an arbitrary confiscation or expropriation from compulsory acquisition is that the 'taking' is for a public purpose and involves compensation. In this, the jurists are, I think, suggesting constitutionalist curbs on legislatures and executives. Governments are free to acquire property, but whenever there is a grievance regarding either of these two vital elements, the judiciary comes into the picture.

The original, that is, the unamended Indian Constitution's property-related provisions implied reliance on the doctrine of eminent domain in its classic form. It guaranteed that no person shall be deprived of his property except by 'the authority of law'(Article 31 [1]); and it made the compulsory acquisition conditional on a public purpose and on payment of compensation (Article 31 [2]).

Article 31 went through a most gruelling discussion in the Constituent Assembly, lasting more than two years. In fact, most of the discussion was around compensation: its quantum, form, and its openness to judicial scrutiny.[21] The formulation of the right went through many drafts and finally the members of the Assembly settled on a version which, while protecting the owners of property from 'predatory legislation', also ensured—or sought to ensure—trouble-free passage of 'socially beneficent measures'.[22] It is another matter that these hopes and intentions ran counter to the judiciary's understanding of what 'compensation' meant and what relation the acquisition-related article (Article 31) had with the structurally vital Part III of the Constitution. Successive governments reacted by resorting to constitutional amendments, which in turn attracted judicial scrutiny, till, through the Forty-second and Forty-fourth amendments, the government's acquisition of property was placed beyond the reach of the judiciary.

The successive constitutional amendments have changed the status of the Right to Property completely and correspondingly increased state powers to 'take' property. Right to Property is no longer a Fundamental Right and therefore does not enjoy special judicial protection. Nor is the state now constitutionally obliged, barring a few exceptions, to pay any compensation.[23] All that the Constitution assures now, through the new Article 300 A, is that no person shall be deprived of his property 'save by authority of law'. This is a phantom of both the right to property in the Government of India Act of 1935 (a Fundamental Right there) and the very first formulation of this right in the Constituent Assembly: 'No property...shall be taken or acquired for public use unless the law provides for the payment of compensation...and specifies the principles on which and the manner in which the compensation is to be made.'[24]

What weighed ultimately with the majority in the assembly was that legislatures, as Nehru said, 'must not be interfered with by the courts of law in such measures of social reforms'.[25] 'Measures of social reforms' obviously referred to the Zamindari Abolition Bills, either pending or being contemplated.[26] Austin and Merillat have given a detailed account of how landlords were seen by many of the Constituent Assembly members as exploitative, pro-British, and, worse, inhibiting agrarian productivity. Their removal was high on the list of the Congress party's priorities. It is true that the Congress election manifesto of 1945 spoke of 'state ownership or control of a wide variety of industries and businesses', along with 'the removal of intermediaries between the peasant and the state';[27] and the Industrial Policy Resolution of the Union Cabinet (1948) asserted the 'inherent right of the state to acquire industrial undertakings' (with 'equitable compensation' in both the cases).[28] But within the Constituent Assembly, it was the property of the zamindars which was being openly or obliquely talked about. A vital distinction between acquiring land for 'public use' and taking away land from the zamindars as part of social reform or social engineering was drawn by both Nehru and Ambedkar at different points.[29]

It is significant that throughout this period, 'compensation' was consistently added as a clause or a qualifier to all the resolutions, drafts, bills, etc. There were radical voices, within the Constituent Assembly and outside, which wondered whether the zamindars deserved any compensation at all. But expropriation was not seriously considered. Some compensation there would definitely be, it was being assured time and again, but the fairness of it should not be the judiciary's concern. The anxiety expressed by several members of the assembly was that the courts, 'manned by irremovable Judiciary not so sensitive to public needs in the social or economic sphere' would frustrate the government's progressive legislation.

I have gone in these details here because a reading of various documents, speeches, bills, and, finally, the provisions of the original Constitution shows that most of the proposals regarding property were operating within the scope of the eminent domain doctrine. But the unexpected incursions of the judiciary made the legislatures build protection around itself, justified as protection of 'parliamentary supremacy'. This trend became stronger in later years (for varied reasons) till, with the Forty-second and Forty-fourth amendments, all the judicial fetters were removed. It is possible to see these developments as a victory for the legislature, representing the will of the people; and within the logic of the established legal-political discourse there is a lot to be said for this reading. Way back, during the framing of the Constitution, Nehru had said: 'Within limits no judge and no Supreme Court can make itself a Third Chamber. No Supreme Court and no judiciary can stand in judgement over the sovereign will of Parliament representing the will of the entire community. If we go wrong here and there it can point it out, but in the ultimate analysis, where the future of the community is concerned, no judiciary can come in the way...'[30]

This finger-wagging, as we know, did not deter the judiciary from intruding on the means being used to shape the 'future of the community'. The question is whether the Parliament's victory was won at the cost of the doctrine of eminent domain. Usha Ramanathan believes that the state's power under eminent domain to compulsorily acquire land has been reinforced by the abolition of the Right to Property as a Fundamental Right.[31] The new provision (Article 300 A) says, 'No person shall be deprived of his property save by the authority of law.' It does not speak of 'due process of law', which would have brought in the judiciary. The relevant statutes, like the Land Acquisition Act (1894), have clauses on 'public purpose' and 'compensation', but that does not amount to a constitutional guarantee. What has happened, I think, is that while the state's power to acquire land remains undiminished, it is removed from the constitutional discourse, which is a historically evolved discourse, of 'citizens' having to make 'sacrifices' for the 'common good'. Shorn of these wrappings, the power stands naked, as an expression of the legislature's will.

A fairly predictable response to these happenings would be to argue for the restoration of the Right to Property to its earlier status of a

Fundamental Right and reviving, through that, the doctrine of eminent domain. But, instead of that, what I propose to do is to explore the utility of the Public Trust Doctrine, invoked by our Supreme Court in a recent case.

III

The Supreme Court case *M.C. Mehta* v. *Kamal Nath and Others*[32] dealt with the case of a private company, Span Motels Private Ltd., which had got on lease some government land situated along the Kullu-Manali road on the bank of the river Beas. The lease, signed in 1981, was for a period of 99 years and the company was permitted to put up a motel in the leased area subject to some environmental conditions. In due course the company encroached on the land around the lease area and rearranged its topography. It also dredged the river basin. The management claimed that this was done to protect the motel from the annual floods of the Beas, and that they were doing nothing more than restoring the river to its original course. These eco-friendly interventions in the surroundings and the encroachment were regularized when Kamal Nath was the environment minister. Leela Nath, a member of Kamal Nath's family, happened to be the main shareholder in the motel company. The motel management, in its affidavit to the court, tried to establish everybody's innocence by stating that the proposal for regularization of the encroachment went through various appropriate levels of the government all the way to the prime minister, bypassing Kamal Nath. The implication was that he did not deal with the file, and so he had no occasion to influence the decision. But the court was not impressed by this show of integrity. It quashed the order regularizing the encroachment, slapped a fine on the motel 'by way of cost for the restitution of the environment and ecology of the area', and ordered the reversal of various changes in the surroundings brought about by the motel management.

In the course of its judgement, the court observed that the notion 'that the public has a right to expect certain lands and natural areas to retain their natural characteristics is finding its way into the law of the land'. Referring to the ecological principle that our world is finite, it lamented that 'current legal doctrine' rarely takes environmental constraints into account (para. 23). The court went on to expound the 'Doctrine of Public Trust', apparently to fill that void. Its order to the motel to pay compensation was based on the 'Precautionary Principle' and the 'Polluter Pays Principle', both of which had already been established by the Supreme Court in the *Vellore Citizens' Welfare Forum* v. *Union of India* case.[33] What was new was the invoking of the Trust Doctrine. Stating categorically that the doctrine is part of the law of the land (para 39.1), the judgement holds the Himachal Pradesh government guilty of a 'breach of public trust' in leasing ecologically fragile land to the motel 'purely for commercial purposes' (para 36).

The State is the trustee of all the natural resources which are by nature meant for public use and enjoyment. Public at large is the beneficiary of the sea-shore, running waters, airs, forests and ecologically fragile lands. The State as a trustee is under a legal duty to protect the natural resources. These resources meant for public use cannot be converted into private ownership (para. 34).

The court's construction of the doctrine, drawing extensively on the American precedents, English Common Law, and an exposition of the doctrine by Joseph Sax in the *Michigan Law Review* (1970),[34] can be summarized as follows:

1. Under the Roman Law, certain things like air, water, forests, etc., are 'either owned by no one or by everyone'. The government is the trustee of those natural resources, with people at large being the beneficiaries of the trust. It is a duty of the government to take affirmative as well as preventive action to maintain and facilitate for the public unimpeded access to nature.
2. Conventionally, the doctrine was understood to be applicable to cases where the Sovereign's action or inaction threatened customary uses of waterways—like navigation, fishing, swimming, etc. But through various judicial interpretations, especially in the US, it came to include other ecologically vital waters as well, and the Indian Supreme Court's judgement in the *Kamal Nath* case extends it further to include 'all ecosystems operating in our natural resources' (para. 33).
3. Although the doctrine has its truly glorious moments when there is a conflict between the public uses and the 'self-interest of private parties' (para. 26), it can be and has indeed been successfully invoked in America even in cases where public projects like railroads, highways, etc., interfere with the public's use of natural resources.
4. 'Public Uses', it is argued, are not to be understood to be fixed once and for all but must be viewed as changing and evolving with the times. Therefore scenic beauty, study of an eco-system, and recreation must also be recognized as public uses and objects of public interest.

Having presented and defended the doctrine, the judgement proceeds:

As a matter of practical necessity the state may have to approve appropriations despite foreseeable harm to public trust users. In so doing, however, the State must bear in mind its duty as trustee...and to preserve, so far as consistent with public trust, its uses protected by the trust (para. 35).

The court acknowledges conflict between ecological preservation and the administrative compulsions to encroach upon nature to satisfy the 'changing needs of an increasingly complex society'. And it continues, '[T]he resolution of this conflict in any given case is for the legislature and not the courts'(para. 35). Using the same Trust doctrine, the American judiciary has been able to force a reconsideration upon the government of its environmentally harmful development decisions, as for example in the Mono Lake case in the Supreme Court of California. But despite the cautious and qualified use of the doctrine, the Indian Supreme Court has incorporated in our legal system a tool to handle at least some cases of environmental degradation, cases arising out of aquaculture, or privatization of rivers and water bodies.

It must be however mentioned here that the court simply announces that the doctrine is part of the law of the land without citing any precedents or referring to any parts of the Constitution with which the doctrine may have relation of derivation or consonance. Thus the doctrine of public trust seems to be simply added to the legal discourse and not interpretatively assimilated to it. While this is a genuine problem, it is not an insurmountable one because it can be interpretatively assimilated into the Constitution. In our system, 'We, the People' are presumed to have given the Constitution to ourselves and, as the Objectives Resolution passed in the Constituent Assembly makes clear, we have adopted the legal fiction of all power having been derived from the people, they being the ultimate locus of sovereignty. From this it should be easy to argue that since all power has been given to the government by the people, natural resources can also be seen to have been given by the people to the state to be held in trust and to be used as trustees.

IV

Walter F. Murphy (1993) has said that while both democracy and constitutionalism value human dignity they go about protecting it in different ways.[35] Given its pessimism about human nature, constitutionalism seeks to limit legitimate governmental action. It 'tries to lower the stakes of politics', thereby reducing the chances that anybody's dignity will be compromised. Democracy tries to achieve the same thing by ensuring equal participation to all in political and governmental processes.[36]

Constitutionalism has been historically closely connected to liberalism and shares with the latter a certain view of human nature. The question for us then is how to justify constitutionalism without necessarily having to argue that human beings are by nature selfish or oppressive towards each other. They might well be so, but it increases the plausibility and the persuasiveness of an argument if it does not have to make large claims about human nature.

An alternative strategy would be to ask whether democracy is a comprehensive ideal. If by democracy we mean political equality among all adult members of a polity, then it is not a value which can by itself give us a complete normative picture of a good polity. It is well known that there are problems with the various mechanisms used to translate the abstract ideal of political equality into the actual equality of political participation. But I do not propose to follow that line of criticism. Quite apart from problems with methods of representation and institutional procedures, it is enough for my purposes here to make the obvious claim that democracy is one of the many values we cherish, and not the only value. And it might be worthwhile to ask what its main limitation is.

It is revealing how so many democrats, when arguing against constitutionalism, have found it difficult to accept the idea of one generation being bound by some earlier one. There is a denial of historical continuity and the suspicion that constitutionalism has nothing to do with history and politics, that it amounts to an anti-political attempt by some wise men from the distant past to set limits to what can be politically done and what cannot be done. Let me try to deal with both these perceptions one by one.

It has been alleged that one of the problems with democracy is that it does not have a sense of time built into its concept.[37] It seems to be more accurate to say that the narratives instituted by democratic politics have a tendency to predominate the public culture and prevent us from attending to the different temporalities of different actions. But morality is inescapably about consequences of our actions. It is therefore normatively required of us that we do not, through our actions, inflict on the next generation consequences they cannot be reasonably expected to welcome. It might be said here that we all make mistakes, that nobody is perfect, and that we need democracy to correct mistakes committed by democratic politics. But evidently, not all wrongs can be undone.[38] In the context of the environmental consequences of developmentalism, we need to remind ourselves that the mistakes we are making are often not 'retrievable mistakes', to use Tocqueville's expression, but mistakes that might take a very long time to correct.[39]

It is also important not to see constitutions and politics as discontinuous with each other. The making of a constitution is itself a political event and the practice of a constitution—the way it is used, invoked, interpreted—is a historical growth. On the whole it represents a certain understanding that has evolved and become dominant in a given society. Therefore if the judiciary comes to insist that the laws and the executive actions pay sufficient heed to environmental issues, it is not helpful to dismiss it as coming from unrepresentative, unaccountable quarters. Environmental concerns have grown steadily and have even found their way into our jurisprudence through the Forty-second Amendment, through India's international obligations by virtue of the Indian government's ratifications of several environment-related treaties and conventions, and through case law predating the *M.C. Mehta* case. The Public Trust Doctrine gives us one more resource to protect our natural resources for ourselves and for posterity. Of course, even before the application of this doctrine it was open to use the 'public purpose' clause of the (original) right to property and, after its transformation into an ordinary right, to exploit the requirement in the Land Acquisition Act that there be demonstrable public purpose for which the government is planning to acquire property. But 'public purpose' includes a vast and heterogeneous list of instances (ranging from housing for the poor to residence for chief minister) and the category itself has been left undefined in the case law, judges and legal authorities generally being of the view that it is better to take it in a flexible and generic sense.[40] It was said by Ambedkar in the Constituent Assembly[41] that 'public purpose' referred to not only governmental purposes like acquiring land for a police station, but also to social purposes, thus greatly widening the scope of the term. (He was referring to the term as used in the Government of India Act of 1935, but the context was the Right to Property article being discussed in the assembly.) In the *Gulam Mustafa* v. *State of Maharashtra* case,[42] the court took the view that it is a mere 'terminological deviation' to try to distinguish between 'governmental purpose' and 'public purpose'. This judicial observation gives latitude to governments in invoking the clause. In *Suleman* v. *J.H. Patwardhan*,[43] the Bombay High Court said that even if the land taken by the government is made available only to some and not the public at large, it does not violate the 'public purpose' requirement, as long as the aim of the acquisition is the 'general interest of the community as opposed to the particular interest of individuals'.[44] On the whole, it seems, once the legislature has declared that a public purpose exists, the courts cannot question whether that purpose is best served through the proposed acquisition.[45] All this seriously limits the scope of legal redressal of grievances against what might be arbitrary use of the powers of acquisition.

Now it may be argued that the judiciary will be handicapped in a similar way even in its application of the doctrine of public trust when it comes to determine what is 'public'. It is therefore important to point out that the 'public' in the trust doctrine is of an entirely different order from the 'public' in the Land Acquisition Act. In saying that the natural resources belong to the public at large, the Public Trust Doctrine does not limit the beneficiaries of the trust to the present generation. It will be contrary to the spirit of the doctrine to say, for example, that air, river water, the seashore, and so on, belong to all the living people, to the present generation.[46] In denying that these can be privately owned, the doctrine cannot also consistently hold that they can be exclusively appropriated by a given generation.

Thus the notion of the 'public' here goes beyond an empirically demonstrable set of people living at a given time. The doctrine cares for the unborn as well as the living[47] and can therefore be seen as doing what democracy, as a 'rule of the living' (Tom Paine) cannot. Holmes has pointed out that the unborn are permanently disenfranchised.[48] Democracy not only does not, but cannot, give equal political representation to the dead, the living, and the unborn. If participation is meaningless without choice, and if every generation determines the choice situation for the succeeding one, then in the very exercise of democracy we might be unwittingly making democracy unattractive or meaningless to the future generation. By putting limits on our legitimate political actions, constitutionalism saves democracy from this debilitating paradox.

NOTES

1. *CAD*, vol. IX, pp. 1644–67.
2. Jon Elster and Rune Slagstad (eds), *Constitutionalism and Democracy* (Cambridge: Cambridge University Press, 1988), pp. 1–2.

3. Constitutionalism has often been described as limited government, the limits being procedural or substantive, as prohibitions or as roadblocks that slow down. See William G. Andrew, *Constitutions and Constitutionalism* (New Delhi: East-West Press, 1971), pp. 13–14; and Elster and Slagstad (eds), *Constitutionalism and Democracy*, p. 2. The survey of arguments for and against constitutionalism is taken from Stephen Holmes, 'Precommitment and the Paradox of Democracy', in Elster and Slagstad (eds), *Constitutionalism and Democracy*, pp. 195–240; and Stephen Holmes, 'Constitutionalism', in Seymour Martin Lipset (ed.), *The Encyclopaedia of Democracy*, vol. 1 (London: Routledge, 1995), pp. 299–306.

4. Holmes, 'Precommitment', p. 210.

5. Ibid., pp. 203–4.

6. Madison, cited in ibid., p. 221.

7. Ibid., p. 216.

8. Ibid., pp. 213–15.

9. Bertrand de Jouvenel, *Sovereignty: An Inquiry into the Political Good* (London and Chicago, Phoenix Books: University of Chicago Press, 1963), p. 171.

10. de Jouvenel, *Sovereignty*, pp. 184–5.

11. Holmes, 'Constitutionalism', pp. 299–306.

12. Holmes, 'Precommitment', p. 197.

13. Granville Austin, *The Indian Constitution: Cornerstone of a Nation* (Bombay: Oxford University Press, 1972), p. 86.

14. Ibid., p. 84.

15. *Bouvier's Law Dictionary* (Kansas City: Vernon Law Book Co., and West Publishing Co., St Paul, Minn., 1914), p. 1011.

16. Ibid.

17. Ibid.

18. Ibid., p. 1012.

19. Ibid.; *American Jurisprudence*, vol. 26 (Rochester, New York: The Lawyers Cooperative Publishing Co., and San Francisco, California, Bancroft-Whitney Co., 1966).

20. 1994 1 SCC 44; pp. 49–50.

21. See *CAD*, vol. IX; Austin, *The Indian Constitution*, pp. 84–99; and Merillat, *Land and the Constitution*, ch. 3.

22. Austin, *The Indian Constitution*.

23. Not all scholars agree with this. Seervai and Tripathi, for example, argue that post-Forty-second Amendment, the right to compensation exists to even a fuller degree than earlier. See Basu, 1988, pp. 801–8 for the contending interpretations.

24. *CAD*, vol. III, pp. 5, 511, cited by Merillat, *Land and the Constitution*, pp. 52–3.

25. *CAD*, vol. IX, pp. 1195–6, cited by Merillat, *Land and the Constitution*, p. 63.

26. Austin, *The Indian Constitution*, p. 89.

27. Ibid., p. 90.

28. Ibid.

29. Nehru, in *CAD*, vol. IX, pp. 31, 1192, cited by Merillat, *Land and the Constitution*, pp. 62–3; and Ambedkar as Law Minister, presenting the First Amendment (1951) in Parliament, cited by Austin, *The Indian Constitution*, p.100.

30. *CAD*, vol. IX, pp. 1195–6, cited by Merillat, *Land and the Constitution*.

31. Usha Ramnathan, 'Displacement and Rehabilitation: Towards a National Policy', *Lokayan Bulletin*, vol. 11, no. 5 (1995), pp. 43–4.

32. AIR (1997) 1 SCC 388.

33. AIR (1996) SC 2715.

34. L. Joseph Sax, 'The Public Trust Doctrine in Natural Resource Law: Effective Judicial Intervention', *Michigan Law Review*, vol. 68 (1970).

35. Walter F. Murphy, 'Constitutions, Constitutionalism, and Democracy', in Douglas Greenberg, Stanley N. Katz, Melanie Beth Oliviero, and Steven C. Wheatley (eds), *Constitutionalism and Democracy: Transitions in the Contemporary World* (New York: Oxford University Press, 1993).

36. Ibid., pp. 5–6.

37. In Elster and Slagstad (eds), *Constitutionalism and Democracy*, pp. 92–7, Elster has discussed Tocquville's views on the relationship between democracy and time.

38. Elster and Slagstad (eds), *Constitutionalism and Democracy*, p. 9.

39. The notion of retrievability here will have to be taken in a relative sense, as something which is a matter of degrees. An economic policy which is environmentally neutral but otherwise bad can ruin the lives of many and in that sense has consequences which are not retrievable. I thank Joergen Hermansson for reminding me of this.

40. See O.P. Aggarwala, *Compulsory Acquisition of Land in India* (Allahabad: The University Book Agency, 1999), pp. 10–13 for case law related to the varying judicial interpretations of 'public purpose'.

41. B. Shiva Rao, *The Framing of India's Constitution: A Study* (New Delhi: Indian Institute of Public Administration, 1968), p. 285.

42. AIR (1976) 1 SCC 800.

43. AIR (1965) Bom 224.

44. O.P. Aggarwala, *Compulsory Acquisition of Land in India*, p. 101.

45. Durga Das Basu, *Commentary on the Constitution of India*, vol. D, (Calcutta: S.C. Sarkar and Sons Pvt. Ltd, 1978), pp. 323–4.

46. A similar point has been made by Edward Berlin, Raismar Anthony, Kessler Gladys, 'Law in Action: The Trust Doctrine', in Malcolm Baldwin and James K. Page Jr (eds), *Law and the Environment* (New York: Walker and Co, 1970), p. 170.
     The trust is perpetual and the public interest that it protects is constant. That public interest requires that man's environment be utilized in a manner that permits the maximum number of people to obtain the benefits of their environment. Those benefits are viewed in the light of future generations of man and not merely as benefits for today.

47. In an interesting and timely article on the Public Trust Doctrine, Lavanyya Rajamani, 'Doctrine of Public Trust: A Tool to Ensure Effective State Management of Natural Resources', *Journal of the Indian Law Institute*, vol. 38, no. 1 (1996) has referred to the Draft International Covenant on Environment and Development, 1995, and Vienna Declaration, 1993, which says that right to development should be exercised in an equitable manner, taking into account the needs of the future as well as the present generation. Rajamani defines 'intergenerational equity' as the principle that 'each generation owes a duty to future ones to avoid impairing their abilities to fulfil their basic needs.'

48. Holmes, 'Precommitment', p. 235.

10
Constitutional Justice
Positional and Cultural

Gopal Guru

The Indian Constitution has been applauded both as a document on liberalism and also as the document of social revolution. Leaders like Ambedkar and Nehru emphasized that an insight into cultural dynamics serves as the precondition for the realization of social revolution. These leaders felt that creating appropriate cultural conditions had a definite bearing on the idea of social justice. As a part of this thinking and imagination, these leaders also thought of constitutions as the sure source of creating these conditions. As we shall see in this essay, the Indian Constitution does contain some relevant provisions and institutional mechanisms to embark on the project of social revolution. The Indian Constitution, as a document on social revolution, is aimed at annihilating man-made hierarchies based on caste, gender, culture, etc. To put it differently, social revolution, 'textualized' in the form of a document seeks to flatten all cultural hierarchies, as seen, for example, in the various titles that existed during the pre-modern period. Thus, at the cultural and social level, the Indian Constitution has abolished all feudal titles, thus facilitating cultural elevation of those whose worth was withered down to the roots. The differential social and cultural values that prevailed in earlier times have now been progressively dissolved in the universal principle of one-person-one-value.

As we shall see in the following pages, the Indian Constitution made several important provisions that could be seen as little else but a definite step forward in creating the background conditions for the realization of social revolution. It is also clear from the Constitution that several provisions laid down in it have suggested the creation of complex structures for achieving justice, freedom, equality, and fraternity. It has been pointed out by some of the eminent commentators on the Indian Constitution that it is the most suitable document that India could have adopted in the given situation.[1] Yet, right from the very inauguration of the Indian Constitution, leaders and scholars have expressed scepticism about this ever-growing document.[2] At another level, the critique of the Indian Constitution has moved from scepticism to what is being termed by some[3] as the complete subversion of this document by some right wing forces in the country. This threat could be seen in the Hindutva demand to review the Indian Constitution.[4] This demand for revision of the Constitution was sought to be interpreted[5] in terms of the inability of the Hindutva forces to realize their politically motivated agenda of creating a Hindu nation within the existing constitutional framework. To put it differently, this demand also needs to be seen in the context wherein the Hindutva forces have shown an increasing sense of impatience with history which has chosen to take a route different from that of Hindutva.

On the other hand, it is quite interesting to note that those radicals who on earlier occasions condemned the Constitution as a bourgeois document have now discovered it to be the most perfect document that one could ever imagine.[6] This affirmation of the Indian Constitution by the Left is motivated by the larger goal of preventing the Hindutva forces from destroying the secular fabric of Indian society. The concern for secularism no doubts warrants the reaffirmation of the Indian Constitution, particularly in the context of Hindutva designs. However, this essay also argues that the concern for social justice too needs to be given a theoretical advantage, as it helps in critically appreciating the role of the Indian Constitution in fair distribution of moral and material resources. It further argues that, along with secularism, there is a need to invoke justice as an evaluative concept for an assessment of the Indian Constitution. Our critique is informed much more by the lopsided implementation of the Indian Constitution inasmuch as it has found it increasingly difficult to extend itself into our civil society that continues to be permeated by social evils. It is on this basis that this essay argues that every successive amendment to the Indian Constitution ironically confirms the discursive capacity of civil society to escape the constitutional attempts that are otherwise aimed at fusing the legal and moral realms of justice. In the context of this broad submission, let me suggest the outline of this essay.

What are the constitutional provisions and institutional arrangements that have been devised to achieve this fusion of the legal and the moral realm of social justice? To what extent have these provisions succeeded in creating cultural conditions within which one could experience mutual recognition? This essay seeks to answer these questions. They become particularly important in a context where the Constitution had to be amended several times to extract this recognition from the recalcitrant members of 'twice-born' civil society. To what extent have the state and its institutions succeeded in augmenting the moral stamina of civil society, so that it could accept the claims for recognition by, for example, the untouchables? In other words, the essay would like to explore to what extent the Indian Constitution and its institutional mechanisms succeeded in promoting the social interaction that otherwise underlies and renews the moral dichotomy between an increasing sense of reverence for the twice-born and an increasing sense of contempt for the lower castes.

    Let me begin by arguing that the idea of social revolution found its resilience in nationalist thinking before it could be formally incorporated into the Indian Constitution. Sardar K.M. Pannikar,[7] and in recent years, Rajeev Bhargava,[8] have argued that social justice formed one of the central organizing and mobilizing principles of the nationalist movement. It is true that social justice did motivate certain social sections, particularly the moderate leaders and the middle classes in the early phase of nationalism, to participate in the freedom struggle. However, with the end of the nineteenth century and the arrival of the twentieth century, the concern for social justice began receding into the background, and was ultimately replaced by the over-centralizing category of self-rule. This shift warrants the need to historicize the concept of justice in terms of the framework of the configuration of power that has a bearing on the historiography of the concept of justice.

    During the freedom struggle, concepts and categories (including social justice) were shaped by two configurations of power: the colonial configuration and the local configurations of power. Within the colonial configuration of power, the upper castes sought to define justice in terms of the discrimination that these elites experienced during the colonial regime in India. These elites articulated their sense of injustice in terms of their relative inclusion or exclusion from the opportunity structures that came up as a part of the imperialist design.[9] They thus found the resolution of injustice in their limited accommodation into the opportunity structures that were provided by the British rulers in India.[10]

Justice was defined in terms of the notion of fair treatment from the colonial rulers. To this extent, the notion of social justice was confined to the moderate stream of nationalist politics. The sociological base of this concept remained primarily middle class in nature, as it was expressed in terms of collaboration and competition. By and large this notion was inward-looking in that it did not look beyond its own narrow interest. Social reforms within the upper castes formed this limited notion of social justice. Although these upper castes had a limited notion of justice, some of the important liberal thinkers like M.G. Ranade had shown a sincere interest in actively supporting the untouchables in their struggle to get justice from the colonial state in India.[11]

Compared to the liberals, the Hindutva notion of justice is built up around a sense of cultural discrimination that the proponents of Hindutva claimed to have faced from the colonial state. Unlike the liberal notion of justice, which emanated from discriminatory distribution of opportunities within the imperial system, the Hindutva forces thought that they were being culturally stamped out by colonial rule. Those with a strong patriarchal taint felt that British interference in the cultural inner space was unjust. Thus, in the case of Hindutva it was the strong sense of cultural suppression that led the former to rouse mass rage against British rule in India.[12] The Hindutva notion of justice was also limited in its reach. It addressed the question of cultural injustice only to the extent that it found British intervention into the Hindu cultural inner space objectionable. This sense of injustice could thus be defined in the background of the colonial configuration of power. It was less likely that they would focus their attention on the issue of social injustice that emanated from the local configurations of power built up around Brahminical Hinduism. And whenever they sought to respond to the question of social justice, it was rhetorical and pragmatic to the extent that it was necessary to meet the challenge of the Christian missionaries on the one hand and the colonial state on the other. They were less worried about the threat of Muslim conversion, as it had lost the institutional framework to attract the people.

While the Hindutva forces sought to seek the nationalist resolution of cultural injustice in self-rule, they however subsumed the question of social justice in this rather centralizing category. As a result, their politics and thinking suggested primacy of self-rule over self-respect. On the other hand, the INC had adopted a rather careful approach towards the question of social justice. In the initial years, Congress did not show any deep interest in caste issues; in fact, some of the Congress leaders took very aggressive stands on the issue of social reform and were stubbornly against even partial accommodation of social justice into the Congress agenda. The extremist wing of the Congress tried to burn the tent of the social conference in Pune in the year 1896.[13] The caste issue had to wait till 1917, when the Congress took it up for the first time.[14] In later years, even during Gandhi's time, the Congress remained sceptical about the social justice question. This scepticism could be understood in terms of Congress politics, which wanted to avoid a fragmenting impact on nationalist solidarity. The Congress treated social justice as an operational category, which they thought could assume a subversive form if not handled with care.

However, it has to be noted here that nationalist politics, led by M.K. Gandhi, had to accommodate the question of untouchability (if not caste)—and hence social justice—in its agenda. Gandhi gave national visibility to untouchability, if not the caste question; however the overall focus was to overshadow the question of justice through an overemphasis on the issue of freedom or self-rule. Why did the Congress and Gandhi take up caste questions? There could be two main reasons for this. First, let us grant that Gandhi was genuinely interested in anti-untouchability issues, but this was because he was personally convinced of the need to eliminate untouchability practices. His confession in his autobiography could be interpreted as his need to moderate his struggle against untouchability when he was engaged in producing a historical conjuncture to produce national solidarity among different social groups. As we know, colonial modernity produces a sense of social justice among different social groups through introducing several opportunities at different levels. Gandhi was convinced that social justice as a political concept could create a fragmenting impact on the nationalist unity of the Indian masses. In order to avoid this impact he had to support the idea of social justice during the freedom struggle. The efforts made by Gandhi to solicit the support of some of the leading industrialists could be seen as a sure step in this direction.

In view of this Congress scepticism, the social justice concept got ontologically linked to the Dalit–Bahujan leaders who organized their thought and action around this concept. They sought to define this concept against the local configuration of power that involved domination by both Brahminical and capitalist forces. Jotirao Phule would call it 'Shetji–Bhatji' (rich merchant–priest) and Ambedkar would call it

'Brahmins and capitalists'. These leaders and thinkers privileged self-respect over self-rule. This primacy could be understood basically in terms of the nationalist failure (Gandhi included) to decisively interrogate the local configurations of power. In fact, the nationalist forces attempted to subsume social justice in the nationalist struggle for independence. The Dalit–Bahujan leaders, on the other hand, linked the struggle for social justice with the nationalist struggle. They imagined the nation without any kind of natural or inherited discrimination between human beings. Their attempts to closely associate idea of justice with nationalism form part of the universal understanding of emancipation.[15] For the Dalit–Bahujan leaders, the local configuration of power becomes the framework within which the Dalit–Bahujan assigns both political and epistemological treatment to the concept of social justice. (I have dealt with this issue at length elsewhere.) For the opposite reason, social justice faced an epistemological blackout by the upper caste leaders during the nationalist movement.

It is on the basis of the political and intellectual engagement of the nationalist leaders that one could then argue that the scepticism of these leaders over the concept of social justice continued to loom large over the making of the Indian Constitution. This is not to say that the Indian Constitution has not made any provision to create suitable conditions for social justice. There are certain provisions that promise to fuse both the moral and legal universe of rights.

I am going to argue that the Indian Constitution has made some attempt to blend both legal/procedural rights and moral rights. The Constitution does seem to be privileging legal rights over moral rights in the sense that it is aimed at extracting a firm commitment to moral rights by enforcing legal rights through institutional mechanisms. Thus the state and judiciary assume far greater importance in this regard. The Indian Constitution already presupposes that the recognition of dignity may not easily come forth from the upper castes; it will have to be forcibly extracted from the recalcitrant members of twice-born civil society. The second assumption that underlies constitutional provisions is that cultural good or recognition is contingent on material good. That is to say, positional good would automatically ensure guarantees of cultural good.

Thus, the Indian Constitution is making two kinds of provisions to achieve this fusion of the moral and the legal. There are groups of provisions aimed at providing opportunities for achieving material parity with others. The constitutional provisions that can help the lower castes to attain material benefits also involve a promise of the reorganization of society along egalitarian lines.

It has been argued by foreign scholars that the Indian Constitution provides elaborate and effective provisions to ensure social justice to the marginalized sections like Scheduled Castes and Scheduled Tribes.[16] Articles 15, 15 (4), 16 (4), and 29 (2), offer two advantages to the SCs/STs and OBCs. First, according to these Articles, the Constitution bans discrimination in government employment and, second, permits the state to make any provision for the reservation of appointments. The Indian Constitution thus provides reservations in several areas like education, employment, land allotments, housing, etc. This is done according to the proportion of the concerned group in the overall population. Articles 330 and 332 of the Indian Constitution provide political reservation to SCs/STs in the Lok Sabha and Vidhan Sabhas. These are provisions that are directly related to the distributive form of justice and are hence aimed at acquiring positional good.

The Indian Constitution has laid down some provisions in order to extract recognition for the lower castes from the upper castes. Thus, Article 17 of the Indian Constitution abolishes untouchability. This article has also enabled the central government and the state governments to adopt acts and implements rules. Thus, the central government formulated the Anti-Untouchability Act in 1955 and subsequently in 1989. The 1989 Act, which is called SC/ST Prevention of Atrocities Act, is obviously much more comprehensive, and arguably more stringent, than the 1955 Act. However, according to constitutional experts like Balgopal, the 1955 Act is still radical in the sense that it treats caste presumptions as the basis for filing First Information Report (FIRs).[17] Preaching and practising untouchability was made an offence. This act was applicable to untouchability practices in public places. Interestingly, the 1955 Act also considered refusal to sell goods and render services on the grounds of untouchability as an offence. The 1955 Act and its improvization in 1977 mostly dealt with cases on a post-facto basis. On the other hand, the 1989 Act is obviously preventive in nature and expects the state to play an interventionist role effectively.

The 1989 Act does not limit itself to the sphere of human rights; it in fact goes beyond this and includes in its framework the issue of humiliation as crime. Thus, insulting anyone or outraging the modesty of women are considered as offences in this act. Scavenging has been treated as a serious offence. According to this act, forcing people to carry human excreta on their head is considered an offence. The Government of India, Ministry of Welfare, has already adopted the Act in 1993, prohibiting the employment of manual scavengers. Governments, both at the state level and central level, have adopted legal and policy measures to ensure dignity for those who are exposed to humiliation and indignity.

It has to be acknowledged that it is not the ethical insight of the state that has led it to take the lead in legal prohibition of scavenging and atrocities. The Dalit assertion for self-respect in certain parts of the country has forced the central and state governments to implement these constitutional provisions in order to ensure cultural justice to the untouchables. Dalits have in many cases taken the lead and sought legal intervention to force the upper castes to acknowledge their comparative worth. Through their constitutional struggles they would like to assert and prove that they must not be reduced to the level of animals. They do this through establishing their right to draw water from public wells. The legal system seems to be responsive to such initiatives, and at times punishes those upper caste persons who deny Dalits access to water.[18]

Thus, the legal system may succeed in extracting confirmation of the constitutional rights of Dalits from the upper castes. However, constitutional provisions tend to achieve only a limited success in extracting upper caste compliance with cultural justice. This is because the upper castes have failed to take the moral lead in offering unconditional recognition to those social groups deprived of this recognition. On the contrary, these upper castes seem to be deploying discursive methods to escape this constitutional obligation.

Let me offer another rather interesting illustration which shows that a state government has to force compliance of the upper castes with the policies that are aimed at providing social justice to Dalits. In the early 1980s, the state government of Maharashtra, led by the Congress party, adopted a novel policy of developing socially mixed colonies of people belonging to different castes and religions. This policy was obviously motivated by the egalitarian concern of eliminating the physical segregation that has existed and continues to exist in India even today. Arguably, the state government made serious moves to eliminate physical segregation based on the ideology of purity/pollution. It sought to narrow the physical gap among different castes and communities through adopting and implementing the policy of mixed housing societies in certain towns and cities in Maharashtra. As a part of this policy, the state planned one such socially mixed colony in Kolhapur town in south

Maharashtra.[19] It is also interesting to note that this was meant for the lower income groups. It is true that the government could achieve some success in terms of reshuffling different caste residents and bringing them together in some degree of physical proximity. But here too the upper castes tried to bribe the house allotment officer with the intention of persuading him to allot the houses in such a way as to produce a little caste enclave (*agrahara*) in an otherwise socially mixed colony. To put it differently, they refused to respond to such a novel scheme primarily because they were interested in forming a little caste enclave of their own caste by excluding the untouchable caste allottees.[20] They even succeeded in achieving the objective of an upper caste agrahara.[21]

In this context it should not be felt that such attempts to produce caste enclaves are driven by the need to keep away strangers. On the contrary, the upper castes seem to be much more motivated by the need to keep the polluting persons away. The upper castes found the caste list that was available with the government officials quite handy to seek segregation so that they could avoid bumping into 'pollutants'. These people managed to escape the state system and succeeded in reproducing an 'agrahara' in a modern context. On moral grounds, the beneficiaries of this particular scheme are not expected to tamper with this state-led 'social revolution'. These members got the houses at radically subsidized prices. To that extent they are not autonomous consumers, and are supposed to be responding to the government policy without seeking any dilution of it. They should have realized that the government subsidy is aimed at promoting physical proximity. The state made genuine efforts to extract a moral commitment to justice that could be realized through developing mixed localities. But the beneficiaries were influenced by caste loyalties rather than a moral commitment to the social policy of the government. Thus the framework of the state does not provide sufficient guarantees to fuse the moral and the legal. The government finds itself helpless in this regard.

The helplessness of the state gets further compounded when it is unable to regulate the private housing market in the direction of social revolution. The state finds it difficult to intervene in the private housing market and force it not to sell housing keeping in mind caste considerations In fact, the private housing market has found sociological preferences to be a source of profit. In different cities and towns one could come across advertisements at housing sites which say 'only for Hindus'.[22] Such advertising may be profitable for the builders or property dealers. The upper caste Hindu residents may offer to pay more for such exclusively 'Hindu' sites that can protect their 'agrahara' from 'polluting Dalits' and also from the minorities. This has implications for justice in a specific sense of the term. It discriminates against those who cannot participate in the so-called 'competitive' market transition despite the fact that they have more than the required capacity to participate. At another level, such restricted logic has implications for the freedom to choose one's habitat. It is only the upper castes who have the freedom to choose a 'decent' habitat.

The Indian Constitution, it seems, does not offer sufficient provisions to turn civil society in the direction of social justice. Does advertising indicating sociological preferences have legal implications? Does a huge hoarding showing a naked torso with a sacred thread involve the violation of Article 17 of the Indian Constitution? One could explore the possibility of some legal intervention in market transactions that practise such subtle forms of discrimination. They tend to morally empower upper caste Hindus, Christians, and Parsis, and to deny Muslims and Dalits, for different reasons, the right to be treated as universal consumers. Thus it is social power rather than economic power that decides associational preferences. This has a doubly crippling impact on the upwardly mobile minorities and Dalits. They feel morally shattered when, on the one hand, the housing market does not find them worthy of any transaction and, on the other, the upper castes find them unworthy of any social/civil association. These individuals have, in a limited individualist sense, every reason to feel frustrated that they cannot move away from their community bonds, which they find burdensome inasmuch as they constrain their individual aspirations. Secondly, they are not welcome in the 'agrahara', which an upwardly mobile Dalit would like to become part of. Taking a cue from Ronald Dworkin, one may find community location to be not a constraining but an enabling context for mutual advancement. Dalit communitarians who have got a stake in identity politics would take a cue from Dworkin[23] and argue that such dissociation from the 'agrahara' might help the Dalits to improve their community wealth and protect their moral resources like community solidarity. This suggestion made by Dowrkin, however, maintains two universes of justice, and this is problematic.

There are other cases where the state has tried to extract a confirmation of the right to dignity of Dalits and Adivasis. The upper castes follow the 1989 Act and thus assign respect to Dalits. This was evident in two cases, which I would like to put it in narrative mode. I, along with my student, went to a village in Barsi taluka of Solapur district in Maharashtra. We went to this village in a jeep. We went to the upper caste 'Ali' (a section of village where people live in a segregated manner). We requested these people to help us to locate the Mahar and Mangs 'Alis'. We asked them whether it is not normal to call these people by their community name. They (the upper castes) said that one could be booked under the 1989 Act for doing so. However, they refused to take us to the Dalit colony, nor could we force them to do so. This shows the limits of constitutional/state intervention. This happens because the inner cultural/moral selves of the upper castes cannot be influenced through these legal/constitutional means. These means could at best bring out compliance more by compulsion and less by conviction. Thus, the legal/constitutional measures could help a section of people to achieve positional good, but it does not automatically follow that they would also get cultural/moral good. How does one understand this tension between legal and moral rights?

It could be understood in terms of the deficiencies that are internal to the Constitution itself; in fact, it is related to the constitutional understanding of untouchability. As it is clear from a reading of the Indian Constitution, untouchability is defined exclusively in terms of those castes which were considered as defiling. Constitutional provisions regarding compensatory discrimination seek to designate castes as Scheduled Castes on the basis of their experience of untouchability.[24] It is interesting to note that in the case of OBC reservation, untouchability becomes a secondary criterion of such classification. In case of OBC reservation, caste is treated as the primary unit of classification. But when constitutional provisions, particularly in the case of Dalits, are operationalized into Acts and rules, untouchability acquires primacy over caste. Thus, OBCs are given reservation not on the basis of untouchability but on the basis some other criterion. I think focusing on the experience of untouchability as the basis for classification has significance for capturing its specificity and its universality. We shall come back to this point a little later. Let us first see what problems one faces in the event of treating untouchability as a criterion for classification.

The experience of untouchability, which forms the basis of all the constitutional provisions and Acts (the 1955 Act, with amendments, and the 1989 Act), insulates the source of untouchability and captures only the sites of untouchability. This is a serious problem that has implications for the effectiveness of all these provisions. An upper caste person with the malignant capacity to inflict insults is the source of untouchability and hence needs to be ontologically associated with untouchability. In other words, it is necessary to treat untouchability as a phenomenon involving both the source of pollution and its object. The source therefore needs to be put in a proper constitutional perspective.

In the present constitutional framework, the source of untouchability (the upper caste male) escapes scrutiny. This happens because he deploys a much more discursive weapon to render a person untouchable, undesirable, and unworthy of any attention and concern. Only the more blatant forms of untouchability are considered to be adequate evidence to implicate a person under various acts, including the 1989 Act. A tormentor may not deploy all the weapons available to him or may deploy them with care. In such cases, it becomes difficult to detect his intention and punish him. One often comes across an upper caste person who avoids taking water from the Dalit host. Dalit hosts cannot force their guests to drink water on moral ground. The upper castes may morally force Dalit hosts to exempt them from taking water from Dalits. They extract this concession by providing reasons that look genuine. When the demand for more and more exemptions increases, it also leads to the increasing Dalit suspicion suggesting that repeated exemption is not innocent but a subtle device to practise untouchability. Thus the framework of friendship becomes discursive, leaving enough room for the phenomenology of untouchability. The Indian Constitution does not have enough capacity to penetrate this discursive realm of untouchability.

The second problem that one finds internal to the Constitution is that while treating untouchability as a criterion for classification, it assumes that truth resides only in the body of the untouchable. This assumption makes the untouchable an object of classification and restriction. One is not very sure whether the Constitution also acknowledges that truth (the logical counterpart of a defiling being) resides in the sacred body of a touchable. As we have already seen in the preceding discussion, the upper castes have the ritual power to define who is touchable and untouchable. It is he who marks the purity/ pollution line. He is the cartographer who is ritually empowered to demarcate conceptual spaces and confine some people within these spaces. It is he who is in possession of the power of touch that he deploys to assign hierarchical meaning to human body. In a kind of peculiar inversion, one finds a touchable rendering himself 'supra'-untouchable.

So 'touch' is in some sense a problem for the touchable as well. It is the touchable who takes all the precautions, because touch could be a source of anxiety in relatively anonymous locations (due to blurring of social morphology) that have become sociologically quite ambivalent. The touchable, in order to avoid touch, is compelled to avoid proximity. It could also be true that an upper caste person may avoid being touched on the grounds that he values his atomized self more than any moral commitment to affectionately touch others. The moral vocabulary of love, care, and concern may not motivate such persons to touch others with social intimacy.

Obviously the Indian Constitution is ill-equipped to generate this moral vocabulary. This has implications for untouchable identity, because the lack of proximity can lead to mutual reification of identities residing at two ends but conceptually bound together. It is beyond the purview of the Indian Constitution to classify people on the basis of the power that resides in the social tension between the touchable and the untouchables. Untouchability as a truth acquires power only when it is incarnated in an active human being. Thus, the untouchable become a 'poison weapon' the moment he touches things like cooked food and water that are considered to be sensitive to an untouchable's touch. We have many incidents where Dalits have deployed this against touchables. The upper castes abandoned many wells after they were touched by the untouchables. An upper caste teacher felled the tree when it was touched by her maidservant. Thus, the onus lies on the touchable to create the conditions for this proximity. The upper castes reserve the right to association. In other words, it is they who decide whom they should associate with. Dalits cannot force the upper caste to touch them. This is difficult because the right to be touched falls in the moral realm in which it is entirely up to a upper caste person whether to accede to the moral/cultural need of a untouchable. The upper castes (religion no bar) reserve the right to walk in and out of social relationships with Dalits. In other words, the upper castes control the distribution of moral/cultural resources that tend to condition the use of the public sphere. Constitutional provisions are found deficient in compelling the upper castes to share these resources with those who require it. The Indian Constitution, even with its punitive provisions, therefore offers a limited promise. It has not succeeded in penetrating the upper caste self which has become morally so hardened.

On the other hand, constitutional provisions and related acts and rules have introduced internal tensions within what could be described as the particular universe of justice relating to the Scheduled Castes. It is interesting to note that untouchability as the criterion for classification has also led to the fragmentation within the sphere of social justice. For example, the rule to limit the reservation of benefits to 'sons-of-the-soil' (that is, domiciled) Scheduled Castes may protect the zone of opportunities for the Scheduled Castes. At some level, this domicile criterion has implications for the notion of spatial justice. This domicile clause tends to restrict the mobility of the Scheduled Castes who would like to compete at the national level or beyond their area of domicile. It is interesting to note that the Lokur Committee established in 1965 took objection to this rule on the ground that it inhibits the mobility of Scheduled Castes. This committee thus recommended the removal of this limiting rule.[25] What were the implications of this domicile clause for untouchability? Did this domicile clause suggest that there is specificity to the practice of untouchability? Did it suggest that Dalits face specific forms of untouchability and that there is hence a need to limit the benefits to those who face extreme forms of untouchability?

Within the liberal framework one may find this domicile clause reasonable inasmuch as it promotes the lexical principle that is aimed at ensuring the percolation of benefits to the more needy Dalits from within the community. Limiting the mobility of the Scheduled Caste, particularly in a context where resources are scarce, would appear just, as it promises that the reservation resources are not siphoned off by a few. But this lexical principle could militate against the moral principle. Let me explain this further. It is considered acceptable to deprive migrant, but more competent, Scheduled Castes of reservation benefits on the grounds that these benefits should reach the needy sons of the soil. But will the Scheduled Caste person who succeeds in entering the protected zone through some other opportunity route enjoy an environment which will be bereft of untouchability? The answer unfortunately is in the negative, particularly in the Indian context where society is permeated with a deep sense of untouchability. Untouchability as suggested by the policy-makers is not simply specific but has a universal character, and is hence dynamic and not confined to a local specificity. It travels faster across time and space. That is to say the caste background of a Dalit officer is reported faster than the officer himself as an ontological being. For example, 80 years ago, Ambedkar's caste background reached his Baroda office faster than his physical self. The Scheduled Castes who have migrated to Delhi are haunted by the anxiety of being discriminated against on the basis of untouchability. Untouchability thus persists and travels across both time and space. If untouchability is all-pervading, one does not understand why Jammu and Kashmir has been made an exception to the 1989 Act.[26] It is ironic to note that those sanitary workers, mostly Valmikis, who were 'taken' by the Raja of Kashmir to that state have not been given citizenship status till today.[27]

In conclusion, one could add that constitutional provisions are necessary for positional good but not sufficient for achieving cultural goods like recognition and dignity. As far as positional goods are concerned one can see a positional change among Indian Dalits and Adivasis. It is also necessary to mention that the credit for this advance is to be attributed more to the protracted struggle that the Dalits have waged from time to time than to the ethical character of the Indian state. Further, the Constitution does not automatically guarantee the benefits of cultural justice; it has to augment its extractive power to force the non-Dalits to acknowledge the achievements of Dalits. However, its implementing institutions have achieved only partial success in extracting grudging respect from the upper castes, which continue to be recalcitrant. In fact, the Constitution consciously or unconsciously creates tensions between the positional and cultural notion of justice. In view of this constitutional deficiency, which was noticed by Ambedkar himself,[28] it becomes imperative to open up the possibility of finding other ways of morally/politically exhausting the adversary of dignity.

Ambedkar is not issuing a warning out of frustration. In fact he is suggesting that positional good is not a sufficient condition of democracy and justice. For him, the moral/cultural good (one-man-one-value) is the defining condition of justice. He thus makes moral good (dignity, recognition) the meta-evaluative concept. He is not only applying cultural justice as the assessing standard, but is going beyond this sphere and applying justice as a standard evaluator of the sphere of larger social relationships where claims for equal worth are framed and articulated. I would come to the conclusion that constitutional practice failed to provide the stable social context that is so necessary for the realization of mutual worth. I would like to further conclude that constitutional practice could not achieve a consensus on the shared meaning of social good or primary good like the right to equal respect and equal concern.

One of the ways to wage a moral and political struggle against these tendencies is to confront the structures of cultural injustice on an everyday basis. Failing to launch such struggles is likely to lead to the reification of the issues of dignity in constitutional documents. Everyday forms of struggle would possibly involve constant and consistent questioning of those who seek to degrade Dalits, Adivasis, and women. This, I think, is a small beginning of a larger struggle of creating a society which will be free from all kinds of malaise.

NOTES

1. Granville Austin, *The Indian Constitution: The Cornerstone of a Nation* (Delhi: Oxford University Press, 1998).
2. Dr Ambedkar, Principal Architect of the Constitution of India, *Collected Writings of Babasaheb Ambedkar*, vol. 13, (Mumbai: Education Department, Government of Maharashtra, 1994), p. 1214.
3. Some leftist organizations like ANHAD have been campaigning in favour of the Indian Constitution. This campaign has been carried out in different states, more particularly in Gujarat.
4. In 2003, Hindutva parties, particularly the BJP, tried to float the idea to review the Indian Constitution.
5. The Left forces opposed this BJP idea of revision of the Indian Constitution. In fact some of the members belonging to leftist organization like SAHMAT and ANHAD carried out the campaign in Gujarat against such a move of revision.
6. Ibid.
7. K.M. Pannikar, *In Defence of Liberalism* (Bombay: Asia Publishing House, 1962), p. 15.
8. Rajeev Bhargava, 'Democratic Vision of a New Republic India, 1950', in Francine Frankel, Zoya Hasan, Rajeev Bhargava, and Balveer Arora (eds), *Transforming India* (Delhi: Oxford University Press, 2000), p. 26.
9. Tapan Roy Choudhury, *Europe Re-considered* (Delhi: Oxford University Press, 1988).
10. Ibid. For further details please refer to Anil Seal's book on *Emergence of Indian Nationalism: Collaboration and Competition in the later Nineteenth Century* (Cambridge: Cambridge University Press, 1968).
11. Eleanor Zelliot, 'Dr. Ambedkar and Mahar Movement', unpublished Ph.D. thesis, University of Pennsylvania, 1969, p. 57.
12. Javeed Alam, *India: Living with Modernity* (Delhi, Oxford University Press, 1999).
13. C.B. Khairmode, *Babasaheb Ambedkaranche Charitra* (Marathi), vol. 4 (Mumbai: Marathi Sahitya ani Sanskrutik Mandal, 1987), p. 34.
14. Marc Galanter, *Competing Equalities* (Delhi: Oxford University Press, 1984), p. 17.

15. Etienne Balibar, *Masses, Classes, Ideas: Studies on Politics and Philosophy Before and After Marx*, James Swenson (trans.) (London: Routledge, 1994), p. 193.
16. Constitutional provision.
17. Balgopal made a presentation on 'Law, Caste and Democracy' in the seminar on caste and democracy, held at Central Institute of English and Foreign Languages (CIEFL), Hyderabad, on 10–12 August 2006.
18. The state government of Maharashtra created such a colony called 'Shastri Nagar' a mixed colony of people belonging to different castes in the city of Kolhapur in southern Maharashtra.
19. Ibid.
20. Ibid.
21. These instructions could be seen in cities like Hyderabad and Chennai.
22. Ronald Dworkin, *Taking Rights Seriously* (London: Duckworth, 1984), p. 237.
23. This could be seen both in the villages as well as in metropolitian cities like Delhi.
24. Galanter, *Competing Equalities*, p. 142.
25. Girish Agrawal and Colin Gonsalves, *Dalits and the Law*, New Delhi: Human Rights Law Network, 2005, p. 104.
26. I got this information from Darshan Ratan Rawan, the president of the All-Indian Swashkar Samaj, 31 December 2006. Also see Agrawal and Gonsalves, *Dalits and the Law*, p. 27.
27. Ibid.
28. Ambedkar, *Collected Works of Babasaheb Ambedkar*, p. 1214.

Section III

11

Containing the Lower Castes
The Constituent Assembly and the Reservation Policy

Christophe Jaffrelot

In one of the most influential studies of the Indian Constitution, Granville Austin[1] has emphasized that this 'cornerstone of the nation' was intended to promote social transformation. He dwells on the progressive overtone of the Directive Principles to make his point. In spite of the remarkable character of this seminal work, this particular aspect of the book is highly questionable. In fact, one could equally convincingly argue that the Indian Constitution reflects the conservative views of the assembly which drafted it. This Congress-dominated Constituent Assembly did not aim so much at emancipating the subaltern groups as at defusing their mobilization by making not-very-far-reaching concessions. This is evident from the debates of the assembly regarding reservations for the lower castes.

In contrast to most post-colonial states, India was already familiar with positive discrimination when it became independent in 1947. The British had introduced reservations in favour of the lower castes as well as tribals (a social group which I shall not deal with in this essay). These policies created new administrative categories which tended to refashion the old notions of 'untouchables' or 'Shudras'. The term 'backward classes', for instance, was first used in the 1870s by the Madras administration in the framework of an affirmative action policy in favour of under-educated groups. When the list of 'backwards' increased and widened, growing from 39 to 131 communities in the 1920s, the untouchables (or Dalits to use today's terminology) claimed the right of being treated as a distinct class. Hence the sharing out of the 'backward' between 'Depressed Classes' (untouchables and tribals) and 'Castes other than Depressed Classes' that was decided in 1925.[2] While Tamil Nadu appears to be a precursor, the Centre gradually moved in the same direction and eventually tried to harmonize the local classifications.

The time-honoured expression of the central government to designate the lower and intermediate castes was 'Depressed Classes', a group for which seats in local and national assemblies were reserved from 1919 onwards. However, after the 1935 Government of India Act, the untouchables were designated as 'Scheduled Castes' and the denomination spread in the provinces of British India. When India became independent in 1947, this group was officially recognized by the Constituent Assembly, whereas the rest of the former 'Depressed Classes' group was often reclassified in a new category, the 'other backward classes'. Both groups were supposed to benefit from programmes of positive discrimination. However, the reservation policy in favour of the Scheduled Castes which resulted from the Constituent Assembly Debates did not enable them to send their own representatives to Parliament, and the assembly largely failed to define the 'other backward classes'. In both cases the constitutional arrangements turned out to be less progressive than the pre-1947 situation.

HOW NOT TO DISCRIMINATE TOO POSITIVELY IN FAVOUR OF THE SCS?[3]

In 1947, the Scheduled Castes benefited from a very complicated system of seat reservation. After the 1932 Communal Award, the conflict between Gandhi and Ambedkar had eventually been settled by the Poona Pact in terms which favoured Gandhi's option but gave substantial compensations to Ambedkar's: in contrast to the separate electorates Ambedkar advocated, the new reservation system did not enable the Scheduled Castes to designate their representatives. However, the Poona Pact established a Scheduled Castes electoral college which was in charge of designating, in each constituency, the four Scheduled Caste candidates who were then allowed to contest the elections. The Scheduled Castes exerted an exclusive influence during the primary elections—this is a very important point. But after that, they were not in a majority in any constituency and the successful Scheduled Caste candidate was, therefore, inevitably elected in large part by the other castes. Besides, the system based on the Poona Pact did not allow the Scheduled Castes to get a representation that was proportional to their number. The 1935 Government of India Act gave them only seven seats out of 156 in the Council of State, 19 out of 250 in the Central Assembly, and 151 out of 1585 in the different Provincial Legislative Assemblies.[4]

Naturally, the Constituent Assembly closely examined this question. In the sub-committee on minorities, Ambedkar, the newly appointed Chairman of the Drafting Committee, had suggested that non-Scheduled Castes Hindu candidates should, before being declared elected, poll a minimum number of votes among voters of the minority communities, including the Scheduled Castes. He alone voted for this resolution. Congressmen objected that it amounted to a reintroduction of the separate electorates through the back door, whereas independent India had to get rid of these divisive influences. The sub-committee decided by a majority of 28 to 3 that there should be no separate electorates.[5,6] Influential Hindu traditionalist leaders such as K.M. Munshi, who was also a member of the Drafting Committee, Seth Govind Das, Rajendra Prasad (the assembly president), and Vallabhbhai Patel rejected any kind of separate electorate because—to use Munshi's words, which recalled Gandhi's arguments in 1932—Scheduled Castes were 'part and parcel of Hindu community'.[7] Another assembly member even mentioned the fact that people had to consider 'the Scheduled Castes as belonging to Hindus [sic]'.[8] They all wanted to continue with the reservation system without any safety clause. They argued together against Ambedkar, who preferred not to attend the plenary session of the assembly where this question was discussed. However, one of his disciples, S. Nagappa,[9] proposed an alternative solution recalling Ambedkar's views. According to this schema, in the constituencies reserved for Scheduled Castes, the candidates winning more than 35 per cent of the untouchables' votes could be declared as victorious. For Nagappa, such a system would have given more legitimacy to the Scheduled Caste MPs and Members of Legislative Assemblies (MLAs):

...today, if we are elected to reserved seats, when there is agrarian trouble, when the Harijans and the agriculturists are at loggerheads and when we go and appeal to these people, these Harijans, they say, 'Get out man, you are the henchmen and show-boys of the Caste Hindus. You have sold our community and you have come here on their behalf in order to cut our throats. We don't accept you as our representative.' Sir, in order to avoid that what I suggested is that a certain percentage of the Harijans must elect the candidate so that he may be able to tell them that he has the backing of some Harijans and he will have the prestige and voice as their representative.[10]

Upper caste assembly members reacted vehemently, all the more so as Ambedkar did not attend this crucial session: his name topped the list of the four Assembly members who had supported Nagappa's amendment, but he had not come to defend it himself. He had probably no hope of having it passed. Nagappa's amendment was not discussed for long[11] because Patel sealed its fate promptly:

So far as the Scheduled Castes are concerned, I do not think very much has to be said on this amendment, because I got a representation from a large majority of the Scheduled Castes representatives in this house, except one or two or three, that they are all against this amendment (Hear, Hear), and Mr Nagappa knew about it. But Mr Nagappa wanted to move his amendment to fulfil a promise or undertaking or at least to show his community that he was not purchased by the majority community! Well, he has done his job, but other people took him seriously and took a lot of time.[12]

Such an ironical speech substantiated Nagappa's plea: the Congress party expected nothing but docility from the Scheduled Castes. Patel even accused the Scheduled Castes of fomenting fissiparous tendencies:

To the Scheduled Castes friends, I also appeal: 'Let us forget what Dr. Ambedkar or his group have done.' Let us forget what you did. You have very nearly escaped partition of the country again on your lines. You have seen the result of separate electorates in Bombay, that when the greatest benefactor of your community [Gandhi] came to Bombay to stay in *bhangi* quarters it was your people who tried to stone his quarters. What was it? It was again the result of this poison, and therefore I resist this only because I feel that the vast majority of the Hindu population wish you well. Without them where will you be? Therefore secure their confidence and forget that you are a Scheduled Caste [...] those representatives of the Scheduled Castes must know that the Scheduled Castes must be effaced altogether from our society, and if it is to be effaced, those who have ceased to be untouchables and sit amongst us have to forget that they are untouchables or else if they carry this inferiority complex, they will not be able to serve their community.[13]

In other words, Patel tells the Scheduled Castes that they should be ashamed of their demands, which almost amount to separatism, whereas their real hero, Gandhi, kept the nation united. For him, it is up to the

Scheduled Castes to regain the trust of the upper castes. The problem lies in the Scheduled Castes' psychology: they must remove their inferiority complex.

Eventually, the Constitution established a system of reserved seats on a population basis for ten years. It was extended in 1959 and again in 1969 and so on every ten years. The key element in comparison to the pre-1947 legacy was that the primary elections system was abolished. This move deprived the Scheduled Castes from some crucial leverage. Article 330 (2) simply established quotas for the Scheduled Castes and the Scheduled Tribes in proportion to their population, which was a positive step compared to the system that prevailed before 1947. But the implementation of these quotas could take many different shapes. In the reserved constituencies where the Scheduled Castes and Scheduled Tribes were in a majority, the seat would be automatically for them. So far as the former were concerned, in 1952, this was the case for only three seats (all in West Bengal) and only one in 1957.[14] However, most of the quota was filled with double constituencies. These double constituencies were located in the places where Scheduled Castes and Scheduled Tribes were in large numbers. There, two MLAs (or two MPs) were returned: one from the non-SC/non-ST candidates, and the other one coming from the SC/ST candidates. So far as the Scheduled Castes were concerned, the system worked as follows: in 15 per cent of the constituencies, in areas where the Scheduled Castes were in large numbers, two seats were contested (in a very small number of constituencies a third seat was reserved for a tribal), and each voter therefore had two ballots (exceptionally three). Even if none of the Scheduled Caste candidates received the largest or the second largest number of votes, the one who came first among them won the reserved seat. However, if two Scheduled Caste (or Scheduled Tribe) candidates came first and second, they won both seats. That is what happened in 1957 in a constituency of Andhra Pradesh where one of the seats was reserved for the Scheduled Tribes. Two tribal candidates came first and second and were elected; the third was V.V. Giri, an influential Brahmin Congress leader who became president of India in 1969. He brought the case before the Supreme Court, which upheld the election results as pronounced by the Election Commission.[15] Interestingly, the system was modified before the 1962 elections, allegedly because the double constituencies were huge, but obviously because the defeat of Giri had shown that both seats could be won by Scheduled Caste or Scheduled Tribe candidates.

Since 1961 there are only single constituencies. In 1961, in 15 per cent of them, where the Scheduled Castes were in the largest numbers, the candidates could only be from their community. But the Scheduled Castes were (and still are) everywhere in a minority. Under the 1961 delimitation of parliamentary constituencies, 75 seats were reserved for representation by the Scheduled Castes. The proportion of the population made up by these castes in these constituencies varied considerably, but they were never in a majority, as evident from Table 8.1:

Table 8.1: Distribution of the constituencies reserved for the Scheduled Castes according to the percentage of Scheduled Castes

Percentage of Scheduled Castes	Number of Constituencies
0–10	4
10–20	25
20–30	33
30–40	10
40–50	3
Total	75

Source: Marc Galanter, 'Compensatory discrimination in political representation', in Economic and Political Weekly, vol. 14, 7–8 February 1979, pp. 438–9.

Besides, 75 per cent of the Scheduled Castes were in non-reserved constituencies.[16] A coalition of high and intermediate castes could very well have their Scheduled Caste candidate returned even if the Scheduled Castes did not vote for him. Now, the Congress had precisely become adept at co-opting Scheduled Caste leaders and at having them returned by mobilizing non-Scheduled Castes voters. As a result, the reservation system did not enable the Scheduled Castes to send vocal, effective representatives to the assemblies. Marc Galanter emphasizes the point:

The design of the legislative reservations—the dependence on outside parties for funds and organisations and the need to appeal to constituencies made up overwhelmingly of others—tends to produce compliant and accommodating leaders rather than forceful articulators of the interests of these groups.[17]

One of the Scheduled Caste leaders co-opted by the Congress, Jagjivan Ram, admitted that 'since one had to depend on the non-Scheduled Caste vote, one went along with the fortunes of the party.'[18]

To conclude on this point, the Constitution has not substantially promoted the emancipation of the Dalits in terms of access to political power. Other aspects of this 'cornerstone of a nation' might have made a stronger impact, like the abolition of untouchability, reservations in education, and job quotas. But in the sphere of political representation, the Scheduled Castes have not earned much from the Constitution; on the contrary, they have lost something: the primary elections which gave them a big say in the designation of the Scheduled Castes deputies. The 'other backward classes' also suffered from the conservative attitude of the Constituent Assembly.

THE (UNACHIEVED) INVENTION OF THE OTHER BACKWARD CLASSES

Nehru used the expression 'other backward classes' during his first speech, on 13 December 1946, before the Constituent Assembly, in his Objectives Resolution. He announced then that special measures were to be taken in favour of 'minorities, backward and tribal areas and depressed and other backward classes'.[19] He did not elaborate further. The Constituent Assembly had, therefore, to clarify the content of this notion.

Within the Constituent Assembly the notion of the 'other backward classes' was taken up by the 'Advisory Committee on Rights of Citizens, Minorities and Tribal and Excluded Area', which was set up on 24 January 1947 to prepare the articles dealing with these matters. The committee chairman, Vallabhbhai Patel, created several sub-committees, and the one in charge of the Fundamental Rights was the first to reflect upon the reservation issue. On the one hand it recommended that 'The State shall not discriminate against any citizen on grounds only of religion, race, caste, sex, place of birth', and that there should be 'equality of opportunity for all citizens in matters of public employment'.[20] On the other hand, Ambedkar, who was one of the sub-committee members, suggested that one of the measures to be taken in favour of the backward groups should be in the form of job quotas: the government should prescribe 'a certain proportion of posts of public service for the minorities—whoever they may be'.[21] The sub-committee's discussions led its members to define these minorities as 'any backward class of citizens which, in the opinion of the state, is not adequately represented in the services under the State'. This clause was eventually voted by the Constituent Assembly and became Article 16(4) of the Indian Constitution.

In the very first constitutional debates a key element of the reservation policy has thus been representation in the state apparatus. The reason why this aspect was emphasized—and not education, for instance—has never been clearly spelled out, but Ambedkar probably had some responsibility in this. For him job quotas in the administration were the best means for empowering the lower castes, and not primarily an employment schema. He was adopting the same approach as the non-Brahmin movement in Tamil Nadu and Maharashtra. In 1944, Ambedkar used his tour in Madras for mobilizing the Dalits on this objective: 'You should realise what our object is [...] It is not fighting for a few jobs and for a few conveniences. It is the biggest cause that we have ever cherished in our hearts. That is to see that we are recognised as the Governing community.'[22] From the outset, access to power was therefore an important motivation in Ambedkar's demand for quotas in the bureaucracy.

The framing of this reservation policy by the Advisory Committee implied that its beneficiaries could be identified. It was easy in the case of the Scheduled Castes and Scheduled Tribes, since they would continue to be enumerated in the census, but they were not the only 'backwards'. In the report that Vallabhbhai Patel, as Chairman of the Committee, submitted on 8 August 1947, the last clause, which dealt with financial alleviation for the 'backwards' sketched the criteria which could be used for defining the OBCs social profile:

Provision shall also be made for the setting up of a statutory Commission to investigate into the conditions of socially and educationally backward classes, to study the difficulties under which they labour and to recommend to the Union or the Unit Government, as the case may be, the steps that should be taken to eliminate the difficulties and the financial grants that should be given and the conditions that should be prescribed for such grants.[23]

Even qualified that way, the notion of 'Backward Classes' remained vague. This worried some of the Constituent Assembly members, especially those from the north, who were much less familiar with it than those from the south where it had been used for quite some time.[24] However the Drafting Committee refused to be more specific. One of its senior members, K.M. Munshi, retorted

it is perfectly clear that the word 'backward' signifies that class of people—does not matter whether you call them untouchables or touchables, belonging to this community or that—a class of people who are so backward that a special protection is required in the services and I see no reason why any member should be apprehensive of regard to the word 'backward'.[25]

By mentioning the untouchables, Munshi made the situation even more confused, since the case was settled so far as the Scheduled Castes were concerned. He was obviously reluctant to delineate the limits of a clear-cut category of 'backward classes', in contrast to his benevolent attitude vis-à-vis the Scheduled Castes, which he was very much willing to help. Moreover, Munshi brought to the attention of the Scheduled Caste assembly members that the quotas in favour of their caste fellows had never posed any problem and that 'we, members who do not belong to the Scheduled Castes, have in order to wipe out this blot on our society, been in the forefront in this matter.'[26] Munshi's discourse prepared the ground for the Congress strategy of co-option of Scheduled Castes people, thus circumventing intermediate castes which may eventually challenge the upper castes' domination. The 'coalition of extremes' pattern referred to by Paul Brass in his study of Uttar Pradesh was taking shape.[27]

Ambedkar also found it unnecessary to spell out more precisely the meaning of the epithet 'backward', but for other reasons. He felt that many Congressmen feared that too broad a definition of the OBCs could transform them into an all-powerful social coalition regrouping the bulk of society:

A backward community is a community which is backward in the opinion of the state Government [...] If the local government included in this category of reservations such a large number of seats [sic], I think one could very well go to the Federal Court and the Supreme Court and say that the reservation is of such a magnitude that the rule regarding equality of opportunity has been destroyed....[28]

In addition to the vagueness that shrouded the Other Backward Classes' category, some Constituent Assembly members regretted that less was done for them than for the Scheduled Castes,[29] who already had the advantage of quotas. But the low castes did not have a spokesman of Ambedkar's calibre. In fact, they were hardly represented within the Constituent Assembly. According to Granville Austin, amongst the most influential persons (about twenty) who were drafting the Constitution, not a single one was from the low castes (11 were Brahmins, 2 Amils, 1

Kayasth, 1 Banya, 1 Rajput, and 1 Scheduled Caste, namely, Ambedkar).[30] As for members of the main sub-committees—those who elaborated the preliminary draft—their composition was not very different.

Table 8.2: Members of the most important advisory committees of the Constituent Assembly by caste (percentages)

Upper Castes	77	Middle Castes	14.2	Scheduled Castes	6.5
Brahmin	45.7	Reddy	3.8		
Amil	1.9	Nair	0.9		
Kayasth	12.3	Kamma	0.9		
Kshatriya	6.6	Chettiyar	0.9		
Vaishya	4.6	Nadar	0.9		
Lingayat	0.09	Gounder	0.9		
Marwari	4.6	Maratha	1.2		
Bhumihar	1.9	Others	2.8		

Source: Granville Austin, The Indian Constitution, Appendix III.

The lower castes were hardly more represented among the members of the Constituent Assembly at large, as evident from Table 8.3.

There were only a handful of OBC deputies among the members of the Constituent Assembly. This is evident from the figures concerning the Hindi belt—that is, Uttar Pradesh, Madhya Pradesh, Bihar, Rajasthan, Himachal Pradesh, and Delhi. These statistics are more reliable than the ones regarding the Constituent Assembly members at large, given the substantial percentage of elected members whose castes and communities could not be identified among the non-Hindi belt deputies. Interestingly, the social opposition of the Hindi belt MPs elected in 1952 seems to be very similar.

In fact, the main advocate of the low castes was Punjabrao Deshmukh, who did not belong to this category but was a Maratha from Amraoti (Maharashtra). In August 1949, he introduced an amendment according to which all the 'classes and communities' of India would be represented within the administration on a population basis. A vibrant plea accompanied his proposal:

It appears to me that the development in India has been lop-sided, one-sided. About 80 per cent of the people take no part as far as your cultural affairs are concerned, so far as the civilised things of life are concerned. There is a black-out so far as they are concerned; an iron curtain between them and the rest;

Table 8.3: Caste and community of the Constituent Assembly members
and of the Lok Sabha members (1952)

Castes and Communities	Constituent Assembly Members	Constituent Assembly Members from the Hindi belt	1952 Lok Sabha Members from the Hindi belt
Upper castes	45	65	65
Brahmin	21.40	26.35	28.6
Rajput	6.66	12.40	10.7
Banya	6.4	8.5	9.7
Kayasth	6.32	9.30	8.7
Bhumihar	1.40	3.10	3.9
Khatri	1.40	2.33	
Amil	0.70	1.55	
Nair	0.70	–	
Other	2.81	1.55	3.4
Intermediate Castes	2.45	0.8	1
Jat	0.35	??	1
Maratha	1.05	0.78	
Reddy	1.05		
Other Backward Classes	3.50	4.9	4.4
Yadav	0.70	1.75	1.5
Vokkaliga	0.70	–	
Koeri	0.35	0.78	
Kamma	0.35	–	
Ezhava	0.35	–	
Other	1.05	2.33	2.9
Scheduled Castes	6.7	9.31	15.6
Scheduled Tribes	1.75	3.1	5.8
Christian	1.40	1.55	
Muslim	9.1	11.6	5.3
Parsi	1.05	1.55	
Sikh	2.46	0.8	2.9
Unidentified	25.26	1.55	
Total	100 (N = 285)	100 (N = 129)	100 (N = 206)

Source: Parliament of India's Who's Who 1950 (New Delhi: Government of India Press, 1950) and S.P. Singh Sud and A. Singh Sud, Indian Election and Legislators (Ludhiana: All India Publications, 1953).

unless every community, especially the larger and more popular communities advance equally and the advanced communities afford them opportunities for development, the advancement of India will be impossible [an argument Lohia made a few years later]. All that I demand is fairness and justice for the millions of people who are not in a position to come forward and compete with you...[31]

So far as the delineation of the 'Backward Classes' was concerned, Deshmukh regretted that they were 'likely to be defined in a very limited and restricted manner' because, he said, 'it is not the claim of only the Scheduled Castes that they are backward, it is not the tribal people alone who should be considered backward; there are millions of others who are more backward than these and there is no rule nor any room so far as these classes are concerned.'[32]

Deshmukh again spoke out in favour of reservations for the lower castes in November 1949 when Article 335 came up for discussion. This article indicated that 'The claims of the members of the Scheduled Castes and the Scheduled Tribes shall be taken into consideration, consistently with the maintenance of efficiency of administration, in the making of appointments to services and posts in connection with the affairs of the Union or of a state.' Deshmukh wanted the OBCs to be mentioned along with the Scheduled Castes and Scheduled Tribes. Thakur Das Bhargava, who was always well in tune with the Congress high command, objected that the Scheduled Castes and Scheduled Tribes should be 'given more rights than the "backward classes"', since they were 'more backward'.[33] Deshmukh replied that the assembly was 'going to exclude the backward classes simply because they have not formed themselves into one group or agitated.'[34] This might well be the truth, but Deshmukh was in a minority.

Deshmukh's proposal of reserving jobs to all the 'backwards' (and on top of it, on a population basis) gave rise to two objections which have since then become classics. First, several members of the high castes insisted that the administration, in order to be efficient, could not afford to recruit persons with little skill. Second, the multiplication of quotas would annihilate rewards for meritorious candidates, as less and less posts would be filled through competitive examinations. Pool Singh, a deputy from the United Provinces, rejected those arguments, replying first that 'equal merit presupposes equal opportunity and I think it goes without saying that the toiling masses are denied all those opportunities which a few literate people living in big cities enjoy,' and, second, that 'if the administration is to be efficient as my friends want it to be, then you must have people in the job who know something about the job and who come from the masses. Otherwise the administration will lose touch with the masses.'[35] These arguments in favour of affirmative action in the government services had few takers in the Constituent Assembly, since even the Scheduled Caste deputies did not take much interest in the discussion and put their own problems forward. Ambedkar concluded the discussion by repeating that it was not useful to define the backward classes in detail as some deputies urged him to:

Everybody in the province knows who are the backward classes, and I think it is, therefore, better to leave the matter, as has been done in this Constitution to the Commission which is to be appointed which will investigate into the conditions of the state of society, and to ascertain which are to be regarded as backward classes in this country.[36]

Ambedkar here referred to one of the proposals spelled out by the Advisory Committee's chairman, Patel, which eventually became Article 340 of the Indian Constitution voted on 26 January 1950:

The President [of the Republic] can by decree nominate a Commission formed by persons he considers to be competent to investigate, within the Indian territory, on the condition of classes suffering of backwardness as well in social as in educational terms, and on the problems they meet, the way of proposing measures which could be taken by the Central or a State Government in order to eliminate difficulties and improve their condition.[37]

In this article, as in Article 16(4), the word 'class' has been preferred to 'caste'.[38] This phrasing reflected the leftist inspiration of Nehru and others, and a widespread idea that India had to move away from caste-like organization. However, that the OBCs had to be identified on the basis of backwardness in social and educational terms left things wide open, and discussions continued on this issue in the early 1950s even though a commission was supposed to decide the case. Ambedkar systematically emphasized the responsibility of caste in social backwardness but Nehru's views were different, and this contrast came out very strikingly in the debate on the first amendment to the Constitution.

This amendment was voted in reaction to the 1951 decision of the Supreme Court in a case involving Madras State.[39] This judgement struck down the state reservations in educational institutions on the ground that it violated Article 15(1) and Article 29(2)[40] where the fundamental principle of non-discrimination was emphasized. The amendment, which was inserted as Article 15(4), stipulated that the state should not be prevented from 'making any special provision for the advancement of any socially and educationally backward classes of citizens or for the Scheduled Castes and the Scheduled Tribes.' The debate in Parliament primarily focused on the definition of the 'backward classes'. Ambedkar made it clear that, for him, what were called backward classes were 'nothing else but a collection of certain castes'.[41] Nehru was much less specific:

We have to deal with the situation where for a variety of causes for which the present generation is not to blame, the past has the responsibility, there are groups, classes, individuals, communities...who are backward. They are backward in many ways—economically, socially, educationally—sometimes they are not backward in one of these respects and yet backward in another. The fact is therefore that if we wish to encourage them in regard to these matters, we had to do something special for them.

[...] We want to put an end to...all those infinite divisions that have grown up in our social life...we may call them by any name you like, the caste system or caste religious divisions etc.[42]

Nehru certainly acknowledged the pernicious influence of the caste system but he did it almost reluctantly—caste does not appear in his first list of factors of backwardness—and for reasons different from Ambedkar's. He regretted the divisive effect of the social structure at a time when he wanted to build a strong, united India, and was not so much concerned by the need to fight caste as a priority objective for achieving social change. For him, economic modernization would eventually eradicate caste and communal feelings—all those legacies of the past that had to be blamed for 'backwardness'.

The First Amendment episode was revealing of the conflicts arising from any attempt at defining social backwardness. What should be the relevant criterion: caste, class, education? The first Backward Classes Commission was appointed in 1953 in order, precisely, to clarify the definition of the OBCs. Its report used the criterion of caste and recommended job reservations for the OBCs, but the report was rejected by the Indian government. Home Minister G.B. Pant resorted to progressive arguments, and opportunistically emulated a typically Nehruvian argument by considering that 'With the establishment of our society on the socialist pattern [...], social and other distinctions will disappear as we advance towards that goal.'[43] Secondly, Pant disapproved of the use of caste as the most prominent criterion for identifying the backward classes. He considered that 'the recognition of the specified castes as backward may serve to maintain and even perpetuate the existing distinctions on the basis of caste.'[44] Pant considered that it had become necessary 'that some positive and workable criteria should be devised for the specification of the socially and educationally backward classes', but he also suggested that ad hoc surveys should be held and that the state governments should be asked to establish their own list.[45] As a result, according to him, social transformation was not to be promoted by the Indian state: it was expected that it should stem from economic development and the policies of the states.

Like the Scheduled Castes, the lower castes have lost more than they have gained in the constitution-making process: before 1947, they enjoyed reservations in the administration and in the assemblies. For instance, in the Madras province, they benefited from a quota of 25 per cent in the administration and in Mysore, they got half of the upper ranks of the bureaucracy and two thirds of the lower ranks.[46] The governments of Madras and other states tried to pursue with these reservations, but these policies were challenged by upper caste litigants who objected that caste-based quotas did not comply with the new, constitutional criteria which relied on class considerations. In 1963, the Supreme Court ruled in favour of these plaintiffs in the famous case, *Balaji* v. *Mysore state* and several programmes of positive discrimination for the lower castes were cancelled.

*   *   *

To conclude, the attitude of the Constituent Assembly regarding the Scheduled Castes and the OBCs hardly subtantiates the idea that the Indian Constitution was a charter for social transformation. So far as the Scheduled Castes are concerned, they have been marginalized in the political arena over the first two decades of the Indian republic, as the fate of Ambedkar's political parties testifies. In addition to the co-option of its most able spokesmen by the Congress, 'Dalit politics' suffered from the fact that in the assemblies the Scheduled Caste MPs and MLAs did not forcefully advocate the cause of their caste fellows since they were not accountable to them: after 1961 there was not even one reserved constituency with a majority of Scheduled Caste voters.[47]

The 'Other Backward Classes' were also affected by the elitist bias of the Congress group in the assembly since the very definition of this new category remained very vague and non-operational. The Constitution, certainly provided that the president should appoint a commission for clarifying the situation and in 1953, Rajendra Prasad appointed the Kalelkar Commission. But its conclusions were rejected by the government because they explicitly defined the OBCs as castes, a notion modern India had to get rid of according to Nehru's government. However, the Kalelkar Commission initiated the crystallization of this category by recommending caste-based positive discrimination. In north India, the Kalelkar Commission helped the low castes to get a form of group consciousness. It was a new step in the process of reshaping caste identity. The next one was accomplished by political actors. From the late 1960s onwards, the OBCs mobilized through the socialist movements and Charan Singh's political parties. The former—especially the parties of Ram Manohar Lohia—were prompt to use reservations as a means for politicizing the lower castes: the unachieved creation of the OBCs by the Constituent Assembly was opening new opportunities to political leaders.[48] But the Constituent Assembly had not done more than pave the way to political developments that it had not dared to explore itself.

NOTES

1. Granville Austin, *The Indian Constitution: Cornerstone of a Nation* (New Delhi: Oxford University Press, [1966] 1999).
2. P. Radhakrishnan, 'Backward Classes in Tamil Nadu: 1872–1988', *Economic and Political Weekly*, 10 March (1990), pp. 509–17.
3. In this section, I concentrate on the seat reservation issue not only because this aspect of positive discrimination was dealt with at length by the Constituent Assembly, whereas other affirmative action programmes—regarding education, for instance—were not considered in the same detailed way, but also because what was at stake there was really the SCs' access to power. Hence the many debates which took place within the assembly.
4. For the province-wise caste break-up, see B.A.V. Sharma, 'Development of reservation policy', in B.A.V. Sharma and K.M. Reddy (eds), *Reservation Policy in India* (New Delhi: Light and Light Publishers, 1982), pp. 15–16.
5. On the sub-committee's debates, see, B. Shiva Rao (ed.), *The Framing of India's Constitution. Select Documents*, vol. 2 (Bombay: Indian Institute of Public Administration, 1967), p. 398.
6. H.J. Khandekar, another Mahar of the Constituent Assembly who was an opponent of Ambedkar since the 1930s when he had supported Gandhi against the demand for separate electorates, felicitated himself in the assembly that Ambedkar had 'given up the idea of separate electorates and [that] he voted for the joint electorates in the meeting of the Advisory Sub-Committee' (*CAD*, vol. XI, p. 741).
7. Speech by K.M. Munshi, on 27 August 1947, *CAD*, vol. V, p. 227.
8. Speech by S.L. Saksena, *CAD*, vol. V, p. 235.

9. Sardar Nagappa, a Mala from Andhra Pradesh, had joined Congress in 1930 and had been elected to the Madras assembly in 1937 and 1946. Within the Constituent Assembly he was the convenor of the Scheduled Castes members. In Delhi, he lived close to Ambedkar's house and saw him quite often: it is because of Ambedkar that he presented his project of 'qualified joint electorate'. Nagappa unsuccessfully contested the 1952 elections as a candidate of the Kisan Mazdoor Praja Party and then rejoined the Congress. R.K. Kshirsagar, *Dalit Movement in India and its Leaders* (New Delhi: MD Publications, 1994), pp. 282–3.

10. Speech on 28 August 1947, *CAD*, vol. V, p. 259.

11. See the much acclaimed speech by D. Velayudan, *CAD*, vol. V, p. 263.

12. Speech on 28 August 1947, *CAD*, vol. V, p. 270.

13. *CAD*, vol. V, p. 272.

14. Election Commission, *Report on the Second General Elections in India, 1957*, vol. 1, (New Delhi: Election Commission, 1959), p. 59; and Election Commission, *Report on the Third General Elections in India, 1962*, vol. 1 (New Delhi: Election Commission, 1965), p. 7.

15. Election Commission, *Report on the Third General Elections*, p. 8.

16. Marc Galanter, 'Compensatory discrimination in political representation', *Economic and Political Weekly*, 14 (7–8), February (1979), pp. 438–9.

17. Marc Galanter, *Competing Equalities: Law and the Backward Classes in India* (Delhi: Oxford University Press, [1984], 1991), p. 549.

18. Interview cited in F. Frankel, 'Caste, land and dominance in Bihar', in F. Frankel and M.S.A. Rao (eds), *Dominance and State Power in Modern India: Decline of a Social Order* (Delhi: Oxford University Press, 1989), p. 83.

19. *CAD*, vol. I, p. 59.

20. Draft of the Report of the Sub-Committee on Fundamental Rights to the Advisory Committee (3 April 1947), in B. Shiva Rao (ed.), *The Framing of India's Constitution*, vol . 2, p. 171.

21. Ibid., pp. 204–5.

22. Cited in *The Liberator*, 26 September 1944. (Typescript found in Ambedkar papers, reel ½, NMML, microfilm section.)

23. *CAD*, vol. V, op. cit., p. 249.

24. For instance, Dharam Prakash, from Uttar Pradesh, suggested that Depressed Classes or Scheduled Castes should be used instead of the nebulous notion of 'backward classes' (*CAD*, vol. VII, p. 687).

25. *CAD*, vol. VII, debate of 30 November 1948, p. 697.

26. Ibid.

27. Paul Brass, 'The Politicization of the Peasantry in a North Indian State–Part II', *Journal of Peasant Studies*, vol. 8, no. 1, October 1980, pp. 3–36.

28. Ibid., p. 702.

29. Chandrika Ram, returned from Bihar, put it like this: 'We have provided so many privileges to Harijans on the ground that they are backward and I fail to

understand why the same argument should not be applied for providing reservations for the backward classes' (Ibid., p. 688).

30. Granville Austin, *The Indian Constitution*, Appendix III.
31. *CAD*, vol. IX, p. 603.
32. Ibid., p. 604.
33. *CAD*, vol. X, p. 548.
34. Ibid.
35. Ibid., p. 616.
36. Ibid., p. 630.
37. *The Constitution of India (As modified up to the 15ᵗʰ August 1983)*, Government of India [no place, no date], p. 178.
38. Article 340 refers to 'socially and educationally backward classes' while Article 16 (4) refers to 'backward classes of citizens'.
39. Another decision of the Supreme Court regarding the Madras state's reservation policy about government jobs and a 1951 Bombay High Court decision were also involved. See 'Analysis of the Judgements of Supreme Court and the High Courts leading to the First Amendment of the Constitution', in Government of India, *Report of the Backward Classes Commission*, Second Part, vol. III (New Delhi, Government of India, 1980), p. 1; and Marc Galanter, *Competing Equalities*, pp. 164–5.
40. Article 29(2) states: 'No citizen shall be denied admission into any educational institution maintained by the State or receiving aid out of State funds on grounds only of religion, race, caste, language or any of them.'
41. *Parliamentary Debates*, vol. XII, 13 (Part II), column 90006.
42. Ibid., column 9616.
43. Government of India, *Memorandum on the Report of the Backward Classes Commission* (Delhi, Ministry of Home Affairs, [s.d.], p. 2.
44. Ibid.
45. Ibid., p. 3.
46. See O. Chinnappa Reddy, *Report of the Karnataka Third Backward Classes Commission*, vol. 1 (Bangalore: Government of Karnataka, 1990), pp. 11–12.
47. Satish Saberwal draws the same conclusion from the situation prevailing in the Punjabi context: 'A constituency at the state level [...] would have a large majority of high caste voters, making the candidates less dependent upon—and therefore less responsive to—the Harijan vote. Support from high caste faction leaders is, therefore, crucial for success at this level [as well as at the level of the parliamentary constituency, one might argue].' S. Saberwal, 'The Reserved Constituency. Candidates and consequences', *Economic and Political Weekly*, 8 January (1972), p. 79.
48. For more details, see Part III of Christophe Jaffrelot, *India's Silent Revolution. The Rise of the Low Castes in North Indian Politics* (New Delhi, Permanent Black, 2003).

12

Affirmative Action for Disadvantaged Groups
A Cross-constitutional Study of India and the US

Ashok Acharya

The theme of affirmative action usually triggers controversies and evokes passionate reactions and debates amongst both adherents and detractors. Irrespective of the context in which it is invoked, the philosophical content of the idea is essentially contestable and complex. As Michel Rosenfeld observes, 'the affirmative action debate is not between persons who are "pro-equality" and others who are "anti-equality". Both the most ardent advocates of affirmative action and its most vehement foes loudly proclaim their allegiance to the ideal of equality.'[1]

In the 1990s, both India and the US experienced a powerful backlash and sharp polarization of views on affirmative action that has produced a lot of acrimony and polemics and little balanced and objective analysis. This essay will attempt to map the different trajectories that policies of affirmative action (hereafter AA) have taken in the world's two large democracies. At a normative level, it will examine how the idea of equality of opportunity and its relationship to AA policies has been differently conceived in both societies.

DEFINING AFFIRMATIVE ACTION

Affirmative action usually entails a state's preferential policy toward particular groups. However, not all preferential policies can be justifiably adjudged as AA. Although the rationale for AA varies from place to place, it largely seeks to address structural inequalities between different groups in societies. In a positive sense, broadly speaking, it invokes ideas of fairness toward disadvantaged groups and of redress for unjust inequalities by way of temporarily redistributing or reallocating scarce goods.

Preferential policy, though used as a substitute for AA, is a broader term and may include either considerations of fairness, political accommodations of groups, or claims of distinct groups in particular territories.[2] For instance, preferential policies may be designed to politically satisfy dominant ethnic majorities or minorities such as the ones for Sinhalese in Sri Lanka, Bumiputeras in Malaysia, Marathas in Maharashtra, Assamese in Assam, or whites in South Africa. Although the political justifications for this may vary, these may be used by a powerful majority or a minority either in a democratic or non-democratic set-up (for example, whites in South Africa) as an accommodative measure to further entrench the groups' position that may result in the exclusion of others. AA is not concerned with these instances or the logic behind them.

In contrast to preferential policy, AA may be defined as a formal effort to provide increased employment and educational opportunities for under-represented and disadvantaged groups at a level sufficient to overcome past patterns of discrimination and present structural inequalities.[3] As a policy it seeks to ensure inclusion of disadvantaged groups that were hitherto excluded from full participation in citizenship. Once this is achieved, its rationale ceases to exist. In aiming to ensure justice for historic deprivations and to secure inclusion into full citizenship rights, AA needs to be both forward and backward-looking.

Marc Galanter chooses the term 'compensatory discrimination' instead of AA to categorize India's preferential policies. The purpose of discriminating on a compensatory basis is 'not exclusion and relegation but inclusion and recompense both for historic deprivations and to offset present handicaps'.[4] This discrimination, however, is a temporary affair, and should cease when inclusion of the excluded groups is achieved. Galanter, like any other advocate of AA policies, is aware that he is discussing a society with a long history of social inequality in which the idea of historical compensation becomes a morally compelling goal. The intuitive sense of justice that he employs is evident too in his painstaking and largely successful defence of such policies, something from which he also draws insights that are useful for Americans.

AFFIRMATIVE ACTION IN INDIA

The colonial policy of ensuring representation rights to the different communities is a crude precursor to AA policies in post-Independence India. Two principles ground the colonial policy of equal representation in political offices and jobs that led to communal or representational quotas: (1) the policy of balance between competing communities, or interests, and; (2) the policy to divide the nationalist front by creating differences. The constitutional scheme of preferences that came to fruition during 1947–50 was, on the contrary, based on the policy of social justice.[5] As a democracy in search of both formal and substantive equality, India had to address on an urgent basis the cause of the historically disadvantaged groups. Whereas the requirements of formal equality meant the equal protection of law against discrimination on morally invidious grounds, the requirements of substantive equality meant recognizing the needs of the more disadvantaged. Both of these commitments—one to individuals stripped of their differences, and the other to groups—run parallel in the Constitution.[6] At a broader level, they complement each other very much like the contents and provisions of fundamental rights and Directive Principles. Some rights have inscribed into them reasonable limits and restrictions.

Articles 15(4) (added by the First Amendment), 16(4), 46, 330, and 332 form the crux of the AA policies in India's Constitution. Article 335, which since the Constitution came into effect has been a subject of controversy and differing interpretations of the judiciary, qualifies the AA provisions by adding a rider that, claims of SCs and STs for federal and provincial jobs are to be taken into consideration 'consistently with the maintenance of efficiency of administration'.

Broadly, three types of preferences are sanctioned by the Constitution. First are reservations—and in the sense used here these denote a broader category than AA—which cover (a) special representation rights of SCs and STs by way of reserved seats in legislatures, and (b) quotas in government jobs and educational institutions. The reservation device, as Galanter notes, is also used to a lesser extent in 'the distribution of land allotments, housing, and other scarce resources'[7]. Second, preferences target a few groups—SCs, STs, and women—with regard to provision of certain expenditures, services and ameliorative schemes such as scholarships, grants, loans, land allotments, health care, and legal aid. In the course of fulfilling its developmental goals and mandate, antipoverty measures including rural development schemes, also target some of the usual beneficiaries of AA. Third, certain preferences take the form of special protections that safeguard vulnerable groups from oppression and exploitation, like measures to prohibit forced labour and others.

In explicitly stating such sweeping and enabling AA provisions, the Constitution thus seeks to strike a balance between formal and substantive equality. From the above account it is partially clear, however, that the state's moral commitments are more towards the SCs and STs than what it loosely defines as backward classes generally. It ought to be noted here that the founders of the Constitution did not give a comprehensive view of social backwardness and who merits inclusion in it. This was left to future governments to define and identify such groups for preferential policies. But otherwise in its dual commitments to both individuals and groups, the Constitution brings into a sharper focus the tension between individuals and groups as proper objects of state policies including those of AA.

During India's constitutional deliberations, equal citizenship for lower caste members meant assuming responsibility to initiate positive policy initiatives to offset historic disadvantages faced by them. Such initiatives underscored the need for AA policies for Scheduled Castes and Scheduled Tribes. Since the early 1990s, by a revision to the initial list of group beneficiaries, AA policies have been extended to include OBCs as well. As AA in India is constitutionally mandated and exists by way of quotas, the extension involves numerical goals in filling educational seats, government and public sector jobs from the listed group beneficiaries— SCs, STs, and OBCs.

AFFIRMATIVE ACTION IN THE US

In contrast to the Indian Constitution, the Constitution of the US contains no reference to AA. Of relevance in the AA debate is the Equal Protection Clause of the Fourteenth Amendment, which provides that no state shall 'deny to any person within its jurisdiction the equal protection of the laws'. The development of the policy owes itself to a few executive orders and congressional state legislative endorsements. The term 'affirmative action' first appeared in Executive Order 10925, which was signed by President John F. Kennedy on 6 March 1961. The Kennedy Executive Order followed a series of orders issued by every president[8] since Franklin D. Roosevelt that required government contractors to agree not to discriminate against employees or job applicants because of race, creed, colour, or national origin. The Kennedy Executive Order additionally mandated that these contractors agree to 'take affirmative action to ensure that applicants are employed, and employees are treated during employment, without regard to their race, creed, colour or national origin'.

On the other hand, the Civil Rights Act of 1964, an anti-discrimination statute, does not contain any mandate that an employer engage in 'affirmative action'. Title VII of the Act makes it an 'unlawful employment practice' for an employer to make employment decisions about an individual 'because of such individual's race, colour, religion, sex, or national origin'. Under very limited circumstances, an employer may base hiring decisions on religion, sex, or national origin if that factor is a 'bona fide occupational qualification (BFOQ) reasonably necessary to the normal operation of that particular business or enterprise'. The act does not include race as a BFOQ nor contemplate that race will ever be an appropriate hiring determinant.

The Supreme Court of the US has on several occasions examined whether AA plans are valid under both Title VII of the Civil Rights Act and the US Constitution. While the theories behind the anti-discrimination mandate of Title VII and the equal protection mandate of the Constitution are substantially similar, the court obviously has a longer history of decision-making under the Constitution. One challenge to observers of developments in the AA arena has been that the court has at times applied different logic in the constitutional cases (which deal primarily with government employers) than in the Title VII cases (which deal primarily, although not exclusively, with private employers). The court's decisions have not been confined AA in employment but cover also AA as it relates to education, minority set-asides for government contracts, and minority set-asides in the transportation and communications industries.

The first and perhaps best known Supreme Court decision on AA is *Regents of the University of California v. Bakke* (1978) where the court agreed with Bakke's claim that the programme of racial preference in admissions violated Title VI of the Civil Rights Act as well as the Fourteenth Amendment of the Constitution. However, the court refused to completely close the question of AA plans in that it would not go so far as to prohibit the university from any consideration of race in the course of its admissions process. In *United Steelworkers of America v. Weber* (1979), Justice Brennan stated the court's position quite clearly: 'We hold

Politics and Ethics of the Indian Constitution

that Title VII does not prohibit such race-conscious AA plans.' Justice Brennan also explained that a 'permissible' AA plan must: (1) mirror the purposes of Title VII ('to break down old patterns of racial segregation and hierarchy'); (2) 'not unnecessarily trammel the interests of the white employees'; (3) not 'create an absolute bar to the advancement of white employees'; and (4) be a 'temporary measure' that 'is not intended to maintain racial balance, but simply to eliminate a manifest racial imbalance' (Weber, 443 U.S. at 208-09). In *U.S.* v. *Paradise* (1980), the majority of the court echoed Justice Powell's opinion when it stated that race-based AA by the government is appropriate when there has been a finding of past government action that was 'long-term, open, and pervasive' discriminatory conduct.

Both the Indian and the American discourses on AA reveal some common patterns with a few differences. The Indian experience is heavily weighted toward the recognition of backward identities needing AA benefits. The American practice, on the other hand, has been exclusively modelled on an individual rights framework with non-discrimination as the major background rationale. In both contexts, however, one observes the popular appeal of the theme of compensatory justice. With regard to the particular forms that AA is endorsed in both societies, one cannot miss that whereas India allows for quotas, the US finds it favourable to consider weaker forms of AA.

From the 1960s to the late 1980s one notices in both societies the gradual evolution of a common pattern of AA justifications—from non-discrimination, to equal opportunity, to some form of equal outcome approach. In the following, I draw selectively on insights from scholars and jurists writing both from Indian and American perspectives.

LIBERAL JUSTIFICATIONS FOR AFFIRMATIVE ACTION

Liberal defences of AA usually encounter the challenge of justifying AA in terms of a common citizenship model. Since such policies require a departure from a framework of rights of individuals toward a conscious recognition of societal inequalities between groups, most arguments with regard to AA do have to take cognizance of the conflict entailed in the individual rights–group rights model. But arguments of liberal equality are not confined to the conflict of rights alone. At issue are other normative considerations such as the appropriate role of the state to ameliorate conditions of social equality; the nature of social justice itself; the morality of concerns regarding past injustices and the need to redress them; the present inequalities that are strengthened by continuing intentional, unintentional, or systemic discrimination; the question of opportunities; the proper means of redistribution; access to resources; fairness of institutions; and so on. Many of these concerns may also be interrelated and intertwined and reflect differently on how we conceive notions of justice toward groups, which bears a necessary relationship to issues of group and individual rights.

The starting point for any analysis for AA is usually non-discrimination, a goal that both supporters and detractors of AA construe as justified and worth defending. However, non-discrimination in itself is not a sufficient ground for advocating AA, although the facts of social discrimination are compelling grounds to consider the need for AA. In what follows I discuss non-discrimination, equal opportunity, and group disadvantage arguments to evaluate the efficacy of AA arguments. All of these three views may be said to lie on a continuum between the two ends of individual and group rights: the non-discrimination argument rests entirely on the individual rights principle and common citizenship model, the idea of equal opportunity maintains an uneasy relationship between commitments to individuals and groups, and the group disadvantage argument, as its very name suggests, lies squarely on the other extreme, that is, in the realm of group rights and group-differentiated citizenship.

THE NON-DISCRIMINATION ARGUMENT

This principle holds that all persons are to be treated with equal consideration. Because differences between individuals based on religion, race, caste, sex, language, and ethnicity (or, the different bases of ascription) are irrelevant for purposes of public policy and depend on morally arbitrary criteria, the state should ensure non-discrimination while distributing goods and opportunities, including if possible, policies that seek to redress past discrimination. Since this logic uses a universalistic language, the appeal of this principle is difficult to miss.[9] Hedged by the notion of individual rights, this principle is a guarantee of ideas such as common citizenship and formal equality. Armed with this kind of a difference-blind logic, the state seeks to protect each citizen equally. The state, and especially the judiciary, is bound, on this view, by a certain form of neutrality and objectivity.

The intellectual forerunner of a difference-blind view, especially in the American context, is Justice John Marshall Harlan's aphorism, postulated in his dissent more than a hundred years ago in *Plessy* v. *Ferguson*, that 'our Constitution is color-blind'. Plessy cannot, however, be credited for establishing social equality between races: since Plessy, and especially after *Brown* v. *Board of Education* in the present century, a difference-blind anti-discrimination view has come to complement both social and political equality.[10] This reasoning has increasingly become commonplace in American legal parlance now and consistent with this interpretation, the Supreme Court has applied the strict scrutiny test, an extreme variant of judicial review, to strike down what it calls 'invidious' racial classifications.[11] Such reasoning has constituted the legal, constitutional, and the moral fibre of American disquisition on attempts to disqualify colour- or race-conscious policies.

What are the Indian parallels to these expressions of difference-blind logic? The prominent Indian expositions on equal rights and common citizenship as reflected, say, in Article 14, the provisions of the removal of untouchability in Article 17, or the different provisions of the Part IV of the Constitution, together with a belief in the wall of separation thesis between religious and political matters, rely on a classical pronouncement of secularism. The reasoning runs somewhat like this: because the Indian state is secular it should not recognize differences based on religion or jati. But this view, as Galanter has rightly noted, is deeply mired in the process of first of all identifying the broad contours of group membership.[12]

How can a principle that is based on equal treatment be used to support special advantages for some on criteria that are held to be morally repugnant in the first place? In other words, how can a policy favour some on the basis of caste (or race) if caste as a distinction is held to be morally arbitrary? Shouldn't such a policy be considered to be impinging on the requirements of formal equality? Galanter is aware of this dilemma and accordingly argues,

[c]ompensatory discrimination may be viewed as an extension of the norms of equal treatment, an extension invited by our awareness that even when invidious discriminatory standards are abandoned there remain subtle and tenacious forms of discrimination and structural factors which limit the application of new norms of equality.[13]

When we speak of the new norms of equality we are obviously referring to the idea of substantive, as distinct from formal, equality. The idea of equal treatment, a fuzzy constitutional norm, may encompass both the above. Galanter's arguments operate at two simultaneous levels: on the one hand, the idea of equal treatment is extended to include AA policies; on the other, such an extension is made possible by a realization that persistent patterns of discrimination and inequality require a necessary articulation of a substantive conception of equality.

From a different angle, the limits of the non-discrimination principle as a tool to combat group exclusion and injustice are suggested by Owen M. Fiss and Iris Marion Young.[14] They argue, taking slightly different routes,[15] that an officially sanctioned policy of colour- and caste-blind formal equality is not enough and that we need to take into account how groups get excluded by a process which is unjust to begin with and that which does not redress the more severe forms of inequality. Young, for instance, argues that discrimination is not the chief injustice that marginalized groups face; for the latter, '[o]ppression, not discrimination, is the primary concept for naming group-related injustice'.[16] The argument of anti-discrimination, in assuming equal treatment, brings into a sharper focus the moral claims of both those who are included and those who are excluded from preferential policies. It tells us very little about how membership in a disadvantaged group may prove crucial to a policy based on differential, and not equal treatment. This logic is very much an American justification; 'an extension', as Galanter rightly notes, 'of classical individualistic non-discrimination principles'.[17] The non-discrimination argument is a weak, or possibly, non-existent defence of AA. Although a laudable goal, it does not tell us much about how to take stock of the continuity of discriminatory practices and what exactly the principle amounts to in relation to concrete policies designed to offset substantive and structural inequalities between groups.

THE EQUAL OPPORTUNITY ARGUMENT

At one level, the equal opportunity argument is closely tied to the anti-discrimination one. This is where both recognize and stress the ideal of individual rights. In a narrow sense, both encapsulate equal treatment between individuals. What this implies is recognizing and protecting legal equality or equal political rights designed to create a level playing field by guarding against discrimination, on the one hand, and on the other, to create formal access to conditions favourable to realizing the full development of human potential. The moment we expand the second part of our argument by taking it as a sort of concern relating to the moral imperatives of equalizing conditions of existence, we realize quite naturally that mere formal access to social goods and opportunities does not suffice. This calls for, hence, not just a regime of equal rights guaranteed by law, but an active involvement in removing obstacles to equalize prospects or chances of success.[18] This enlarged vision is a wider and more robust version of equal opportunity. Following their roles to realize formal and substantive equality, we may call them formal and substantive equal opportunity.[19]

Depending on how narrowly or widely one defines equal opportunity, there are distinct responses to AA. The narrow or the weak view, for instance, is what I have called above formal or (the-careers-open-to-talents) meritocratic equality of opportunity, an idea that holds that absent discrimination, offices should be open to talent. This restricted view, however, does not address the advantages persons have by virtue of differences in their upbringing, family resources, and everything else that contributes to a privileged starting point in life. This way of looking at what equal opportunity implies is hardly a justification for AA: instead, it argues how AA policies negate the possibility of careers being open to talents. Indeed, this cuts across moral principles that seek to establish AA.

In its stronger version, equality of opportunity promises individuals equal life chances to fulfill their goals.[20] Despite the fact that an expanded view strongly endorses a redistributive strategy, including AA policies, this has not helped evolve a singular approach that may translate equal life chances for all without succumbing to principled contradictions. In other words, the term 'equal life chances' implies very broadly both equal means and equal prospects of success. The two senses are, however, dissimilar in actual application and depending on the context we either refer to means- or prospect-regarding equality of opportunity. Let me unpack these concepts. Means-regarding equal opportunity refers to the possession of identical instruments or boxes of tools on the part of, let's say, two individuals or groups to attain an end-good, or goal. Prospect-regarding equal opportunity, on the other hand, emphasizes identical probability on the part of both to attain the same good. Whereas the first is content with providing the means for success, the latter is interested, not in the equal enjoyment of instruments that are crucial for, but in the equal possibilities of success.[21] A conservative account of equal opportunity usually captures the meanings associated with the means-regarding variety, which in turn does not always guarantee even chances of success between persons competing for scarce goods. Justified in a competitive market-driven society operating under a given system of values, it lays emphasis on merit and efficiency; means-regarding equality can only ensure that all competitors possess the wherewithal, that is, the instruments or the boxes of tool, to attain a scarce good.

Justifications for equal opportunity often conflate the two meanings. Much of legal scholarship, especially the American vintage, has sought to justify AA on the basis of equal opportunity understood in a sense where the state undertakes certain special programmes to ameliorate the conditions of those, for instance, who have borne the brunt of past discriminatory practices. But there remains a certain ambiguity regarding the proper classification of such policies. While recent rhetoric is usually informed by a notion of equalizing prospects, the practice falls somewhere between equalizing means and prospects.

The classic statement that justified the policy of AA by broadening the referent of equality in American rhetoric is that of Lyndon B. Johnson who, responding to the civil rights movement, argued that the policy of colour-blindness and political freedom for blacks is not enough:

You do not take a person who, for years, has been hobbled by chains and liberate him, bring him up to the starting line of a race and then say, 'you are free to compete with all the others', and still justly believe that you have been completely fair. Thus it is not enough just to open the gates of opportunity. All our citizens must have the ability to walk through those gates...We seek not just freedom but opportunity—not just legal equity but human ability—not just equality as a right and a theory but equality as a fact and as a result.[22]

Despite its ambiguity with regard to what it actually connotes, equality of opportunity is a powerful idea. It has a dimension with a very radical import, one that enhances the chances of all citizens to compete equitably for scarce goods. For serious proponents, the road to equalizing opportunities, of contemplating a fair starting point in individual lives, inevitably ends up in equalizing conditions in natal families. Logically, this is tantamount to a radical redistribution of resources, something that may be appealing and even morally required under ideal conditions, but at a huge cost to the liberty and autonomy of the family as James Fishkin argues.[23] Under non-ideal circumstances, however, the state assumes a temporary responsibility not to equalize unequal conditions between all (which is seemingly impossible), but to equalize rates of success between unequals. This aspect of equal opportunity best captures what we earlier discussed as prospect-regarding equality of opportunity.[24]

278 Politics and Ethics of the Indian Constitution

And it is this variant that is used as a public justification for stronger versions of AA.

Echoes of this logic in the Indian context reverberate in the constitutional debates and judicial discourse especially in the second quarter of the country's independence. At issue is the debate over Article 16: whereas Article 16 (1) generally makes the case for a provision of equality of opportunity, Article 16 (4) circumscribes the article to make room for state intervention for reservation of jobs for 'any backward class of citizens'. Reservation of jobs for backward classes, hence, constitutes in the constitutional discourse, an extension of the principle of equal opportunity to attain a desired representation of positions for people less advantaged. But this did not stop the opening of the floodgates by the judiciary to probe whether or not Article 16 (4) is consonant with, or an exception to, the general provisions of equal opportunity.

Many legal wrangles, as late as *Indira Sawhney* v. *Union of India* (1993), have deliberated on this question. The judicial consensus so far seems to be supportive of the constitutionality of Article 16 (4) and the view that it is not an exception, but substantially qualifies the import of equality of opportunity contained in Article 16 (1). Whereas in earlier judgements—especially, *Devadasan* v. *Union of India* (1964)—Article 16 (4) was argued to be an exception to the main provisions of Article 16, in a judicial debate that was locked by the competing claims of the inviolability of basic fundamental rights and the role of the state to ameliorate the conditions of the less privileged, latter-day interpretations starting from *State of Kerala* v. *N. M. Thomas* (1976) have largely accepted the close conformity between what counts as equality of opportunity and AA. But this 'doctrinal shift', as Galanter notices especially in Justice Mathew's judgement, involves stretching the meaning of equality of opportunity to include 'not only formal equality with fair competition', but 'equality of result'.[25] This argument, which we will later see as the staple of the Mandal report, in a certain sense also pre-empts the latter: For the 'expanded' version of equal opportunity in Justice Mathew's arguments, the one which justifies reservations, also enables a 'categorical' expansion in the sense that reservations may be extended to 'all members of the backward classes', and not just confined in scope to the SCs and STs.[26] Galanter argues that Thomas 'opens [a] Pandora's box: compensatory classification is available—perhaps incumbent—to succour all the disadvantaged'.[27] But what is more, Thomas succumbs to a pattern of 'patronage and dependence' which then becomes responsible to treat members of Scheduled Castes as the 'passive recipients of government largesse, rather than as active participants in their own improvement'.[28] In order to enable them to become active participants, a useful reconceptualization of Article 16 should have dwelt on 'age-waivers, fee concessions, travel allowances, coaching schemes, lowering of minimum marks, and other provisions that typically accompany reservations and often exist apart from reservation per se'.[29]

Such provisions would have brought about, what we argued before, an equalization of means: of providing the less endowed the wherewithal to compete equitably for scarce goods. The Indian judiciary and the state have, however, opted for the less cumbersome method: equalizing prospects of success between caste groups. This rhetoric at a certain level, by juxtaposing itself to what it pejoratively denounces as formal equality of opportunity, has tended to take the expansionist view, that of equality of results. It is tempting to subject this trend to a probing analysis. Suffice it to be noted at this point, however, that a version of equal opportunity that equalizes prospects of success between two blocs or categories of groups justifies itself by a rough measure of compensation to offset historical injustices, whereas, a policy of equalizing means of success may not be so backward-looking, and need not moreover endorse the stronger versions of AA.[30] However, we first need to be satisfied about the rationale for what justice requires in cases where there are huge disparities between groups of people. How should we, in other words, compensate disadvantaged groups that experience unequal circumstances? Under what circumstances may we utilize a prospect-regarding equality of opportunity between groups or alternatively equality of results to offset handicaps faced by members of the disadvantaged ones?

THE GROUP DISADVANTAGE ARGUMENT

With features that are attractive both to the Indian and American situations, the group disadvantage argument is presented most cogently by Owen M. Fiss. This argument, as its name suggests, has less to do with a conception of rights that are individual-based, and more with the social conditions of group existence. There are obvious problems in identifying social groups if by groups we mean collectivities, that have a sense of belongingness and interdependence. Such criteria, though important, are subjective in nature and are largely dependent on how groups define themselves. However, very often membership in certain groups, especially those that experience concrete social disadvantages, is something that may be imposed from the outside, the larger society, and may not necessarily be an internal affair. Hence, aside from the subjective and internal, in the context of disadvantaged groups, we come to terms also with their objective and external aspects. When we are referring to the objective aspect we are basically looking into the experiential conditions of disadvantages that are fairly concentrated and cumulative.

The theoretical structure underlying Fiss' work underscores the rationale for using the group disadvantage principle, as against the anti-discrimination principle, as the real mediating principle of the Equal Protection Clause in the American Constitution. This, Fiss argues, helps to broaden the referent of equality while taking a fuller account of social reality regarding the disadvantages of racial membership. On Fiss' account, blacks merit to be viewed as a disadvantaged group and hence by that logic are eligible for preferential considerations. But why just blacks? Fiss pleads that blacks are indeed a very special type of group; they are 'America's perpetual underclass': a group that suffers from being very worse-off, in addition to having had to endure being at the lowest rung for several centuries. Fiss reasons:

It is both of these characteristics—the relative position of the group and the duration of the position—that make efforts to improve the status of the group defensible. This redistribution may be rooted in a theory of compensation—blacks as a group were put in that position by others and the redistributive measures are owed to the group as a form of compensation. The debt would be viewed as owed by society, once again viewed as a collectivity.[31]

A rough but appropriate parallel to the blacks' situation is that of the Dalits in India who comprise 16.5 per cent of the population or roughly 138.2 million people as per the 1991 census. Dalits in India, closely analogous to the blacks in the US, are in a sense the worst-off group that has occupied the lowest rung in the social hierarchy for centuries. According to the 1991 census, the literacy rate among the Dalits is 37.41 per cent compared to the general literacy rate of 52.21 per cent. A vast majority of Dalits—81.28 per cent—live in rural areas, and almost 50 per cent of them are landless agricultural labourers. Their present lot compounds historical factors of exclusion, centuries of sub-human existence, and a clear statement of lack of self-respect. Clearly any redistributive strategy, including AA, cannot in the Indian context wish away the reality of these complex, enduring, structural inequalities.

Keeping in mind these normative considerations, the Constituent Assembly set about the task of devising a complex array of preferential policies for the Dalits. Invoking the same principle, Galanter concedes the usefulness of 'compensatory discrimination' to offset disadvantages that are concentrated and cumulative.

The idea of compensation evokes, too, the logic of substantive equality, one that closely borders on the idea of equality of results. Owing to the unequal circumstances that disadvantaged groups find themselves in, the mere presence of a policy of non-discrimination and equal treatment does not suffice. Where disproportionate shares of goods have already been cornered by the more advantaged groups, a more equitable redistribution becomes morally imperative. However, this redistribution does not involve a start-from-scratch process under an ideal setting which keeps in view the needs of all groups or individuals. The redistributive strategy under non-ideal circumstances that interests us here, on the other hand, acknowledges the messy realities of accumulated injustices meted out to particular groups that still experience in the present situation gross inequalities of a cumulative nature. A part of this strategy is to mitigate the conditions of the disadvantaged groups on a fast-paced, short-term track so as to bring about a noticeable change in their fortunes, changes that equalize outcomes between unequal groups. A justification for AA on an equal outcome approach involves not only egalitarian considerations per se, but also the added normative requirement of compensating for past wrongs. When making a case for compensation for disadvantaged groups we bridge the important divide that separates equality of opportunity from that of equality of results. It is somewhat like recovering what Lyndon Johnson implied in his famous foot-race aphorism that fairness requires more than a commitment to impartial treatment, 'not just equality as a right and a theory but equality as a fact and equality as a result'.[32] When used to offset intended and discernible disadvantages recognizable in particular groups, justifications for AA undergo a shift from what we had earlier discussed as prospect-regarding equality of opportunity to equality of results.

Aside from an argument to reinforce the compensatory theme, there are other plausible ways of presenting different versions of equality of results. The latter also represents arguments made on behalf of quotas and proportional equality. Quotas, the stronger version of AA, specifically relate to numerical set-asides, of particular allocations to jobs, places in universities, or seats in legislatures. It may be both, proportional or disproportional to the relative percentage of the beneficiary group to the total population. When the former, quotas become indistinguishable from a sense of proportional equality:[33] both use the equal outcomes approach to distribute goods on a proportional basis. Let's say if beneficiary groups J and K constitute 18 and 25 per cent of the general population, then on an equal outcomes rationale both of them deserve 18 and 25 per cent of jobs, seats, etc.[34] This rationale becomes morally compelling under conditions of a glaring disparity: for instance, where both J and K occupy, let's say 3 and 5 per cent of jobs, considerably lesser and disproportionate to their relative strengths in the overall population. On the other hand, the logic of proportional equality can be extended to the whole of the population as was done comprehensively in the Communal Government Orders of Madras in 1927 and 1947 to cover all caste groups on a proportional basis so as to benefit the non-Brahmin majority.[35] But where unused for a long period, accumulated quotas could be so huge that they simply might be disproportional in size to the relative population of the group.

There can be a wide range to how one may use the idea of equal outcomes in practice. The idea can have different implications depending on how it—as compensatory distributions, quotas, proportional equality, or a combination of any of these two—is sought to be used. In the Indian case, I argue next that by enhancing quotas, we are seriously compromising considerations of equal opportunity. The American example, on the other hand, reveals that there is a powerful backlash against AA policies and a Supreme Court that increasingly looks more conservative in recent times compared to the 1970s and 1980s is reinforcing this. A very narrow definition of equal opportunity and non-discrimination informs the contemporary judicial discourse in the US.

INDIA: POLITICAL FAIRNESS AND THE LIMITS OF QUOTAS

The implementation of the Mandal Commission report, which implied an extension of quotas by 27 per cent for the benefit of the OBCs over and above the existing level of quotas at 22.5 per cent already mandated for SCs and STs, raised a political storm in 1990. The then Janata Dal government headed by V. P. Singh was accused of pandering to the OBC vote bank. A crossfire of political and academic debates surrounded concerns regarding the extended scheme of AA for OBCs. At the surface level, the debate concerned the moral appropriateness of AA: those who did favour AA defended the caste-based quotas, with or without extensions; those who did not favour AA of any sort argued against a regime of unfair quotas, the unfairness of which they thought was intensified by extensions to less deserving groups. At another and what may be construed as deeper level serious questions were raised regarding Mandal's criteria for determining caste backwardness. Save some,[36] most were not interested in analysing Mandal's normative justifications that made a case for quota extensions. Central to the report's recommendation is the background understanding of social justice and what that entails for AA.

In opting for an 'expansive' view with regard to who belongs to the middle stratum of the caste hierarchy, the report identifies 3743 castes, which following the 1931 census is roughly 52 per cent of the population, as backward. Using a controversial toolkit of caste backwardness,[37] it favoured proportional equality between those that it considered as backward and the rest that were fortunate enough to be 'forward'. But since the Supreme Court in its landmark decision in the *Balaji v. State of Mysore* (1963) case had decreed an upper ceiling of 50 per cent as the limit for the total quantum of reservations,[38] the report was constrained to recommend only 27 per cent of reservation for OBCs, so that together with the quotas for SCs and STs it did not exceed the 50 per cent limit. Had there been no such upper limit the report, relying on the rationale of proportional equality, would have in all likelihood recommended a further increase of 52 per cent reservations. How does the report justify its argument for proportional equality?

The key mantra of the report lies in a wishy-washy notion of equality of results. Following the work of Herbert J. Gans,[39] the report makes a tripartite distinction between equality of opportunity, equality of treatment, and equality of results. Using the narrow view of equality of opportunity (see above), it says that Article 16 (1) is in fact a libertarian, and not an egalitarian, principle and, in any case, this conception does not take us far in giving due consideration to the needs of the disadvantaged. Similarly, equality of treatment by its implication of uniformity of justice doesn't differentiate between the advantaged and the disadvantaged. Hence, the only true egalitarian ideal that ensures justice to the disadvantaged, according to the report, is the idea of equality of results.[40] That begs the question, how is equality of results to be realized? Equalizing resources, or rights, or both? With regard to rights, we have already observed above how under a group-disadvantage principle certain stronger versions of AA could be justified. We will consider the efficacy of that for OBCs shortly. But let me first address the issue of equalizing resources. Under ideal circumstances, this would be a laudable scheme and would involve, as Dworkin's work[41] (1981) suggests, a comprehensive system of distributive justice that compensates for unequal circumstances. Is this feasible? And does it merely involve short-term compensations such as AA? Gans himself answers these questions in ways, which the Mandal Commission neither acknowledges nor incorporates in its report. Shortly after dismissing the two other conceptions of equality, Gans moves on to analyse the infeasibility and unattractiveness of the ideal of equality of results:

Equality of results can produce sameness; when everyone is equal with respect to a given resource, every person has the same amount of that resource, and if all resources were equalized, everyone would be uniform on all counts. Such uniformity is neither desirable nor achievable; a society in which everyone had an equal amount of the same resources would probably be deathly boring, but in any case it is not achievable. For one thing, human beings differ in many characteristics, and not all these differences can be erased by an equality of resources. For another, in a society with a division of labor, sameness is impossible because people fill so many different roles.[42]

The question that interests us next is to consider whether or not the OBCs are disadvantaged enough to merit AA? Is their situation comparable to those of SCs and the STs? Although the report does argue about certain indicators about social and educational backwardness in general, a large part of its conclusions as regards who merits inclusion in this category is derived from subjective assessments that are methodologically flawed and suspect.[43] What is difficult to sustain from the group disadvantage principle is the inclusion among OBCs of prominent well-entrenched, powerful, land-owning, dominant castes, euphemistically called the 'creamy layer'. Writing much before the report was implemented, André Béteille[44] did point out that the 'moral basis' of the claims for special treatment for Dalits was quite different from those that were made in favour of the OBCs. The same difference holds true even today. Since not all OBCs experience the same disadvantages, and those who do more than the rest do not compare well with groups whose disadvantages are fairly concentrated and cumulative, the rationale for AA is truly suspect.

What about the other issue regarding empowerment that is used on behalf of OBCs? This view, as pointed out by V. P. Singh above, entails an equalization of power. Does equality of results necessitate a sort of proportional equality to enhance equal outcomes between merely unequal blocs/groups? While this argument is fundamentally flawed in terms of what democratic justice might require, let us engage it on its own terms—that of equality. Strict equalization of outcomes for different groups implies that we are engaging the notion of prospect-regarding equality of opportunity between blocs. Is this fair? I have already argued above why this seems compelling as a justification for AA. Where disadvantages across groups are unequal, what consequences arise if we extend the logic to many more groups and create a larger bloc of AA beneficiaries? That, I argue, is grossly unfair: when the size of the bloc gets larger, unequal prospects within the blocs increases. This is a common sociologically based refrain against AA policies in general: the argument here is that instead of benefiting the more deserving within the bloc, an expanded bloc creates more opportunities for the less deserving to corner the benefits. Furthermore, once vested interests get ossified, such arrangements tend to diverge from policies that also aim to enhance the means-regarding equality of opportunity between individuals.[45] However, the real risk of stretching the ideal of equality of results seems to me to be a compromise with even a substantive version of equality of opportunity within and across blocs. The purpose of the above exercise was to caution against the detrimental consequences that are unleashed by unreasonable numerical games of quotas which instead of mitigating inequalities, create other (and possibly more severe) forms of unequal deprivations.[46]

What does the Constitution require us to do in this context? In a very interesting observation, Galanter reminds us that the Constitution requires us to ameliorate the conditions of the SCs and STs. This he likes calling our 'national commitments'. An expansion of these constitutional commitments will entail a dissolution (or dilution) of 'the original and distinctive national commitment to the core beneficiary groups, the Scheduled Castes and Scheduled Tribes'.[47] One of the ways to ensure that this dilution does not take place is to lay down principled justifications like the group-disadvantage argument for what needs to be defended as stronger versions of AA.

It will be instructive for our purposes to revisit the Constituent Assembly Debates to find out the nature of deliberations that characterized the issue of quotas. Defending a version of prospect-regarding equality of opportunity in access to public services and government jobs between different caste communities, B.R. Ambedkar, the Dalit chairman of the drafting committee in the Constituent Assembly, argued against extensive quotas, as this would compromise the principle itself.

Supposing, for instance, reservations were made for a community or a collection of communities, the total of which came to something like 70 per cent of the total posts under the State and only 30 per cent are retained as the unreserved. Could anybody say that the reservation of 30 per cent as open to general competition would be satisfactory from the point of view of giving effect to the first principle, namely, that there shall be equality of opportunity? It cannot be in my judgment.[48]

It is evident from Ambedkar's comments above that he drew a line on the limits of quotas. Political fairness toward disadvantaged groups requires that where quotas exceed its mandate, it needs be mediated by narrower versions of equal opportunity arguments. This is not only found defensible in India's constitutional interpretation as part of its original commitments but can normatively relate to the precarious balance that exists in political theory between liberty and equality.

US: JUDICIAL BACKTRACKING AND POLITICAL BACKLASH

In a reversal of trends beginning late 1980s/early 1990s, and especially in *City of Richmond* v. *J.A. Croson Co.* (1989), the court struck down the city's minority set-aside plan because Richmond had not made a preliminary finding of past discriminatory action by anyone in the Richmond construction industry. The court refused to accept the effects of past societal discrimination as a compelling enough reason to justify race-conscious action by the municipal government. After the retirements of Justice Brennan and Justice Thurgood Marshall from the court, the court has increasingly adopted an approach that is unsympathetic to AA policies. In *Adarand Constructors, Inc.* v. *Pena* (1995), which involved a Congressional AA programme that provided a financial incentive to government contractors who hired minority subcontractors, the court applied strict scrutiny to this race-based programme and found that it violated the Fifth Amendment to the Constitution. The court confirmed that a finding of systemic and egregious discrimination by the government would justify a race-based remedial programme so long as the programme was a narrowly tailored remedy.

Following the Supreme Court's Adarand decision, President Bill Clinton ordered a comprehensive review of federal programmes that made distinctions on the basis of race or ethnicity. The Department of Justice concluded after the review that AA based on race or ethnicity was still appropriate in those cases in which the federal government had a factual basis on which to assume that past discrimination had taken place, and that some limited consideration of race as a factor may be appropriate if no other reasonable means of including minority participation was available.[49]

The Supreme Court has declined two important opportunities to review cases AA in light of its Adarand decision. The first of these, *Hopwood v. Texas* (5th Cir. 1996), involved an AA plan by the University of Texas law school that was designed to increase the number of minorities in its entering class. The Supreme Court refused to review the decision of the Fifth Circuit Court of Appeals, which had struck down the programme as unconstitutional.

Reflecting the shifts in public opinion, the Supreme Court now takes a dim view of such group preferences and entitlements. The Constitution, says Supreme Court Justice Sandra Day O'Connor, protects 'persons, not groups'. Justice Antonin Scalia states that 'under our Constitution, there can be no such thing as a creditor or a debtor race'. 'Government cannot make us equal', says Justice Clarence Thomas. 'Affirmative action programs stamp minorities with a badge of inferiority' no matter how competent they are or how hard they work. The beneficiaries of special treatment, says Justice Thomas, too often 'develop dependencies or adopt an attitude that they are entitled to preferences'.

Quotas in the US are generally considered strong, extreme, and undesirable forms of AA. The usual criticism against quotas, also understood as minority set-asides, is that it creates more harm than it attempts to do good, is divisive in nature, and does not help those for whom it is intended. As Bickel notes,

[A] racial quota derogates the human dignity and individuality of all to whom it is applied; it is invidious in principle as well as in practice. Moreover, it can easily be turned against those it purports to help. The history of the racial quota is a history of subjugation, not beneficence. Its evil lies not in its name, but in its effects: a quota is a divider of society, a creator of castes, and it is all the worse for its racial base, especially in a society desperately striving for an equality that will make race irrelevant.[50]

The judicial backtracking on questions of AA have been matched by popular initiatives in two American states to do away with AA: California (Proposition 209, 1996) and Washington (Initiative 200, 1998), passed initiatives designed to prohibit the use of AA in state matters. Significantly, these initiatives were directly voted on by the populations of each state (as opposed to being enacted by the states' legislatures) and in each state the vote easily exceeded the 50 per cent majority required for passage. California's Proposition 209 prohibits the government from 'giving preferential treatment to any individual or group in public employment, public education, or public contracting on the basis of race, sex, color, ethnicity or national origin'. The wording of the Washington Initiative 200 is modelled after Proposition 209 of California.

CONCLUSION

The most important conclusion we derive from our study establishes that there is wisdom in justifying AA for structurally disadvantaged groups, true for both India and the US. However, one notices that in the Indian context there is a strong temptation (running concurrently with vote bank considerations) to apply flexibility to the definition of disadvantaged groups resulting in a weakening of the idea of equal opportunity. In the American context, the equal opportunity argument tied to the non-discrimination theme, is being used both in academic and judicial rhetoric to undermine whatever remains of AA policies.

NOTES

1. See Michel Rosenfeld, *Affirmative Action and Justice* (New Haven: Yale University Press, 1991), pp. 2–3.
2. The distinction that I draw between affirmative action and preferential policies is meant to highlight the contrasting rationale between what constitutes as fair (as in the case of AA) and that which may or may not be so (the case of preferential policy). For a helpful discussion of preferential policies, see Donald L. Horowitz, *Ethnic Groups in Conflict* (Berkeley and Los Angeles: University of California Press, 1985) and Thomas Sowell, *Preferential Policies: An International Perspective* (New York: William Morrow and Co., Inc, 1990). In the Indian context, the differences between the two forms of preferential policies that I highlight are covered as two distinct types of 'preferential policies' in Myron Weiner and Mary F. Katzenstein, *India's Preferential Policies: Migrants, the Middle Classes, and Ethnic Equality* (Chicago: University of Chicago Press, 1981).
3. This is a revised version of AA used in Congressional Digest (1996).

4. Marc Galanter, *Competing Equalities: Law and the Backward Classes in India* (Delhi: Oxford University Press, 1984 [1991 with new preface]), p. 3.

5. See André Béteille, *Society and Politics in India: Essays in Comparative Perspective* (London: Athlone Press, 1991), pp. 205–6.

6. See, Llyod I. Rudolph and Susanne Hoeber Rudolph, *In Pursuit of Lakshmi: The Political Economy of the Indian State* (Chicago: University of Chicago Press, 1987). However, Béteille's reading of the constitution puts more emphasis on the rights of the individual. 'In the Indian Constitution the individual is the principal, though not the sole, bearer of rights and responsibilities, and citizenship is an unmediated relationship between the individual and the state' (Béteille, *Society and Politics in India*, p. 222) His readings of the articles of equality (14–17) are meant to stress 'the centrality of individual rights, treating religion, race, caste, sex, etc. as possible impediments to their full exercise' (ibid., p. 223; emphasis in original). The only exceptions that Béteille would allow to such a view of the Constitution are the special provisions related to affirmative action. See more generally ch. 9 of *Society and Politics in India*.

7. Galanter, *Competing Equalities*, p. 43.

8. President Lyndon B. Johnson (Executive Order 11246 of 1965), President Richard Nixon (Executive Order 11478), and President Bill Clinton (Executive Order 13005).

9. See Owen Fiss, 'Groups and the Equal Protection Clause', in Marshall Cohen, Thomas Nagel, and Thomas Scanlon (eds), *Equality and Preferential Treatment* (Princeton: Princeton University Press, 1977), p. 105.

10. See Andrew Koppelman, *Antidiscrimination Law and Social Equality* (New Haven: Yale University Press, 1996), pp. 1–2.

11. Recent decisions informed by a colour-blind logic are *Richmond v. J.A. Croson Co.* (1989) and *Adarand Constructors, Inc. v. Pena* (1995). In both of these, the court struck down affirmative action programmes thereby narrowly circumscribing the use of race as a factor in public policy. See Scott Cummings, 'Affirmative Action and the Rhetoric of Individual Rights: Reclaiming Liberalism as a "Color-Conscious" Theory', *Harvard Blackletter Law Journal* 13, 1997, p. 193.
    Contrast this to the 'benign' classifications used in earlier judgements to justify AA.

12. See Marc Galanter, 'Secularism East and West', *Comparative Studies in Society and History*, 7, 1965, pp. 133–59.

13. Galanter, *Competing Equalities*, pp. 552–3.

14. Fiss, 'Groups and the Equal Protection Clause', pp. 84–154. Iris Marion Young, *Justice and the Politics of Difference* (Princeton: Princeton University Press, 1990).

15. Young seeks to identify various forms of group injustices and as a result has an expanded notion of marginalized groups than Fiss' account allows.

16. Young, *Justice and the Politics of Difference*, p. 195.

17. Galanter, *Competing Equalities*, p. 553.

18. Edwin Dorn argues that since equal opportunity refers to scarce goods, we cannot speak of legally enforceable rights as we would, for instance, while referring to equal protection guaranteed by the Fourteenth Amendment. See Edwin Dorn, *Rules and Racial Equality* (New Haven: Yale University Press, 1979), p. 111.

19. Note, however, that Rawls distinguishes them as formal and fair equality of opportunity. Formal equality of opportunity, understood as ensuring equal legal access to all advantaged social positions, Rawls argues, does not guarantee that every person has a fair chance to attain them. To give others a fair chance in terms of the fair equality of opportunity principle in the Rawlsian scheme entails that 'those with similar abilities and skills should have similar life chances'. Hence, the second part of Rawls' difference principle establishes that social and economic equalities are to be so arranged so that they are 'attached to offices and positions open to all under conditions of fair equality of opportunity'. See John Rawls, *A Theory of Justice* (Cambridge, MA: Belknap Press, 1971), pp. 73, 83.

20. Cf. Amy Gutmann and Dennis Thompson, *Democracy and Disagreement* (Cambridge, MA: Belknap Press, 1996). Extending a perspective of deliberative democracy, Gutmann and Thompson argue that 'fair opportunity' does not mean equal life chances, nor 'equal chances for jobs and other similar goods...it requires that each qualified applicant receive equal consideration for the job' (ibid., p. 311; my emphasis). But their understanding of equal consideration falls somewhere between a well-developed anti-discrimination and a meritocratic equality of opportunity. An ideal of equal consideration of interests may, in Gutmann and Thompson's analysis, have nothing to do with opportunity per se, but spell out in general what constitutes a well-developed theme for a ground-level impartiality.

21. For this view, see Douglas Rae, *Equalities* (Cambridge, MA: Harvard University Press, 1981), ch. 4. For discussions below on this dichotomy, I follow Rae's analyses.

22. Lyndon B. Johnson's address (1965) in Lee Rainwater, and William L. Yancey, *The Moynihan Report and the Politics of Controversy* (Cambridge, MA: MIT Press, 1967), p. 126. For a historical analysis of the changing rhetoric of equality in the American context, see Celeste M. Condit and John L. Lucaites, *Crafting Equality: America's Anglo-African Word* (Chicago: University of Chicago Press, 1993).

23. See generally, James Fishkin, *Justice, Equal Opportunity, and the Family* (New Haven: Yale University Press, 1983).

24. Douglas Rae defines it thus: 'Two persons, j and k, have equal opportunities for x if each has the same probability of attaining x' (Rae, *Equalities*, p. 65).

25. Galanter, *Competing Equalities*, p. 386. Justice Mathew argues: 'If equality of opportunity guaranteed under Article 16 (1) means effective material equality, then Article 16 (4) is not an exception to Article 16 (1). It is only an emphatic way of putting the extent to which equality of opportunity could be carried viz, even up to the point of making reservation' (ibid., p. 386).

26. Galanter, *Competing Equalities*, p. 387. Justice Krishna Iyer, however, is at variance with Justice Mathew's views. The former is more circumspect about who qualifies under Article 16 (4); stating that not all backward caste groups qualify to be recognized within its ambit, he argues that the legitimate classification can only be made on behalf of the 'harijans', a group which faces 'social disparity [that is] grim and substantial'(ibid., p. 387).
27. Galanter, *Competing Equalities*, p. 393.
28. Ibid., p. 391(my emphasis).
29. Galanter, *Competing Equalities*, p. 389.
30. As a non-compensatory and possibly stronger defence of AA, equality of opportunity looks not at the past, but at the future. This view is concerned with the evolution of an egalitarian society in the positive sense; whereas, the compensatory defence is still locked in the past and hence, essentially backward-looking. See Bowie E. Norman and Robert L. Simon, *The Individual and the Political Order: An Introduction to Social and Political Philosophy*, 3rd edn (Lanham, MA: Rowman & Littlefield Publishers, Inc., 1998), ch. 9.
31. Owen, 'Groups and the Equal Protection Clause', p. 127, original emphasis.
32. Rainwater and Yancey, *The Moynihan Report and the Politics of Controversy*, p. 126.
33. For a defence of this view and an argument based on proportional group equality in the Indian context, see M.P. Singh, 'Jurisprudential Foundation of Reservations', in Vinay Ch. Mishra (ed.), *Reservation Crisis in India: Legal and Sociological Study on Mandal Commission Report* (New Delhi: Bar Council of India Trust, 1991) pp. 245–74.
34. Such a constitutional justification, as noted above, already exists for reservation of legislative seats for SCs and STs at both the federal and provincial levels in accordance with the terms of Articles 330 (2) and 332 (3).
35. See Galanter, *Competing Equalities*, p. 365. For an account of caste mobilization and early reservation in South India, see Sunita Parikh, *The Politics of Preference: Democratic Institutions and Affirmative Action in the United States and India* (Ann Arbor: University of Michigan Press, 1997), pp. 80–4. On the costs that this policy has entailed, see Dharma Kumar, 'The Affirmative Action Debate in India', *Asian Survey*, 1992, XXXII (3), pp. 294–8.
36. See Galanter, *Competing Equalities*, Preface to the 1991 edn and André Béteille, 'Distributive Justice and Institutional Well-Being', *Economic and Political Weekly*, XXVI (11&12; annual), 1991, pp. 591–600.
37. For a brief but incisive criticism of Mandal's use of caste criteria, see Galanter, *Competing Equalities*, Preface to the 1991 edn, p. xviii.
38. Although the Supreme Court in this case argued for lesser percentages of approximately one-third shares as 'reasonable', both the provincial governments and the high courts have taken the 50 per cent limit as a permissible 'flat maximum' (Galanter, *Competing Equalities*, pp. 402–3).
39. Herbert Gans, *More Equality* (New York: Pantheon Books, 1973).
40. Long after he had ceased to be in power, ex-prime minister V.P. Singh in a lecture delivered at Harvard University on 29 September 1995 defended his

policy of implementing AA for OBCs echoing the same logic that the report had expounded on: 'If equality has indeed to be realized then we have to ensure equality of results and take concrete measures for the same. Mere provision in the Constitution that we are equal does not make everyone equal. Till power is shared equally inequality will remain' (V.P. Singh, 'Affirmative Action in India' [Text of the Harvard lecture], *Mainstream*, XXXIV (24), 1996, p. 11).

41. Ronald Dworkin, 'What is Equality? Part 2: Equality of Resources', *Philosophy and Public Affairs*, 10(4), 1981, pp. 283–345.

42. Gans, *More Equality*, p. 65.

43. See Galanter, *Competing Equalities*, Preface to the 1991 edn, pp. xviii-ix and P. Radhakrishnan, 'Mandal Commission Report: A Sociological Critique', in M.N. Srinivas (ed.), *Caste: Its Twentieth Century Avatar* (New Delhi: Viking, 1996), pp. 203–20.

44. André Béteille, 'The Problem', (Reservations), *Seminar* 268, 1981, pp. 10–13.

45. 'The broader the class of beneficiaries and the more expansive the benefits, the greater the danger that the essentially transitional arrangements contemplated by the Constitution will ossify into permanent arrangements' (Galanter, *Competing Equalities*, Preface to the 1991 edn, pp. xxii).

46. This is the reason why I further argue that there are moral limits to what political compromises should achieve. Political compromises arrived between groups sometimes drastically fail to address what's fair and the line between what counts as AA and preferential policies tends to get erased. Hence, a compromise formula of let's say 37.5 per cent doesn't address questions of fairness. Compare the views of E.J. Prior ('Constitutional Fairness or Fraud on the Constitution? Compensatory Discrimination in India', *Case Western Reserve Journal of International Law*, 28 [1], 1996, pp. 63–99) who advocates a lowering of the quotas for OBCs to pacify all groups. However, Prior is right to argue in my view that the report's 'proportional reasoning is unsound and not substantiated by the Constitution' (ibid., p. 96).

47. Galanter, *Competing Equalities*, Preface to the 1991 edn, pp. xxi-xxii. This argument informs Galanter's overall analysis.

48. *Constituent Assembly Debates (CAD)*, vols 1–12 (Delhi: Lok Sabha Secretariat, 1967).

49. U.S. Department of Justice, 1996.

50. Alexander M. Bickel, *The Morality of Consent* (New Haven: Yale University Press, 1975) p. 133.

SELECT REFERENCES

Austin, Granville, *The Indian Constitution: Cornerstone of a Nation* (Oxford: Clarendon Press, 1966).

Chalam, K.S., 'Caste Reservations and Equality of Opportunity in Education', *Economic and Political Weekly*, XXV (41), 1990, pp. 2333–9.

Congressional Digest, 1996, 75 (6–7) (June-July).

Cunningham, Clark D. and N.R. Madhava Menon, 'Race, Class, Caste...? Rethinking Affirmative Action', *Michigan Law Review*, 97 (5), 1999, pp. 1296–1310.

Das, Bhagwan, 'Moments in a History of Reservations', *Economic and Political Weekly*, XXXV, (43 & 44), 2000, pp. 3831–4.

Gupta, Dipankar, 'Positive Discrimination and the Question of Fraternity: Contrasting Ambedkar and Mandal on Reservations', *Economic and Political Weekly*, 2 August 1971–8.

Iyer, Ramaswamy R., 'Towards Clarity on Reservation Question', *Economic and Political Weekly*, XXVI (9-10), 1991, pp. 495–500.

Jain, Harish C. and C. S. Venkata Ratnam, 'Affirmative Action in Employment for the Scheduled Castes and the Scheduled Tribes in India', *International Journal of Manpower*, 15 (7), 1994, pp. 6–25.

Jalali, Rita, 'Preferential Policies and the Movement of the Disadvantaged: The Case of the Scheduled Castes in India', *Ethnic and Racial Studies*, 16 (1), 1993, pp. 95–120.

————, 'Affirmative Action Policies and their Ramifications in India', in Michael A. Burayidi (ed.), *Multiculturalism in a Cross-National Perspective* (Lanham: University Press of America, Inc, 1997), pp. 153–85.

Jenkins, Laura D., 'Preferential Policies for Disadvantaged Ethnic Groups: Employment and Education', in Crawford Young (ed.), *Ethnic Diversity and Public Policy: A Comparative Inquiry* (New York: St Martin's Press, 1998), pp. 192–231.

Mandal Report, *Reservations for Backward Classes: Mandal Commission Report of the Backward Classes Commission* (Delhi: Akalank Publications, 1980 [1991]).

Manor, James, 'How and Why Liberal and Representative Politics Emerged in India', *Political Studies*, 38, 1990, pp. 20–38.

Mansbridge, Jane, 'Should Blacks Represent Blacks and Women Represent Women? A Contingent "Yes"', *The Journal of Politics*, 61 (3), 1999, pp. 628–57.

Mendelsohn, Oliver and Marika Vicziany, *The Untouchables: Subordination, Poverty and the State in Modern India* (New Delhi: Cambridge University Press, 2000).

Menski, Werner, 'The Indian Experience and Its Lessons for Britain', in Bob Hepple and Erika M. Szyszczak (eds), *Discrimination: The Limits of Law* (London: Mansell Publications Ltd, 1992), pp. 300–43.

Nesiah, Devanesan, *Discrimination With Reason? The Policy of Reservations in the United States, India and Malaysia* (New Delhi: Oxford University Press, 1997).

Newell, W. R., 'Affirmative Action and the Dilemmas of Liberalism', in Michael W. Combs and John Gruhl, *Affirmative Action: Theory, Analysis, and Prospects* (Jefferson, NC: McFarland & Co., Inc., 1986), pp. 44–60.

Parekh, Bhikhu, 'A Case for Positive Discrimination', in Bob Hepple and Erika M. Szyszczak (eds), *Discrimination: The Limits of Law* (London: Mansell Publications Ltd, 1992), pp. 261–80.

Shah, Ghanashyam, 'Social Backwardness and Politics of Reservations', *Economic and Political Weekly*, XXVI (11–12), 1991, pp. 601–10.

Sheth, D.L., 'Reservations Policy Revisited', *Economic and Political Weekly*. XXII (46), 1987, pp. 1957–62.

Sorabjee, Soli J., 'Equality in the United States and India', in Louis Henkin and Albert J. Rosenthal (eds), *Constitutionalism and Rights: The Influence of the United States Constitution Abroad* (New York: Columbia University Press, 1990), pp. 94–124.

Varshney, Ashutosh, 'Is India Becoming More Democratic?' *The Journal of Asian Studies*, 59 (1), 2000, pp. 3–25.

Wilson, Prince E., 'Discrimination against Blacks in Education: An Historical Perspective', in William T. Blackstone and Robert D. Heslep (eds), *Social Justice & Preferential Treatment: Women and Racial Minorities in Education and Business* (Athens: University of Georgia Press, 1977), pp. 161–75.

Section IV

13

Religion and the Indian Constitution
Questions of Separation and Equality

Gurpreet Mahajan

This essay tries to understand the conceptual framework that governs issues of religion in democratic India. It focuses almost exclusively on the constitutional design and through the latter reflects on that which is distinctive of state–religion interactions in India. In independent India, responses of the state to questions of religion and its attitude towards religious communities have been among the most controversial issues and they have elicited a wide range of responses. While some analysts have been critical of the incursions of religion in the public domain and the close association between state and religion in one form or another, a few have accused the state of partisan behaviour. The majority community has accused it of favouring the minorities, and the latter have in turn blamed it for neglecting their interests.

To intervene in this debate and to make sense of what was characteristic of secular India, it is imperative to turn to the Indian Constitution. One needs to begin with the normative framework and the principles that shaped the place of religion in the polity. This task gains some urgency because assessments of the state–religion interface have overwhelmingly been influenced by the way secularism and equality have been interpreted and applied in other countries. Since these perspectives have been helpful neither in making sense of the problems which confront contemporary India nor in apprehending the relation between state and religion in the country, the following pages reflect upon the specifics of the Indian Constitution. They try to outline the framework that is enunciated here on issues of religion. The constitutional structure has in the post-Independence era been interpreted in a variety of ways. The attitude of different religious communities to the constitutional design as well as its interpretation by the state and its institutions have not however been included here. The essay, as I said at the very outset, is narrowly focussed. It dwells only on the framework that is articulated in the Indian Constitution, and here too it speaks primarily of the place accorded to religion and religious communities in the public domain, for it is this that has given a distinctive form to secularism in India.

I

Commentaries on the Indian Constitution almost always begin with the statement that the key features of this document are taken from other constitutions. Analysts from Granville Austin to Durga Das Basu all preface their discussion with the note that the chapter on Fundamental Rights was drawn from the American Constitution, the Directive Principles of State Policy from the Constitution of Ireland, and the parliamentary system from Britain. There is no doubt that in the deliberations of the Constituent Assembly the constitutions of these and many other European states were discussed at some length. Individual members debated the experiences of these nations and some even tried to incorporate specific clauses from these texts. Nevertheless what emerged from these considerations was a document whose foundational principles and norms were to a large extent quite distinct. On several crucial issues the Constitution of independent India endorsed a position that was significantly different from the perspective that was expressed by the dominant liberal framework of that time. To take an example: even though the idea of including a chapter on Fundamental Rights was influenced by the American Constitution, the rights that were granted to citizens and communities as well as the notion of individual and state that informed the thinking on rights was largely without precedent. While exploring the Indian Constitution it is necessary to underline this dimension. Indeed the experiences of post-Independence India and the challenges that confront it can best be understood by attending to the distinctiveness of the constitutional design.

II

There are several issues on which the approach of the framers of the Indian Constitution was quite distinctive but perhaps nowhere more than on the question of equality. The members of the Constituent Assembly saw caste and religious identities as the most significant sources of discrimination in society, and through a democratic system they wished to counter these. They visualized democracy as a framework where ascribed identities would neither be a basis for allocating political rights nor of disadvantaging any citizen in the public domain. In conceiving democracy in this form they reflected the sentiments of contemporary liberalism. However while constructing a framework for ensuring equality for diverse castes and religious groups they differed widely from much of the liberal discourse.

The goal of social non-discrimination or equality could have been pursued in a variety of ways. The framers of the Indian Constitution could have followed the American example and provided equality before the law. In fact, as Granville Austin points out, in a 'traditional and hierarchical society that did not recognize the principle of individual equality', this itself would have been quite revolutionary.[1] Yet, the members of the Constituent Assembly decided not to settle for this. Even as they provided 'equality under the law' and 'equal protection of the law' they felt that (a) a general assertion of formal equality was inadequate; and (b) formal equality was not always sufficient for ensuring equal treatment or even equal opportunity. A general assertion of formal equality does not pinpoint practices that a society must regard as being discriminatory and unacceptable. The framers felt that certain social practices, on account of their wide acceptability, may continue, even though they treat some unfairly. This is something that has since been argued forcefully by feminist scholarship and needs no further elaboration. It is sufficient to say that it is only when certain structures of discrimination are identified that the principle of formal equality can be a tool of emancipation. When, for instance, excluding women from the public domain was not identified as a site of discrimination, political and civil rights granted to individuals as citizens continued to exclude women. However, when this form of exclusion came to be challenged, women could invoke the idea of formal equality to claim equal rights of participation. The framers of the Indian Constitution recognized this, and they specified a number of caste-related practices that would not be accepted in society. It would perhaps have been sufficient to locate certain sites of discrimination, but in their enthusiasm the framers made a list of unacceptable or discriminatory practices, and in doing so embodied the principle of formal equality in a fairly distinctive way.

In addition to giving some concrete substance to the idea of formal equality, the Constituent Assembly members deviated from the accepted liberal norm in yet another significant way. At a time when the free world was wary of attempts to differentiate between citizens, the members of the Constituent Assembly asserted that equality before the law was insufficient for ensuring equal opportunity and equal treatment to all. To ensure that castes and communities that were previously excluded and segregated from the rest of society are included into the political system, it singled out Scheduled Castes and Scheduled Tribes for special treatment. The Constitution reserved seats for them in the education system, government jobs, and legislative bodies at all levels.

Besides the Scheduled Castes and Scheduled Tribes, the Constitution gave special attention to religious communities. It recognized the presence of diverse and historically distinct communities within the polity, and assured each of them that their cultures and identities would be protected in independent India and that they would each be treated equally. In other words, it tried to promote equality between different religious communities by acknowledging their separate and distinct character and by protecting the distinctiveness of each. Religious communities were conceived here as being separate but equal, and it is on these terms that they were included within the polity. Much more importantly, the framers accepted, at least implicitly, that Hindus constituted a majority and that in a framework of formal equality this community may come to dominate the political and cultural domain. Hence, they pursued equality for diverse communities by implicitly making a distinction between the majority and the minorities, and accorded to the latter special treatment that would enable them to express, and perhaps even sustain, their distinct identity. This was the general principle that informed the Indian Constitution and set it apart from other liberal polities of that time.

III

The Indian Constitution could have opted for a different framework while dealing with the issue of religion and religious communities. There were before it at least two other models, one derived primarily from America and the other from the experiences of countries such as Britain, Germany, and Sweden. The former combined disestablishment with the policy of separation, while the latter continued with the practice of an established religion even as it simultaneously extended the liberties granted to other non-recognized faiths. Each of these was discussed in the Constituent Assembly, and there was strong support for each. In different ways, Nehru,

Pant, and Patel favoured a system in which the citizen rather than her community identity would receive priority. Even though they wished to assure the minorities that they would be treated as equals, they believed that this might well be achieved by conceiving individuals as citizens, and granting rights to them in that capacity. While moving a resolution for the constitution of the Advisory Committee on Fundamental Rights, Pant stated:

I cannot however refrain from referring to the morbid tendency which has gripped this country for the last many years. The individual citizen who is really the backbone of the State, the pivot, the cardinal centre of all social activity, and whose happiness and satisfaction should be the goal of every social mechanism, has been lost here in that indiscriminate body known as the community. We have even forgotten that a citizen exists as such. There is the unwholesome, and to some extent a degrading habit of thinking always in terms of communities and never in terms of citizens. (Cheers). But it is after all citizens that form communities and the individual as such is essentially the core of all mechanisms and means and devices that are adopted for securing progress and advancement. It is the welfare and happiness of the individual citizen which is the object of every sound administrator and statesman. So let us remember that it is the citizen that must count. It is the citizen that forms the base as well as the summit of the social pyramid and his importance, his dignity and his sanctity, should always be remembered.[2]

This vision did not however go unchallenged in the Constituent Assembly. Several members, particularly K.T. Shah, K.M. Munshi, and the representatives of different minority communities, drew attention to community memberships. They spoke of the need to supplement rights of citizens with rights of communities, and underlined the significance of religious identity to the self. Eventually, it was the perception of the latter that prevailed. While concessions were made to the former view, the Constitution nevertheless placed religion and community in the public domain.

The Indian Constitution dealt with the issue of religion by endorsing the principle of non-establishment of religion but without advocating the separation of religion from politics. Put simply, it said 'no' to established state religion and 'no' to the policy of 'separation'. This meant that the state was to have no religion of its own, but religion was not also viewed as a personal or private matter: it was placed squarely in the public domain and the state was expected to be involved in a variety of ways with religion. While non-establishment assured different religious communities, particularly the minorities, that the state would not endorse any religion as its own, non-separation gave a special status to religion and religious communities in the public domain. It placed certain obligations upon the state without disallowing state regulation of the public domain, including certain spheres of religious community life.

It is necessary at the present juncture to underline this difference in the approach to issues of religion because discussions on secularism in India and the accompanying analysis of state–religion interactions almost always revolve around the question of separation. The only difference being that some theorists lament the absence of distance between state and religion,[3] while others question the possibility of separating religion from politics here.[4] Against this vast body of literature it is important to underline that India did not pursue equality or the path of secularism by endorsing the policy of separation. Although it asserted that the state shall not espouse any religion, this was not an endorsement of the path of separation.

In America dis-establishment went hand-in-hand with the policy of separation. Indeed the two elements were so combined that we customarily assume that the absence of state religion suggests that religion will not enter into politics and, vice versa, the state will keep itself away from religion. However it is essential to distinguish between these two fairly distinct elements. Dis-establishment indicated that the practice of established state churches would be discontinued and that the federal government would not give recognition to any church as the official national church. The doctrine of separation, on the other hand, stipulated a specific relation between the state and religious groups and institutions. It suggested that the state will not determine or dictate religious beliefs, and that it will not be involved in the activities of religious communities and institutions. Not only will it disengage itself from their religious activities, it will also distance itself from all other kind of work in which they are engaged. Thus, even if religious groups establish schools and hospitals, these organizations will have the liberty to function in accordance with the law but will not receive any financial or other support from the state. In fact till the first decade of the twentieth century, public buildings, parks, and related facilities were not open for use by religious bodies.[5] Although other voluntary groups and associations could access and use public places for their work, religious groups were assiduously kept away, and this was one of the issues that led these groups to complain of discrimination by the state. In a nutshell, separation stipulated such a divide between state and religion/religious institutions and groups.

The framers of the Indian Constitution decided not to follow the path of separation. In this regard they were by no means unique, for several European countries created conditions for religious tolerance and non-discrimination without following the policy of separation. England continued with the practice of an established state religion. Even as it removed the legal barriers that prevented members of non-recognized faiths from participating in political and public life, it retained the Church of England as the official national church. Likewise, Sweden retained support of the official Evangelical Lutheran Church, but created room for greater religious liberty by extending formal recognition to the Roman Catholic Church and the Protestant Church to ensure a greater degree of religious freedom. In many of these countries the officially recognized religion/s enjoyed a special status in society and polity, and members of religious institutions were actively involved in a variety of activities, from having representation in education boards to providing religious education in schools. Independent India followed neither the English nor the American model. It chartered a different route wherein non-establishment of religion was combined with the absence of separation.

A number of reasons dictated this choice. Non-establishment was clearly intended as an assurance to minority communities that they would be equal partners in the polity. Even though there were pressures to conceive the state as a 'Hindu State' since Pakistan was to be a 'Muslim State', the leaders of the Indian National Congress, who played a critical role in the Constituent Assembly, maintained that the country had an obligation to the minorities who had chosen to stay on in India. It had to assure them that the state of India would not establish or endorse any religion as its own. This was the minimum guarantee for religious non-discrimination. The question of separation, on the other hand, was influenced as much by historical and pragmatic considerations as it was by a conception of the self. In an environment where religious communities were politically mobilized and extremely assertive, it would have been exceedingly difficult to keep religion out of the public domain. In any case separation would have meant that religious communities and their various activities would not receive any support from the state. Almost all communities—the 'Hindu' majority as well as the minorities— wished to avoid this. Since several temples, especially in erstwhile princely states, were supported and managed by the ruler, the majority community underlined the need to provide continued support to them. Minority communities too made demands for direct and indirect assistance of the state for their non-religious activities, and, quite obviously, these demands could not be accommodated within the framework of separation.[6]

Considerations of this kind merited attention in the discussions within the Constituent Assembly, as they were backed by the belief that religion was a constitutive element of personal identity. To put it somewhat differently, the policy of non-separation was not simply a reluctant concession made for the sake of peaceful coexistence or tolerance; rather it was based on the claim that religion is not simply a private or a personal matter: it has a public dimension and the state needs to take cognizance of that. The public nature of religion placed certain obligations upon the state, particularly since the Constitution sanctioned not only the right to religious worship but also the right to religious practice. The latter meant that religion would no longer be restricted to a specific space or territory in the public arena. If religious practice entailed that members of a community have the liberty to immerse the idol of Durga in running water, or to gather for a holy dip in Ganga on the day of full Kumbh or at Allahabad on the last day of the month of 'Shravana', the state would have to accommodate that. It would have to make arrangements to facilitate the observance of these practices. The right to religious practice thus gave religion and religious groups an opportunity to be highly visible in the public arena, to carry processions outside of their designated place of worship, and to stamp their presence in the public domain. What is perhaps equally important is that it bestowed a special status upon religious leadership. Practices were to be determined and directed by religious leaders. Their voice, and not that of the individual, was the authoritative one in this regard. When it came to issues of religious practice, the state was, at least implicitly, expected to discuss and negotiate with the religious leadership. The state could of course establish certain norms in the interest of public order, health, and morality. It could also initiate social legislation to promote equality for all. Yet, the recognition it bestowed upon religious leadership in matters of community life certainly privileged their voice.

High visibility and presence in the public domain was one reason why religion was not treated as a subject of the private sphere. The other equally significant component of the thinking was that religion is a kind of group engagement, and it must be treated like other forms of collective and associational life. In other words, religious groups and collectivities must be treated on par with all other groups and associations in society. Religious groups could, like any other association, engage in competitive politics, form parties, and express their point of view. The work undertaken by religious groups, particularly social and welfare-related work, could receive assistance from the state. The Constitution in fact specified that educational institutions set up by religious communities would be eligible for state funds. Even though it placed no obligation upon the state to give them funds, these institutions could also receive state support. The state was expected to treat educational institutions run by religious communities like any other educational institution and not discriminate against them.

State support to religious communities, treating religious communities like other associations, and granting these communities the right to form parties and participate in the political arena were measures that manifested, and followed from, the basic rejection of the policy of separation. Non-separation thus bought religion frontally in the public arena, but at the same time also allowed the state to engage with matters of religion as also with the affairs of religious communities. To put it in another way, non-separation meant that religion could have a strong presence in the public domain and religious communities could have access to public resources and facilities even in the pursuit of their religious work. And vice versa it implied that the state need not dissociate itself from religion or the affairs of religious communities. It could, in principle, interfere in matters of religion and regulate religious life. The Constituent Assembly took cognizance of this possibility and, even as it endorsed the policy of non-separation, placed certain limitations upon state interference in religion. Limitations were placed to protect the religious liberty of all communities. Indeed, one might say that the Constitution aimed to treat all communities as equals not by separating religion from politics but by guaranteeing religious liberty to all.

IV

The principle of religious liberty to all was the operative norm by which India pursued the goal of religious non-discrimination. Instead of following the path of separation, it framed a secular polity by acknowledging the existence of different religious communities and asserting that they would each be treated as being distinct, or separate, and equal. The Constitution quite unambiguously identified Hindus, Muslims, and Christians as distinct religious communities, each with a separate culture, religious practices, and personal laws. At the time of framing the Constitution, Sikhs and Parsis were also included as minorities. The former was separately represented in the Sub-Committee on the Rights of Minorities and even though the Parsi community was not formally represented in this committee, R.K. Sidhwa pleaded their case.[7] Consequently, in the proposals endorsed by the committee, provision was made for representation of the Parsis as a minority community.[8] The committee did not consider separate representation for the Buddhists, but subsequently they too were recognized as a distinct community. On the other hand, the Jain community made frequent representations to be treated as a distinct religious group; however these requests were not acceded to. It is only later that the Minorities Commission made a positive recommendation for treating them as a separate community.

The recognition of minority religious communities was from the outset a subject of some controversy. Even when communities were recognized as separate minorities, they were not always unambiguously separated or designated as distinct religions. For instance, the Sikhs and Buddhists were recognized as separate minorities, yet for purposes of personal law and 'temple entry' they were incorporated within the fold of Hinduism. Over the years the issue of recognition as a separate community has become more complex as the Supreme Court has for a variety of reasons acknowledged a whole range of sects within Hinduism as separate sects and declared them as minorities.[9] The boundaries that have remained more or less firm are those that separate Hinduism from Islam and Christianity. What the Constitution provided was for these and other recognized minority religious communities to be treated as equal. It also assured them that their distinctiveness would be acknowledged and protected in independent India.

Treating the recognized religious communities as equals meant that they would enjoy more or less the same degree of religious liberty. While religious practices and activities of religious communities were subject to some restrictions, it was said that the religious liberty of each of these communities would be equally protected. Each would enjoy the same rights with regard to religion. However, since the Constitution functioned on the assumption that the culture of the majority may prevail in the public domain, it made special provisions for the minority religious communities. To protect their distinctiveness it gave them the right to establish institutions to conserve their culture and language. Although no obligation was placed upon the state in this regard except to ensure that these institutions have the necessary freedom to exist, yet the right to conserve one's language did indirectly imply that minorities had claims that must be recognized, if not also acknowledged, by the state.

The commitment to religious liberty for all placed certain limitations upon the state and its interference in the sphere of religion. As was noted earlier, the policy of non-separation brought religion in the public and political domain but at the same time it also permitted state involvement and intervention in matters of religion. In retrospect it appears that non-separation sat well with the two contending perspectives within the Constituent Assembly: one demanding a strong state for checking the communal and separationist aspects of religion, and the other asserting the rights of religious communities in the public domain. It allowed the former to regulate religion and at the same time it gave the latter an opportunity to seek equal rights for religious communities in the public arena. So both parties supported it, but there still remained the question of balancing the two contending claims. The Constitution-makers had to determine both the nature and extent of permissible state intervention, and they also had to stipulate the rights and liberty that religion and religious communities may exercise and enjoy.

The Constituent Assembly struck a balance by giving them the right to profess, practise, and propagate their religion and by allowing them access to public resources and the freedom to participate in the political arena. It brought the state in and allowed it to regulate religion and the activities of religious institutions, but in certain designated spheres only. The question of religious belief and worship were more or less sheltered from state intervention, but the state could regulate religious practices in the interest of protecting public order, morality, and health. This gave the state fairly extensive powers to regulate religious activities. In addition it allowed the state to regulate non-religious affairs of religious institutions. Here the Constitution made a distinction between religious and non-religious activities of religious institutions and organizations. Even though no sharp distinction was made in this regard, it reinforced the commitment to protect the religious liberty of all communities. Indeed the Supreme Court of India has interpreted it in this spirit and checked state interference in such matters as appointment of the 'Mahant' and appropriation of trust funds for specific purposes.

The one issue on which the Constitution gave power to the state to intervene in religious practices was 'temple entry'. While the principle of religious liberty was applied to curb state intervention in religion, it was not to stand in the way of caste equality. In some ways, the Constitution-makers placed the goal of ensuring equality, at least social and political equality, for members of all castes above everything else. It was to be accommodated along with other concerns, certainly with the commitment to religious liberty for all communities. Consequently, the Constitution opened Hindu places of worship to members of all castes. In addition to this, it also allowed the state to initiate legislation for social welfare. This was a concession to the women representatives who had objected to the inclusion of a right to religious practice as against religious worship. Nevertheless it did give the state another lever to intervene in matters of religion and to initiate such legislation as may promote equality for all citizens.

To conclude, the Constitution of India created room both for religion in the public domain as also for state intervention in matters of religion. In fact it placed certain obligations upon the state. In particular, it called upon the state to not discriminate against religious institutions and exclude them from public resources. State involvement in religious institutions and, to some extent, in facilitating the practice of religion thus flowed from the constitutional design. The Constitution also made a distinction between the majority and the minority communities. Although the boundaries it drew between these two kinds of communities have since been redrawn, nevertheless it operated with a framework that separated the majority and the minority. Lastly, with regard to the minorities, the Constitution did not adopt a proactive approach. That is, it did not direct the state to ensure that the culture and language of these communities survives and is protected, yet it assumed that the minorities would like to 'conserve' their culture and identity. In other words, it legitimized the desire of minority communities particularly to preserve their culture.

V

It is not surprising to find that two issues have dominated the discussions on religion in the post-Independence period. First, the presence of religion in the public domain; and second, state intervention in matters of religion. Although these are issues that deserve a more detailed analysis than in possible here, let me nevertheless touch upon them very briefly. The Constitution of India, as was mentioned earlier, rejected the policy of separation. It consciously placed religion in the public domain. It also made no distinction between the private and public lives of state functionaries. Indeed its implicit assessment of the importance of religious identity to the self implied that individuals must not be expected to efface that identity. Hence, the issue was one of fairness or dealing with different religious communities equally, rather than negating or suppressing the religious identity. Yet, even as the Constitution operated with this vision, disputes arose on this issue almost immediately and were reflected in the differences between Prime Minister Jawaharlal Nehru and President Rajendra Prasad. Nehru, who frequently associated religion with superstition, obscurantism, and blind faith, wanted that public functionaries should not associate themselves with any religion or religious activity. He wrote to Prasad about this at the time when the latter was to join the inauguration ceremony of the reconstructed Somnath temple. The differences between them on this and other issues remained, in part because what Nehru desired was not the formal norm endorsed in the Constitution. He favoured separation and hoped that others would be persuaded to accept this, but that was not to be. However, the differences that surfaced at the very outset cast a long shadow. It once again brought in the issue of separating religion from politics and this has remained a recurrent theme in debates on secularism in India.

The issue of state intervention is, in some ways, a more complex one. It has raised a number of questions, the most important being whether the state has intervened unduly in the affairs of the Hindu religious community while sparing the others. Since the Constitution operated with the majority–minority framework, it is hardly surprising that there has been greater caution about legislating for the minorities. This is not to say that the Hindu state could not legislate for the Muslims and other minorities but that such actions could easily be misconstrued as attempts to assimilate the minorities, and the constitutional warning in this regard has been at times heeded. What is also worth remembering here is that the various institutions of the state have not always acted as a single unit. On a number of occasions the interventions of legislative bodies at various levels have been severely curtailed by the Supreme Court. Further, on several occasions the court has ruled to protect Hindu religious practices and sheltered them from state intervention.

Relatively speaking, it is in making available public resources to different religious communities that state officials and different governments have been most arbitrary. The policy of non-separation gave governments the freedom to patronize some communities—to extend or withdraw its largesse—and this was something that was not open to review by any other body. Whether this has helped to protect minority religious communities is a question that must be left for a separate discussion. However, even as we analyse the changes introduced by the ideologues of Hindutva, one needs to remember that non-separation was the constitutional mandate. We may debate whether this has served the larger goal of equal liberty for all, but surely bringing religion into the public sphere or into politics is not a new phenomenon. The terms of the debate on secularism in India therefore need to be rethought, both to understand the changes being introduced by a government that is inclined to give a clear cultural identity to the nation-state as well as to apprehend the path that India followed in pursuing equality for all groups and communities.

NOTES

1. Granville Austin, *Working a Democratic Constitution* (Delhi: Oxford University Press, 1999), p. 7.
2. Reproduced in B. Shiva Rao, *The Framing of India's Constitution: Select Documents*, vol. II (Delhi: Indian Institute of Public Administration, 1967), pp. 62–3.
3. See, for instance, K.N. Panikkar (ed.), *Communalism in India* (Delhi: Manohar, 1991); Tavleen Singh, 'The Secular Myth', *Seminar*, vol. 304 (1985), pp. 25–8.
4. See T.N. Madan, 'Secularism in its Place', *The Journal of Asian Studies*, vol. 46, no. 4. (1987), pp.747–59.
5. See Leo Pfeffer, *Church, State and Freedom* (Boston: The Beacon Press, 1953).
6. See Shiva Rao, *The Framing of India's Constitution*, pp. 309–86.
7. Ibid., pp. 318–22.
8. See 'Report of the Sub-Committee on Minorities', 27 July 1947, in Shiva Rao, *The Framing of India's Constitution*, pp. 396–400.
9. See Gurpreet Mahajan, *Identities and Rights: Aspects of Liberal Democracy in India* (New Delhi: Oxford University Press, 1998), pp. 86–109.

14
Passion and Constraint
Courts and the Regulation of Religious Meaning

Pratap Bhanu Mehta

INTRODUCTION

This essay is an attempt to look at moments in Indian constitutional practice that might be described, for want of a better term, as Hobbesian. Thomas Hobbes had with single-minded clarity argued that the exercise of private judgement posed a formidable challenge for the state in at least three respects. First, the exercise of private judgement in matters such as what constitutes a threat to one's life lead to the chaos and anarchy in the State of Nature. The chaos of the State of Nature was for Hobbes not simply a consequence of vainglory run amok. It was a product of the fact that when it is left up to each one of us to decide when our life is in danger, we are all, given the inherent uncertainties that attend to such judgements, likely to make pre-emptive strikes against others. Lots of individuals making pre-emptive strikes cannot but result in chaos, in a state of affairs where life is nasty, brutish, and short. One of the things we do in setting up a state, Hobbes argued, is to give up the right to private judgement. The sovereign produces order and regularity not only because it possesses a coercive mechanism but also because it is the sole judge of what constitutes a threat to society. Only when we *authorize* the state to make judgements on our behalf can a well-ordered society be produced.

Despite the fact that modern states, and those governed by liberal constitutions, place a great stress on civil liberties, the scope of these liberties is circumscribed by the Hobbesian imperative of reason of state.

It should come as no surprise that all liberal constitutions, not just the Indian Constitution, have some difficulty in protecting civil liberties when the survival of society is seen to be at stake. Almost all states, even the most liberal ones, have had to formally uphold the Hobbesian idea that the state is the final authority empowered to make judgements about when society is imperilled. Under such circumstances, the state can exercise its prerogative to suspend civil liberties that citizens can enjoy only so long as the state is not in mortal danger. Most states are Hobbesian in this respect: they recognize the principle of necessity which justifies the right of every sovereign state to take all reasonable steps needed to protect and preserve the integrity of the state. But the crucial point is that the state—and not citizens acting in a private capacity—is the final judge of when it is in such danger.

It is fair to say that this doctrine has been one of the principal threats to civil liberties, and Indian courts have given the executive very wide latitude in interpreting what reasonable steps are necessary to protect the integrity of the state. It would be tedious to rehearse the long list of measures—emergency powers, disturbed areas acts, prevention of terrorism acts, preventive detention, and so on—which ought to, on any interpretation, be considered a violation of civil liberties. No court has seen fit to challenge the executive's authority seriously in these matters, and I do not propose to discuss them in this essay. This is in part because I think it is, for the reasons Hobbes powerfully articulated, difficult to argue in *purely formal and legal terms* that the state ought not to have authority in matters pertaining to its own survival. Yet, as Gajendragadkar noted in *Gopalan*, the crucial issue is not the state's legal authority to invoke the doctrine of necessity; the crucial issue is to work at creating circumstances under which the invocation of necessity is rendered transparently irrelevant.

But there are two more aspects to the Hobbesian imagination that are relevant here. The second sense in which private judgement was an issue for Hobbes was that the exercise of our right to judgement should not take such a form that it puts the public purposes of the state in jeopardy. In the Hobbesian imagination, peace was one such paramount public purpose; modern states have expanded the list of public purposes to include justice, public order, and so on. But Hobbes went further. He argued that a sovereign could, in order to make contending religious doctrines congruent with the purposes of the state, acquire authority over the interpretation of religion. The sovereign was to be entrusted with the task of not only promulgating public purposes, but also preaching a form of religion that was compatible with those purposes. I argue in this essay that Indian constitutionalism has taken this Hobbesian mandate seriously. Constitutional practice has not only set the content of public purposes, it has also taken upon itself the task of interpreting religious doctrine. The practice of Indian constitution-alism not only articulates the public values that need to be taken as authoritative constraints on behaviour; it also seeks to regulate the meaning of religion. I argue that Indian constitutional practice is forced to fix the meaning of religious terms because of an internal tension within its conception of religion. On the one hand constitutional practice requires that religion be made subordinate to public purposes. On the other hand it wants to claim that these public purposes do not impinge upon religious freedom. The only way in which it can square this circle is by interpreting religion in such a way that its requirements and the demands of the state turn out to be congruent. And the only way of achieving this happy congruence is by *regulating* and trying to control the meaning of religious doctrine.

The third sense in which a Hobbesian sensibility looms large is this. Hobbes argued very powerfully that in order for the state to work we should not be in the grip of fears that could override the fear of violent death. Religious doctrines, in this view, imperilled the stability of the state because their doctrinal content made us fear things like everlasting torment and hell more than the fear of violent death. This made us immune to the possible punishments a state had to offer (because we feared even greater punishment in hell) and made it impossible for us to think with any clarity about our earthly interests. In order for a state to function, human beings had to be relieved of a whole set of fears instilled by religion and Hobbes went on to construct a theology of what a religion without fear would look like. But the claim that certain religious ideas distort the functioning of reason by playing on the passion of fear, I argue, underlies much of Indian jurisprudence on restrictions on speech relating to religion. I examine three classes of restrictions relating to speech: the first that protects religion against offensive speech, the second that upholds the constitutionality of speech aimed at conversion, and the third that excludes religious speech from politics via the Representation of People's Act. I argue that underlying these disparate classes of restrictions is a picture of moral agency—a Hobbesian picture— of the ways in which our passions are aroused and our reasoning impaired by speech involving religion. These cases also show the way in which the states attitude to religion is Janus-faced: it can protect and acknowledge the importance of religious interests and at the same time exclude them from the public sphere.

REASONABLE PLURALISM AND HAVING ONE'S CAKE AND EATING IT TOO

The fact that citizens disagree a good deal is often said to provide the basic starting point of *liberal* constitutionalism. Whatever its precise content, the 'fact' of reasonable pluralism is often thought to provide the central argument for liberal toleration. To use an influential formulation, *reasonable pluralism* obtains when:

The society in question is one in which there is diversity of comprehensive doctrines, all perfectly reasonable. This is the fact of reasonable pluralism, as opposed to the fact of pluralism as such.

In addition, Rawls argues,

It is the fact that free institutions tend to generate not simply a variety of doctrines or views, as one might expect from people's various interests and their tendency to focus on narrow points of view. Rather it is the fact that among the views that develop are a diversity of reasonable comprehensive doctrines.

Reasonable pluralism is produced due to what Rawls calls the burdens of judgement. These burdens relate to the complexity of evidence, the indeterminacy of many important concepts, and the elusive nature of justifying one's beliefs. The burdens of judgement are meant as an explanation for why disagreement can arise between reasonable persons; why the exercise of reason is compatible with a wide range of comprehensive doctrines.

The epistemological status of our disagreements is, however, difficult to articulate. For example does the burden of judgement show that reason under-determines belief in the content of comprehensive doctrines? I am tempted to say yes, but hesitate in the face of implication that if I say yes, I am in effect saying that reason alone is insufficient to tell me which comprehensive doctrine to believe, given that there seems to be a large number of reasonable ones. While reason can show the shortcomings of many doctrines, it is insufficient to determine which particular one an individual should choose. But then what would explain why people choose the particular doctrines that they do? You might offer a whole range of explanations: cultural, psychological, etc., for how people come to have the beliefs that they do. But the central fact remains: by the argument from the burdens of judgement, we are forced to admit that people believe more than *reason* warrants. But then why call such beliefs *reasonable*?

On the other hand claiming that the burdens of judgement do not show that reason under-determines belief in the content of comprehensive doctrines leads to a puzzle. Suppose that reason tells us to believe p, the beliefs constitutive of a particular comprehensive doctrine. If p is reasonable, then for it to be reasonable the belief *not-p* should be rejected. But if reasonable pluralism is to make sense, there must be a p of which reasonable pluralism suggests that *not-p* is reasonable too. Otherwise there is no basis for describing the situation as one of reasonable *disagreement*. But to say that we have reason to believe both p and *not-p* is just to say that reason cannot decide one way or the other. So reason does under-determine belief in comprehensive doctrines. The burdens of judgement might lead therefore not to the doctrine of *reasonable* pluralism, but something more akin to reasonable scepticism.

Confronted with the above dilemma we could say the following: those who are in disagreement would, if they are presented with the truth about the burdens, agree that these showed that they would be unreasonable not to agree, that is, not to agree that the burdens show that *nobody's* comprehensive doctrine can be shown to be more reasonable than everyone else's. Each person thus has to accept that this applies to them, that their belief is no longer supported by sufficient reasons. This might amount to saying that reason requires that they abandon their beliefs.

The difficulty is that the burdens of judgement have to show two opposite things. They have to show why people reasonably believe what they believe, while also not having enough reasons to show why others who disagree with these beliefs are wrong. There is an incongruity in this. On the one hand the burdens of judgement make pluralism reasonable at the collective level: they show why no one doctrine can win a decisive victory over others. On the other hand, individuals continue to hold onto their particular comprehensive doctrines; at an individual level their belief remains undiminished despite the burdens of judgement.

But to believe of a specific set of beliefs that it is contradicted by beliefs no less reasonable means that one no longer has sufficient reason to continue holding the belief.

There is a notorious ambiguity in Rawls' formulation of the idea 'reasonable'. Is reasonable an adjective that describes beliefs or believers? To be a reasonable *person* is just to recognize that one's own comprehensive doctrine alone does not give sufficient justification to use coercion in its name. But reasonable in this sense is tied to an acceptance of a central tenet of political liberalism itself. But if this is the foundational sense of reasonable, we end up in a circle: political liberalism is justified because reasonable people endorse it, but their endorsement of political liberalism is what makes persons reasonable.

It is plausible to argue, as Rawls has done, that something like the liberty of conscience can be derived directly from the burdens of judgement.

Reasonable persons see that the burdens of judgement set limits on what can be reasonably justified to others, and so endorse some forms of liberty of conscience or freedom of thought....It is unreasonable to use political power to repress comprehensive views that are not unreasonable.

The argument goes something as follows: because the burdens of judgement limit what can reasonably be justified to others, you can reasonably reject my comprehensive doctrine; you are therefore justified in rejecting any use of political power designed to impose my comprehensive doctrine as a private individual on you, as another such individual. But notice that this argument does not require reasonable pluralism. All it requires is some scepticism about the *relative* standing of comprehensive doctrines. Liberty of conscience simply follows from the fact that there are no sufficient reasons for me to choose one doctrine over another.

The challenge for a certain version of liberal constitutionalism is this. On the one hand the different comprehensive doctrines of believers in a society must matter enough to set the terms of the problem and require protection. On the other hand they cannot matter so much that those who hold them are justified in imposing them upon others. This is not, strictly speaking, a contradiction. But it provides the background for three interesting tensions. First, is the line between reasonable pluralism and scepticism a bright one? Does not the claim that there are no sufficient reasons for our beliefs shade over into the thought that we do not have good reasons for our beliefs as such. If a comprehensive doctrine cannot be publicly justified to others, what is the sense in which it is a justified set of beliefs to hold? Second, does liberalism require, at the individual level, a form of psychological uncoupling? We are required both to be attached to our first-order beliefs and to have a second-order view about their insufficiency. The more individuals are wedded to the thought that their private judgements give them sufficient reasons for actions, the less feasible this will be. Third, this discussion is around the question of the scope of private beliefs and judgements in liberal theory. I had, in the discussion above, raised doubts about how far partisans of comprehensive doctrines could go in drawing inferences from their own beliefs, and how these inferences could be accommodated from an external standpoint, such as that required by the philosophy of public justification. What is the force of the claim that 'X' is a good reason for me, even though 'X' cannot be justified to others? Where does the authority for the term 'good' come from in this claim? The doctrine of reasonable pluralism undercuts itself unless the force of the term 'reason' at work in the formation of private judgements could be kept separate from the concept of 'reason' which tells us that the burdens of judgement exist. If this is not the case, reason will either fail to produce a disagreement, or fail to produce belief which give rise to disagreement, since it brands both a belief and its contrary as reasonable.

The point of this philosophical discussion is to found thought that any version of liberal constitutionalism is likely to embody an inner tension. First, such a version of constitutionalism often aims to draw its legitimacy from the fact that it protects the right to private judgement and from the fact that it will allow a variety of reasonable comprehensive doctrines to flourish in society without hindrance. On the other hand, liberal constitutionalism will have to limit the scope of private judgement in a number of ways. The scope of private judgement and beliefs must be such that they do not impede the legitimate purposes of the state that can be publicly justified. The wider the domains of life over which the comprehensive doctrine claims authority, the more likely it is to come into conflict with the public purposes of the state. Second, the place of pluralism in liberal constitutionalism is an uneasy one. Either reasonable comprehensive doctrines converge on the fundamentals of a liberal polity, in which case it is difficult to describe the resulting society as one marked by deep *disagreement*; or what makes liberal constitutionalism work is a second-order scepticism or indifference about our beliefs.

All this would have been pretty obvious to a liberalism more bloody-minded than Rawls'. Such liberalism would stake its ground not on the acts of reasonable pluralism but on a straightforward defence of liberty and equality. The aspiration of such liberalism would not be to get around the facts of disagreement by recourse to an appeal to neutrality or impartiality. Such liberalism would not minimize the tensions between itself and various contending comprehensive doctrines within civil society. As I argue above, defending liberal constitutionalism on the grounds that it best protects reasonable pluralism is at best disingenuous. Either the scope of the comprehensive doctrines tolerated is more limited than liberals acknowledge, or political liberalism implodes.

Why is all this of relevance to Indian constitutionalism? I want to suggest the argument that the justificatory foundations of the Indian Constitution, and the practices of interpretation that have grown up around it, are based on something of an illusion similar to the one that a doctrine such as Rawls' political liberalism falls prey to. There has been an attempt, in official self-presentation, to minimize the potential conflict between the claims of various comprehensive doctrines in society (religions) on the one hand and the liberal and ameliorative aspirations of the Constitution on the other. The Indian Constitution has to take religion as both an object of reform and at the same time claim that the state and public purposes do not pose a threat to the exercise of religion. On the one hand Indian courts have had to restrict the scope of the domains over which private judgements can be exercised. But the Indian courts have had to justify the narrowing of the scope of comprehensive doctrines in the names of those religious doctrines themselves. It turns out, as the mythology of our courts goes, that there is very little conflict between vying comprehensive doctrines in civil society and the requirements of liberal constitutionalism. I argue that the courts are forced to make this argument because they see it as the only way in which free exercise of religion can be made compatible with the requirements of liberal constitutionalism; and the prospects for this argument working depend entirely upon the fact the courts take on the regulative role of themselves defining the true meaning of comprehensive doctrines.

In order to see this in some detail, take a feature of the Indian Supreme Court's engagement with religion that many scholars—especially those who work in the framework of comparative constitutionalism—find particularly odd. Indian Supreme Court judges not only routinely consider questions of law; they also actively participate in the reinterpretation of religious doctrine, especially, though not exclusively, of Hinduism. Such active participation in the reinterpretation of religious doctrine by secular judges of a modern state committed to a version of liberal constitutionalism arouses many misgivings. It certainly sits at odds with some prominent views of church–state relations in American constitutional law. For example, Laurence Tribe in his influential textbook argues that the most clearly forbidden church–state entanglement occurs when institutions of civil government use the legal process in order to discover religious error or to promulgate religious truth.[1] Tribe's claim is of course ambiguous in an interesting way. A reference to religious error or religious truth can be taken in two senses. It may refer to promulgating the truth *of* a particular religion, or it could refer to the state promulgating a particular truth *about* a religion. Even if the state were not advancing the claims of a particular religion, would it be legitimate for the state to promulgate a specific interpretation of a particular religion? What would be the rationale for doing so?

In this essay I do not examine this question directly. Rather, I give a brief account of why the institutions on the Indian stage and the courts in particular came to be the agency through which public purposes were not just articulated, but internal religious reforms were also carried out. I then explore some implications of this finding. What does the fact that the Indian state has sought to regulate the meaning of Hinduism—and other religions—and has acquired the authority to do so tell us about the distinctive manner in which the Indian polity constitutes religion? I argue that the court has to find a strategy both of acknowledging the importance of religion and limiting its scope, affirming its truth and denying that its dictates have to be authoritative guides to public purposes.

No constitutional culture can entirely escape the thorny problem of defining religion and thereby regulating its meaning. As Kent Greenwalt has argued, there is a paradox at the heart of the free exercise and establishment clauses in the American case. Sometimes courts have to determine whether or not a policy places a substantial burden on the free exercise of a religion. This might require the court to have not just a definition of religion but also to determine whether a particular practice counts as falling under that definition. In making these determinations, courts can of course favour some religions over others, but they can also regulate the meaning of a particular practice within a religion by attaching more or less significance to that practice. For this reason it has been a presumption of American constitutional law that the courts must not, as far as it is possible, determine religious truth or even whether claimants are faithful to a religious tradition.

Where are the legitimate boundaries to be drawn on the state's interference in religious matters? What would the freedom of religion amount to if the state had broad powers to regulate religion in the name of social reform?[2] In some ways these questions arise in any constitutional context with varying degrees of urgency. But in contemporary discussions—as the example of Rawls suggests—the tensions between the free exercise of religion and the secular purposes of the state are often minimized. Our prevalent metaphors for talking about regimes of religious toleration often disguise the stakes. No secular state, as is now familiar, can be neutral or impartial among religions, because the state determines the boundaries within which neutrality must operate. Similarly, another metaphor used by Amy Gutmann—which describes the separation of Church and state as a two-way accommodation whose purpose is to protect religion from the state as much as it is to protect the state from religion—does not adequately acknowledge the fact that the a two-way accommodation metaphor works only when vast areas of religious practice have already been ceded to the state, arguably to the point where religious practice becomes socially less consequential.

The two-way accommodation metaphor also belies the fact that all states extensively regulate religion; one might say that they define the normatively permissible boundaries of religion. Particular aspects of religion are given protection, recognition, and support; others are the subject of indifference; and many aspects are curtailed and proscribed. But, as Marc Galanter pointed out, there are different modes of regulating and shaping religion. One, which might be called external regulation, often favoured by liberals, goes something like this. The state promulgates its public purposes: it defines the areas where these public standards will prevail, where they will override competing assertions of religious authority; and leaves it up to religion to accommodate itself to these standards. But another mode of regulation might be more internal. The state might try and reformulate religious traditions from within. The state might do this in one of two ways. It might try to define what the proper practice of a particular religion requires. It could go even further and argue that the public secular purposes are themselves the best expression of particular religious doctrines or are at least congruent with it.

Indian legislatures and the courts in particular have done much more of the latter than their corresponding American counterparts, and this essay in part seeks to understand the reasons for this. (This is not to deny that Indian courts have also externally regulated religion.) The Constitution gives the state broad powers to regulate religious freedom, if such regulation can be justified in terms of public purposes, including the maintenance of public order, morality, and health. There have been periods in the Supreme Court's deliberations where the court has been quite deferential when the state has invoked public purposes to regulate religious activity. It has not interrogated the state's invocation of the public order clause nearly as much as it ought to.

But it is the court's frequent attempts to grasp the internal levers of reform within religions that is of interest here. The Indian Supreme Court has, in some sense, taken to heart Hobbes' recognition that the control of public meanings of religion was the essence of the civil sovereign's role: it has tried to install itself as the true measure of the meaning of a religion. Why would the courts go to great lengths to determine the internal content and meaning of religion and argue that *those* provide reason for going along with public purposes? One obvious answer might simply go as follows. Indian courts like to find support for their reformist agendas within the Hindu scriptures and traditions themselves. This is simply a way of bolstering their authority, by giving Hindus reasons that are internal to the tradition itself, to go along with the courts' and legislature's reform agenda. This motivation is certainly part of the story, but it is, as I shall argue, only a part of the story. It does not examine the question of how courts come to have the authority to not only promulgate public purposes to which religion must conform but also the authority to determine what the truth about a particular religion is.

I proceed in the following steps. I discuss some instances where the Supreme Court has sought to fix the meaning of Hinduism as part of its strategy to grasp the internal levers of reform. I discuss the different ideological functions this performs. In particular it allows the state to maintain the potentially misleading fiction that the political requirements of a liberal constitution are not only compatible with but are also sustained by a variety of comprehensive doctrines.

ALL GOOD THINGS GO TOGETHER

Indian courts are faced with the obvious question: which practice is entitled to constitutional protection under the freedom of religion clauses? Defining religion is a complex problem; defining what counts as a *Hindu* religious practice is an even more thorny issue. Yet, if the constitutional right to the freedom of religion is to be tested, the court is required to have a definition of a religion so that it can assess when *religious* freedom is being violated. The Indian Supreme Court's most often cited definition of religion is from an Australian judgement and it goes:

There are those who regard religion as consisting principally in a system of beliefs or statements of doctrine. So viewed religion may be either true or false. Other is more inclined to regard religion as prescribing a mode of conduct. So viewed a religion may be good or bad. There are others who pay greater attention to religion as involving some prescribed form of ritual or religious observance.[3]

This account acknowledges that religion has an ambit wider than simply belief.[4] In the very first case dealing with this question, *Commissioner of Hindu Religious Endowments, Madras v. Sri Lakshmindra Tirtha Swaminar,* popularly known as the *Shrirur Math* case the Supreme Court acknowledged that the Constitution not only guarantees freedom of religious belief but also freedom of practice. In determining whether a practice counts as a religious practice, the courts have consistently rejected an assertion test. According to this test, a practitioner could simply assert that their particular practice was a religious practice and all the courts would have to do is establish the existence of such a practice. The Supreme Court, in a unanimous opinion in the *Shrirur Math* case, rejected this test. More significantly, this case also provided the first formulation of a staple of Indian jurisprudence on religion: the essential practices test. In order for it to be established that a policy or law violates the freedom of religion, it must be shown that the policy in question violates an essential practice of religion.

Ever since the *Shrirur Math* case, the notion of 'essential part of religion' has acquired critical importance. Later judgements have held that the Constitution's protection of freedom of religion extends only to its essential part. For example in *Durgah Committee, Ajmer v. Syed Hussain Ali,* only the essential and integral part of religion has constitutional protection. This excludes secular matters disguised as religious but also, in the words of Justice Gajendragadkar, the key architect of this doctrine, 'superstitious beliefs and practices which may be extraneous and unessential accretions to religion itself'. The courts seem committed to some Ciceronian idea of *religio* cleansed of *superstitio*, to the search for a pure religion whose theology turns out to be compatible with the civil theology of the Commonwealth. Debates over secularism often overlook the fact that even secular purposes can in some ways remain anchored in religious ones. And the Indian Supreme Court takes it upon itself to show how.

The essential practices test serves a number of purposes. On the one hand it allows the courts to determine whether or not a practice is a candidate for protection under the Constitution's freedom of religion guarantees. For instance, does the setting up of a trust for providing milk for cobras in a temple precinct count as a *Hindu religious* trust. The courts argued that a trust formed to feed milk to reptiles could not be so counted.[5] But the logic of the essential practices test has given the courts wide authority to define, interpret, and regulate the meaning of religion. For example, take cases involving questions such as: does an individual or a cult or sect form part of Hinduism or not? In numerous such cases, the courts have identified the essential practices of both the sect in question and Hinduism, and have on that basis determined whether or not that sect belongs to Hinduism. The stakes in defining whether or not a sect belongs to Hinduism were quite high, as I shall discuss below. But the essential practices test has also allowed the courts to do more. They have been able, in theory at any rate, to minimize the conflict between the free exercise of religion and the secular purposes of the state, by constructing an argument to the effect that the practices being regulated were not essential to that religion in any case. By distinguishing the essential from the non-essential aspects of religion, the courts seek to narrow the gap between the guarantees of free exercise of religion and the public purposes served by the state. Recall that the two-way accommodation doctrine works only if religious authority is confined to particular domains. The distinction between essential and non-essential potentially narrows the range of activity that might otherwise be deemed as the free exercise of religion. The net result, as Derrett put it, is:

The Courts can discard as non-essentials anything which is not proved to their satisfaction—and they are not religious leaders or in any relevant fashion qualified in such matters—to be essential, with the result that it would have no constitutional protection. The Constitution does not say freely to profess and propagate the *essentials* of religion, but this is how it is constructed.[6]

But the Supreme Court has also used the essential practices doctrine to make a more far-reaching move. In many instances the court has argued that the secular, public purposes of the state *just are* the best expression of the free exercise of the particular religion in question. The courts can claim that if one properly understood the essentials of religion, one would find that those deemed essential would support or justify the legitimate public objectives of the state.

How do the courts determine what is essential or integral to a religion? The Supreme Court's deployment of the distinction between religion and superstition, or essential and inessential, arouses immense legal controversy. The obvious criticism is that one person's superstition is another person's religion. Justice Mukherjee's injunction in the *Shrirur Math* judgement—what constitutes the essential part of the religion is primarily to be ascertained with reference to the doctrines of religion itself—raises as many questions as it answers. The Supreme Court's methods here may be described as a combination of inspired ad-hoccery and fidelity to texts. In some cases the courts will try to ascertain the traditional beliefs and customs of the parties involved, although usually there are enough disagreements amongst the parties to make this test less than useful. Often the most vital evidence the courts will use is textual. But the courts' use of the texts of a tradition itself involves complex hermeneutic assumptions that we shall discuss below.

Shastri Yagnapurashdasji v. *Muldas Bhundardas Vaisya*, also known as the *Satsang* case, gives a representative glimpse into the court's modus operandi. The petitioners in this case claimed that temple-entry legislation, passed in Bombay in 1947, the objective of which was to open Hindu temples to untouchables, did not apply to them because they were not Hindus. In effect, this was an attempt to subvert the social reform of Hinduism and its attempts to be more inclusive by starting a new religion. The issue before the courts was whether the Satsangis could claim exemption from the temple entry legislation by declaring themselves to be of a religion different from Hinduism. As Derrett stressed, the case was significant for a variety of reasons. On the one hand, given the insidious history of caste oppression in the name of Hinduism, opening up temples to untouchables was the key plank of social reform. On the other hand the court was put in the position of saying why it was that the Satsangis could not declare themselves to be not Hindus. The question therefore was whether the Satsangis were Hindus, and this meant considering who was a Hindu.

The court, in declaring the Satsangis to be Hindus, first argued that the teachings of the sect were identical with Hinduism properly understood; second, that the founder of the sect, Swami Narayan, was simply one in a long series of reformers of Hinduism who carried the spark of divinity. In order to prove their distinctiveness, the Satsangis had claimed, first, that their sect gave women *diksha* (initiation), which was unusual; second, that they admitted Muslims and Parsis to diksha (members of these religions could become full members of the sect without ceasing to be Muslim or Parsi); and, third, that the founder of the sect was worshiped as a god in the temples of the sect.

The court dismissed the first claim swiftly: although historically unusual there were no theological impediments within Hinduism to initiating women. On the second the court argued that the fact merely shows that the Satsang philosophy preached by Swami Narayan allows followers of other religions to receive the blessings of his teachings without insisting upon their forsaking their own religion. In a sense this attitude of the Satsang sect is consistent with the basic Hindu religious and philosophical theory that many roads lead to God. The court then, in typical fashion, went on to cite the Bhagwad Gita's claim to the effect that those who are devoted to other deities thereby worship Krishna himself. This does not mean of course that Muslims and Parsis who participate in such activities are, by extension, Hindus for legal purposes, because their participation does not by itself raise any question of their conversion. The Muslim and Parsi community may disown them, but the law as constituted would not declare a Muslim to have lost the benefits of their personal law by joining in a multi-religious spiritual community.[7] On the third point—the worship of Swami Narayan as divinity—the court was blunt: there was nothing in Hinduism proscribing that.

But the crucial point in the judgement was this: was not the state's regulation of entry to temples a violation of the constitutional freedom of the denomination to manage their own affairs? Was not control over participation in temple services a religious act and therefore deserving of constitutional protection? In an earlier case, *Sri Venkatarama Devaru v. State of Mysore*,[8] the court had considered the very same question. In that case the court upheld the Temple Entry Act, but acknowledged that it may violate religious freedom.[9] In effect the court was imposing a form of external regulation on religion. But in the *Shrirur Math* case, the court had this to say:

The Satsangi's apprehension about the pollution of the temple is founded on superstition, ignorance and *complete misunderstanding of the true teachings of Hinduism and the real significance of the tenets and philosophy taught by Swami Narayan himself.*

Having begun its judgement with an acknowledgment that Hinduism was diffuse and indefinable, the court managed to conjure up the true teaching of Hinduism that enabled it to discern what was essential to the tradition and what was not. This enabled the court to argue that progress, democracy, and egalitarianism were at the heart of a properly interpreted Hinduism. The judgement, penned by Justice Gajendra-gadkar, contained a lengthy discussion of the definition of Hinduism, which relied heavily on modern Indian philosophical reconstructions of Hinduism that stressed its progressive capacity for internal reform, its compatibility with the doctrine of social equality, and its tolerance for a variety of outlooks. On these grounds the judgement could argue that any discrimination against untouchables in Satsangi temples was a misunderstanding of both Hinduism and the Swami Narayan's teaching.

Examples such as this can be multiplied. In *Seshammal* v. *State of Tamil Nadu*,[10] Tamil Nadu legislation abolishing the hereditary appointment of temple priests was challenged on the grounds that it interfered with the priests' constitutional right to the freedom of religion. In this instance the courts took it for granted that the sacred texts on which this practice was based, the Agamas, were authoritative in relation to the particular temple in question. It then went onto uphold the Tamil Nadu legislation on the basis of a reinterpretation of Agama texts. The court argued that the Agama texts in question laid down some qualifications a priest must meet, but the *mode* of appointment (hereditary entitlement) was of secular, not religious, origin, and therefore opens to regulation. In the *Shah Bano* case the Supreme Court tried to acquire the same interpretive authority over the Koran, with predictably disastrous results. The point is that the courts have gone to inordinate and implausible lengths to show that the requirements of justice have a basis in the different comprehensive doctrines. In doing so the court not only renders the different doctrines compatible with one another, it implicitly denies that there *could* be serious disagreement.

It should evidently be clear that Indian judges engage in extensive scriptural exegesis, almost as if this were the source of law and legitimacy. In doing so the judges interpret the true meaning of religious traditions, and, conveniently enough, their interpretations and reinterpretations make religious traditions with modern ideals of social reform. The act of interpreting religious texts has a dual purpose: on the one hand the courts are able to demonstrate that the authority of their rulings rests upon both modern constitutional provisions and structurally sanctioned foundations; on the other hand the courts offer internal reasons to Hindus to the effect that there is little in the content of social reform efforts that is a threat to their religion, as understood in its essentials.

In some ways it may be easy to dismiss the vast efforts the courts expend upon interpreting religious texts as simply a veneer that gives added support to the conclusions they would have arrived at anyway. On this view it is simply a contortion of the tradition, or another instance of judicial myth-making, to suppose that many wonderful modern values like democracy and equality can be produced out of traditional scriptures. But a more benign view might suppose that Hindu discourse has never been monolithic and that if often reinterprets itself in new lights. Indeed there are long-standing indigenous interpretive traditions of ancient texts that unrecognizably alter the meaning of the original text in the act of interpretation. The indeterminacy of the sign is the oldest interpretive gambit in the books. The role of interpretation amounts to this: if offers society the means whereby it can discover itself in fact.[11] In some ways, then, it is as besides the point to assert that modern reformist goals contradict Hinduism as it is to assert that they are compatible with it.

If one finds what Indian judges do with religious texts odd or arbitrary, one need only to see that at least in formal terms their procedures are not radically different from what, at least on some views, judges do in American law. Dworkin, for instance, argued that judges generally offer a new statement of law as improved reports of what the law, properly understood, already is. They claim, in other words, that the new statement is required by *a correct perception of the true grounds of law, even though this has not been recognized previously or has even been denied.*[12]

In some ways Indian judges discover the true grounds of religious law even when these have not been hitherto recognized. Of course, unlike judges interpreting law, judges interpreting scripture may not always have access to legislative intent. And judges interpreting ancient scripture are more apt to emphasize the thought that the truth they have discovered existed from time immemorial. But once the complexities of textual interpretation are taken into account, the contrast between modern and traditional/religious law becomes a matter of degree; arguably the difference between modern judicial reasoning and classical Hindu religious interpretation is formally less than we might suppose.[13]

What are the ideological functions performed by the interpretation of texts by Indian judges? What are the advantages and disadvantages of such a strategy? One could simply say that Indian judges are forced to interpret scripture out of necessity. Due to the thickness of Hinduism and the extensive reach of its obligations on vast areas of social life, both the Indian state and, by implication, Indian courts do not have the luxury simply to impose external regulation on religions; they have to reformulate the religion from within. In some ways what Indian courts do would be analogous to an American court not only upholding legislation that required some churches to ordain women as priests, but then going onto suggest that this comported well with the true meaning of the Bible. This would probably be seen a violation of religious freedom, and the courts meddling in biblical hermeneutics would seem gratuitous indeed. While many might think that the exclusion of women is in some sense unjust, there is also the recognition that at this juncture its social and public consequences are not onerous enough to warrant interference in a religious practice. But Indian courts face an acute dilemma: the potential conflict between the public purposes of the state and considerations of modern conceptions of justice on the one hand and freedom of religion on the other are much greater, and the social consequences of not intervening in religion can be monumental. But extensive interference violates freedom of religion, and too little interference would violate the ameliorative aims and public purposes of the state. The courts have tired to square this circle by in effect saying that interventions that look like violations of religious freedom are, if properly considered, not really so. To make that argument work, they have to interpret religious doctrines by their own lights, and in doing so reconstitute them.

But ideological functions of these interpretations extend beyond the legal issues at stake. For one thing, the courts reinterpretations find a way of overcoming tradition without making tradition despicable. They draw sustenance from and articulate a version of Hindu traditions much in line with the reform movements at the turn of the century, which allow Hindus to make their peace with the modern world. Should this matter? Clearly in a political and psychological sense this is important. It provides societies complex ways of negotiating with post-colonial insecurities about which I say something below. But more importantly, and normatively speaking, these accomplished two goals: the first is that the state, rather than positioning itself in hostility to religion, became the vehicle for the democratization of religion.[14] In a sense the democratic state was the vehicle through which the community of believers acquired interpretive authority over many of the requirements of their religion.

The extent to which the courts' decisions are democratic is of course open to debate. It has been argued that their interpretations often reflect the biases of middle class Hindus; and there are general reasons for being suspicious of the courts setting themselves up as the embodiments of the popular will. But in a very general sense, as I suggested above, the courts can claim that in a parliamentary system, where the courts' decisions are easy to override legislatively, the courts' decisions and interpretations can, unless challenged, claim some presumptive status to represent the views of the community of believers. The second, which has in retrospect turned out to have some negative consequences, is that this process of reinterpretation also provided the means of the consolidation of a more unified Hindu identity than had probably existed previously. In its consequence modern Hindu law is creating something that traditional Hinduism has never been: one single territorially based community welded together to a coherent body of law by a uniformity of laws overriding particular customs. The boundaries of this community are marked by the definition of a Hindu contained in these statues. The process of reform and the inclusion of lower castes and untouchables serves a dual purpose. On the one hand it ostensibly advances the cause of social justice. On the other it seeks to create a unitary Hindu identity.

Although this is not the place to discuss this, in some ways the paradox of modern Hinduism is this: the very process of social reform has also helped the consolidation of Hindu *identity*. Indeed, the very normatively salutary elements that Justice Gajendragadkar identified as elements of true Hinduism—progressivism, tolerance, and a capacity for reform— are now being politically mobilized in a discourse of intolerance. Of course the consolidation of this identity had various sources, but its availability as a legal category has surely helped the process. And finally, this construction of the true aspirations of the Constitution as being compatible with the essence of religious practice has obscured the ways in which the actual practices of believers are *not* compatible with the requirements of liberal constitutionalism.

But the quote from Derrett raises the following question: How do judges, who are not religious leaders in any sense of the term, acquire the authority to interpret religion and regulate its meaning? Part of the answer has of course to do with the nature and character of Hinduism. Although historically the practices of Hindus have denied that many people—lower castes in particular—had any such interpretive authority, it is never clear *who* actually did. So the state, rather than wresting the right to regulate religious affairs away from a church, more or less filled in the vacuum in different ways, according to the ideology that underpinned it. Although this is not the occasion to make this argument at any length, I have argued elsewhere that Indian religious and political identities were, in some significant sense, constituted through the state.

But in order to fully understand how judges acquired this authority, one has to come to terms with the recent history of the relationship between the state and religion; and for that one has to turn, as always, to colonial origins. This is not the occasion to go into a full discussion of the origins how the courts came to be authoritative interpreters of scripture.[15] But I hope I have said enough to make this point. Indian constitutionalism has, in a Hobbesian manner, sought to regulate the meaning of religious doctrine. Indian courts tell us not only what public purposes ought to be authoritative constraints on behaviour but also which interpretation of religious doctrine should be considered authoritative. This has enabled to position constitutionalism to perform two functions simultaneously: protect religion and regulate it.

PASSION AND CONSTRAINT

The problematic and contradictory status of religion comes out nicely in the courts' attitude to speech involving religion. In Indian law many of the restrictions on religious speech and speech about religion comes from provisions in the law. For example Article 295 of the Indian Penal Code, a remnant from colonial times, makes punishable whoever with deliberate and malicious intention of outraging the feelings of any class of citizens attempts to insult the religious beliefs of that class. There are laws restricting religious speech. Some state enactments, notably in Madhya Pradesh and Orissa, regulate speech whose object is conversion. The use of religious speech is regulated in the context of elections. Under the Representation of People's Act, certain kinds of appeals on the basis of religion are deemed to be corrupt practices. Under Article 123 (2) any attempt to induce a candidate or elector to believe that he or she will be rendered the object of divine displeasure; the appeal by a candidate to vote for or refrain from voting on ground of a candidate's religion, race, caste, or languages; and the use of or appeal to religious symbols are all instances of corrupt practice.

Are these restrictions constitutional? The courts have dealt with these questions rather perfunctorily. In the case of Article 295—that makes offences against religion punishable—the courts beginning with *Ramji Lal Modi* v. *State of U.P.* have adopted the following strategy. The first is to say that most attempts to insult a religion have a tendency to disrupt public order; and since our Fundamental Rights to free expression under Articles 19 and 25 can be regulated on grounds of maintaining public order, any 'insult' to religion can therefore be regulated. This resolution assumes two things that the courts have not on the whole shed light on. Why assume that every attempt to insult religion must have a tendency to disrupt public order? But the courts have read the public order exceptions in Articles 19 and 25 too broadly. It has generally been assumed that as soon as a restriction is said to be associated with public order, the courts need not pursue any further questions. This has constantly posed a threat to freedom of expression, as the recent controversy over the banning of D.N. Jha's book on the history of beef eating testifies.

The second case is that the case law shows that the courts have interpreted Article 295 as more than simply an attempt to prevent the disorders occasioned by insults to religion. For example, in one of the early cases—*N. Veerabrahama* v. *State of Andhra Pradesh*—a ban against a rationalist critique of the Bible was upheld. This critique had claimed that the Pentateuch had not been written by Moses; that the Bible was full of incongruities and inconsistencies; that since nobody can be born of a virgin, Jesus must have been the result of an adulterous union for which the immaculate conception theory was a cover-up, etc. From the court proceedings it is very clear that there was no real threat to public order. But the rationale for upholding the ban was simply that it might cause emotional distress. As the majority opinion put it, put the justification for the argument does not matter as what consequences it would have upon the religious susceptibilities of the Christian community who hold the Bible sacred. Another judge added: 'All the citizens of India are guaranteed freedom of religion and freedom of conscience. And each has a right to pursue his own way of attaining salvation, unhampered and without interference from others—as for example by the book in question.'

This judgement seems to give a rationale for Article 295 that goes beyond simple considerations of public order. Nor is it simply an attempt to avoid mental distress to Christians. The last sentence of the judgement is significant: 'each citizen has a right to pursue his own way of attaining salvation, unhampered and without interference from others—as for example by the book in question.' This yields an underlying picture of moral agency. It implies, first, that criticism of a religion is an obstacle to its free exercise. Indeed an image that the court uses is that a book is an obstacle almost the way in which physical coercion might be. What the courts have done has given a rather odd content to what freedom of religion might mean: freedom of religion means freedom not to be confronted by criticism of religion; it is a right to be left alone, a right not to be subject to any unsolicited influence. I think there is a deeper assumption underlying this judgement: religion is a subjective matter; in matters of religious truth nothing is to gained from any engagement with, least of all a conflictive encounter with, the beliefs of others. In matters of religion, at any rate, truth is not to be arrived at by, as Mill put it, the rough process of a struggle between combatants fighting under hostile banners. But what is interesting is that the courts seem to think that religion is sufficiently important to warrant protection from easy abuse or criticism by others. Indeed, it is sufficiently important to provide the basis for the state occasionally banning books that are deemed offensive to religion. On the other hand it is not important enough that it can provide the basis for public arguments.

As an aside I should mention that the precedent in *Veerbrahamna* inspired a whole series of cases. There was an important case in Uttar Pradesh—*Lalai Singh Yadav* v. *State of U.P.*—in which the plaintiff alleged that Ambedkar's writings were republished with malicious intent. Ambedkar's writings were alleged to be offensive because they insulted Hinduism, denied the divine origin of the Vedas, and promoted disharmony amongst the castes. Another notorious case in Bengal— *Chandanmal Chopra* v. *State of West Bengal*—demanded that the Koran be banned because it offended the religious sensibilities of those who worship idols. Both cases were thrown out—the Ambedkar case on the grounds that he did not really mean to offend Hindus (*that* might be an insult to Ambedkar), and the Koran case on two separate grounds: first that it was a sacred object and entitled to protection, and second that the Koran read in context did not really insult any religion. In this case, the judge rightly construed the petition as itself an insult to Islam undertaken with malicious intent and ordered that the petitioner be punished. What is striking about these seemingly frivolous cases is this: the judges were of course correct to throw out these cases but in the process they were compelled to go to great lengths to deny that anyone could have any reason to find the doctrines contained in the texts under question 'offensive'. The substance of both these decisions was correct. But there is a certain awkwardness in the court's implicit assumption that nothing in one religion can be offensive to another. In this instance, the court was articulating another aspect of our constitutional mythology—namely that, properly construed, the contents of any comprehensive doctrine are quite compatible with those of any other. Again, the only way to make this argument stick is by the state defining and regulating what these religions *really* mean. Again, the courts bring about convergence by claiming interpretive authority and redefining religion by their own lights.

As is well known, the Supreme Court gave a notoriously contorted ruling in *Rev. Stainslaus v. State of Madhya Pradesh*. This case challenged two state acts that regulate activity aimed at conversion on the grounds that these acts violate Article 25 of the Constitution that specifically mentions the right to propagate religion. The Supreme Court upheld the acts against this challenge. The acts in the *Stainslaus* case did not prohibit all attempts at conversion, only attempts by force, fraud, or inducement. But 'force' was defined broadly to include threat of divine punishment or displeasure, and inducement to include the offer of gift or gratification that would include 'intangible benefits'.

The court—in a typically casuistical fashion—suggested that these acts did not violate the right to propagate religion. It first drew a distinction between an attempt to convert from simply transmitting a religion by the exposition of its tenets. The distinction, if one can make any sense of it at all, seems to turn largely on the motive of the speaker. If a person spoke to transmit tenets, he may not be punished; but if he harboured hopes that the person being addressed would accept the truth of his religion and convert, he would not be protected from punishment. In support of its decisions in the *Stainslaus* case, the Supreme Court said that if Article 25—which protects the right to propagate—were to give a right to convert another person to one's own religion, that would violate another person's right to religious freedom.

It has to be remembered that Article 25(1) guarantees freedom of conscience to every citizen, and not merely to the followers of one particular religion, and that in turn, postulates that there is no fundamental right to convert another person to one's own religion because if a person purposely undertakes the conversion of another person to his religion, as distinguished from his effort to transmit or spread the tenets of his religion that would impinge upon the freedom of conscience guaranteed to all citizens of the country alike.

The Supreme Court construed the freedom of religion clause simply as the right not to be targeted; conversion by another is objectionable because it conflicts with some notion of what is the proper way for important changes to come about in an individual's life. The freedom of conscience just is the freedom to develop without any outside influences that cause pain. To have a right to exercise one's religious beliefs just is the right not to have one's sensibility offended, either by speech deemed insulting or being the target of conversion.

Article 123 of the Representation of People's Act prohibits undue influence on voters. Such undue influence includes threatening a voter with excommunication and causing him to believe that he will become the object of divine displeasure. Such conduct interferes with the free exercise of electoral rights. I want to leave aside the issue of excommunication for the moment and focus on the appeals to divine displeasure. One difficulty in applying this test is this: how does one distinguish between appeals to divine displeasure from appeals to religion generally? The same difficulty of course arises in the conversion case as well. What if the transmitting of tenets, which is allowed, carries the implication that divine displeasure will follow if the tenets are not followed? Surely almost all religious appeals carry the thought that the persons being appealed to would be better-off if they heed the appeal than if they do not.

The courts have had some difficulty with this question. One clear way of identifying whether a threat of divine retribution is being exercised is to see if the candidate associates himself with some authority that might be in the position of authoritatively determining when divine displeasure would accrue. As it turns out, this has been easier to establish in the case of Sikh candidates than almost any other community. I do not have firm proof of this, but my impression is that an overwhelming number of cases tried under the divine displeasure clause have involved *Farmans* (directives) from the Akal Takht to which candidates had imprudently given their consent.

The most interesting aspect of the ways in which the courts construe the threat of divine displeasure clause is that the courts reason that threatening anyone with divine displeasure puts great pressure on the threatened person, and deprives them of the capacity of exercising their rational judgement. In judgement after judgement on this issue, the courts argue that a suggestion of divine displeasure deprives a person of their abilities to make a choice. In cases like *Ram Dial* v. *Sant Lal* (1959) and *Harcharan Singh* v. *Sajan Singh* (1985), the court argued that after the leader of a sect had spoken, it practically left the voters with no choice. Religious appeals in this sense are like drugs or alcohol: they impair our capacity to choose.

In some ways this argument is a non sequitur. The intent of the statute seems to be to exclude certain kinds of religious appeals. There might be good reasons for excluding such appeals. The principal one might be the Hobbesian insight that, in order to discharge our obligations to the state faithfully, we have to be relieved of all those sources of authority that induce even more fear in us than the state might. Whether or not an appeal to divine authority impairs the voters' ability to choose is certainly debatable, but it is neither here nor there. What is significant is the fact that the courts frequently refer to it. Why? The logic of this claim is made more apparent in conversion cases: in *Yulitha Hyde* v. *State of Orissa*, the court wrote: 'Threat of divine displeasure numbs the mental faculty; *more so of an undeveloped mind* and the actions of such a person thereafter, are not free and according to conscience.' In cases involving the Representation of People's Act, the same assumption is made throughout.

If this analysis is correct, we can see a fairly stable set of assumptions about citizens which underlie three different domains that require abridging religious speech or speech about religion: offence against religion; attempts at conversion; and the exclusion of religious appeal from elections. The courts assume throughout that citizens are, when it comes to receiving religious speech or speech about religion, incapable of managing the impressions they receive—to use an old stoic concept. If the insult is to one's religion, or an exhortation is made in the name of religion, we are incapable of receiving the expression on our own terms; incapable of managing our own responses; condemned to receiving these expressions unfreely and helplessly; incapable as it were, of self-discipline. We can manage our impressions, exercise our religious choices, and practise judgement only when left alone. Hence the courts' emphasis on the right to freedom of religion also means the right to freedom from other people's religion. Our choices are impaired or faculties numbed, more so because we have undeveloped minds.

It is undoubtedly the case that the limitations on missionary activity were initiated to protect Hinduism, but this is legitimized on a deeper set of assumptions concerning citizen capabilities, ones that surface in a wider range of discourses. Reading two sets of court judgements—on election cases and conversion cases—one cannot help but feel that the references to citizen incapacity are a bit like the man looking for the key under the lamp-post, not because he had lost it there but because that area happened to be lighted. The displacement onto religion as being, or being uniquely, debilitating of choice simply masks the various conditions that impair the choice in the first place. And taken together they also point to the tensions implicit in the state's attitude toward religion. Religious belief is sufficiently important to warrant protection from having to seriously confront another religion; yet it is irrelevant for public discourse.

The Representation of People's Act (RPA) is associated with a complicated case history that deserves further exploration. One could give a possible Rawlsian rationale for the act in the following terms: public reason requires us to give up appeals to our own comprehensive doctrines; it is therefore legitimate to exclude appeals to religion from politics. But there are two difficulties with this argument. The first is— as Upendra Baxi has argued in connection with the RPA— that excluding religious appeals is a way of saying that a modern state has no political room for questioning its own foundational presuppositions. The second difficulty is more practical. The RPA has the consequence of putting the courts in the difficult position of ascertaining the distinction between a religious and a non-religious appeal. The courts have rightly been criticized, in numerous cases, for letting manifest appeals to religion stand by redefining those appeals as appeals to culture or history. The courts have determined that 'Om' is not a religious symbol; in *Bhairon Singh Shekhawat v. State of Rajasthan*, the courts determined that an election speech promising to build a temple at Ayodhya did not involve an appeal to religion. The grounds on which the court made the determination are of some philosophical interest. The court reasoned, much as Tom Nagel has argued, that in religious matters one cannot make the distinction between my believing something to be true and it actually being true. But since the claim that there was a Hindu temple at the site of the Babri Masjid in Ayodhya can be historically ascertained, claiming that it should be rebuilt does not involve an appeal to religion. Or even more notoriously, in the *Hindutva* cases the court determined that an appeal to Hindutva was not a religious appeal.

I do not want to go into a detailed discussion of these cases. But I hope the following points are clear. The function of the RPA has been to, in effect, give the courts the authority to decide what is religious and what is not; thereby the courts acquire the authority to regulate the meaning of religion. There was much outrage at Justice Verma's claim in the Hindutva cases that an appeal to Hindutva was not an appeal to religion. Yet very few of the critics went on to ask an even more fundamental question. Why have the courts acquired the authority to regulate and fix meanings of terms, much as Hobbes enjoined his sovereign to do? Why does the practice of Indian constitutionalism require the state not only to promulgate public purposes but also to fix the meanings of religious doctrines? Given that the courts have been using their power to nominally define religious content in a variety of domains, it should not come as a surprise that it chose to interpret Hindutva in a particular way. After all, the advantage of nominalism is, as Hobbes argued, that it allows the sovereign to fix the meaning of terms. I suggest that our investments in giving the courts this authority have complicated roots. This is in part because our courts have been the medium through which we have tried to sustain the happy illusion that a deep pluralism of comprehensive doctrines is compatible with the public purposes of a liberal state. This has often obscured not just the true requirements of a secular state but has also exempted religion from criticism. The courts can square circles—at least by definition!

NOTES

1. Laurence Tribe, *American Constitutional Law* (Mineola, NY: The Foundation Press, 1988), p. 1232. See also Richard Epstein, 'Religious Liberty in the Welfare State', *William and Mary Law Review,* 31 (1990), p. 402. Epstein writes that it is one thing for a religious institution to yield its traditions through internal change in order to keep the consent and loyalty of the governed. It is quite another for outsiders to impose their own external standard of right and wrong on these bodies.

2. Within the Indian Constitution there is a significant tension. On the one hand the Constitution guarantees a broad range of religious freedoms. Articles 25 and 26 of the Constitution state that, subject to certain specified conditions, all persons are equally entitled to freedom of conscience and the right freely to practise and propagate religion; and that every religious domination is, amongst other things, entitled to manage its own affairs in matters of religion. On the other hand the Constitution empowers the state to engage in significant social reform of religion.

3. *Adelaide Company of Jehovah's Witnesses Inc v. Commonwealth,* 67 C.L.R. 116, 1943, p. 123.

4. One of the implications of this wider definition of religion is that Indian courts are less apt to take recourse to a distinction familiar in American law between a belief and actions consequent upon that belief. In some instances constitutional protection is then extended to the former and not the latter.

5. The Indian Supreme Court is confronted with awkward judicial issues: Are the Kabir Panthis Hindus? Is a fanatical sect like the Ananda Marga a religious denomination? How many *kirpans* is a Sikh obligated to wear? Are there religious injunctions against photographing women? Do all these involve the essential practices test?

6. J. Duncan Derrett, *Religion, Law and the State in Modern India* (Delhi: Oxford University Press, 1996 reissue), p. 447.

7. The question of conversion is a tricky and contentious one in Indian law, and I will not go into it here. There is however the interesting case of a community, the Ismaili Khojas, whose holy books speak, along Hindu lines, of the ten incarnations of Vishnu, but declare the last one to be the Most Holy Ali. The courts declared that there could be a family of Hindu beliefs that could be governed by Muslim law.

8. AIR 1958 SC 255.

9. Under ceremonial law pertaining to temples, who are entitled to enter them for worship, where they are entitled to stand, and how the worship is to be conducted are all matters of religion. Ibid., 265.

10. AIR 1972 SC 1586. Interpretation of the Agams was also at issue in a further series of temple entry cases. See *Kalyana Das* v. *State of Tamil Nadu* AIR 1973, Madras 264.

11. Robert Lingat, *The Classical law of India*, trans. J. Duncan Derrett (Berkeley: University of California Press, 1973), p. 144.

12. Ronald Dworkin, *Law's Empire* (London: Fontana, 1986), p. 6.

13. I argue this at greater length in *The World Subverts the Word: Reflections on Dharma.*

14. I should add the obvious caveat that I do not take this democratization to be an accomplished fact, but a slow ongoing process. Here I simply mean the proposition that most adherents of the religion no longer deny, at the level of ideological justification, the normative validity of modern egalitarian norms.

15. I have given an account of this in my 'Reason and Authority in the Indian Courts', in Steve Macedo (ed.) *New Perspectives on Toleration and Identity.*

15

Rights versus Representation
Defending Minority Interests in the Constituent Assembly

Shefali Jha

INTRODUCTION

Proponents of constitutionalism and individual rights as bulwarks against the slide of democracy into the tyranny of the majority are often taken to task by democratic theorists for ignoring the design of representative institutions as a means of achieving the same goal. Why should not the danger of majoritarianism be tackled first, or also at the level of alternative mechanisms of representation? This seemed to be one of the important debates, among several others, running through the Indian Constituent Assembly from 1946 to 1949. Each of the representative models suggested for forestalling majoritarianism—for example, proportional representation or reserved seats for minorities—were rejected; but instead of trying to shore up or strengthen representation by proposing some alternative anti-majoritarian representative scheme, the solution proposed to allay the fears of minority groups was a set of rights which included not merely individual rights but a few collective rights for minorities as well.

In presenting this interpretation of part of what was going on in the Indian Constituent Assembly, let me begin with one of these rights, the right to freedom of religion, which reads as follows:

Freedom of conscience and free profession, practise and propagation of religion: (1) Subject to public order, morality and health and to the other provisions of this part, all persons are equally entitled to freedom of conscience and the right freely to profess, practise and propagate religion.[1]

When the right to religious freedom was first discussed in the Fundamental Rights subcommittee of the Constituent Assembly in April 1947, the members of this subcommittee disagreed sharply over whether religious freedom was to be defined as a freedom to 'worship' or as a freedom to the 'practise' of religion. Rajkumari Amrit Kaur argued that the infringement of the rights of women and of Dalits was part of the practice of several religions of India, and so to have a right to 'practise' religion in a chapter guaranteeing the Fundamental Rights of all Indian citizens would be an anomaly. She recommended that only a much narrower right to religious 'worship' be granted.[2]

Amrit Kaur represented, in the Constituent Assembly, the kind of nationalist position that has been called 'statist':[3] Indians were constituting themselves into a nation by all becoming members of the same state. The new Indian citizen was to be identified as just that—a citizen of India, with all markers of extra-political identity, like sex, religion, language, and culture, being attenuated by conscious state policy. If this was the goal, the worst mistake the Constituent Assembly could make would be to highlight the extra-political aspects of one's person, by giving cultural and educational rights to minorities, by reserving seats for women or minority religious groups in legislatures, or by consciously placing religion in the public domain[4] by defining religious freedom widely as a right to the 'practise' of religion.

Amrit Kaur and her supporters espoused their position consistently. The Constituent Assembly was to ensure all of the following: a right only to religious 'worship'; the establishment of the uniform civil code as a Fundamental Right; the forbidding of religious instruction in any state (or state-aided) schools; the recognition by the state of no minority, whether religious, linguistic, or sexual; and no political safeguards for any minority. The new Indian state was to be made up of individuals, not of communities. Pant's oft-cited words bear repeating here:

[T]he individual citizen who is really the backbone of the state [should not be] lost here in that indiscriminate body known as the community. We have even forgotten that the citizen exists as such. There is the unwholesome, and to some extent degrading habit of thinking always in terms of communities and never in terms of citizens.[5]

In the more metaphorical language of another member, '[t]he state is above all gods. It is the god of gods. I would say that a state being the representative of the people, is god himself.'[6] The first loyalty of every

Indian citizen, then, should be to this state, and to ensure that, other identities were to be weakened. It was imperative then that a narrow right to religious 'worship' be granted so as to relegate religion to the private sphere.[7]

This 'statist' position was constantly confronted not only by its polar opposite—with some members insisting, for instance, on the broader right to religious 'practise', on the inclusion, in the list of Fundamental Rights, of the right to be governed by the personal laws of one's religion, and on all kinds of cultural, educational, and political safeguards for religious minorities—but also by a third middling position. In this essay, I want to take up this third position, represented by a person like K.M. Munshi, who while advocating a broad right to the 'practise' of religion, as well as educational and cultural rights for religious and linguistic minorities, rejected outright any reservations for these minorities in legislative bodies of the new state on the grounds that such a step would dangerously strengthen extra-political identities. Is this inconsistency in Munshi's stand, and of others like him, to be rationalized by simply accusing them of being communal?

I think that a more interesting explanation is contained in the words of H.C. Mookerjee, the chairman of the Minorities Sub-Committee, who, expressing his disapproval of those members protesting the rejection, in the Advisory Committee's Report on Minorities of 11 May 1949, of reservations in the legislatures for religious minorities, said:

There are certain people who really feel alarmed over the future of their communities. Such people want to come to the legislatures because they think they can safeguard the interests of the groups to which they belong...But when we have passed the different fundamental rights which guarantee religious, cultural, and educational safeguards which are justifiable, safeguards which can be decided in a court of law, I feel that the presence of people belonging to certain groups is not necessary.[8]

In other words, once the rights to religious and cultural expression had been granted, what was the need of ensuring that Parliament, for example, was more representative of religious minorities? A similar trade-off of rights against representation can be assumed in the supposed compromise brokered with the Christian community: they gave up their demand for reservations in the legislatures in return for the right to 'propagate' their religion.

Initially, however, in the Constituent Assembly Debates there is no sense of representation and rights being perceived as substitutes of each other. At the beginning of the sessions, the framers of the Indian Constitution sought to protect the right to religious freedom not only by focusing on the right itself, both as an individual as well as a collective right, but also by advocating robust representative institutions. Not only were reservations in legislative bodies demanded for religious minorities, but the system of proportional representation was also advocated over simple majority/plurality rule as the electoral system for independent India, all in the name of religious freedom.

It is only later that the trade-off begins to become evident, and this raises questions about the normative as well as the causal assumptions of the members.[9] Normatively speaking, why is the goal of 'secular democracy' used to deny representative safeguards but not cultural group rights: why does the concept of 'secular democracy' have space for one but not the other? In order to ensure that groups do not get discriminated against, that everyone's interests have an equal chance of being furthered, whether she belongs to a majority or a minority community, is it better to ensure a system of collective rights or to demand a certain kind of representative system? What is the causal connection between group interests and rights, and between these interests and a certain system of representation? Is not a robust representative system one of the safeguards of rights? If some members saw that they could not obtain both, on what grounds did they decide which one to settle for? If a robust representative system is one of the best safeguards of rights, why did the struggle to establish it eventually fail?

This essay will look at both prongs of the strategy used in the Constituent Assembly to defend religious freedom. First, we will discuss the demand for proportional representation and reservations in the legislatures, following which we will also look at the sharp disagreement over how the several articles guaranteeing the individual as well as the collective rights to religion were to be framed.

REPRESENTATION OR PROPORTIONAL REPRESENTATION

Early in 1947, B.N. Rau, the constitutional adviser to the assembly, to facilitate the work of drafting the Constitution, circulated a questionnaire about the salient features of the Constitution to members of the central and provincial legislatures. After each of his questions, Rau provided notes with examples of how things were done in other countries. In his section on the legislature, Rau asked: 'What provision should be made for the adequate representation of different communities and interests?'[10] In his note to this specific question, Rau mentioned the US with no provision, and Ireland with a system of proportional representation for the lower house. Hardly anyone replied to this questionnaire, and of those who did, K.M. Panikkar wrote: 'Reservation strictly on population basis for Muslims, Sikhs, Anglo-Indians, Indian Christians and Scheduled Castes. Special constituencies for women, labour and universities.'[11] S.P. Mookerjee's answer was: 'Reservation of seats to important minority communities on the basis of population, joint electorate and adult franchise.'[12]

Rau's next question was on the 'composition, franchise, electorate, constituencies, methods of election, and allocation of seats in respect of the union legislature'.[13] In his note, Rau mentioned the first-past-the-post system of the US, and proportional representation for the lower houses of Switzerland and Ireland. In their answers, Panikkar and Mookerjee mentioned proportional representation for the upper house and direct election by simple majority for the lower house.

It has been noted that as early as the Motilal Nehru Committee Report of 1928, the system of proportional representation had been seen as the best answer in India to community-based claims.[14] Proportional representation had been advocated, of course, as early as the nineteenth century in Britain, with Thomas Hare seeking to replace the British first-past-the-post or plurality system—criticizing it as inadequately representative—by his kind of proportional representation system, in which the voters could vote not only for the party but also for the individual candidate. Proportional representation has been preferred over the plurality system because it results in a greater proportionality between the number of votes a party obtains and the number of seats it gets in the legislature. It is supposed to be specially suited to societies with minorities, because often these minorities do not receive enough votes to get, under a plurality system, any seats in the legislature. Under the proportional representation system, parties representing minority interests would also get a place in the legislature.

The Advisory Committee's first report on minorities was taken up for discussion in the Constituent Assembly on 27 August 1947. Earlier in the year, when the Minorities Sub-Committee began its work, it came up with proposals to establish—for religious minorities and for the

Scheduled Castes—separate electorates, reservations in legislative bodies, ministries, and the civil, military, and judicial services of the government, as well as a minorities commission. When these proposals were discussed in the sub-committee in July 1947, by which time the question of partition had been decided and the Muslim League members had also joined the Constituent Assembly, the demand for separate electorates and for reservation in the ministries was given up. Muslims, Sikhs, Indian Christians, and Scheduled Castes were granted reservation in the legislatures, in proportion to their population, for 10 years, and there were also to be reserved seats in the services for the Scheduled Castes, Muslims, Sikhs, the plains tribes of Assam, and Anglo-Indians. Provision was made for a special minority officer at the Centre and at each of the provinces as well.

In August, the Advisory Committee modified these safeguards by rejecting any reservation for the minorities in the government services, by holding over the question of reserved legislative seats for the Sikhs and by allowing reserved representation for Indian Christians in the central legislature and in the provincial legislatures of Madras and Bombay alone. It was when these recommendations were discussed in the Constituent Assembly later in the month that the demand for proportional representation first came up. When the method of election for the legislatures was under consideration, D.H. Chandrasekhariya moved an amendment that 'provision be made for conducting all elections on the system of proportional representation by single transferable vote'.[15] Justifying his amendment, Chandrasekhariya emphasized representativeness as a fundamental principle of democracy: 'Modern democracy, as we all know, is generally a representative democracy which means that our legislatures should properly and fully reflect the public opinion of the country.'[16] The voting rule of simple majority would 'make room only for the success of one party'.[17] Proportional representation, on the other hand, would make 'our legislature truly democratic and representative of all important elements and interests in the country'.[18] Chandrasekhariya said that he was not concerned with the representation of communal minorities alone; he was equally taking up minorities 'based on political considerations or economic ideologies or even territorial differences'.[19] In a democracy worth its name, '[w]hatever may be the nature of a minority, it ought to find a place in the legislature adequately.'[20] His amendment was however, negatived after hardly any discussion, with one member claiming that his proposed voting rule would have the same effect as separate electorates.

Proportional representation came in for serious discussion only when the Draft Constitution's articles relating to minority safeguards were debated in the Constituent Assembly in December 1948.[21] At that time, we find Sardar Hukam Singh insisting that 'if separate electorates are detestable and if reservation of seats is objectionable, then some method has to be devised by which the rights of minorities can be safeguarded.'[22] The only option left to ensure the adequate representation of the minorities in the legislature was the mechanism of proportional representation. It would certainly safeguard against that 'pervading evil of democracy—the tyranny of the majority'.[23] Anyway, reservations were problematic in that they carried the taint of communalism. Moreover, with reservations and joint electorates, it was still not guaranteed that 'stooges' from the minority community would not be elected. In contrast, the electoral rule of proportional representation would ensure that no one's votes would be wasted; further, '[Proportional representation] is not based on religious grounds and it applies to all minorities, political, religious and communal. Without any sacrifice of democratic principles, it can afford protection to communal minorities also. Without any spirit of communalism, representatives of political and communal minorities can be elected.'[24] This was Kazi Syed Karimuddin's argument for replacing reserved seats in the legislature with proportional representation, and K.T. Shah also recommended using proportional representation under the device of the single transferable vote.

Those who supported proportional representation differed over whether cumulative voting or the single transferable vote was to be used in this system. Anyway, the discussion over proportional representation was of no avail because the assembly again opted for reserved seats in the legislature for minorities.

When the Minorities Sub-Committee took the unprecedented step of dropping the provision of reserved seats even after it had been approved by the assembly, and then presented its changed report through the Advisory Committee to the assembly in May 1949, Z.A. Lari again suggested that instead of separate electorates which were 'positively dangerous',[25] and reservation of seats in the legislature, which was 'ineffectual and having the taint of separatism',[26] the purpose of protecting the interests of the minorities could be better served if 'elections are held under the system of cumulative votes in multi-member constituencies'.[27] Quoting B.N. Rau, Lari asserted: 'One of the best safeguards for minority rights and interests is the system of election by proportional representation.'[28] Citing the contrast between Northern Ireland and Eire, he claimed that the political problems of the former were the result of proportional representation being given up there, whereas Eire had continued with that electoral method.

In India, the system of proportional representation would ensure that the votes of the minorities would get counted, whomever they voted for. Without this safeguard, democracy would allow the majority to ride roughshod over minorities:

The twin principles of democracy are, one that the majority must in the ultimate analysis govern, and second, it is the right of every individual to have some voice in sending his representative to a representative institution, and thereby have some share in selecting a government, to which he owes and renders obedience.[29]

Citing John Stuart Mill's advocacy of the fundamental principle of democracy, 'that every political opinion must be represented in an assembly in proportion to its strength in the country',[30] Lari accused the simple majority rule of disenfranchising 49 per cent of the country's voters.[31]

Lari claimed that elections under the rule of proportional representation would have the three advantages of enabling Parliament to be 'the mirror of the national mind', of consolidating the state by ensuring that 'minorities will not have grievances about their representation', and ensuring that opposition in the house would be based on large national issues.[32] Lari's proposal was, however, shot down mainly on the ground that this voting rule was too difficult for a country such as India with a large illiterate electorate, although one member also feared that it would have the same adverse effect as separate electorates. This rejection was basically a repetition of the reasons that Ambedkar had given against proportional representation in December 1948: that it presupposed literacy on a large scale; that it would lead to the fragmentation of the legislature into many groups and would increase instability; and that it was not suited to a parliamentary form of government.

SEPARATE ELECTORATES AND RESERVED SEATS

The first report that the Minorities Sub-Committee filed in July 1947 did not, of course, mention proportional representation at all. Instead the sub-committee focused on mechanisms like separate electorates and reservations in the legislatures to prevent the 'tyranny of the majority'. The Draft Constitution of February 1948, following the recommend-ations of the Minorities Sub-Committee, reserved seats in Parliament and state legislatures for Muslims, Scheduled Castes, Scheduled Tribes, and Indian Christians for 10 years. I have already in an earlier piece described the process by which this reservation (except for Scheduled Castes and Scheduled Tribes) was finally rejected by the Constituent Assembly in May 1949, after the about-turn of the Advisory Committee on this issue.[33] Here I would just like to add to the discussion the argument that Nehru made while applauding the assembly's decision to give up reserved seats for the minorities. Accepting first that '[t]here is some point in having a safeguard of this type or any other type where there is autocratic rule or foreign rule',[34] Nehru pointed out that India was however now going to be a self-governing democracy. Whereas some members had earlier defined this 'democracy' as an equal voice for every citizen, Nehru's definition of democracy was: 'if it is a democracy, in the long run or in the short run, it is the will of the majority that will prevail.'[35] Given this, minority safeguards, such as reservations, would perhaps protect the minorities 'to a slight extent but at the cost of forfeiting that inner sympathy and fellow feeling with the majority, which is dangerous',[36] since, as Nehru repeated, 'in the very nature of things, in a democracy, the will of the majority will ultimately prevail.'[37]

Contra Nehru, looking at these attempts to strengthen the representative institutions of democratic India, it is tempting to imagine these members being prescient about most legislators being elected on a minority vote in independent India. At the national level, for example, if we take the last three Lok Sabha elections, on average, over 67 per cent of Members of Parliament have won on a minority vote.[38] This certainly calls for some reform of the existing electoral rules. It is interesting to note, however, that the much maligned Constitution Review Committee, even while accepting the 'inadequate representation of Muslims in parliament' as one of the serious problems with India's electoral system,[39] rejected outright any reform of the electoral system in the direction of proportional representation on the grounds that this will further divide the Indian polity:

The idea of any form of proportional representation will aid in the divisive tendencies, as it will now pay the politician to appeal to a small group if he feels that he has a good chance of getting their vote en-bloc...It will then pay the political party to address itself to narrow interests because that may be the only safe way for it to ensure itself a few seats in the house. It should never be enough in such a diverse society as India to maximize support among a narrow grouping and then rely on being needed as part of a coalition government. On the contrary, a party must appeal broadly across the electorate.[40]

This can be done, according to the commission, with a majority system, with run-offs continuing till a candidate obtains a majority of the vote. Like the commission, scholars the world over are discussing ways in which electoral institutions can be so designed or modified to ensure that it is electorally disadvantageous to appeal to only parochial loyalties.

Since ethnic (or religious) hatred is often mobilized by political leaders in response to what they see as routes to power, it is important...to shape the incentives for gaining power in ways that will produce a different result. What is needed in ethnically divided societies, are systems that affect the behavior of elites from one group toward the grass-roots members of other groups. This can be achieved in a variety of ways, all of which require politicians to compete for votes among ethnic groups other than their own.

One example of a solution that is given is that of—contra the Constitutional Review Committee—the proportional representation system.[41]

These asides apart, the point of this and the preceding part of this essay was to show that, for many members of the Constituent Assembly, for protecting the right to freedom of religion of every Indian, the system of representation used was moot.

RIGHTS FOR LINGUISTIC AND RELIGIOUS MINORITIES

We must now look at some of the debates in the Constituent Assembly around religious and cultural rights, but since I have already, in an earlier article,[42] discussed several of these debates, here I will just take up the controversy over whether cultural and educational rights were to be given only to linguistic, or also to religious minorities.

The battle over a system of representation more adequate to safeguarding the interests of religious minorities was lost, apparently because the struggle to establish collective rights for minority religious groups was won even in the teeth of strong opposition. Initially cultural rights for linguistic groups alone, and not for religious groups, were acceptable. Jayaprakash Narayan, for instance, held that the 'secularisation of general education...necessary for the growth of a national outlook and unity'[43] required that the cultural and educational rights guaranteed in the constitution should be confined only to linguistic minorities. On the same lines, Damodar Swarup Seth suggested:

The only minorities to be recognised should be those based on language: recognition of minorities based on religion or community was not in keeping with the secular character of the state. If such minorities were granted the right to establish and administer educational institutions of their own, it would not only block the way to national unity but would also promote communalism and an anti-national outlook.[44]

It was with similar reservations in mind that G.B. Pant had earlier, in an April 1947 meeting of the Minorities Sub-Committee, suggested that the cultural and educational rights of minorities be included among the non-justiciable Directive Principles. Rajkumari Amrit Kaur had similarly proposed that religious minorities not be allowed to set up separate educational institutions, nor state aid be provided to these institutions.

As these articles were finally framed in the Minorities Sub-Committee, however, they reflected the point of view of the other side. The draft rights defined minorities in terms of religion as well as language and gave them the right to establish and administer educational institutions. The Constituent Assembly also passed these articles in the same form in May 1947: 'All minorities, whether based on religion, community or language shall be free in any unit to establish and administer educational institutions of their choice,'[45] which were then entitled to state aid just as any other educational bodies. When these articles were discussed a second time in the Constituent Assembly on 7 December 1948, the debate crystallized around two positions. On the one hand were members like Lokanath Misra who pointed to the danger of such articles attenuating or weakening the unity of India. Misra wanted to preface the first article on cultural and educational rights with the words 'without detriment to the spiritual heritage and cultural unity of the country, which the state shall recognise, protect and nourish',[46] so that the recognition of cultural rights would not endanger national unity. Damodar Swarup Seth repeated his earlier argument that only linguistic and not religious minorities be recognized, for to recognize religious minorities would not only endanger secularism and national unity but also promote communalism and anti-nationalism.

On the opposite side were ranged members fighting for strengthening these cultural and educational rights further. Z.A. Lari protested vehemently at the Drafting Committee's changing of the phrasing of the right even after it had been approved by the assembly. In May 1947, the first clause of the right had been passed by the assembly as: 'Minorities in every Unit shall be protected in respect of their languages, script and culture, and no laws or regulations may be enacted that may operate oppressively or prejudicially in this respect.'[47] The Drafting Committee changed this to 'Any section of the citizens residing in the territory of India or any part thereof having a distinct language, script and culture of its own shall have the right to conserve the same.'[48] Lari argued that, as now phrased, the first right was 'of no effect at all. It states a truism, it is not a fundamental right at all'.[49] He called it 'a paper transaction and nothing more',[50] because all it entitled a body of citizens to was to use their language in their private intercourse. The real issue was the entitlement to use one's own language in elementary education given at state expense, and in order to ensure this Lari wanted the clause back to the form in which it had been passed by the Constituent Assembly when it was first discussed.

Lari pointed out how in UP, where Hindi and Urdu were commonly used, a recent order of the government had forbidden education in Urdu. He gave the example of his own six-year-old son who was no longer permitted by his teacher to study mathematics in Urdu. According to the order, provision could be made in schools for instruction in Urdu, only if a majority of parents so wished, and here Lari hit the nail on the head in his complaint that 'when a facility is made for a minority which is less than 50 per cent, to make that facility dependent on the will of the majority is a denial of that facility.'[51] Lari's complaint made sense in the context of the justification that K.M. Munshi had provided earlier in his defence of cultural and educational rights: 'This minority right is intended to prevent majority control legislatures from favouring their own community to the exclusion of other communities.'[52]

CONCLUSION

A constitution does at least two things: setting down a form of government with its powers, it also places certain matters beyond the limits of those powers. A constitution can, for instance, forbid a democratic government to interfere with the religious freedom of its citizens. When a constitution sets down a democratic form of government and duly emphasizes the representative institutions of that democracy, it may do so to better safeguard the rights of the citizens. In fact, it is only 'liberal rights-based constitutionalism' which is blind to the truth that 'the protection and realization of rights' does not come from merely allowing rights to override the ordinary political process, but is equally a matter of the 'institutional design' of that political process.[53]

Why did a person like Ambedkar, who advocated a narrow right to religious worship and who was ambivalent about collective rights for religious minorities, yet insist on better representation for religious minorities in the representative bodies of the new state? Did the focus on representation and the seeming neglect of the right to religious freedom flow from the view that it was more important for religious freedom to secure a place for religious minorities in the ongoing, never-ending process of deliberation and negotiation which would take place in the Indian state's legislative bodies? Those who insisted on defining religious freedom broadly as the right to religious practice,[54] and were also more open to collective rights for religious groups, were strangely also among the members adamantly resistant to better representation for religious minorities. In denying the religious minorities the additional safeguard of better representation, were these members unwittingly giving in to a view of democracy as majoritarianism, which would eventually prove antithetical to religious freedom? Or were they instead trying to argue that the open-endedness of democratic deliberation could also be subverted by certain kinds of representation? If representative mechanisms are set up such that democratic decision-making becomes just 'bargained accommodation between different interest groups', then that certainly also undermines the openness of democratic deliberation. If this was their motivation for rejecting proportional representation, separate electorates, and reserved seats, then that would imply that these members had a different view of the purpose of representation in a democracy—but this is something which needs further investigation.

NOTES

1. Clause (1), Article 25 of the Indian Constitution, 1950.
2. In an earlier letter to B.N. Rau, Amrit Kaur had explained her rejection of a right phrased in terms of the 'practise' of religion and her insistence on 'freedom of religious worship': 'As we are all aware there are several customs practised in the name of religion, e.g., *purdah*, child marriage, polygamy,

unequal laws of inheritance, prevention of inter-caste marriages, dedication of girls to temples. We are naturally anxious that no clause in any fundamental right shall make impossible future legislation for the purpose of wiping out these evils. As worded, clause 16 (on religious freedom) may even contradict or conflict with the provision abolishing the practice of untouchability.'

3. See A. Sen, 'Secularism and Its Discontents' in K. Basu and S. Subrahmanyam (eds), *Unravelling the Nation* (New Delhi: Penguin, 1996), p. 26.

4. See Gurpreet Mahajan, *Identities and Rights: Aspects of Liberal Democracy in India* (Delhi: Oxford University Press, 1998), pp. 68–70, for usefully distinguishing the two separate questions which were being decided here: the 'non-establishment' of any state religion, and the restriction, or not, of religion to the private sphere.

5. B. Shiva Rao, *The Framing of India's Constitution: Select Documents* [hereafter cited as SD], vol. II (Nashik: Government of India Press, 1968), pp. 62–3.

6. *CAD*, vol. VII, p. 865.

7. Tajamul Hussain insisted, for instance, that only a right to 'practice religion privately' be granted. *CAD*, vol. VII, p. 816.

8. *CAD*, vol. VIII, p. 299.

9. I am grateful to Pratap Bhanu Mehta for reminding me to look more seriously at both the normative as well as the causal assumptions of the Constituent Assembly members.

10. *SD*, vol. II, p. 513.

11. Ibid.

12. Ibid.

13. Ibid.

14. I.A. Ansari, 'Minorities and the Politics of Constitution Making in India', in D.L. Sheth and Gurpreet Mahajan, *Minority Identities and the Nation State*, p. 122. I am indebted to this article for directing my attention to some of the discussions in the Constituent Assembly on proportional representation. I am also grateful to Rochana Bajpai for letting me look at her work on representation in the Constituent Assembly.

15. *CAD*, vol. V, p. 273.

16. Ibid., p. 274.

17. Ibid.

18. Ibid., p. 275.

19. Ibid., p. 274.

20. Ibid.

21. Most articles of the Constitution were discussed twice in the assembly, the first time during 1947, and the second time in the form that they were given by the Drafting Committee which finished the first draft of the Constitution in February 1948.

22. *CAD*, vol. VII, p. 1250.

23. Ibid., p. 1233.

24. Ibid., p. 1235.

25. *CAD*, vol. VIII, p. 283.
26. Ibid.
27. Ibid.
28. Ibid., p. 284.
29. Ibid., p. 283.
30. Ibid.
31. Ibid.
32. Ibid., p. 286.
33. Shefali Jha, 'Secularism in the Constituent Assembly Debates, 1946–1950', *Economic and Political Weekly*, 27 July 2002.
34. *CAD*, vol. VIII, p. 330.
35. Ibid.
36. Ibid.
37. Ibid.
38. National Commission to Review the Working of the Constitution, 'Review of Election Law, Processes and Reform Options (Consultation Paper)', January 2001, p. 53.
39. See *The Times of India*, 4 October 2001, p 5.
40. National Commission, 'Review of Election Law, Processes, and Reform Options', p. 57.
41. I. Shapiro, 'Group Aspirations and Democratic Politics', in I. Shapiro and C. Hacker-Cordon, *Democracy's Edges* (Cambridge: Cambridge University Press, 1999), p. 218.
42. See Jha, 'Secularism in the Constituent Assembly Debates'.
43. B. Shiva Rao, *The Framing of India's Constitution: A Study* (Nashik: Government of India Press, 1968), p. 276.
44. Shiva Rao, *The Framing of India's Constitution*, p. 277.
45. *CAD*, vol. III, p. 503.
46. *CAD*, vol. VII, p. 892.
47. *CAD*, vol. III, p. 503.
48. *CAD*, vol. VII, p. 893.
49. Ibid., p. 894.
50. Ibid.
51. Ibid., p. 902.
52. *CAD*, vol. IV, p. 367.
53. R. Bellamy and D. Castiglione, *Constitutionalism in Transformation: European and Theoretical Perspectives* (Oxford: Blackwell, 1996).
54. The controversy over religious 'worship' and religious 'practise' is another fascinating example of how closely battles were fought on the floor of the Constituent Assembly.

16

Minority Representation and the Making of the Indian Constitution*

Rochana Bajpai

INTRODUCTION

Recent years have seen an upsurge of interest in the rights of minority groups in liberal democracies. In India, one of the oldest and most intricate regimes of group preference exists within a polity broadly committed to liberal democratic norms. The Constituent Assembly Debates (1946–50) mark a decisive turning point in state policies of minority rights in India. Since the late nineteenth century, an array of preferential policies had been instituted by the colonial state[1] as well as by some princely states,[2] primarily for groups characterized as minorities and 'backward'. The chief components of the colonial regime of group preference were political safeguards: provisions for special representation in the legislatures and quotas in the public services. Over time, these had been extended to a variety of groups, including Muslims, Sikhs, Indian Christians, Anglo-Indians, Scheduled Castes, and tribal groups.

During the deliberations of the Constituent Assembly, the colonial regime of group preference was fundamentally recast. While the first

* This is a slightly revised version of a paper presented at the Conference on the Philosophy of the Indian Constitution, Goa 2001. It is based on Rochana Bajpai, 'Recognising Minorities: A Study of Some Aspects of The Indian Constituent Assembly Debates, 1946–1949', unpublished M.Phil. thesis, University of Oxford, 1997; versions of the argument have been presented at the APSA Boston, 1998 and published as Rochana Bajpai, 'Constituent Assembly Debates and Minority Rights', *Economic and Political Weekly*, XXXV (21–2), 27 May 2000, pp. 1837–45.

draft of the Constitution had included reserved seats in legislatures and quotas in government employment for religious minorities, by the time of the final draft these provisions were dropped and legislative and employment quotas came to be restricted mainly to the Scheduled Castes and tribal groups.[3] Curiously, this remarkable development has received little scholarly attention. In the scant scholarship on this question, the withdrawal of political safeguards for religious minorities during Constitution-making has been explained mainly in terms of the partition of the country.[4] This traumatic event, it is argued, hardened opinion within the Indian National Congress against groups that represented communal interests. Moreover, the Congress no longer had to conciliate a powerful Muslim League and had few real checks in the way of pushing through its agenda. The political parties representing the two main religious minorities pressing for political safeguards—the Muslim League and the Sikh Panthic Party—were in disarray, and could not offer a united front resisting the revocation of safeguards.

Elsewhere, I have argued that while Partition and the changed balance of power that ensued are important, these are not, as is commonly believed, sufficient for explaining the retraction of political safeguards for religious minorities.[5] During the making of the Indian Constitution, the existing normative basis of group preference was fundamentally recast, and this is crucial for an adequate understanding of the forms that political safeguards would eventually assume. This essay focuses on one type of political safeguard, namely, special representation in the legislatures—the most significant and controversial element of the colonial regime of group preference. It offers a detailed reconstruction of arguments over the main group representation mechanisms considered by the Constituent Assembly: separate electorates, proportional representation, and reserved seats in legislatures. I will argue that in the nationalist vocabulary, there was a normative deficit in the case of *group representation* as such, and this enables us to understand better the retraction of legislative quotas for religious minorities during Constitution-making.[6]

Dominant approaches in historical and social science scholarship have tended to regard the principles professed by politicians in defence of positions as little more than smokescreens for their more 'real' interests, and as irrelevant for explanations of political outcomes. This essay follows Quentin Skinner's position on why our explanations of political outcomes should take seriously the principles professed by politicians.

Skinner suggests that political actors are constrained to behave in ways that appear to conform to principles invoked to legitimate them.[7] Further, politicians cannot manipulate legitimating principles wholly at will, for their availability and applicability is limited by prevailing social usages. The existing legitimating vocabulary thus shapes and constrains the possible range of political actions and is relevant to explanations of political outcomes.

The essay is divided into four parts. The first section discusses the usage of the term 'minority' in claims for preferential treatment in the Constituent Assembly Debates. The second section delineates the contours of nationalist opinion on political safeguards for minorities. The third section offers a detailed analysis of the debate in the Constituent Assembly over three types of minority representation mechanisms: separate electorates, proportional representation, and reserved seats in legislatures. The concluding section draws out the implications of the analysis of political representation for the character of the legitimating vocabulary and the fate of political safeguards during Constitution-making.

DEFINING MINORITIES

The Constituent Assembly began its proceedings as scheduled on 9 December 1946, with the Muslim League boycotting its sessions.[8] In the assembly's deliberations, the minorities question was regarded as encompassing the claims of three kinds of communities: religious minorities, backward castes, and tribals, for all of whom safeguards in different forms had been instituted by the British and princely states in the colonial period. The representatives of most groups claiming special provisions in some form emphasized that the group was a minority of some kind. The employment of the term 'minority' did not denote the numerical status of the group as much as the claim that the group suffered from some kind of disadvantage with respect to the rest that entitled it to special treatment from the state. In minority claims, numerical status was invoked most frequently to denote numerical strength of a group which made it a force to reckon with, and entitled it to safeguards over other smaller groups. The representatives of each group advanced reasons why their group was more eligible for safeguards or deserving of greater representation than any other, on grounds, for instance, that it was numerically superior, more backward than others, more distinct from the majority in its cultural practices, and so on.

Several representatives from religious minority communities voiced concerns regarding the submergence of a distinct cultural identity in independent India. Considerations about cultural autonomy were sought to be rendered compatible with the nationalist elite's concerns regarding national unity by arguing that it was only through the retention of their own distinct cultures that members of these communities would be able to contribute effectively to the nation.[9] These arguments drew upon early nationalist conceptions, which regarded communities, defined in religious, caste, and linguistic terms, rather than the individual citizen as the building blocks of the nation.[10]

Most untouchable representatives in the Constituent Assembly also claimed minority status but emphasized that untouchables were a different type of minority from the religious minorities. It was stressed that Scheduled Castes were a 'political minority',[11] that the term 'minority' in the case of Scheduled Castes did not connote numerical disadvantage but rather, entitlement to special treatment on account of social and economic backwardness.[12] Not all Scheduled Caste representatives claimed minority status and concomitant 'political safeguards' for the community. Some argued, in keeping with dominant nationalist opinion, that reserved quotas in legislatures and public employment were undesirable, and that the solution to the problems of these groups lay in the removal of economic and social disabilities.[13]

The most vocal tribal representative in this period, while claiming that his group was entitled to special provisions, chose not to term tribes 'minorities'.[14] Tribal claims resembled those of the Scheduled Castes on several counts. Representatives of both groups would declare that they were the original inhabitants of the land, and that their claims were thereby antecedent to all others.[15] In both cases, arguments for special treatment referred to a history of injustice and exploitation by Hindu society, and invoked compensatory justice in favour of preferential treatment.[16] However, there were also differences: the pronouncements of tribal representatives were distinguished by an emphasis on the importance of land in tribal life and its link to cultural identity.[17] In contrast, the claims of the Scheduled Castes in this period lacked the element of territoriality. These were dominated by their concern regarding inclusion in the administrative and governing elite of the country and access to positions of political power generally, an aspect which was implicit in the self-description of 'political minority'.

While the appellation 'minority' was popular among the representatives of almost every group claiming special provisions in the Constituent Assembly, nationalist opinion regarded the term unfavourably and consistently sought to restrict its usage. K.M. Munshi proposed an amendment to define the term minority more narrowly in order to exclude the Scheduled Castes from its ambit as well as to define the Scheduled Castes as a part of the Hindu community.[18] In later stages of Constitution-making, the term 'minorities' would be removed altogether from constitutional sections dealing with provisions of group preference.[19]

NATIONALIST OPINION AND POLITICAL SAFEGUARDS

Nationalist opinion in the Constituent Assembly recognized both individuals as well as groups as subjects of rights.[20] This would be reflected in the future Indian Constitution, where cultural and educational rights of religious minorities are enshrined as justiciable fundamental rights, and assume the form of the rights of individual members of minority communities as well as that of minority group rights.[21] Congress pronouncements in the Constituent Assembly continually reiterated support for the cultural, educational, and linguistic rights of minorities, as a means of enabling minority groups to protect their distinct cultural identities.[22]

Political safeguards, however, were a different matter. While these were included in the Report on Minority Rights adopted by the Constituent Assembly in August 1947 and in Part XIV of the Draft Constitution published in February 1948, nationalist opinion was hostile to such provisions from the outset. Political safeguards for minorities were reluctantly admitted as temporary, transitional measures, necessary until 'backward' sections of the population were brought up to the level of the rest, or until groups accustomed to 'privileges' under the colonial system had adjusted to the new order. In the dominant nationalist opinion, however, the ideal was always visualized as a situation in the future where political safeguards for minorities in the form of reservation in the legislatures and services would no longer be necessary. Such safeguards were regarded as corrosive of the fundamental principles on which the new nation state was to be constituted: secularism, equality and justice, democracy, and above all, national unity and development. While analytically distinguishable, these concepts were deployed together and interdependently in political arguments. Nationalist opinion encompassed a range of ideological positions, and there were several distinct arguments from the standpoints of national unity and development, secularism, justice, and democracy against political safeguards.

The strongest opposition to political safeguards in this period unsurprisingly stemmed from national unity concerns. This was usually accompanied by a particular understanding of the history of political safeguards where these appeared as instruments of a colonial divide-and-rule policy.[23] At least three related national unity concerns can be discerned.[24] First, political safeguards were seen as a threat to the political unity and integrity of the country. Recent history was perceived as providing conclusive evidence in support of this position, with religion-based separate electorates in particular regarded as the direct cause of the traumatic partition of the country.[25] The paramount task facing the assembly was that of containing civil strife and consolidating political unity, and it was argued that history had shown that political safeguards were inimical to this goal. Political integrity and stability were the dominant national unity concern in this period.

A second national unity concern pertained to common nationhood—a sense of belonging to the same nation. Nationalist opinion recognized that the new state had to create a sense of common nationality among its citizens which would transcend group identities based on 'caste, creed, and religion' that divided them. Safeguards involved the recognition of group identities in the political realm that it was felt would promote identification with particular groups at the cost of the nation. Nationalist opinion in this period looked upon group identities with suspicion, as 'distinct from, and potentially in competition with, common citizenship identities'.[26] Having recently formed the basis of an alternative nation-state, religious identities were seen as a particular threat to the national identity. But caste, regional, and other ascriptive groups were also viewed as competing loci for citizens' affections, detracting, in proportion to their strength, from a common citizenship identity. A sense of common nationhood was regarded as a prerequisite both for the political integrity of the nation and for the successful functioning of a democracy.[27]

Third, political safeguards not only encouraged identification with groups rather than the nation, but the content of the group identities that these promoted was antithetical to the *kind* of national identity favoured in this period. Political safeguards were instituted for groups defined in terms of ascriptive criteria of religion, caste, and tribe, whereas the national identity in dominant nationalist opinion was defined in secular liberal democratic terms which avoided references to ethno-cultural criteria.[28] The ascendant conception of the Indian nation in our period was the modernist one, where the nation was conceived of as a political community, united by its commitment to common political ideals of secularism, democracy, rights, equality, and justice.[29] Moreover, these ideals were construed as *precluding* the recognition of ethno-cultural criteria, particularly religious criteria, in the political domain. The recognition of cultural group identities in the political sphere was considered a pre-modern legacy that was inconsistent with the task of building a modern nation-state, where the cultural affiliations of individuals were irrelevant for purposes of citizenship.[30] Political safeguards thus undermined national unity in several ways: by endangering the political integrity of the nation, by inhibiting the development of a common nationality, and by undermining the creation of a modern, secular democratic citizenship. Characteristically of nationalist doctrines, minority groups were perceived to be a 'part' of the 'organic whole' that was the nation, and were advised not to put their 'narrow', 'petty' group concerns above the 'larger', 'common' national interest. In nationalist opinion, the nation was usually conceived in terms of biological metaphors, referred to, for instance, as an 'organic whole', a 'body politic'—in other words, as being 'natural', in contrast to the artificially created minorities. Political safeguards were referred to variously as 'concessions' and 'crutches', and a symptom of 'ill-health' in the polity.[31]

Political safeguards were also opposed on grounds that these were privileges or concessions that involved departures from justice.[32] In such characterizations justice was construed in liberal terms of equal individual rights, which were seen to imply that all individuals should have the *same* rights. Differences in the political rights of individuals deriving from their cultural group membership were seen to contravene the state's commitment to treat all its citizens as equals.[33] Individuals rather than groups were seen in dominant nationalist opinion as the primary subjects of rights. Several Congress representatives lamented the importance accorded to community and the neglect of the individual citizen in political claims.[34]

Another set of arguments in nationalist opinion against political safeguards invoked the value of secularism. In terms of the state's stance towards religion, most arguments in the Constituent Assembly emphasized that secularism did not imply that the state was hostile to religious belief. Further, a secular state was not a state that was incognizant of the importance of religious faith in society, nor was a secular state zealous of inculcating scepticism towards religious belief among its citizens. Speeches in this vein argued simultaneously that a secular state did not imply secularism of this kind as well as that a secular state could not assume such a stance in a country like India that was dominated by religious beliefs. For instance, proposing an amendment that gave the president the option of taking his oath of office in the name of God, a proposal which was supported by representatives of the religious minorities and incorporated into the Constitution, K.M. Munshi stated:

A secular state is not a Godless state. It is not a state which is pledged to eradicate or ignore religion. It is not a state which refuses to take notice of religious belief in this country...We must take cognisance of the fact that India is a religious minded country. Even while we are talking of a secular state, our mode of thought and life is largely coloured by a religious attitude to life...the state in India cannot be secular in the sense of being anti-religious.[35]

A secular state did, however, imply some forms of separation between state and religion.[36] First, a secular state was construed in terms of dis-establishment—the notion that the state would not have an official religion. Second, secularism was regarded to imply the exclusion of religion from the political domain: religion, it was argued, should be a 'personal matter' for citizens, restricted to their individual and associational private practices.[37] A third conception of secularism as separation was that of state impartiality between different religions: secularism meant 'that the state or the government cannot aid one religion or give preference to one religion as against another...not that it has lost faith in all religions'.[38]

Two main arguments in support of nationalist conceptions of secularism as separation between state and religion can be identified. First, secularism was regarded as a requisite of equal citizenship in a situation where citizens professed a variety of faiths. It was argued that the state had an obligation to treat its citizens as equals, to not discriminate between them on grounds of (religious) group membership.[39] The assumption was that, given a situation of religious pluralism and the importance of religion in people's lives, this obligation would be compromised if the state identified with or gave preference to any particular religion. An amendment was proposed, explicitly stipulating state neutrality in matters relating to religion, in order that '…all classes of citizens…have the same treatment in matters mundane from the state.'[40] Key liberal concerns were thus intimately bound up with the meaning and justification of secularism in the Constituent Assembly Debates.

The requirements of equal citizenship were, however, not the only considerations motivating conceptions of secularism as separation between state and religion. Separation was also regarded as a critical imperative, as 'mixing religion and politics' was dangerous from the standpoint of the survival of the new nation-state. The recent violent partition of the country was portrayed as a direct consequence of the colonial policy of 'mixing religion and politics'. It was felt that if conflicts about religious doctrines were played out in the arena of the state, the state would be torn apart.[41] Therefore, the state, in order to save itself and in order to achieve the consolidation of the nation, had to keep clear of matters concerning religion.

While religion was to be excluded from the affairs of the state, a secular state also implied religious freedom for individuals and groups. Interestingly, religious freedom was most prominently invoked in conceptions of a secular state in the speeches of proponents of Muslim Personal Law in the Constituent Assembly. Many Muslim representatives argued that religious personal laws which governed areas such as marriage, divorce, and maintenance were an essential aspect of religion, and ought as such to be granted immunity from state interference.[42] These claims were rejected by the Constitution-makers, which was not surprising, given that the reform of Hindu personal law loomed large on the political agenda.[43] In dominant nationalist opinion, secularism was not—unlike in the speeches of Muslim proponents of personal law—*identified* with religious freedom.[44]

Thus far we have seen conceptions of secularism in terms of the state's stance towards religion. Connotations of secularism in the Constituent Assembly Debates, however, did not pertain to religion and state alone. The ideal of secular, liberal nationalism captured in the popular slogan 'irrespective of caste, creed, race or community' was of a polity where ascriptive affiliations of any kind would become irrelevant in the political domain. This ideal, moreover, required not just the exclusion of ascriptive affiliations from the political domain, but also the creation of a new secular ethos and secular citizenship identities, where people would cease to see themselves as members of this or that community and regard themselves as Indians 'first and last'. The implication of secularism in the project of nation-building is clearly evident: ascriptive affiliations were viewed simultaneously as anti-secular and as expressions of anti-national sentiments. It may be recalled that the pejorative term 'communal' was opposed to both 'secular' and 'national' in nationalist discourse of this period.[45] In the nationalist scheme, secularism was the envisaged solution to the problem of the creation of a unified nation-state and a common national identity out of a diversity of competing allegiances of religion, caste, and language.[46]

In its elaboration by the modernizing nationalist elite of the Constituent Assembly exemplified by Nehru, secularism had another inflection.[47] Here, ascriptive affiliations were viewed as vestiges of a pre-modern era that processes of modernization and development would make redundant. It was held that nation, rather than religion or caste, provided the appropriate basis for identity in the modern era. The nation in this period was backed both by the force of self-evident legitimacy as well as historical necessity. S. Radhakrishnan declared: 'The present tendency is for larger and larger aggregations. Nationalism, not religion, is the basis of modern life.'[48] To define the nation without reference to ascriptive criteria was considered to be the mark of India's coming of age.[49] Religion and other ascriptive identities, it was argued, had acquired importance only as a result of the machinations of the colonial regime and Indian vested interests. This importance would wither away once the country was rid of imperialism, the problems of economic injustice were addressed, and there occurred a diffusion of education and a scientific temper among the Indian people. Until then, cultural identities and claims for safeguards based on these were regarded as out of step with the times, and as distractions from the real and more pressing tasks of tackling issues of development and attending to the basic needs of the common man.[50] Recent history has shown only too well that Nehru's confidence in the withering away of religious and other communal identities was misplaced. What is less often recognized, however, is that the mistaken causal claim, namely that processes of modernization and secularization would make for secular attitudes and identities, was based on a conceptual confusion: the identification of a scientific temper with a secular outlook.[51]

In the debates over political safeguards, the vocabulary of liberal–secular nationalism was interwoven with indigenous cultural and historical idioms. The most salient instance was the conception of the tolerance and the generosity of the house and the majority community towards the minorities, which was increasingly in evidence in political speeches after the partition of the country in 1947. This theme, explicitly or implicitly, evoked filial norms—the the majority community was cast in the role of the responsible, easygoing, benevolent, and self-sacrificing older brother—indulgent, protective, and accommodating of even the excessive and unreasonable demands of his younger and weaker brothers, the minorities.[52] There was frequent elision between the majority community and the major party, both overwhelmingly numerically preponderant in the country and the assembly respectively, both generous beyond the call of justice in allaying the misapprehensions and insecurities of the minorities. The theme of the tolerance and generosity of the house/the majority community towards minorities also invoked in some cases notions of the 'age-old civilizational traditions' of (Hindu) India of the accommodation of diverse religious groups. Secularism as tolerance and generosity towards minorities carried connotations of forbearance and self-restraint; it implied 'that the numerical majority, the Hindus, would not use their power to give Hinduism a favoured place over other religions'.[53] Arguments about minority safeguards in the Constituent Assembly Debates frequently drew their normative force from the simultaneous invocation of a secular liberal–democratic idiom and traditional filial and feudal values.

THE NATIONALIST RESOLUTION OF THE MINORITIES QUESTION: THE CASE OF POLITICAL REPRESENTATION

The question of political safeguards for minorities was referred to the Advisory Committee on Fundamental Rights, Minorities, Tribal and Excluded Areas in the Constituent Assembly, whose creation had been mandated by the Cabinet Mission Plan of 16 May 1946. Its first report on minority rights of August 1947 proposed a number of measures. While rejecting some of the central components of the British system of minority safeguards, such as separate electorates and weightage, it offered an alternative set of political safeguards. A system of joint electorates with representation for communities in proportion to their population was proposed for a period of ten years. The Instrument of Instructions to the President and Governor suggested the 'desirability of including members of important minority communities in Cabinets as far as practicable'.[54] A general declaration was adopted to the effect that 'in the All India and Provincial Services, the claims of all the minorities shall be kept in view in making appointments to these services consistently with the consideration of efficiency of administration.'[55] A provision was made for a Special Minority Officer at the central and provincial levels to report to the legislatures regarding the working of various safeguards for minorities.

This report was adopted by the Constituent Assembly in August 1947 and incorporated in the Draft Constitution published in February 1948. In a comprehensive reversal, amendments were adopted to each of these articles during discussions on the Draft Constitution in October 1949, effectively removing religious minorities from the purview of these safeguards and restricting the scope of these articles mainly to the Scheduled Castes and the Scheduled Tribes. The abolition of special representation provisions for religious minorities was pivotal. Once this was accomplished, the removal of other political safeguards for religious minorities followed swiftly, almost as a matter of supplementary adjustment.

Separate electorates, various forms of proportional representation and reserved seats in the legislatures were the chief mechanisms proposed for enabling minority representation during the career of the Constituent Assembly.[56] This section analyses the debate in the Constituent Assembly over these three group representation provisions, with a view to illuminating the fate of political safeguards during Constitution-making.

CONFLICTING CONCEPTIONS OF REPRESENTATION:
THE CASE OF SEPARATE ELECTORATES

One of the most forceful demands for political safeguards in the Constituent Assembly was to be found in arguments for separate electorates put forward by Muslim League representatives during discussions on the first Report on Minority Rights in August 1947.[57] The case for separate electorates was built around a contention over the concept of representation and typically invoked the following arguments. First, representatives asserted that minority groups were a permanent feature of every human society, and not, as nationalist opinion claimed, a contrivance of colonial machinations and vested interests. There were fundamental and irreducible differences between communities, at least along lines of religion. To deny the existence of minority communities, B. Pocker Sahib Bahadur (Muslim League, Madras) declared, was going 'against the facts of human nature and having before us ideologies that are impossible for realization. Human nature being what it is, there are bound to be minorities...'[58] Second, the fact that distinct minority communities existed along lines of religion meant that these differences had to be represented in political institutions. As the legislature made laws which affected all communities, it was 'necessary that in that legislature the needs of all communities should be ventilated'.[59]

Two points are significant here. To begin with, this was a claim that the entities relevant from the standpoint of representation were religious groups rather than individuals; the political interests of individuals were seen to derive from their religious group membership. Two, while bearing a superficial resemblance to the democratic idea that those affected by decisions should participate in their making, unlike in our present-day institutions, representation here was not necessarily about popular participation in decision-making.[60] Separate electorates had thus far operated in a colonial framework of circumscribed democracy, where political participation was limited and legislative bodies played a largely advisory rather than law-making role, acting as sounding boards for various sections of Indian opinion.[61]

Third, group representation was thought to imply the presence of members of the group in legislative assemblies: the fact that culturally distinct groups existed had to be reflected in the social composition of legislatures, in what legislatures looked like. The mechanism of separate electorates does not, strictly speaking, require that representatives elected belong to beneficiary groups, only that the electorate be constituted of group members. But in its practice in India, the former had almost always been the case, and it was assumed to be an aspect of separate electorates by its advocates in the Constituent Assembly. The underlying notion here was that of descriptive representation, where representation was seen as requiring a correspondence between the characteristics of the representative and those she represented.[62] Further, descriptive group representation was advocated here as a means of enhancing substantive representation. Different religious communities had distinct needs and preferences and it was not possible for members of other communities, no matter how well-informed and well-intentioned they were, to adequately understand, and thereby to effectively represent, the interests of the community in policy-making, particularly in the prevailing climate of distrust between communities.[63] Advocating separate electorates, B. Pocker Sahib Bahadur held:

...as matters stand at the present moment in this country, it will be very difficult for members of particular communities, say the non-Muslims to realize the actual needs and requirements of the Muslim community...even if a non-Muslim does his best to do what he can for the Muslim community, to represent their views, he will find it impossible to do so because he is not in a position to realize, understand, and appreciate the actual needs of members of that particular community, so long as he does not belong to that community...How would Hindus feel if Muslims were to represent their grievances in the legislature and provide effective remedies as regards, say, temple entry, marriage customs etc?[64]

Fourth, it was argued that if minorities were to be represented, electoral constituencies had to be organized so that they could choose their representatives. Group representation would not be authentic, and hence not effective, unless the person representing the community was chosen by members of that community alone.[65] As B. Pocker Sahib Bahadur put it, under a system of joint electorates,

...it is that person whom the majority community backs that will be elected...the mere fact that a particular member belongs to a particular community is not a guarantee that his views represent the views of that particular community. That particular community, if at all it has to be represented, has got to elect the right man from among the members of that community.[66]

In other words, for minority representation to be achieved, it was necessary but not sufficient that the representative belong to the minority community. To be a 'true representative', one who genuinely represented the views of the community, she had to be chosen by the community. Separate electorates were defended as the best mechanism for securing this end, which reserved seats for groups in legislatures could not in themselves ensure. The case for separate electorates thus went beyond the descriptive view that representation could be achieved simply by virtue of belonging to the same group; it reflected a concern that representatives be accountable primarily to the group they were supposed to represent.[67]

The proposals for separate electorates were, predictably, rejected in the house: these had already been rejected by the Report on Minority Rights. Nationalist opinion was opposed to the conception of representation implicit in the case for separate electorates in each of the aspects discussed above: in terms of the entities to be represented (groups or individuals); the function of representatives (advocacy of a group's concerns or participation in democratic decision-making); who could do the representing (members of the group or any citizen); and how group representation was to be achieved (separate or joint electorates).

Three main sets of arguments were put forward against separate electorates. In one set of arguments, separate electorates were considered incompatible with the nationalist ideal of a secular state. Congress representatives argued, in contrast to the advocates of separate electorates, that in a secular state the interests relevant from the standpoint of political representation were those of individual citizens, not of religious groups:

To give the right of suffrage to a section of the people on religious basis is something which the world does not understand. After all, we do not come here to legislate about religions. We come here to legislate and make laws to see that peace is maintained in the country on a country-wide basis. It is not a question of one or the other section being considered. It is the whole country which has to be taken into consideration when we legislate. So the idea of getting representation from religious sections is simply ridiculous. We have had it till now but we cannot continue it because the future constitution is not meant to be a constitution of religions. A State cannot be a confederation of so many religions or sects or groups.[68]

It was assumed that with regard to secular national issues there were no significant differences in the interests of individuals along religious lines. The conception of secularism implicit here was that of the exclusion of religion from the political domain. Religion-based separate electorates were thought to undermine a secular state in several respects—through the recognition of religious affiliations for electoral purposes; as these implied that the political rights of citizens would differ depending upon their religious group membership; as it was felt that separate electorates would entrench the role of religion in the definition of political identities and inhibit the emergence of common, secular citizen identities; and, finally, as religion was thought to be a medieval relic, out of place in a modern state. So representation along religious lines was simultaneously anti-secular and anti-national.

In a second set of arguments, separate electorates were opposed as undemocratic. One objection held that separate electorates detracted from 'true democracy', because they gave some groups special privileges with regard to political representation:

...unadulterated democracy...means a true representation of the people; true without any weightage, without any favour; without any disregard of the rightful privileges of any section of the people or any individual...if we put obstacles in the way of any or stop the passage of others or give privilege to others, that will mean that the democracy or the representation of the people will not be as true and pure as it ought to be in an unadulterated democracy.[69]

The underlying democratic norm here was that of political equality. Political equality was thought to require equal political rights for all individuals irrespective of the religious group to which they belonged, and was identified with the equally weighted vote for all individuals (one person, one vote).[70] Territory rather than religious group was regarded as the appropriate basis of representation; territorial representation was equated with the representation of individuals rather than groups. Separate electorates for minorities appeared as undemocratic from the standpoint of this proceduralist and individualist conception of democratic representation. This line of criticism was similar to the claim that separate electorates undermined secularism because they violated equal citizenship. Here, differentiated political rights implied by separate electorates were regarded to contravene democratic citizenship.

A second objection to separate electorates on democratic grounds contrasted the role of representatives under a colonial regime with a democratic political system. Separate electorates, it was held, might have been relevant in a colonial framework, where assemblies were primarily advisory bodies with few decision-making powers, and the role of representatives was largely in acting as advocates for their respective communities. In a democratic system—such as the one that Constitution-makers were fashioning, where legislatures were law-making bodies— the role of representatives was different:

...it is not merely a question of advocacy now...It is a question of having an effective decisive voice in the affairs and in the deliberations of the Legislatures and the Parliament of this free country. Even if in an advisory capacity one were a very good advocate, he cannot be absolutely of any use...if the Judge whom he has to address does not appreciate his arguments...and there is no possibility of the Advocate ever becoming a Judge.[71]

The demand for separate electorates was portrayed as resting on a misapprehension of what was entailed by the transformation of the political system from an undemocratic colonial regime to democratic, independent India.[72] In a democratic framework, it was argued, separate electorates would be harmful to minorities. Vallabhbhai Patel held:

Assume that you have separate electorates on a communal basis. Will you ever find a place in any of the Ministries in the Provinces or the Centre? You have a separate interest. Here is a Ministry or a Government based on joint responsibility, where people who do not trust us, or who do not trust the majority cannot obviously come into the Government itself...You will exclude yourselves and remain perpetually in a minority.[73]

Implicit here was a particular conception of democracy. The democratic norm appealed to was that of popular sovereignty, where laws were made by those subject to them. This ideal was institutionally embodied in representative government, which, in turn, was identified with the procedures of majoritarian parliamentary government, where the mechanism of decision-making was majority rule. Further, in contrast to the case for separate electorates, the assumption was that there were no permanent majorities or minorities in legislatures, only temporary, issue-based ones—thus, religious minorities could be part of legislative majorities. From the standpoint of this conception of democracy, separate electorates were undemocratic, because they cast minority representatives in the role of advocates rather than authors of law. They were also harmful to minorities—separate electorates, it was held, would isolate minority representatives from the main body of legislators, preventing them from forming majority coalitions in the legislatures that alone would allow them to enact their preferences into policy. As such, separate electorates would give minority groups a voice in the legislature, while depriving them of any effective policy influence.[74]

A third set of arguments against separate electorates in nationalist opinion, the most prominent in this period, was based on national unity. Separate electorates were historically associated with a policy which had denied the existence of an Indian nation and was widely believed to have caused its dismemberment by sharpening differences between Hindus and Muslims. Different concerns of national unity were invoked. Separate electorates had become synonymous with political separatism in this period, and their continuation was regarded as incompatible with the political unity of the country and the maintenance of civil peace. Further, it was felt that the perpetuation of separate group representation would keep different groups apart and thus sabotage the nationalist project of the creation of a common political community and national identity. Joint electorates, it was argued, would promote communication and trust across different groups, and strengthen citizenship identities:

We expect if there is to be joint electorates, we will come together sometime. Under the joint electorate system a Hindu can represent the Muslims and a Muslim the Hindus...If I do not come on his vote, if I am not his representative, what on earth is there to bind me to him?[75]

Conceptions of secularism and democracy discussed above formed part of the vision of the common good, on the basis of which citizenship was to be defined in the new nation. From a nationalist standpoint, separate electorates challenged the idea of a national community and a common good.

CHANGING BASES OF MINORITY CLAIMS: THE CASE OF PROPORTIONAL REPRESENTATION

Various forms of proportional representation were also proposed to enable minority representation, at different stages of the framing of the Constitution, primarily in the context of the election of members to the lower house and the formation of the Cabinet. Initially, proportional representation was chiefly advocated to supplement reserved seats, as a means of giving members of minority groups a greater voice in the election of minority representatives. Increasingly, however, proportional representation came to be favoured as an alternative to reserved seats in legislatures for minorities. Legislative quotas under joint electorates were regarded as an illusory safeguard which on account of the electoral disadvantage of minorities in mixed constituencies under a first-past-the-post-system, could not ensure that the person elected was a 'true' or 'real' representative of the community.[76] Proportional representation was also advocated as a mechanism which would enable the representation of minority political *opinion*, and, as one of its consequences, enable more representatives from minority communities to be elected.[77] While both claims for proportional representation were based on the notion of pictorial adequacy, its implications in the two cases were somewhat distinct, resting on the composition of assemblies in terms of social groups in the first instance, and in terms of political opinion in the second.[78]

The arguments invoked in the case for proportional representation were substantially similar in the different proposals advanced during the career of the Constituent Assembly. Proportional representation was justified on democratic grounds in three related types of arguments. First, it was argued that a first-past-the-post electoral system resulted, in effect, in the disenfranchisement of large portions of the electorate. Proportional representation was more democratic as it enabled a more adequate realization of the democratic right of every individual in a democracy to be represented by a person of her choice. Z.H. Lari, the most vocal supporter of proportional representation during the career of the Constituent Assembly, argued:

The twin principles of democracy are that everybody has a right of representation and the majority has the right of govern [sic]. The electoral system must be such as to ensure representation to everybody. This is the significance of adult franchise but the method adopted really amounts to the disenfranchisement of 49 per cent of the voters...I am talking of political minority. Even political minorities are entitled to be represented in representative institutions...It is better for us to adopt this principle [proportional representation by single transferable or cumulative voting] which is more progressive in instinct and which is really democratic...[79]

In such arguments, the appeal was to the democratic norm of political equality. This was construed here in terms of 'an equal chance of voting for a winning candidate.'[80] Proportional representation was more democratic than a first-past-the-post electoral system, as, unlike the latter, it ensured that the vote of each individual counted towards the election of a candidate. The central claim implicit here was that inequalities in political outcomes, such as those between the representation of majority and minority opinion in legislatures, violated procedural equality, the equal political rights of individuals. The theoretical basis of this move is problematic: the principle of political equality is compatible with a range of institutional mechanisms which distribute opportunities for political influence as well as actual political influence differently: inequalities in outcomes do not necessarily prove that procedural equality has been violated.[81] What is significant for our purposes here is that in the disenfranchisement argument, the case for minority representation was cast in terms drawn from the nationalist vocabulary. Minority representation was defended not on grounds that distinct *social groups* had a right to be represented in the legislature, as had been the case in arguments for separate electorates, but rather on democratic grounds, with democracy construed here in liberal terms, as characterized by equal *individual rights*. Further, the identification of equal political rights of individuals with an equal chance of voting for a winning candidate meant that proponents of minority representation could portray their concern with electoral outcomes, as a matter concerning democratic procedures, and in particular, the one-person-one-vote principle that formed the keystone of nationalist conceptions of democracy. Both moves towards individual rights and procedural equality brought arguments for minority representation closer to the nationalist framework.

A second democratic argument for proportional representation was that it would make assemblies more representative of the diversity of political opinion in society. Here too, proportional representation was favoured because it meant that each person's vote would count towards the election of a successful candidate. This, however, was considered more democratic not because it enabled each individual to elect a person of their choice, but because it would result in assemblies which were more representative of the diversity of political opinion in society.[82] Democracy was construed as implying that the legislature should mirror the different shades of political opinion in society in proportion to their strength. Z.H. Lari argued:

...Those who have read the writings of Mill must have been impressed by his advocacy of fundamental principle of democracy, that every political opinion must be represented in an assembly in proportion to its strength in the country, and naturally so...But if you adopt a method by which only 51 percent of the people alone are represented in the legislature, it ceases to be the mirror of the nation. Now the question is, does the method of representation adopted by this House...implement the principles of democracy?[83]

The representativeness argument was commonly seen to follow directly from the disenfranchisement argument, as a logical extension of the 'right of each individual to be represented'. While both arguments invoked the principle of political equality, its implications in the two cases were distinct: political equality in the disenfranchisement argument implied that majority and minority preferences should have an *equal* chance of being adopted; and in the representativeness argument it implied that majority and minority preferences should be represented in proportion to their *strength*.[84]

Importantly, the representativeness argument, like the disenfranchisement argument for proportional representation, drew upon nationalist conceptions of democracy and representation. In contrast with the case for separate electorates, these arguments did not assume that there were permanent and essential differences between religious groups; that the political choices of individuals derived from their religious group membership; that representatives had to belong to the group concerned; or that constituencies had to be defined along lines of religion. While desirable, the legislative representation of religious and other ascriptive minorities was to be achieved by focusing not so much on the social identity of representatives but the procedure for electing them, a position much more congenial to nationalist opinion.

A third type of democratic argument held that proportional representation would mitigate the tendency of a parliamentary system for the concentration of power in one party. The term 'tyranny of the majority' was frequently employed in such arguments, to refer to the disposition of legislative majorities to act in disregard of opposing political views. Majoritarian tendencies were portrayed as one of the great dangers to democracy in a parliamentary system under a first-past-the-post electoral system.[85] By enabling the representation of minority opinion, proportional representation would save the parliamentary system from the undemocratic tendencies immanent within it. Mahboob Ali Baig Sahib Bahadur was a prominent advocate in the Constituent Assembly of this line of argument for proportional representation:

[This] will enable peoples and parties in the country, who hold views different from the majority party, to be represented in the legislatures. Can you think of any parliamentary democracy where there is no opposition? Unless there is opposition...the danger of its turning itself into a Fascist body is there...[86]

Proportional representation, it was argued, would make for a stronger opposition, increase the likelihood of coalition governments, and necessitate greater consultation with minority political opinion, all of which would strengthen democracy.[87] Again, it is significant that democracy was construed here, in line with nationalist opinion, in terms of the ideals of popular rule and political equality and the institutions of parliamentary government. Proportional representation was defended on the grounds that it would make the parliamentary system more democratic by ensuring that the majority party was more responsive to the electorate and less prone to disregarding popular preferences and the rights of individuals and minorities.

While I have focused so far on democratic arguments, the case for proportional representation also invoked other concepts from the nationalist vocabulary. It was argued that proportional representation would facilitate minority representation without giving explicit recognition to religious and other ascriptive identities in the political realm. As such, unlike mechanisms such as separate electorates or reserved seats for religious minorities, proportional representation was consistent with secular principles.[88] Proportional representation was also defended as strengthening national unity. A parliament which was representative of the different shades of political opinion in society, it was suggested, would generate a stronger sense of belonging to the nation among political and communal minorities, and thereby enhance the stability of the state. Z.H. Lari held:

I concede that a minority must aspire to be an integral part of the nation...The minority must claim only such safeguards as are consistent with this aspiration...the adoption of this method is in the national interest and that for three reasons. 1. Parliament must be the mirror of the national mind: otherwise it will not have the respect which is due to it. 2...where national interest is preserved or is not jeopardized or imperilled it is necessary to consult minority opinion. If you do that it necessarily leads to consolidation of the State...3...If you have proportional representation you will have an opposition in the House. You will have a party not on a communal basis but based on large national issues.[89]

The proposals for proportional representation put forward for elections to the lower house of Parliament and the constitution of the Cabinet were rejected by the assembly.[90] In some cases, proportional representation was seen as a way of smuggling in separate electorates indirectly, and opposed on grounds that it shared the flaws of communalism and separatism of separate electorates. In other cases, proportional representation was seen as impracticable in an illiterate country. The most important concern, however, appears to have been government instability. B.R. Ambedkar argued:

...proportional representation would not permit a stable government to remain in office, because Parliament would be so divided into so many small groups that every time anything happened which displeased certain groups in Parliament they would on that occasion, withdraw their support from the government, with the result that the government...would fall to pieces. Now, I have not the least doubt in my mind that whatever else the future government provides for, whether it relieves the people from the wants from which they are suffering now or not, our future government must do one thing, namely it must maintain a stable government and maintain law and order.[91]

The belief that a strong and stable government was necessary for achieving national unity thus weighed against proportional representation.

The fact that proportional representation increasingly replaced separate electorates as the favoured mechanism for minority representation was significant. It suggested that minority claims were increasingly put forward in forms more acceptable to nationalist opinion than separate electorates. The arguments advanced for proportional representation also increasingly invoked the central concepts of the nationalist vocabulary, those of democracy, secularism, equal rights, and national unity. Both the institutional mechanisms and the arguments for minority representation moved closer to the nationalist framework during the course of the assembly's deliberations.

RECASTING GROUP REPRESENTATION: RESERVED SEATS IN LEGISLATURES

Reserved seats in legislatures for minorities under joint electorates had long been the form of political safeguard favoured by nationalists as an alternative to separate electorates, and these were endorsed in early deliberations. On what grounds were these defended in nationalist opinion? The first point of note is that even when reserved seats in legislatures were endorsed, these were regarded as 'temporary' and 'transitional' provisions, admitted for a short period of time. The ideal was always visualized as a situation in the future when reserved seats would no longer exist. Like separate electorates and proportional representation, these too were seen as detracting from secularism, democracy, justice, and, above all, national unity and development. When the Constituent Assembly accepted proposals for reserved seats in August 1947, S. Radhakrishnan pressed for the inclusion of the following caveat:

...we must declare our objective—that it is our desire to set up here a homogeneous, democratic, secular State, and those devices which were hitherto employed to keep the different sections of society apart have to be scrapped; if we now provide for certain compromise measures, it is simply because we wish to reckon with the past. We have to effect a compromise between the ideal we have in view and the actual conditions which have come down to us...[Let us] say that it is not our desire to maintain these minorities as minorities...The measures of compromise are transitional....[92]

The next point of note is that reserved seats in legislatures for religious minorities, even as temporary provisions, lacked a principled defence in nationalist opinion. The most common argument in their favour was that religious minorities needed time to adapt to the change from the colonial system where they had been accustomed to certain privileges. In fact, several nationalist arguments against separate electorates and proportional representation were directed not at these institutional mechanisms *per se* but at special representation for religious minorities as such. The colonial assumption that religious differences must be taken into account in the fashioning of representative institutions was rejected, and little attempt was made by nationalists to elaborate an alternative rationale for minority representation in the edifice they were fashioning. So, even as these were incorporated into the Draft Constitution of 1948, it remained unclear whether—and if so, how—reserved seats in legislatures for religious minorities had a place in the nationalist vision of the common good. When reserved seats in legislatures for religious minorities were withdrawn in 1949, Nehru commended their abolition as 'a historic turn in our destiny', confessing that he had never been convinced about the provision:

Reluctantly we agreed to carry on with some measure of reservation...but always there was this doubt in our minds, namely, whether we had not shown weakness in dealing with a thing that was wrong...doing away with this reservation business is not only a good thing in itself ...It shows that we are really sincere about this business of having a secular democracy.[93]

While a detailed analysis of the debates on special provisions for the Scheduled Castes and Scheduled Tribes is outside the scope of this essay, a few points deserve mention. Although reserved seats in legislatures for these groups were also opposed as detracting from ideals such as secularism and national unity, there were arguments in favour of such provisions in nationalist opinion. Broadly speaking, reserved seats in legislatures in the case of the Scheduled Castes and Scheduled Tribes were defended on the grounds that access to political power would enable the economic and social advancement of these groups. This, it was argued, would in turn facilitate the reduction of vast socio-economic inequalities in society, the closer integration of these groups with the rest of the population, and the development of the nation. So unlike in the case of religious minorities, reserved seats in legislatures for the Scheduled Castes and Scheduled Tribes did have a principled defence in nationalist opinion as temporary mechanisms, and were defended on grounds of justice, national unity, and development.

Two features need to be noted of the normative basis that was fashioned in the nationalist framework for political representation for 'backward sections'. First, *only* grounds relating to backwardness were seen as creating legitimate claims for legislative quotas; further, these were regarded as attaching to 'backward castes' and tribes, but *not* to the religious minorities. In nationalist opinion, the case for special treatment of Scheduled Castes and Scheduled Tribes was constantly sought to be distinguished from the religious minorities. It was emphasized that these groups were characterized not by religious or cultural difference but by socio-economic disabilities. Nehru held:

Frankly I would like this proposal to go further and put an end to such reservations that still remain. But...I realise that in the present state of affairs in India that would not be a desirable thing to do...in regard to the Scheduled Castes... I do not look at it from the religious point of view or the caste point of view, but from the point of view that a backward group ought to be helped and I am glad that this reservation will also be limited to ten years.[94]

Thus even when reserved seats in legislatures were admitted for both types of groups, those for the Scheduled Castes and Scheduled Tribes had a distinct basis in the nationalist vocabulary from religious minorities, one which derived from 'backwardness'.[95]

Second, the grounds on which reserved seats in legislatures for the untouchables and tribal groups were accommodated in the nationalist framework had little to do with *representation* as such. We have seen that in the case of religious minorities, nationalist opinion was hostile to the view that the social identity of representatives was relevant for representation: belonging to a community was not considered either necessary or sufficient for the adequate representation of its interests. This applied in the case of the Scheduled Castes and Scheduled Tribes as well: nationalists were not conceding here what they had rejected in the case of religious minorities. There was, for instance, no affirmation in nationalist arguments that 'backward' groups had a distinctive perspective which merited representation,[96] or that members of these groups were in a better position to understand and thereby represent their interests.

Reserved seats in legislatures for the Scheduled Castes and Scheduled Tribes were defended in nationalist opinion not as a means of securing a voice for these groups in the legislatures but as one among a range of measures for improving the socio-economic conditions of the disadvantaged, as 'a form of political "affirmative action"'.[97] How exactly reserved seats in legislatures would improve the socio-economic conditions of the beneficiaries was not specified, but political representation as such was not seen as playing a key role in the process.

Recast as a temporary affirmative action mechanism in the nationalist framework, the envisaged role of political representation was one of reducing rather than preserving group difference.[98] While reserved seats in legislatures for the Scheduled Castes and Scheduled Tribes were amenable to such an interpretation, those for the religious minorities were more problematic, given their association with the representation of the interests of culturally distinct groups. Lacking legitimacy in the nationalist scheme, their existence in the Indian Constitution was precarious from the outset.

CONCLUSION

In conclusion, I want to draw out some implications of the analysis of debates on minority representation for the legitimating vocabulary on group rights and the fate of political safeguards during Constitution-making. First, arguments advanced from diverse political and ideological positions within national opinion employed a shared normative vocabulary, comprising secularism, democracy, equality and justice, national unity, and development. There were different conceptions of these concepts: for example, some conceptions of secularism in nationalist opinion accorded primacy to the notion of equal citizenship, others to religious freedom, and yet others to a modern nation-state. Further, conceptions of secularism, democracy, justice, national unity, and development were mutually dependent, drawing upon each other for their connotations and normative force. So the nationalist vocabulary can be seen as a grid of interlocking concepts: all arguments in nationalist opinion invoked one or other of these concepts, and each of these concepts was defined in relation to the other elements of the vocabulary.[99] Second, the nationalist vocabulary comprised liberal norms. Notions of equal individual rights, religious freedom, state neutrality, and equality of opportunity substantially informed conceptions of secularism, democracy, and justice in the Constituent Assembly Debates.[100] Third, while minority claims for political safeguards initially relied on an earlier colonial language of group entitlement, as the deliberations progressed these increasingly came to be aligned closer to the nationalist vocabulary. In the process a shared legitimating vocabulary was forged, one which was employed in arguments both for and against group rights. So in the deliberations of the Constituent Assembly, we can discern a new legitimating vocabulary coming to be established as the framework for political debate on group rights.

The dominant nationalist interpretation of the key concepts of this vocabulary was hostile to political safeguards for minorities. This essay has focused on special representation in legislatures, the most significant area of minority claims in the colonial period. However, the debates in the Constituent Assembly on other political safeguards reveal a similar pattern. Quotas in the public services for example were regarded as undesirable in general, albeit admissible as temporary affirmative action provisions for 'backward sections'. Colonial policy on political safeguards had been based on a twofold rationale.[101] These had served as a means of adjusting the balance between different communities in representative bodies, public services and other arenas, as well as of improving the socio-economic conditions of disadvantaged groups. In nationalist vocabulary of our period, by contrast, there was no support for balancing the numbers of members of different communities in public institutions *per se*. Political safeguards were considered acceptable only for tackling 'backwardness', which was in turn associated with lower castes and tribes but not religious minorities.[102] This is crucial for an adequate understanding of the dissimilar fate of political safeguards in the case of religious minorities and 'backward classes', in particular, how special representation provisions for religious minorities, which had initially been accepted, came to be removed in the final stages of Constitution-making.

NOTES

1. Group representation provisions in central legislatures were first introduced by the colonial state in the constitutional reforms of 1909, which granted separate electorates to Muslims. The Government of India Act of 1919 extended separate electorates to Sikhs, Indian Christians, and Europeans. In the Government of India Act of 1935, a total of eighteen communal and functional groups were granted special representation. Reservations in government appointments for Muslims were first recognized by the colonial state in 1925. The policy was formalized and extended to other communities

under the Government of India Act of 1935. See B. Shiva Rao, *The Framing of India's Constitution: A Study* (Delhi: Indian Institute of Public Administration, 1968).

2. Some of the earliest instances of policies of group preference in government employment are to be found in the caste-based reservation schemes instituted by the princely states, such as Kolhapur and Mysore. See Susan Bayly, *Caste, Society and Politics in India From the Eighteenth Century to the Modern Age* (Cambridge: Cambridge University Press, 1999).

3. In constitutional drafts and deliberations, political safeguards comprised provisions for reserved seats in legislatures, quotas in government employment, reserved posts in the Cabinet and administrative machinery for the supervision and protection of minority rights. All minority groups hitherto preferred were included in the initial proposals and the first draft of the Constitution published in 1948. By the final draft, political safeguards were limited to the Scheduled Castes and Scheduled Tribes; some temporary provisions for the Anglo-Indians were also retained.

4. See for instance, Ralph Retzlaff, 'The Problem of Communal Minorities in the Drafting of the Indian Constitution', in R.N. Spann (ed.), *Constitutionalism in Asia* (Bombay: Asia Publishing House, 1963); and I.A. Ansari, 'Minorities and the Politics of Constitution Making in India', in D.L. Sheth and Gurpreet Mahajan (eds), *Minority Identities and the Nation State* (Delhi: Oxford University Press, 1999).

5. Rochana Bajpai, 'Constitution-making and Political Safeguards for Minorities: An Ideological Explanation', in M.R. Ansari and D. Achar (eds), *Discourse, Democracy and Difference* (New Delhi: Sahitya Akademi, 2008, forthcoming).

6. The terms 'nationalist opinion' and 'nationalist vocabulary' are heuristic categories. Nationalist opinion was not monolithic, and it included representatives belonging to minority communities. It is part of my argument that an increasing number of non-Congress minority representatives came to espouse the nationalist vocabulary during the course of the assembly's deliberations.

7. From this perspective, no assumptions need to be made that the actors sincerely believe in the principles they profess. See Quentin Skinner, 'Some Problems in the Analysis of Political Thought and Action', 'Meaning and Context', in James Tully (ed.), *Meaning and Context: Quentin Skinner and his Critics* (Cambridge: Polity Press, 1989); Quentin Skinner, 'Language and Social Change', in Tully (ed.), *Meaning and Context*. In this essay, unlike in Skinner's account, the focus is not on how the norms professed by individual actors constrain their actions, but rather on how a shared normative vocabulary is forged through debate and shapes policy outcomes.

8. The Muslim League never lifted its boycott of the Constituent Assembly. The League representatives began participating in the work of the assembly from the fourth session, in July 1947, after the decision to partition the country had been announced. Some Sikh members had also initially expressed reluctance

to join the assembly, but had come around after negotiations with the Congress. See Granville Austin, *The Indian Constitution: Cornerstone of a Nation* (Oxford: Clarendon Press, 1966).

9. See, for instance, the statements of Rev. Jerome D'Souza, *CAD*, Official Report, 12 vols (Delhi: Lok Sabha Secretariat, 1946–50), vol. III, p. 296; and Sardar Ujjal Singh *CAD*, vol. I, p. 107.

10. See Gyanendra Pandey, *The Construction of Communalism in Colonial North India* (Delhi: Oxford University Press, 1990), chs 6–7.

11. See, for instance, P.R. Thakur, *CAD*, vol. I, p. 139; and S. Nagappa, *CAD*, vol. II, p. 284.

12. See, for instance, V.I. Muniswamy Pillai, *CAD*, vol. V, p. 202.

13. See, for instance, Dakshayani Velayudan, *CAD*, vol. I, pp. 151–2; also *CAD*, vol. V, p. 264. Ambedkar and Gandhi were emblematic of the adversarial positions in the debate over whether the Scheduled Castes should be considered a separate minority or a backward section of the Hindu community. Gandhi had vigorously opposed proposals that the Scheduled Castes be treated separately from the Hindu community for purposes of representation, most notably the Communal Award of 1932 that offered Scheduled Castes separate electorates.

14. Jaipal Singh: 'I do not consider my people as a minority...the Depressed Classes also consider themselves as Adibasis, the original inhabitants of this country. If you go on adding people like the exterior castes and others who are socially in no man's land, we are not a minority. In any case, we have prescriptive rights that no one dare deny.' *CAD*, vol. I, p. 144.

15. See, for instance, S Nagappa, *CAD*, vol. II, p. 284.

16. See, for instance, Jaipal Singh: 'I leave to the good sense of the House...that, at long last, they will right the injuries of 6000 years.' *CAD*, vol. II, p. 317. For similar statements made by Scheduled Caste representatives, see for instance, S. Nagappa, *CAD*, vol. I, p. 284.

17. Speaking in support of a proposed clause that permitted restrictions on the Fundamental Right of all citizens to reside, settle, or acquire property in any part of the country '...as may be necessary in the public interest including the protection of minority groups and tribes', Jaipal Singh argued: '...land is the bulwark of aboriginal life...Equality sounds well; but I do demand discrimination when it comes to the holdings of aboriginal land.' *CAD*, vol. III, pp. 462–3.

18. Speaking in support of this amendment, K.M. Munshi said: '...my amendment seeks to clarify the position that so far as the Scheduled Castes are concerned, they are not minorities in the strict meaning of the term; that Harijans are part and parcel of the Hindu community, and that safeguards are given to them to protect their rights only till they are completely absorbed in the Hindu community.' *CAD*, vol. V, p. 227. The amendment was adopted.

19. During discussion of the revised draft of the Constitution on 16 November 1949, an amendment was adopted which stipulated the substitution of

the word 'minorities' by the words 'certain classes' in all instances of its usage.

20. See the speeches during the discussion of the Objectives Resolution; for instance, Shri Purushottamdas Tandon, *CAD*, vol. I, pp. 66–7; Vijayalakshmi Pandit, *CAD*, vol. II, p. 261.

21. Each individual has the freedom to profess, practise, and propagate his religion (Article 25), every religious group or denomination has the right to establish and maintain institutions for religious and charitable purposes, to manage its own affairs in matters of religion, to own and acquire movable and immovable property, and to administer such property in accordance with law (Article 26). Further, any section of citizens of India that has a distinct language, script, or culture has the right to conserve the same (Article 29.1). All minorities, whether based on religion or language, have the right to establish and administer educational institutions of their choice (Article 30.1). Every Congress resolution on the Fundamental Rights of citizens since the 1931 Karachi resolution had included guarantees for the protection of the culture, language, and scripts of minorities in its list of Fundamental Rights.

22. It is however, important to note that while minority groups were granted cultural and educational rights, these were not interpreted by the Constitution-makers as creating a constitutional entitlement to state support.

23. See, for instance, R.V. Dhulekar, *CAD*, vol. II, p. 285.

24. These distinctions are adapted from Will Kymlicka and Wayne Norman (eds), *Citizenship in Diverse Societies* (Oxford: Oxford University Press, 2000), p. 31.

25. For instance, Purushottamdas Tandon held, 'In politics [the Congress party] refuses to recognise any differences on account of religion. We ask Sir Stafford Cripps and other British leaders: If a hundred years or for that matter twenty years ago, the right of separate elections were given to different sects of your country, what sort of government would you have had today? Would you not have had continuous civil wars?', *CAD*, vol. I, p. 66.

26. Kymlicka and Norman (eds), *Citizenship in Diverse Societies*, p. 35.

27. Pandit Govind Vallabh Pant argued: '... If in a democracy, you create rival loyalties, or you create a system in which any individual or group, instead of suppressing his extravagance, cares nought for larger or other interests, then democracy is doomed.' *CAD*, vol. II, p. 224.

28. On the conception of the nation-state and national identity in India, see D.L. Sheth, 'The Nation-State and Minority Rights', in D.L. Sheth and Gurpreet Mahajan (eds), *Minority Identities and the Nation State* (Delhi: Oxford University Press, 1999); Bhikhu Parekh, 'Discourses on National Identity', *Political Studies*, 42(3), 1994, pp. 492–504.

29. It is important to note that the 'nation' had not been regarded as antagonistic to ethno-cultural 'communities' in early nationalist visions of the nation. Prior to the 1920s, the nation had been envisaged as a composite of communities defined in religious, regional, and caste terms, reflected in the equation Hindu

+ Muslim + Christian + Parsi + Sikh. See Pandey, *The Construction of Communalism*.

30. Renuka Ray argued: 'After all...it is not a question of minorities and majorities on a religious basis that we should consider in a democratic secular State...we have stood aside helplessly while artificially this problem of religious differences—an echo of medieval times, has been fostered and nurtured and enhanced by the method of political devices such as separate electorates in order to serve the interests of our alien rulers. Today we see as a result our country divided and provinces like my own dismembered...We have submitted to all this so that at least in the rest of India that remains with us now we may go ahead in forming a democratic secular State without bringing in religion to cloud the issue.' *CAD*, vol. V, p. 268.

31. See, for instance Somnath Lahiri, *CAD*, vol. I, p. 137.

32. See, for instance, Biswanath Das: '...it is very very unfortunate that the minority communities do not demand mere justice, equity and fairplay but claim safeguards and weightages under third party domination.' *CAD*, vol. II, p. 345. Interestingly, women representatives in the Constituent Assembly were some of the strongest opponents of political safeguards on liberal justice grounds. See for instance, Hansa Mehta's statement: 'The women's organisation to which I have the honour to belong has never asked for reserved seats, for quotas or for separate electorates. What we have asked for is social justice, economic justice and political justice. We have asked for equality.' *CAD*, vol. I, p. 134.

33. Mahavir Tyagi argued: 'These minorities cannot be recognized because in a country whose administration is supposed to be run on the basis of justice alone, there is no question of minority or majority. All individuals are at par...We cannot recognize religion as far as the State is concerned.' Quoting Jinnah, he said, '...even in that State he says religions will not be taken notice of by the State. Every individual will be an individual and Hindus will lose their Hinduship as far as their political rights and privileges are concerned...We are one nation which stands for justice. We will legislate in a manner that will be a guarantee against all injustice, and we shall not recognise any sections.' *CAD*, vol. V, p. 219. For liberal arguments on how the right of each individual to be treated as an equal is compatible with, and may under some circumstances require, unequal treatment, see Ronald Dworkin, *Taking Rights Seriously* (London: Duckworth, 1977); Will Kymlicka, *Multicultural Citizenship: A Liberal Theory of Minority Rights* (Oxford: Clarendon Press, 1995).

34. Pandit G.B. Pant held: 'There is the unwholesome and to some extent a degrading habit of thinking always in terms of communities and never in terms of citizens. But it is after all citizens who form communities and the individual as such is essentially the core of all mechanisms and means and devices that are adopted for securing progress and advancement. So let us remember that it is the citizen that must count. It is the citizen that forms the base as well as the summit of the social pyramid.' *CAD*, vol. II, p. 312.

35. *CAD*, vol. VII, p. 1057. See also Rev. Jerome D' Souza's statement, *CAD*, vol. VII, p. 1059.

36. For distinctions between different forms of separation between state and religion, see Rajeev Bhargava, 'Is Secularism a Value in Itself?', in I. Ahmad, P. Ghosh, and H. Reifeld (eds), *Pluralism and Equality* (Delhi: Sage, 2000); on conceptions of secularism in the Constituent Assembly, see James Chiriyankandath, 'Creating a Secular State in a Religious Country: The Debate in the Indian Constituent Assembly', *Commonwealth and Comparative Politics*, 38(2), July 2000, pp. 1–24; Shefali Jha, 'Secularism in the Constituent Assembly Debates, 1946–1950', *Economic and Political Weekly*, 37(30), 27 July–2 August 2002, pp. 3175–80.

37. Renuka Ray argued: '...at least in the rest of India that remains with us now we may go ahead in forming a democratic secular State without bringing in religion to cloud the issue. Religion is a personal matter. Religious differences might have been exploited as a political expedient by the British, but there is no room for that in the India of today.' *CAD*, vol. V, p. 268.

38. M. Ananthasayanam Ayyangar, *CAD*, vol. VII, pp. 881–2.

39. K.M. Munshi asserted: 'A secular state is used in contrast with a theocratic government or a religious state. It implies that citizenship is irrespective of religious belief, that every citizen, to whatever religion he may belong, is equal before the law, that he has equal civil rights, and equal opportunity to derive benefit from the state and to lead his own life and nothing more.' *CAD*, vol. VII, p. 1057.

40. K.T. Shah opined: '...with the actual profession of faith or belief, the State should have no concern. Nor should it, by any action of it, give any indication that it is partial to one or the other.' *CAD*, vol. VII, p. 816. The amendment was not carried. The Congress' Karachi Resolution of 1931 had explicitly proposed religious neutrality on the part of the state.

41. Thus, for instance, B.R. Ambedkar opined, speaking against the proposals that religious instruction be provided in state schools: '...it seems to me that we should be considerably disturbing the peaceful atmosphere of an institution if these controversies as to the truthful character of any particular religion and the erroneous character of the other were brought into juxtaposition in the school itself.' *CAD*, vol. VII, p. 884. While cultural and educational rights of minorities are outside the scope of this essay, the debates on these provisions involved conceptions of secularism as separation between state and religion. State funding of educational institutions providing religious instruction was regarded as illegitimate, as it would involve the state in purveying religious tenets. It was resolved that the state could provide aid to minority educational institutions that imparted religious instruction, although there was no obligation upon the state to do so. However, institutions maintained wholly out of state funds were prohibited from giving religious instruction.

42. It was held, for instance: 'This secular State which we are trying to create should not do anything to interfere with the way of life and religion of the people...People seem to think that under a secular State, there must be a

common law observed by its citizens in all matters, including matters of their daily life, their language, their culture, their personal laws. That is not a correct way to look at this secular State. In a secular State, citizens belonging to different communities must have the freedom—to practise their own religion, observe their own life and their personal laws should be applied to them.' *CAD*, vol. VII, pp. 540–1, 544. Secularism, as invoked by the proponents of Muslim Personal Law, drew upon conceptions of secularism as de-politicization of religion. Here, secularism as separation of state and religion was construed to imply that religion in a secular order should be free from state interference. A secular order was one in which citizens would have full religious freedom, including the freedom to live by the tenets of their religious personal law. A secular state would be excluded from the domain of religion and would lack the authority to intervene in matters regulated by religious personal law.

43. See, for instance, B.R. Ambedkar, *CAD*, vol. VII, pp. 781–2.
44. Nevertheless, the identification of secularism with religious freedom would remain in political discourse, and was to become the dominant connotation of secularism in the Shah Bano debate.
45. See Pandey, *The Construction of Communalism*; also Thomas Pantham, 'Indian Secularism and Its Critics: Some Reflections', *The Review of Politics*, 59 (3), 1997, pp. 523–40.
46. On this point, see A. Embree, *Utopias in Conflict: Religion and Nationalism in Modern India* (Berkeley and Los Angeles: University of California Press, 1990); Niraja Gopal Jayal, *Democracy and the State: Welfare, Secularism, and Development in India* (Delhi: Oxford University Press, 1999).
47. For secularism in the writings and speeches of Nehru, see Neera Chandhoke, *Beyond Secularism: The Rights of Religious Minorities* (Delhi: Oxford University Press, 1999).
48. *CAD*, vol. II, p. 254.
49. Embree, *Utopias in Conflict*, p. 55.
50. On the subject of political safeguards for minorities, Nehru reportedly said that the Draft Constitution had 'certain definite communal elements'. 'What the final decision will be about that I cannot say. I hope personally that the less reservation there is the better.' Quoted in Retzlaff, 'The Problem of Communal Minorities', p. 66.
51. On this point, see Akeel Bilgrami, 'Two Concepts of Secularism: Reason, Modernity and Secular Ideal', *Economic and Political Weekly*, 29(28), 1994, pp. 1749–61. For an alternative reading of Nehru, see Sunil Khilnani, 'Nehru's Faith', *Economic and Political Weekly*, 37(48), 30 November 2002, pp. 4793–9.
52. Naziruddin Ahmad, speaking in support of minority representation, argued: '...the Hindu community who can be collectively described as the elder brother has in a generous mood conceded for the period of ten years—I should consider that period quite sufficient—that they (Muslims) should get a reserved representation. It seems to me that it implies that the great Hindu community are willing for this period of ten years to listen to what difficulties and

complaints, apart from the justice or otherwise of these complaints, of the Muslim community...No danger or harm can follow from this in the period of ten years if the elder brother listens to the grievances of the younger brother. These grievances and difficulties may be real or exaggerated, they may be due more to fear and suspicion rather than to any real reasons...' *CAD*, vol. V, pp. 269–70.

53. Embree, *Utopias in Conflict*, p. 87.

54. *CAD*, vol. V, p. 246.

55. *CAD*, vol. V, p. 249. Some special provisions of a temporary nature were also made for the Anglo-Indian community in the spheres of representation, education, and the services. This report was regarded as representing the high watermark in Congress' concessions to minorities, made several months after the partition of the country, when the need for conciliating the minorities, particularly the Muslims, had greatly diminished. See Retzlaff, 'The Problem of Communal Minorities', pp. 64–5.

56. Different combinations of these mechanisms were proposed: for instance, reserved seats in conjunction with separate electorates or some form of proportional representation which would enable members of minority communities to have a greater voice in the election of their representatives to reserved seats. For an illuminating discussion of different types of institutional mechanisms for the representation of minority parties and social groups in the context of the electoral system in India, see E. Sridharan, 'The Origins of the Electoral System: Rules, Representation and Power-sharing in India's Democracy', in Zoya Hasan, E. Sridharan, and R. Sudarshan (eds), *India's Living Constitution: Ideas, Practices, Controversies* (Delhi: Permanent Black, 2002).

57. Demands for separate electorates were also put forward on behalf of Sikhs and Scheduled Castes during the assembly's deliberations.

58. *CAD*, vol. V, p. 212.

59. *CAD*, vol. V, p. 213.

60. Mohamed Ismail Sahib noted: 'It enables you, it enables the Government to know what the respective people have got in their mind and then enables you to cure those grievances and those troubles.' *CAD*, vol. VIII, p. 281.

61. See Farzana Shaikh, *Community and Consensus in Islam: Muslim Representation in Colonial India, 1860–1947* (Cambridge: Cambridge University Press, 1989), pp. 74–5.

62. On descriptive representation, see H. Pitkin, *The Concept of Representation*, (Berkeley: University of California Press, 1967); Anne Phillips, *The Politics of Presence* (Oxford: Clarendon Press, 1995). Drawing upon Pitkin's notion, Farzana Shaikh has argued that the Muslim's League's demands for institutional mechanisms such as separate electorates for Muslims stemmed from a notion of representation as a descriptive activity. She contrasts this with conventional liberal–democratic notions of representation, where the focus is not on the personal attributes of representatives as on the activity of representation (Shaikh, *Community and Consensus in Islam*.) My analysis however, suggests

that a sharp contrast between descriptive and substantive representation is misleading. Descriptive representation can be a means of enhancing the substantive representation of a group's interests in policy-making, and was seen as such by proponents of separate electorates.

63. On the general point, see Jane Mansbridge, 'What Does A Representative Do? Descriptive Representation in Communicative Settings of Distrust, Uncrystallized Interests, and Historically Denigrated Status', in Kymlicka and Norman (eds), *Citizenship in Diverse Societies* (Oxford: Oxford University Press, 2000).

64. *CAD*, vol. V, p. 213.

65. Ambedkar had voiced similar concerns in his Note on Minorities of 1947. See also S. Nagappa's speech in support of his proposal that candidates for reserved seats poll at least 35 per cent from the Scheduled Castes in order to be declared elected. *CAD*, vol. V, pp. 259–61.

66. *CAD*, vol. V, pp. 212–13. See also Chaudhari Khaliquzzaman, *CAD*, vol. V, pp. 221–2.

67. Contra Shaikh, *Community and Consensus in Islam*, it is important to emphasize that in the case for separate electorates, descriptive representation was necessary but not sufficient for group representation.

68. Mahavir Tyagi, *CAD*, vol. V, p. 218.

69. See, for instance, Mahavir Tyagi, *CAD*, vol. V, pp. 218–19.

70. On how political equality is compatible with differentiated political rights, see Charles Beitz, *Political Equality: An Essay in Democratic Theory* (Princeton: Princeton University Press, 1989).

71. Pandit G.B. Pant, *CAD*, vol. V, p. 223.

72. Arguing that separate electorates would be suicidal for minorities, Pandit G.B. Pant said: 'Do the minorities always want to remain as minorities or do they ever expect to form an integral part of a great nation and as such to guide and control its destiny? If they do, can they ever achieve that aspiration and that ideal if they are isolated from the rest of the community?...The minorities if they are returned by separate electorates can never have any effective voice...will you be satisfied with the pitiable position of being no more than advocates—if advocates alone you wish to be—when your advocacy will be treated, if not with scorn and ridicule, but in any case with utter disregard and unconcern, which is bound to be the case when those who are the judges are not in any way answerable to your electorate?' *CAD*, vol. V, pp. 222–4.

73. *CAD*, vol. VIII, p. 350.

74. It is important to emphasize that it was from the standpoint of a particular interpretation of democracy that separate electorates were undemocratic and harmful to minorities. There were other possibilities, available at the time, in which this would not necessarily be the case: for example, consociational type of power-sharing mechanisms and decision-making by consensus rather than majority rule.

75. Ananthasayanam Ayyangar, *CAD*, vol. V, p. 216.

76. For instance, Kazi Syed Karimuddin argued: 'Even a false convert, or a hireling of the majority party could come in by the votes of the majority party...There is no chance under this system for any real representatives of the minorities to be elected...If at all the majority community want to protect the rights of the minorities, let them introduce the system of proportional representation...without any sacrifice of democratic principles the minorities can be protected....' *CAD*, vol. VII, p. 243. Sardar Bhopinder Singh Man held: '...at the time of forming these constituencies, particular care should be taken to make them plural constituencies. The right which you have conferred on the minorities can be preserved only if you make the constituencies in such a way that they should be able to represent themselves.' *CAD*, vol. VII, p. 1249.

77. For instance, K.T. Shah argued in support of proportional representation that it 'is not intended so much to perpetuate communal minorities, as to reflect the various shades of political opinion which after all, should be reflected in your Legislature, if you desire to be really a democratic government....' *CAD*, vol. VII, p. 1238.

78. This distinction draws upon Phillips, *The Politics of Presence*, p. 49. Phillips criticizes Pitkin's discussion of the limits of descriptive representation for ignoring the distinction between these two kinds of proportionality, between the mapping of opinion and the mapping of people.

79. *CAD*, vol. VII, p. 209. See also Kazi Syed Karimuddin, *CAD*, vol. VII, p. 1233.

80. Phillips, *The Politics of Presence*, p. 107.

81. For a critique of the claim that individuals who vote for candidates who do not win are disenfranchised, see Brian Barry, 'Is Democracy Special?', in P. Laslett and J. Fishkin (eds), *Philosophy, Politics and Society* (Oxford: Blackwell, 1979). As Phillips, *The Politics of Presence*, notes, in order to give citizens equal actual power over political outcomes, we may need to assign unequal weights to their preferences.

82. This distinction between the disenfranchisement and representativeness arguments draws upon Phillips, *The Politics of Presence*.

83. Z.H. Lari, *CAD*, vol. VIII, p. 282.

84. Phillips, *The Politics of Presence*, p. 107.

85. Several minority representatives spoke against parliamentary democracy and advocated a Presidential system.

86. *CAD*, vol. VII, p. 1245.

87. Some Muslim League representatives put forward proposals for the constitutional recognition of the opposition, arguing that this was necessary since, in the prevailing climate of opinion, criticizing the majority party, the Congress, was perceived as tantamount to sedition.

88. Kazi Syed Karimuddin argued: '[Proportional Representation] is not based on religious grounds and it applies to all minorities, political, religious or communal...without any sacrifice of democratic principles, it can afford protection to communal minorities also. Without any spirit of communalism, representatives of political and communal minorities can be elected.' *CAD*,

vol. VII, pp. 1234–5. See also Sardar Hukam Singh, *CAD*, vol. VII, p. 1250.

89. *CAD*, vol. VIII, p. 286.

90. Proportional representation by the single transferable vote was accepted by the house as the mode of election for the president as well as the constitution of the Council of States, the Rajya Sabha.

91. *CAD*, vol. VII, p. 1262.

92. *CAD*, vol. V, pp. 283–4. See also Vallabhbhai Patel's speech in the House, introducing the first minority report, *CAD*, vol. V, pp. 199–200.

93. *CAD*, vol. VIII, pp. 329, 332.

94. *CAD*, vol. VIII, p. 331. In a similar vein, Jagat Narain Lal held: '...the Scheduled Castes have been given reservation not on grounds of religion at all; they form part and parcel of the Hindu Community, and they have been given reservation apparently and clearly on grounds of their economic, social and educational backwardness.' *CAD*, vol. VIII, p. 308.

95. On this point, see also Gurpreet Mahajan, *Identities and Rights: Aspects of Liberal Democracy in India* (Delhi: Oxford University Press, 1998).

96. This draws upon Melissal Williams, *Voice, Trust and Memory: Marginalised Groups and the Failings of Liberal Representation* (Princeton: Princeton University Press, 1998); Mansbridge, 'What Does A Representative Do?'; and Kymlicka, *Multicultural Citizenship.*

97. Kymlicka, *Multicultural Citizenship*, p. 141. Scheduled Caste representatives who had criticized reserved seats in legislatures as ineffectual from the point of view of group *representation* defended these in later stages of Constitution-making as a mechanism for improving the economic conditions and educational and employment opportunities of untouchables. They continued to back reserved seats in legislatures, in contrast with most religious minority representatives, whose support dwindled once it became clear that these would not be an effective instrument of group representation.

98. Thus, for instance, Vallabhbhai Patel stated: '...the Scheduled Caste has to be effaced altogether from our society, and if it is to be effaced, those who have ceased to be untouchables and sit amongst us must forget that they are untouchables...We are now to begin again. So let us forget these sections and cross-sections and let us stand as one, and together.' *CAD*, vol. V, p. 272.

99. This formulation draws upon Michael Freeden, *Ideologies and Political Theory: A Conceptual Approach* (Oxford: Clarendon Press, 1996), and is elaborated in Rochana Bajpai, 'The Legitimating Vocabulary of Group Rights in Contemporary India', unpublished D.Phil. thesis, University of Oxford, 2003.

100. In nationalist opinion of this period, liberal individualist norms were mostly deployed against political safeguards for minorities. Here, the Indian Constituent Assembly Debates illustrate the close association of liberal norms and nation-building also found in other contexts.

101. Marc Galanter, *Competing Equalities: Law and the Backward Classes in India* (Delhi: Oxford University Press, 1984), p. 363.

102. For example, opposing the amendment moved by Sikh representatives that all minority groups receive special consideration in the matter of appointments to the public services as provided in the first draft of the Constitution, Vallabhbhai Patel held: 'After all, what is the Sikh community backward in? Is it backward in industry, or commerce or in anything?' *CAD*, vol. X, p. 249.

Contributors

Ashok Acharya, Department of Political Science, University of Delhi.

Rochana Bajpai, Lecturer in the Politics of Asia/Africa, Department of Politics and International Studies, School of Oriental and African Studies, University of London.

Upendra Baxi, Professor of Law, University of Warwick.

Rajeev Bhargava, Director, Centre for the Study of Developing Societies (CSDS), Delhi.

Peter deSouza, Senior Fellow, Centre for the Study of Developing Societies (CSDS), Delhi.

Gopal Guru, Professor of Political Science, University of Delhi.

Christophe Jaffrelot, Director of CERI (Centre d'Etudes et de Recherches Internationales) at Sciences and research director at the CNRS (Centre National de la Recherche Scientifique), Paris.

Shefali Jha, Associate Professor, Centre for Political Studies, Jawaharlal Nehru University, New Delhi (on leave till July 2008).

Gurpreet Mahajan, Professor, Centre for Political Studies, Jawaharlal Nehru University, New Delhi.

Pratap Bhanu Mehta, President, Centre for Policy Research, New Delhi.

Nivedita Menon, Reader, Department of Political Science, University of Delhi.

Aditya Nigam, Fellow, Centre for the Study of Developing Societies (CSDS), Delhi and Visiting Fellow, Shelby Cullom Davis Center for Historical Studies, Department of History, Princeton University.

SANJAY PALSHIKAR, Reader, Department of Political Science, University of Hyderabad.

SUHAS PALSHIKAR, Professor, Department of Politics and Public Administration, University of Pune.

THOMAS PANTHAM, former Professor of Political Science, Maharaja Sayajirao University of Baroda.

BHIKHU PAREKH holds the Centennial Professorship at the Centre for the Study of Global Governance, London School of Economics.

VALERIAN RODRIGUES, Professor, Centre for Political Studies, Jawaharlal Nehru University, New Delhi.

Index